# Queen Victoria's
# SKETCHBOOK

# Queen Victoria's
# SKETCHBOOK

MARINA WARNER

BOOK CLUB ASSOCIATES
LONDON

First published 1979 by
Macmillan London Limited

This edition published 1980 by
Book Club Associates
by arrangement with Macmillan London Ltd

Photoset by Filmtype Services Limited, Scarborough
Printed by Sackville Press Billericay Limited

# Contents

# *Acknowledgements*

The publishers and I most gratefully acknowledge the permission of Her Majesty The Queen to sift the many sketchbooks of Queen Victoria in the Royal Collection, and to match sketches with entries in Queen Victoria's Journal.

I owe an enormous debt of gratitude to Sir Robin Mackworth-Young, K.C.V.O., the Royal Librarian, to Jane Roberts, Curator of the Print Room, and to the Deputy Curator, Charlotte Miller. Everyone in the Royal Archives was helpfulness itself: my deepest thanks go to Jane Langton, M.V.O., Elizabeth Cuthbert, Sheila de Bellaigue and Frances Dimond. The House Governor at Osborne kindly allowed me to visit the Queen's apartments, and I am indebted to Edward Sibbick for his encyclopaedic information on the house and its collection.

Lady Longford gave me invaluable advice on the finished manuscript; Daphne Bennett also was most generous with her comments; Dr Roy Foster, besides helping me through-out with bibliographic references, also read the manuscript.

Elizabeth Johnston's research for the Royal Performance exhibition at Windsor in 1977 provided the first inspiration for this book, and later she gave me her enthusiastic support. Victoria Moger helped me greatly by researching aspects of Victoria's theatre-going, and child-bearing and rearing in her day. Bernard Nevill invited me to read Queen Alexandra's bound volumes of *The Graphic* magazine, and Christopher Wood helped me place Victoria's watercolours in the context of their day. My sister Laura Warner's work on Italian opera was an illumination.

My special thanks go also to all who helped me while I was writing by looking after my son Conrad. It is to him that I dedicate this book.

Marina Warner
*London, 1979*

# Introduction

*In 1845 the Danseuses Viennoises danced before the Queen in her own theatre — Her Majesty's in the Haymarket — in the Pas des Moissoneurs, from the ballet* Käya, ou l'Amour Voyageur.

*In sketches such as this Victoria expressed her gaiety and her tremendous love of life.*

Queen Victoria personified to an uncanny degree the values of the era that is justly called after her. Over the sixty-three years of her reign she was the cynosure of all eyes, and her influence governed the direction, ambition and ideals of the subjects under her. In the first sense of the word, she was the cliché of her age, the cast from which it took its unique imprint. She was thrifty, but capable of largesse; she was affectionate, even passionate, but rarely unbridled and never wanton; she was a devoted mother, but had decided ideas about the duties of children. The deadliest sin in her view was sloth, and the parable most suited to her nature and the character of her times is that of the talents, with its stern warning that native gifts should never lie buried and unused.

But Victoria was not puritanical, and she made her industry serve her pleasure. She kept, with infectious enthusiasm, a journal of her life from 1832 until her death in 1901; her voluminous correspondence to friends, relations, and later to her children when they married and left home, bubbles over with news, plans, hints and solicitude. She tackled with gritty dedication the heaps of despatches in the boxes sent by her ministers; she received guests continually; she played the piano and sang; and in between, she painted.

For Queen Victoria was an artist. The first date on a small sketchbook in the Royal Collection is 1827, the last, inscribed in a wobbly hand on a loose sheet of paper, is 1890. There are over fifty of her albums and sketchbooks, and only very few of the drawings and watercolours which fill them have been reproduced before. She has been, until now, an unknown example of a marvellous and extinct breed: the Victorian amateur watercolourist.

Victoria drew and painted to chronicle her daily life. She was an amateur not in the later pejorative sense of Sunday painter, but because she had no higher aim than to seize the fugitive moment. She very seldom created a picture from imagination, and the contemporary Pre-Raphaelite movement never touched her. She certainly had a gift, particularly for a quick, lively likeness of one of her children or her friends, but she made no claims to profound portraiture. If art had been her first vocation, she would have failed; because it was a hobby amongst many, she distinguished herself.

Apart from their intrinsic charm Queen Victoria's paintings and drawings have a historical importance. She was the monarch who ruled during the epoch of which we are the direct heirs, as beneficiaries and as victims, and her art forms a distant yet audible accompaniment to the policies that were carried out under her rule. Through her sketches of genre scenes and picturesque peasantry we see the age's bafflement at the reality of poverty. Her tender portraits of her children announce the clear ascendancy of the family as an institution to be given all protection — the Victorians were the first to legislate for the rights of married women and children. Her watercolours of Germany reveal the love and fascination she felt for her mother and her husband's country, and her loyalty to Albert's conception of his homeland was reflected in the conduct of foreign policy. Her attraction to exoticism, dark-eyed and dusky, is part of the dream that took the English to Africa, India and all points faraway.

Victoria was too practical to adopt the confessional tone, too dedicated to self-improvement to make an exhibition of herself. Yet she also had a prodigal capacity for self-revelation. Her drawings and her paintings are guileless, as she was. Their strength is her strength: impetuosity, quick decisiveness, spontaneity, loyalty to her own perception, obstinacy in her likes and dislikes, readiness to admire, to enjoy and to praise.

2 V. f. Nov: 30th
1833 Lehzen.

# ONE

# Kensington Palace

In 1865, when Queen Victoria was a widow of forty-six, the Mock Turtle sighed to Alice that he had only taken 'the regular course' of lessons. 'What was that?' Alice asked. The curriculum the Gryphon and the Mock Turtle then described would not have been unrecognizable to the Queen of England. It resembled, in almost all particulars, the education she received at Kensington Palace from her early childhood to her accession at the age of eighteen in 1837. 'Reeling and Writhing, of course', said the Mock Turtle. In later years Victoria admitted in a memoir: 'I was not fond of learning as a little child — and baffled every attempt to teach me my letters up to 5 years old — when I consented to learn them by their being written down before me.'

'And then the different branches of Arithmetic', proceeded the Turtle. Louise Lehzen, Victoria's governess, must have taught her charge the rudiments of mathematics; but in the diary Victoria kept from 1832 until her death there is no record that any branch of arithmetic held any appeal for her.

*Louise Lehzen, created a Hanoverian baroness by King George IV in 1826, was the most important influence on Victoria's childhood. She became devoted to the Princess with maternal and possessive intensity.*

11

'What else had you to learn?' asked Alice, perhaps equally impatient to pass on to other subjects. 'Well, there was Mystery . . . ancient and modern.' History was one of Victoria's delights. Guided principally by her mother's brother, King Leopold of the Belgians, Victoria read widely in memoirs and manuals, from Sully to the French Academician Gaillard's history of Franco-Spanish tensions. But, as she explained to Uncle Leopold: 'The history of my own country is one of my first duties.'

Victoria's schooling in history was intense, but not systematic. Lehzen would read aloud to the little Princess morning and night while her hair was being brushed by her maid, so that she should always employ her time profitably and also learn not to chatter in front of domestics. The governess, daughter of a Lutheran pastor, was strict but not joyless: her taste, fortunately for Victoria, was lighter than that of Uncle Leopold. She began by reading stories to the small girl, and history was served later in the delectable form

*A small red leather sketchpad with horizontal pages was given to Princess Victoria by Lehzen in 1827, when she was eight years old. In it she drew this picture of herself, with her hair fresh out of screwpapers.*

*One of Victoria's earliest drawings from her first sketchbook, before Richard Westall's tuition had begun to tell.*

of Walter Scott's writings — exciting and romantic, certainly, but also deeply instructive of the historical and social forces that toss all individuals, be they queens or commoners. It was Lehzen who defended Victoria's pleasure in reading contemporary travels and memoirs. On the diary of the famous actress Fanny Kemble, Victoria commented: 'There are some fine feelings and descriptions . . . but upon the whole it is pertly and sometimes *even* vulgarly written.'

In *Alice*, to the Mock Turtle's account the Gryphon adds that he had been taught 'Laughing and Grief'. Victoria learned no Greek, and when, on a visit to Oxford in 1832, she was shown Queen Elizabeth I's Latin exercise book, she was awed. 'She was of my age (13)', she wrote in her diary. But when the Mock Turtle had counted off on his flappers Mystery and Seaography, he came to the accomplishment included in the 'regular course' of all Victorian children of gentle birth. 'Then Drawling', he said. 'The Drawling-master was an old conger-eel, that used to come once a week: *he* taught us Drawling, Stretching, and Fainting in Coils.'

In 1827, when Victoria was eight years old, she received her first drawing lesson from Richard Westall, R.A. From then on until his death nine years later, he called at Kensington Palace twice a week to give her hour-long lessons. But Mr Westall, of whom we shall hear more later, was only one of a team of visiting instructors in the polite arts. There was Madame Bourdin, Victoria's dancing teacher; Mrs Anderson, her music and singing mistress; John Sale, impresario and organist at St Margaret's, Westminster, who taught her piano; and others for French, German and Italian, languages being considered an essential part of her education. Her chief tutor was the Very Rev. George Davys, Dean of Chester, who was responsible for her education as a whole and for her religious instruction. He came for two hours most mornings, but sometimes, Victoria records ruefully, for the whole day. The Duchess of Northumberland was her official governess, ranking above Lehzen, though Lehzen retained her considerable influence over Victoria right up to the painful time when first Lord Melbourne, and later Prince Albert, replaced her in the young Queen's strong affections.

It was Lehzen who taught Victoria to keep a meticulous account of her daily schedule. Her first Journal opens with the inscription, written in sepia ink in a vigorous, sloping and angular hand: 'This book Mama gave me, that I might write the journal of my journey to Wales in it. — Victoria, Kensington Palace, July 31'. But when such refreshing material as a journey was lacking, the diary has a sad, clock-punching look: 'I awoke at 7 and got up at $\frac{1}{2}$ past 7. At $\frac{1}{2}$ past 8 we breakfasted. At $\frac{1}{2}$ past 9 came the Dean till 11. At $\frac{1}{2}$ past 12 we lunched . . . At $\frac{1}{2}$ past 2 came Mr Westall till $\frac{1}{2}$ past 3 . . . '

Westall came to teach the Princess drawing and sketching (but not painting in oils). She reports sometimes that he was pleased with her work, and that she admired him; she saw 'some great beauties by Westall, my master' at Downton Castle, near Shrewsbury (where they still are). But only after his death in 1836 did Victoria pay him generous, emotional tribute, and then she was moved more by pity for his financial state than by ardour for a master who had truly

*Lehzen, the Princess's first regularly available sitter, inspired portraits which reveal that assurance of line and spontaneity of approach which remained Victoria's strongest artistic qualities.*

PV 1 Lehzen .

a sketch
from nature
2 V. j. R.P. character
1833.

inspired her. 'He was a very indulgent, patient, agreeable master, and a very worthy man . . . I have had every reason to be satisfied with him; he was very gentlemanly in his manners and extremely punctual and exact in everything he did.'

Richard Westall came from artistic stock. His father William was a melancholy man, who travelled with the explorer Matthew Flinders on his voyage to the Pacific, and provided the beautiful, grand illustrations of the natives, flora and fauna of Australia for the expedition's report to the Admiralty. Richard was apprenticed to a silver engraver, and later studied at the Royal Academy schools. He began as a portrait painter, but in the first quarter of the century he concentrated on illustrating editions of the poets. The cleanly chiselled lines of the engraver survived in all his later draughtsmanship. The study drawings he produced for his pupil to copy are distinguished by an exquisite delicacy of contour, set down upon the paper with a lightness and assurance that belies his age and his ill-health.

Though Westall could never be considered first rate, his drawings echo those of the greatest of his older contemporaries, John Flaxman, William Blake and Henry Fuseli. He shares with them a firmness of outline, and a leaning towards exaggerated facial expressions — knitted brows, rapt eyes, and dramatic gestures contained within a formal style, expressed with none of the impressionism of the later romantics. But the imagination and energy of Blake or Fuseli is entirely missing. Though in later years Westall adapted himself successfully to the needs of the times, abandoning the classics for the new authors, illustrating Goethe's *Faust*, Byron's *Don Juan* and Walter Scott's poems, he remained a peaceable artist, strikingly skilful but lacking in fire.

Princess Victoria was his first and only pupil. She had an artistic talent inherited from both sides of her family. Her grandfather George III was a collector of genius but also an accomplished draughtsman, as were his daughters, Augusta Sophia and Elizabeth. On the Coburg side, the Duchess of

*Lehzen encouraged Victoria to make genealogical tables of the English sovereigns. It was when the young Princess saw her own name added to the bottom of the tree that she realized how close she was to the throne.*

17

Kent had herself painted a *trompe-l'oeil* conservatory at the Rosenau in Coburg, her home before her first marriage. This talent Westall undoubtedly fostered with patient attention and some generosity.

Victoria copied Westall's drawings, of horses, of hands, of eyes. His lessons stuck: she always relied on her linear technique and was adept at catching the expression in a subject's eyes, at setting down the movement of a pony, or using a hand gesture to capture mood. Westall was also fond of genre painting, and he did a number of finished studies for Victoria — of a peasant girl drawing water at a well, a mother teaching her child, a begging urchin given alms by a mother holding her baby — and thus he instilled in her a

*On her mother's birthday, 17 August, Victoria often presented her with a highly finished watercolour copied from her drawing master Richard Westall. These Tyrolese peasants with their prettily coloured local costume show his influence clearly.*

*This careful study of the horse Shrewsbury was also copied from Westall as a present for Mama.*

Shrewsbury.

conventional, picturesque approach to scenes of ordinary life about her, often spoiled by pretty-pretty colouring. She never succeeded in shaking off this tradition and achieving a more committed realism. But through his attachment to scenes of humble life, Westall taught the Princess to use her eyes. Her observation of details of dress, for instance, is strong in all her work.

On New Year's Day and on the birthday of 'Mama', Victoria several times made a fair copy of one of Westall's compositions as a present for her. For a girl in her teens, she was very sure with her pencil and her brush, but it is clear that her application soon waned, for if there are two figures in

Westall, there is usually only one that bears the legend, 'P.V. *del*. K.P.' — Princess Victoria *delineavit* Kensington Palace. Sometimes she made copies for charity; some of these survive, adding lustre to Victoria's reputation in places as far flung as the University of Auckland, New Zealand, while the composition's originator, Westall, is almost forgotten. One drawing was presented by Victoria to the United States Embassy in exchange for Fenimore Cooper's autograph.

An artist's career was even more precarious in the early decades of the nineteenth century than it is now, and Westall was in great straits. He was supporting a blind sister on his meagre income, and some dabbling in picture-dealing had gone awry. But he refused to accept payment for the lessons he gave the future Queen, though his sister received help from the Duchess of Kent. To Victoria, who was tender-hearted towards others' misfortunes, his penury was very bitter. 'He died in the *greatest* state of *pecuniary* distress', she wrote. 'This killed him. It *grieves* and *pains* me beyond measure that I could not alleviate his sufferings.' He told her mother that he was dying of a broken heart. 'Oh! this is sad, very very sad! to think that one whom I saw so often, knew so well, and who was so ready to oblige me, should *die* in want and overwhelmed by grief is grievous indeed!' In one of the very few passages of her diary as a Princess that betrays her knowledge of the great fortune awaiting her, Victoria continued: 'I could no more, as I had hoped, at a future time, make him comfortable and render his old days cheerful and without those worldly cares which . . . have brought him to the grave in a peculiarly distressing manner.' Westall left a letter for the Duchess of Kent, Victoria's mother, to be opened after his death. In it he begged her to settle £100 a year on his sister. This the Duchess of Kent naturally did, though the household at Kensington Palace was itself beset by all sorts of financial problems, caused partly by King William IV's dislike of his sister-in-law, and partly by the unscrupulousness and mismanagement of the Comptroller of the Duchess of Kent's household, the opportunist Sir John Conroy.

*Westall's* Hagar and Ishmael in the Desert *was exhibited at the Royal Academy in 1834. Victoria made several versions of it to be sold for charity, at such functions as 'the Fancy Fair in aid of the Fund for the Relief of Distressed Foreigners' held in Hanover Square.*

Westall has left us one of the most attractive portraits of Victoria ever painted, among the hundreds that were executed in the course of a long and strenuously recorded life. He painted the eleven-year-old Princess with her pencil poised in her hand, holding out her sketching book professionally at arm's length to gauge perspective, her wide-brimmed straw bonnet flung off at her feet. She is sitting in the shade of a tree, by a classical urn, with a running stream beside her. It is an idyllic scene of tranquil rural pleasures, and a fine painting, reflecting the influence of Sir Thomas Lawrence, with whom Westall had lived in the 1790s. But it is without doubt a pretty fantasy. There is no evidence that Princess Victoria was ever allowed out sketching in this carefree manner. Her drawings are strictly schoolroom work, interpretations of books she was reading, such as Walter Scott's *Marmion*, or academic imitations of Westall, or of German artists admired by her mother, such as Moritz Retzsch, whose illustrations of Schiller and Goethe appear regularly in her diary lists of presents received.

Victoria's upbringing was sheltered and closeted, even by those standards that came to be called Victorian. The life of this eldest legitimate descendant of the vast family of George III was infinitely precious; after the death of the Duke of Kent in Victoria's first year the fatherless Princess was closely guarded. Lehzen or the Duchess of Northumberland always sat in on her lessons. Her mother also attended. Victoria recalled in 1872 that she had never had a room of her own, but slept in her mother's room until 1837 when she became Queen. When she went downstairs, her hand was held so that she should not fall; when Leigh Hunt glimpsed her watering flowers in Kensington Garden, he noted that she was followed about by a footman in livery like 'a gigantic fairy'.

When in later years she looked back on her childhood, Queen Victoria always emphasized two aspects: the frugality and the loneliness. In 1872 she wrote: 'We lived in a very simple plain manner . . . Tea was only allowed as a great treat in later years.' To her eldest daughter Vicky, she wrote in 1858: 'I had led a very unhappy life as a child; had no scope

*Richard Westall was strongly influenced by the great portraitist Sir Thomas Lawrence, as is shown in this idyllic portrait of the Princess sketching outdoors, with Fanny her favourite dog at her feet.*

for my very violent feelings of affection — had no brothers and sisters to live with — never had a father — from my unfortunate circumstances was not on a comfortable or at all intimate or confidential footing with my mother (so different from you to me) — much as I love her now — and did not know what a happy domestic life was!'

One of the few people who alleviated this crushing solitude was her half-sister Feodore, daughter of the Duchess of Kent by her first marriage to Charles, Prince of Leiningen. But Feodore was twelve years older than Victoria, and in 1828 she left Kensington Palace for Germany to marry, leaving Victoria alone with her tutors, Lehzen and Mama. As Feodore recalled in a letter to the Queen in 1843: 'When I look back upon those years, which ought to have been the happiest in my life . . . I cannot help pitying myself. Not to have enjoyed the pleasures of youth is nothing, but to have been deprived of all intercourse, and not one cheerful thought in that dismal existence of ours, was very hard. My

P.V. del
K.P. June 13ᵈ
1837.

Princess of Leiningen,
drawn from nature.

only happy time was going or driving out with you and Lehzen; then I could speak and look as I like. I escaped some years of imprisonment, which you, my poor darling sister, had to endure after I was married.'

Because she responded in a way that Mama could not, Feodore received the torrent of Victoria's pent-up emotion. The Duchess of Kent, twice-widowed, a German living for the first time in England, an anxious and overprotective custodian of the future monarch, was an immensely biddable personality, and it was Victoria's great misfortune that her mother chose to be bidden by the self-seeking Sir John Conroy. When Feodore came to stay at Kensington Palace in the summer of 1833, Victoria's fifteenth year, she and her first two children, Eliza and Charles, radiated light and warmth through the gloom and tension. Feodore was a beautiful young woman, with a gentle and serene countenance, large brown eyes and a handsome straight nose, snowy sloping shoulders greatly admired at the time, and a frivolous, beribboned, ornamental taste in clothes and head-dresses. As Victoria recalled later, after Feodore had aged: 'She was very lovely then . . . and had charming manners . . .'

On the day her sister and the two children were leaving, Victoria's skills broke down, but the results convey vividly the extent of her grief. As soon as they had gone she sketched Eliza, in the little shift she had worn as she washed herself that morning, and again, in her travelling dress. In her diary, Victoria raced over fourteen pages — by far the longest entry till her Coronation — as she cried over the pain of parting: 'It is such a VERY VERY GREAT HAPPINESS for me to have my DEAREST most DEARLY BELOVED sister with me in my room . . . How I love her I cannot say . . . It is TOO DREADFUL for me to think that in an hour I shall not see *Dearest* Feodore's *dear kind* sweet face, and the *little beauty* Eliza jumping about, and *good honest* Charles running about the room, any more. . . . I was so dreadfully affected with grief at thinking of parting, that I fell round her [Feodore's] neck and we both cried *bitterly* and pressed each other in our arms *most tenderly*. . . I sobbed and cried most violently the whole morning.'

*Dear little Eliza in her travelling-dress which she wore the morning she left us. from nature.*

*A. D. ½ P.*

*Saturday 26th July 1834. The day dearest Feodore went.*

*When Victoria's half-sister Feodore left after a visit with her two small children in July 1834, the Princess was desolate, and immediately sketched from memory Eliza in her travelling clothes.*

Eliza died of tuberculosis, aged twenty, and Victoria, with the coolness of distance and new loves, was able to comment: 'She had rather an unbendable character which made her mother fear she might *not* be happy in the future.' But her earlier effusions had not been merely the expressions of conventional sentimentality; Princess Victoria was clear-sighted in her assessment of character, and never more so when she said that as a child she had no scope for her passionate nature. She was hungry for company, for young company, and her high spirits demanded an outlet. Three years later, when her other half-nephews, Ernest and Edward, the small children of Feodore's brother Charles of Leiningen, came to stay, Victoria again responded with delight at the ordinary demonstrativeness of children: 'Edward was beyond everything funny. He calls me Lisettche, and a number of other odd names. . . . He has no *respect* for me, I fear, at all.' As soon as such visits were over, the stilted tone returned to the diary as she set down the hourly tedium of lessons, interrupted only by mealtimes with the Conroys, rides in the park and ministrations to the many dogs on whom Victoria lavished her starved affections.

The Conroys are ever-present in the daily routine of Kensington Palace; above all, their daughter Victoire, who was a little older than Victoria and was produced, as many unfortunate children are, specifically to be a friend and playmate. She never wins a word of praise or affection from the Princess. She is merely there, and Victoria bleakly states her encroaching ways: 'Victoire stayed from 3 till 6.' 'Victoire dressed here for dinner.' On Victoire's birthday Victoria notes that she went to see her, but says nothing of her gift (if she gave one), though gifts given and received take up large portions of the diary. When they go riding together, Victoria, who rode with the verve she showed in so many other areas, merely comments: 'Victoire rode first on the wrong side Gossamer, then Sylph.'

*Right: Victoria craved gaiety: fancy dress provided it, and she and Victoire Conroy, a constant companion, often created costumes out of shawls and borrowed necklaces, and came down to dinner as 'a nun' or 'an old Turkish lawyer' or an 'Italian brigand's wife'.*

Dash /our dog./
From nature. Jan: 11th 1836.

*Left: The only thing Sir John Conroy did that Princess Victoria appreciated was to give her mother a King Charles spaniel, Dash. Victoria took him over immediately; when he died she buried him under the epitaph:*

*Reader*
*If you would live beloved*
*And die regretted*
*Profit by the example of*
*DASH*

A Nun
Sister Victoire

P. V. del.
Claremont
18ᵗʰ Jun: 1837.

Portrait of Miss
Victoire Conroy

P.V. del.
Dec: 1836.
Claremont.

Miss Victoire Conroy
from
nature.

*Sir John Conroy (above) was ambitious for a Regency which would give him power over the Queen through her mother, and he used his daughter Victoire (left) to help spread rumours that Victoria was immature, unhealthy and incompetent to reign.*

The Conroys' likenesses, taken down in the inky silhouettes then fashionable as a parlour game, appear together in one of Victoria's albums, entitled with unconscious aptness, 'A Collection of Shades'. The five years recorded in the diary until the accession, when the whole Conroy tribe were forbidden to appear at court, show no improvement in her relations with Victoire, though she continued to pass some of the enforced hours of her companionship in drawing portraits of her.

There was one aspect of the 'Kensington System', Sir John's plan for Victoria's upbringing and his own advancement, that Princess Victoria at first enjoyed. For although Mama allowed Conroy to persuade her that the heir presumptive to the throne must not see her royal relations but be kept aloof from Court, alone at Kensington Palace, she also agreed with him that Victoria should be seen by her future subjects. So began in 1832, each autumn, a series of triumphal progresses through the countryside. King William IV was infuriated by the honours that Conroy insisted upon: the royal salutes at Portsmouth — 'the popping must stop', said the King — the official greetings committees and the escort of county yeomanry that accompanied the Princess's carriage. But Victoria, at least to begin with, during the journey to Wales of 1832, enjoyed getting out and seeing new people and new sights and making friends, some of whom remained for life. In this way she made the acquaintance of the Pagets, on their estate of Beaudesert. Many different Pagets were to wait on her as Maids of Honour and Equerries; at the age of fourteen Victoria enjoyed their frivolity and sophistication, and Lord Alfred Paget became one of her favourite dancing partners. Later the clan did not altogether meet with Albert's approval.

The young Princess proceeded from one great Whig English country house to another, down roads strewn with dahlias — for it was October — under arches on which, as she described, disingenuously trying to disguise her pleasure, her name was written 'not in ink, but with flowers and pink bows'. She visited Buxted Park, the seat of Lord Liverpool,

P. B.B.
Ramsgate.
23ᵈ Oct: 1836.

Lady Catherine Jenkinson.
Drawn from nature

*Lady Catherine Jenkinson (left), daughter of Lord Liverpool, often accompanied Victoria on her 'royal progresses' to different parts of England.*

*Riding was one of the Princess's chief pleasures, and though custom demanded that she ride sidesaddle, she went with greater brio than is suggested by her sketch of a riding party (below right) in decorous Tunbridge Wells.*

and met his daughters the Ladies Louisa and Selina Jenkinson, who played the harp and the piano after dinner and gave excerpts from operas. Louisa was later a train-bearer at her Coronation, and Lord Liverpool was the only Tory — with the august exception of the Duke of Wellington — who was invited to her wedding, for through the friendship formed during these early years he understood the Princess's abilities and supported her against Conroy. At Chatsworth she watched a charade, her first encounter with a game that met all her love of gaiety and dressing up and later became a staple entertainment of her family gatherings. The word 'Kenilworth', from Scott's novel, was mimed in four costume tableaux, and the characters recorded in her sketchbook. On a visit to Hardwicke Hall nearby, she saw the window through which Mary Queen of Scots was spied upon, and noted it was 'very singular'.

*A riding party.*

A. J. D. J. W.
Feb: 13. 1834.

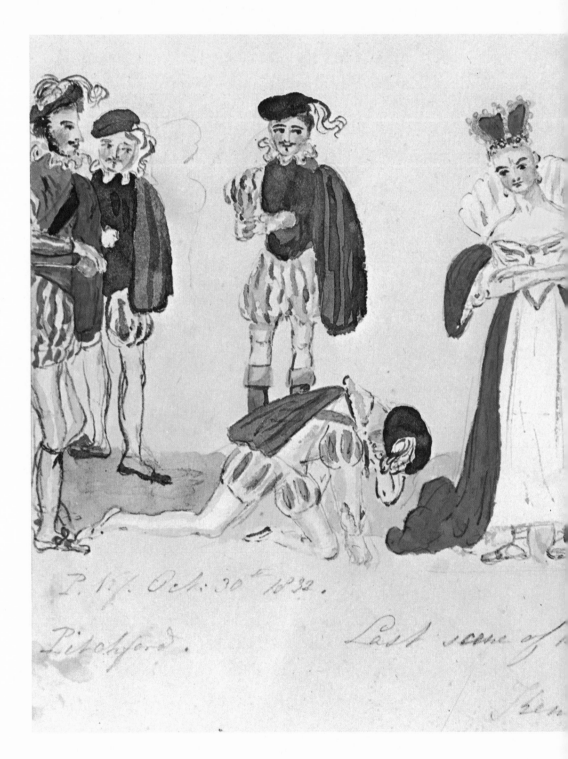

*charade at Chatsworth*

Deceased Queens were not the only objects of the Princess's curious scrutiny. She complained to Uncle Leopold when he sent her an extract about the government of Queen Anne: '[I] must beg you, as you have sent me to show what a Queen *ought not* to be, that you will send me what a Queen *ought to be.*' She had met Donna Maria da Gloria, Queen of Portugal, at a children's party given by King George IV, but Victoria was only eight years old at the time. When she met her again, in Portsmouth during a yachting trip, Victoria was fourteen, and she noted Donna Maria and her stepmother the ex-Empress of Brazil, then only twenty-one, with some care, and made drawings on her sketch pad. 'Donna Maria', she wrote, 'is only a month older than I am

*Previous page: Staying at Chatsworth House in Derbyshire in the autumn of 1832, Victoria saw her first game of charades played by the large house party. She did not take part, but the occasion made a vivid impression on her and* tableaux vivants *remained a favourite pastime all her life.*

*Victoria observed with close interest two young queens whom she met when she was fourteen: Amelia, the ex-Empress of Brazil (left), and her 'very stout' stepdaughter Donna Maria da Gloria of Portugal (below right).*

and is very kind to me . . . she is grown very tall but also very stout . . . She has a beautiful complexion, and is very sweet and friendly. She wore her hair in two large curls in front and a thick fine plait turned up behind. The Empress . . . has beautiful blue eyes, and has a fine tall figure . . . She was simply dressed in a grey watered moiré trimmed with blonde.' Artlessly, and with perfect good nature, the girl who knew she would one day be Queen of England was taking stock of the first two young queens she had ever met. Four years later, and more discerning, Victoria disliked comment on the 'likeness' between herself and Donna Maria, for Maria's education was 'one of the worst that could be.'

P. Veil.
Nov: 1836. Ramsgate.

Boulogne fishermen
from recollection.

The scarring of early industrial England was not lost on the Princess as her carriage bowled along towards the great ancestral houses, but her instinct was to dismiss such ugliness. Though she drew her fellow passengers, and the horses' dancing heads from the carriage, she did not record the figures of misery which she must have seen on her travels. But in the course of a stay at St Leonards, during which the boredom of the repetitious days hangs pall-like over the diary, Victoria's fount of strong feelings was again tapped. There had been a shipwreck off the coast and six men had drowned. Victoria, like a newspaper reader today, was hungry for more details of adversity. 'The wind blows a hurricane, the sea is mountains high and deluges of rain', she wrote. 'Another body of one of the poor men was found quite close here this morning, and they carried it past the windows.' When by chance, out walking with Lehzen, the Princess saw one of the widows, she was fascinated: 'Mrs Covely . . . stood on the steps. She had a cheerful countenance with rosy cheeks and fine teeth. She was in deep mourning and had a widow-cap on.'

39

The Disconsolate

J⁺ L. Hk d.
2ᵈ Jⁿ 1835.

*Left: Victoria rarely drew from imagination, but after six men drowned trying to rescue goods from a shipwreck near St Leonards, she drew this idealized portrait of a 'disconsolate' widow.*

Mrs Covely went straight into the sketchbook; but so did an imaginary figure, inscribed 'The Disconsolate'. Ignoring the 'blooming and cheerful appearance' of Mrs Covely as unfitting, Victoria summoned up that persistent morbidity that was to become one of her most difficult and dominating traits of character. Yet Mrs Covely is one of the very few people Victoria drew outside her own narrow circle. She was not in the least haughty, and at times showed strong powers of empathy, but this natural responsiveness seems to have been staunched in later life.

Just before she became Queen, she made friends with a family of gipsies encamped on the road near Claremont House, the English home of her uncle Leopold. She was

*Right and overleaf: In 1836, at Christmas, a family of gipsies set up camp near Claremont House where Victoria was staying. She was fascinated by them, especially by the formidable appearance of the tribe's mother, Sarah Cooper (right): 'There is so much mind and soul in it . . . I do so wish I could take her likeness from nature! What a study she would be!'*

*Instead she made many watercolours 'from recollection'.*

Sarah Cooper
Gipsy woman near Claremont.
from recollection.
P.V. del.
Claremont
Dec: 1836.

P.V. del.
Dec: 12th 1836.
Claremont.

Gipsy women near Claremont.
from recollection.
(The same women is on the other side.)

P.V. del:
Claremont.
Dec: 1836:

Gipsy woman & children
near Claremont.
from recollection.

The woman called Sarah Cooper & the
children (her nephews & nieces) called: Dinah,
Job, Britannia, Emmeline, Helen &c.

deeply stirred by them, and became their impassioned defender. When a baby was born to one of the young women, Victoria made certain that food and blankets were provided. Though the child had no father, she wanted to call him Leopold after her uncle, but dared not suggest it, not because she thought it improper for a bastard — she never gives an inkling of such prejudice — but because the gipsies did not ask her to be sponsor. 'It is *atrocious*', she wrote in high indignation in 1837, 'how often these poor creatures have been falsely accused, cruelly wronged, and greatly ill-treated.'

The gipsies distracted her from life at home. Kensington Palace was silent, gloomy and tense, and she passed most of her 'very unhappy life as a child' shut up inside it. But even the Conroys did not prevent her — though they almost always came with her — from discovering the intoxicating interest, the abiding elation of 'the Play'.

M.me Taglioni, as la Sylphide & others. Albert as James, as they appeared in the ballet of la Sylphide at the King's Theatre this season.

# TWO

## Souvenirs de l'Opéra

*Marie Taglioni, 'goddess of the dance', was the creator and personification of romantic ballet.*

Princess Victoria was stagestruck. She is perhaps the first little girl on record, and certainly the most august, to have languished for the heroines of the boards with the intense identification described in such classics as *Ballet Shoes*. For London in the late 1820s and 1830s saw the flowering of romantic ballet; to London came the most celebrated interpreters of Italian opera, then in its salad days with Bellini, Rossini, Donizetti; here too was carried on the lively tradition of melodrama, performed with full-blooded gusto by the spirited heirs of Kean and Kemble. Victoria was there, sometimes as often as three times a week, sitting in her box after dinner, surrounded by her faithful retinue of Mama, Lehzen and the Conroys. Day after day in her diary she copies out playbills, dashes off enthusiastic summaries of plots and highlights, despatches an ugly actress with a single blow, or enthuses fulsomely about her favourites. The young critic's ready-reckoner of praise was simple: 'I was very much amused', closes her account of an evening's pleasure; or 'I was *very very much amused*', or 'I was VERY VERY MUCH AMUSED' (two underlinings), or 'I WAS VERY VERY MUCH AMUSED INDEED' (three underlinings).

By the time she was fourteen, Victoria was in thrall to ballet. Over half her collection of dolls consists of dancers in different roles, and these are, contrary to common belief, almost the only real characters she brought to life in this way. The other dolls, given grandiose names and stories — the thrice-married Harriet Arnold, Duchess of Parma, and the twin-bearing Countess of Rothesay — are imaginary. But the ballerinas whom she saw inhabited the ethereal sphere fit for dolls, and she and Lehzen together made a troupe from tiny five-inch Dutch figurines, dressed them in miniature

*Miss Woolford, one of the first circus dancers, was married to Andrew Ducrow, the eccentric and tempestuous creator of the modern circus spectacular.*

*Myself — 1845.* *Mazourka.*

*In* Eoline, ou La Dryade, *a ballet Victoria saw at Her Majesty's in 1845, Eoline is bewitched by her wicked lover the gnome Rubezahl, and 'like the bird fascinated by a serpent . . . yields'. Together they dance 'a fantastic mazourka', the Mazourka d'Extase.*

replicas of the costumes they had worn on stage, and arranged them in pairs according to their favourite ballet stories. Tiny rosettes of ribbon, edgings of gold braid, pinafores of veiling, cross-laced corsages, silk slippers a quarter of an inch long, head-dresses with beads and plumes, minute reticules attached to wrists, bandeaux set with a gem — all were worked by Lehzen with the Princess's assistance, or sometimes by Victoria herself, supervised by the governess. They formed a strikingly charming catalogue of the contemporary ballet repertory, and in particular of Victoria's idol, the greatest ballerina of her day and the creator of the romantic sublime in nineteenth-century dance, Marie Taglioni.

49

O.V.d.K.P.
July 13ᵗʰ 1834.
Mˡˡᵉ Taglioni
as she appeared in the ballet of Le Pouvoir de la danse ou la Nouvelle
Therbijenne

50

*Right: 'La Tyrolienne', a pas de trois from Rossini's opera* William Tell, *was a favourite divertissement at benefit nights. Victoria thought Paul Taglioni, Marie's brother (half hidden to the right), 'the most splendid man-dancer I ever saw'.*

*Left: Filippo Taglioni was the first choreographer to make dancers seem lighter than air, and his daughter Marie the first to alight on points. 'Taglioni danced quite exquisitely', wrote Victoria, '. . . she positively almost flew'.*

'Lehzen finished for me . . . at about 6, a lovely doll, representing La Sylphide, which I saw in town', writes the Princess in her Journal. The ballet *La Sylphide*, the prototype of the 'ballet blanc', was created for Taglioni by her father Filippo, the most inventive and dedicated choreographer of his day. For the role, Eugène Lami designed the costume that has become synonymous with romantic ballet: the multi-layered white skirt of tulle, caught into a satin bodice and cut off at the knee so that the dancers' legs are seen.

Marie Taglioni was half Italian, half Swedish. She was trained by her father, and became the pioneer of dancing on points. 'She danced quite beautifully, quite as if she flew in the air, so gracefully and lightly', wrote Victoria after seeing her in *La Sylphide*. 'When she bounds and skips along the stage, it is quite beautiful. Quite like a fawn. And she has grace in every action. The motion of her arms and beautiful hands are so graceful, and she has such a sweet expression in her face . . .' Later, making a literary effort, the Princess commented: 'It seemed as if some sylph had taken her form and lighted upon earth.'

Victoria was not alone in her delight: Taglioni's new technique inspired her audience to an extent rarely achieved by avant-garde revolutions in the arts. Thackeray wrote to his mother from Paris: 'They have a superb dancing damsel yclept Taglioni who hath the most superb pair of pins, & maketh the most superb use of them that ever I saw dancer do before. Then there is Paul [Taglioni, Marie's brother and frequent partner] who will leap you quite off the perpendicular & on the horizontal & recover his feet with the greatest dexterity.' Victor Hugo dedicated a book '*A vos pieds, à vos ailes*'. Berlioz, seeing Taglioni at the height of her international fame in 1843, was no less transported by 'this gentle and melancholy joy, this chaste passion, this swallow's flight over the surface of a lake'. The first company to run coaches between London and Windsor in two hours painted Marie Taglioni on the doors of their vehicles; Victoria herself named a new fast horse after the dancer. When the Princess's dolls had been put away as childish things, she took to fancy dress for dinner: 'I dressed myself up as La Naiade, as Taglioni was dressed, with corals in my hair'.

Victoria's love of Taglioni was not only composed of admiration for her agility and her gentle 'all-ways smiling' countenance. Taglioni was ethereal and vulnerable, modest, even austere. The Parisian chant, '*Est-ce femme, ou est-ce l'air?*' accurately reflects Taglioni's almost spiritual appeal, her fulfilment of the aesthetic ideal of disembodied existence. Victoria was not incapable of earthier tastes: she admired, for example, Taglioni's principal rival, Fanny Essler — famed for the vigorous sensuality of her interpretations — in her most passionate role of all, the Cachucha, with castanets. But usually she found Essler coarse. Taglioni's combination of excellence and naivety tallied exactly with Victoria's conception of womanliness to which, contrary to the wilfulness and impetuosity of her nature, she would like to have conformed.

A fascinating aspect of the romantic ballet is that it embodied a fragile, often doomed, ideal of the feminine while choosing as themes rousing stories of struggle. Taglioni

*Marie Taglioni was idolized but not idealized by Victoria. Her blend of sweetness, austerity, naivety and skill had the quality of genius. 'She has grace in every action', wrote her worshipper. 'The motion of her arms and beautiful hands is so graceful, and she has such a mild sweet expression in her face.'*

Mlle Taglioni as La Sylphide.                    P.V.p. 1833

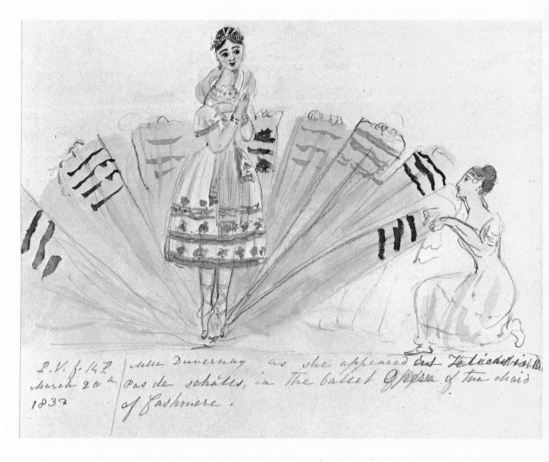

*P.V. f. 14.2 | Mlle Duvernay as she appeared [...] [...]*
*March 20th | Pas de schalls, in the ballet [...] of the maid*
*1837 | of Cashmere.*

created *The Revolt of the Harem*, which set a minor fashion for ballets portraying female emancipation in exotic settings — in this case, the Alhambra. Victoria saw another dancer, Mrs Honey, in *The Revolt of the Naiades* and was much taken with the Amazon scenes: 'The scenery is excessively pretty and the scenes of the coral retreat, of the Naiades bathing, the Stalactistic Hall with the Fête of the Water Queen, and the Revolt and Jeu de guerre are quite beautiful', she wrote. This evening at the Adelphi rated three underscorings.

But the ballet that concentrated all aspects of the formula dear to Victoria was *Le Dieu et la Bayadère, or The Maid of Cashmere*, to music by Auber. Victoria sketched both Taglioni and Pauline Duvernay, whom she also much admired, in the principal role. Her favourite scene came at

*Victoria painted Pauline Duvernay after seeing her do the shawl dance from* Le Dieu et la Bayadère *to music by Auber.*

the end, when the 'unknown' man in the palanquin reveals himself to be the 'god', rescues the maiden, and 'takes her up to heaven'. Far away settings, barbarian costumes, exquisite and faint-hearted heroines, toweringly heroic males materializing at the last minute, put the young girl soon to be Queen into a state of blissful surrender.

In the nineteenth century it was the fashion to vary the evening's entertainment in the theatre. In one night — the benefit or gala of an artiste, for example — she might see part of an opera, some solo arias, a *tour de force* from one ballet and a scene from another, performed by the foremost interpreters, themselves versatile. After dinner Victoria and her party would leave Kensington Palace to take their seats in their usual box after the curtain had gone up. As a rule they rose before the end, though the Princess was often enjoying herself so much that she left with reluctance.

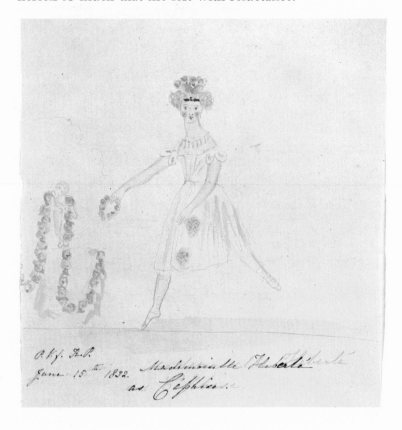

*Heberlé, a pioneer interpreter of romantic roles, had 'immense force and power', wrote Victoria, who saw her only once; she 'was like a young deer in her actions, but her style was quite different to Taglioni's.'*

P.V. del: Pt.
April 1837.

Mr. Charles Mathews
as Dapperwit in The Rape
of the Lock.

*Charles Mathews (left), here in the role of Dapperwit in John Oxenford's adaptation of* The Rape of the Lock, *was in Victoria's opinion 'the most delightful and amusing actor possible'. With his wife Eliza Vestris, he evolved a new informal and naturalistic style of acting, in such comedies as* Riquet with the Tuft *(right), written for them by Charles Dance and James Planché.*

One inspired impresario who struggled gamely for many years in different theatres against appalling financial odds was Eliza Vestris. At the Olympic, Madame Vestris produced plays, cast them, acted and sang herself, and invited dancers and singers to provide divertissements between the acts. Victoria's loyalty to her and to her husband, the actor Charles Mathews, lasted until Vestris's death in 1856; she went often to see them perform, and invited them to Windsor for private theatricals. Her taste in such matters was sound. Even Lord Melbourne, always cutting and usually bored by the theatre, commented about Vestris: 'It's very rare to see a good actress. It's very rare to see a good anything, that's the fact.'

P.V. del. K.V.
(April 16th 1837. from recollection) Mme Vestris - as Belinda. &c —

Victoria admired (and drew) the best-looking and the most accomplished performers: Ellen Tree, who '*acted very well indeed*' in *The Red Mask, or the Council of Three*, a historical melodrama by James Robinson Planché; Fanny Kemble — not as Juliet, the role in which she made her spectacular début, but as Lady Macbeth in which she was also a great success; John Cooper, who 'looked EXTREMELY WELL' in Addison's forgotten drama about Henri IV, *The King's Seal;* and other famous names, Charles Mathews and Charles Macready. But Victoria's judgement was not always reliable. After she saw the famous production of Shakespeare's *King John* for which Planché designed costumes that for the first time aimed at historical verisimilitude, *King John* always ranked in her estimation above *King Lear* or *Hamlet*.

One of the very few Shakespearean scenes she drew is the famous final submission of Katherina in *The Taming of the Shrew*. The dramatic contest for mastery between a strong woman and a strong man appealed to her, as did the play's lesson, that males prevail. In later life Victoria liked to reiterate that the proper order of nature had been reversed by her queenship and precedence over Albert.

*Pd. d. Vy R.
March 12th
835.* Mr Bennett, as Grindoff the Miller, & Miss Taylor a
born off by Grindoff in the "Miller" & Claudine
his men in the 2 act.

Victoria's sketchpad recalls high moments of melodrama: she was inspired for instance by the death-defying selflessness of the noble savage Rolla, hero of *Pizarro*, Sheridan's rodomontade against the Spaniards. One of the best parts, she thought, was 'when he comes on all bleeding and places the rescued child in Cora's arms and falls down dead.' The blowing-up of the powder magazine at the end of *The Miller and His Men*, a family favourite by Isaac Pocock with music by Henry Bishop, earned several underlinings and a sequence of excited drawings. The dialogue of the last scene is characteristic:

*Grindoff, robber-king and villain of Isaac Pocock's melodrama* The Miller and His Men, *abducts the senseless heroine into his mountain lair (above). But Lothair, hero and true lover, anticipates his every*

*move and saves Claudine (above right); as they make their escape Grindoff's hideaway is blown up, with all his banditti followers trapped inside.*

Wolf:   (*With a shout of great exultation*) Ha! Ha! You strive in vain!

Karl:   Cowardly rascal! You will be caught at last. (*Shaking his sword at Wolf*)

Wolf:   By whom?

Karl:   Your only friend, Beelzebub . . .

Wolf:   Foolhardy slave, I have sworn never to descend from the spot alive, unless with liberty.

The spot, his robber's lair, explodes, dynamited by Karl and his righteous supporters.

P. V. del.
Dec: 26th
1836 in.
Claremont
26 Dec
1836.

Mlle Duvernay as
Florinda,
in "the Devil on two sticks."
1st Act.
from recollection.

Henry Crabb Robinson, who kept an ardent amateur's diary of theatregoing from 1811 to 1866, commented as a specialist in 'horrid' spectacles: 'The melodrama of *The Miller and His Men* interested me as all Banditti occurrences do. The scenes however — and in such pieces these are the most material parts of the exhibition — are not so horrid as I have seen before. And the plot is not so well contrived. In such pieces a gross and palpable probability is a great requisite. And here one does not see . . . what end is answered to blow up the magazine at last.' When Victoria took Prince Albert, whose stomach was much more refined, to a revival, she records in all ingenuousness that he said he was interested but kept his praise for the music.

Victoria's interest in the theatre did not wane as she grew older, but it never reached the intensity of her girlhood passion for the ballet. Ballet and opera were mixed in the long programmes offered by Drury Lane, the King's Theatre, and later Covent Garden, and from the age of about fifteen onwards the Princess's affections gradually shifted from Taglioni towards the greatest singer of the day, Giulia Grisi. Taglioni was sadly neglected. Indeed Queen Victoria does not seem to have been aware that her childhood idol was scraping a living in the 1870s giving lessons in 'social dances and deportment for the aristocracy', or that she died in poverty in 1884. In 1837, Victoria, chafing at a long exile from London during the season, had written to Uncle Leopold: 'we shall have been *six months* in the country next Thursday . . . and I am sure you will stand by me for my having my seasons fully, as you may understand that my *Operatic* and *Terpsichorean* feelings are pretty strong . . .' But she was certain that she preferred 'the Opera by far to the ballet. Grisi far surpasses Taglioni in my estimation.'

Grisi's ascent to the position of *prima donna assoluta* marks a moment in the history of opera as revolutionary as Taglioni's use of the first padded ballet shoe in the history of ballet. In both cases Victoria was there, enthusiastic, spontaneous and committed. She spent £600 in one year — 1839 — on her boxes. Three quarto albums in the Royal Library at Windsor

63

*Signor Rubini, Signora Grisi & M. Ivanoff,*
*Neocles, Pamira & Cleomene,*
*(L'Assiedo di Corinto)* P.V.d. R.P. *June 27ᵗʰ 1834.*

*Signora Grisi & M. Ivanoff*
*Pamira & Cleomene*
*(in L'Assiedo di Corinto)* P.V.d. R.P. *June 27ᵗʰ*

record the Princess's impressions. Volume I is inscribed in a careful copperplate hand over pencilled rules:

Souvenirs de l'Opéra
Sketches from Recollection
Mᴌᴌᴇ. Giulietta Grisi &c.
by P.V.
1835
1836

Inside, Victoria pasted drawings of figures from the productions she saw, from operas still in repertory today — Bellini's *Norma* and *I Puritani*, Donizetti's *L'Elisir d'Amore*, Rossini's *Cenerentola* and *La Gazza Ladra* — but also from entirely forgotten works, such as Rossini's *Otello* which was eclipsed by Verdi's later version; the Italian-born composer Michael Costa's *Malek Adel*, with a crusader theme; and the Irishman Michael Balfe's *Maid of Artois*, written specially for the legendary singer La Malibran. Victoria's drawings are

*The modern tradition of faithful, historical costuming in opera was begun in Victoria's time. In 1834 she saw the première of Rossini's* L'Assiedo di Corinto *and noted carefully (above) Grisi's plaits, Ivanoff's scimitar and turban, Rubini's Greek bolero and skirt, and (right) the splendid eastern exoticism of the famous bass Tamburini in the role of Mahomet, Emperor of the Turks.*

repetitive, for as she always sat in the same box, her vantage point for sketch after sketch was identical. Clumsy as they are, they constitute a fascinating souvenir of the performers, their costumes and gestures. It is a sad loss to theatre history that settings interested her so little, for she rarely drew scenery. It was the human voice as an instrument for expressing emotion that bound her to opera.

Signor Tamburini & M.dme G. Grisi
as
Mahomet & Pamira.
in L'Assedio di Corinto. p.V.d.K.S.
June 22 1834.

Victoria's first interest in opera coincided with the emergence of the soprano as the dominant solo performer. Grisi's glory was made possible by the death in 1836 of the then unsurpassed Malibran, otherwise Maria Felicitá García; she died suddenly in Manchester at the age of twenty-eight. Malibran was a natural contralto, but her father, the Spanish tenor Manuel García, had trained her to add a soprano's super-register, giving her a voice of extraordinary range. Malibran intoxicated her audiences: her low notes, held very very long, were thrilling; her impassioned renderings — she tore her glove to shreds as Mary Queen of Scots in Donizetti's *Maria Stuarda* — shocked and enthralled those who heard her. The cruel struggle between the castrato singer, who had hitherto dominated opera — and topped the bill — and the emergent soprano is well caught by an anecdote of Malibran's début in London at the age of sixteen. The castrato Velluti was so scared that she would outshine him on stage that he would only sing plain notes in rehearsal. But Malibran, hearing his embellishments for the first time during the performance, copied them effortlessly, adding several florid decorations of her own. '*Briccona*' (rascal), hissed the poor castrato in the girl's ear.

That was in 1824. A decade later, at Princess Victoria's sixteenth birthday concert, a present from her mother and surely one of the most dazzling collections of musical talent ever made for a private recital, there was no thought of inviting a castrato. The fashion for their particular timbre and tone was over. Instead Malibran, Grisi and all the other great interpreters — Luigi Lablache the bass, Rubini, Tamburini and Ivanoff — performed for Victoria. Malibran arrived late, 'dressed in white satin with a scarlet hat and feathers'. Victoria noted: 'Her low notes are *beautiful*, but her high notes are thick and not clear. I like *Grisi by far better* than her.' Malibran's sudden death stunned her hundreds of *aficionados*, and intense poetic tributes such as Alfred de Musset's 'Stances à la Malibran' commemorated her gift. Even Queen Victoria conceded that 'in point of cleverness and genius there is not a doubt that Malibran far surpassed Grisi . . . '

*Above: The voice of La Malibran was the most famous in Europe at the time of her premature death in 1836, the year Victoria drew this portrait.*

*Right: Victoria thought that Norma in Bellini's famous opera was her adored Giulia Grisi's best role.*

P.V. del.
1836.–

M.me Grisi as Norma & M.lle Assandri as Adalgisa
in Norma.— Finale to 1st Act:

But Grisi was her favourite, not least because of her beauty. Victoria was delighted when she saw the singer out riding in the Park: 'She is pale off the stage, but has not at all a delicate appearance. On the contrary she has a very slight pinkish hue over her face. She looks very pretty and mild.' Three days later, at the première of Donizetti's *Marino Faliero* (based on Byron's play), Victoria was gripped by Grisi's intensity: 'Elena then stares wildly about her, her hand raised to her head, and giving a frantic scream falls prostrate and lifeless to the ground . . . I know no singer I like as well as Grisi. She is perfection (to my feeling). She is *very pretty* and is

M.me Grisi as Elena in Marino Faliero.
Act 3.° Scene 1.st Elena. "Dio clemenza."

*The poet Théophile Gautier said that under Grisi's spell opera was transformed into a tragedy and a poem. Victoria could never see or hear her enough, and remained alive to every nuance of the singer's famous powers of intensely emotional expression.*

*Above: Albertazzi, an English soprano whom Victoria admired for 'her voice of great compass', seen here as the Crusader in* Malek Adel *by Michael Costa.*

*Above right: Victoria was upset when Grisi, in the role of Elena in Donizetti's* Marino Faliero, *'did not look quite so pretty as usual, as she had combed her hair too low into her face . . .'*

an *exquisite* singer and *charming* actress!' She was enraptured by Grisi's generosity in applauding warmly a rival, Albertazzi — now forgotten — in Rossini's *Cinderella*. 'She is a good-natured creature, Grisi', wrote her adorer. A special bow Grisi made to her box gave her the greatest pleasure, and the singer's appearance in person at her birthday treat, 'that delicious concert', inspired a litany of adulation. 'Such a lovely mild expression . . . such beautiful dark eyes with fine long eyelashes . . . Her beautiful dark hair . . . She is very quiet, ladylike and unaffected in her manners.' Victoria dressed herself for a ball with 'a wreath of white roses like Grisi has in the Puritani' — her favourite opera, usually referred to as '*dear* Puritani'.

The singers Grisi, Lablache, Rubini and Tamburini became known as 'the Puritani Quartet' after their unrivalled collaboration in Bellini's emotive Romeo and Juliet story set in Roundhead England. The member of the Quartet whom Victoria came to know best was Luigi Lablache, the monumental basso. Lablache had a genius for *opera buffa*

roles, to which his great size but nimbleness suited him, as
well as for *opera seria*, in which, as the Druid in *Norma* or the
leading Roundhead in *I Puritani*, he dominated majestically.
Although Lablache delighted the Princess, he did not make
her heart flutter as Grisi did. Yet she drew him more often
than any other figure. One particular scene from Rossini's
*Otello* recurs many times: Lablache towering over the tiny
figure of Grisi as Desdemona while she pleads for understanding from her father Elmiro. '*Se il padre m'abbandona, da chi
sperar pietà?*' ('If ever my father abandons me, from whom
else can I hope for pity?') was a line carved deep in Victoria's
memory, it seems. Once again her imagination was captured
by a scene of female vulnerability, intensified here by
Desdemona's psychological orphanhood. Victoria, who
chose to write to Uncle Leopold in Italian that he was not just
'il mio secondo padre', but '*solo* padre', seems to have felt for
the plight of the fatherless children around whom the plots of
so many romantic operas are built. Amina, Grisi's role in
Bellini's *Sonnambula* — one of Victoria's favourite operas —
is a foster-child; Norma's lover Pollione, by whom she has
two children, leaves them orphans not through his death, but
his infidelity.

It would be misleading to give a neurotic edge to
Victoria's love of romantic opera. She revelled in its humour
too, liking particularly Lablache's Don Magnifico in *Cinderella*, and his comic improvisations in the one-act *opera buffa* by
Gnecco, *La Prova di una Opera Seria*. Almost incoherent with
pleasure, Victoria described the scenes: 'Signor Lablache was
*beyond* every thing! He looked so funny, in his huge
powdered wig and bad brown silk coat and sword. And
acted — Oh! *inimitably*! He personated the distracted
composer when Corilla [Grisi] sings out of tune *exquisitely*
. . . When he . . . walks with bent legs . . . and imitates her
voice; she then does the same to him, and they both dance.
Grisi valsed about the stage by herself in a *very funny manner*
. . . Lablache kept us continually laughing . . . '

When Victoria learned that the Vernon family, whom she
met on her journeys in the north of England, had been

*Left: Bellini's* I Puritani, *set in the English Civil War, was Victoria's favourite opera of all; 'dear Puritani', she called it. She heard it sung by the historic and unsurpassed 'Puritani quartet' — Grisi, Lablache, Rubini and Tamburini.*

receiving lessons from Tamburini, her resolve to be taught properly herself must have stiffened. In 1836 Lablache himself came to Kensington Palace, and for twenty years continued to coach the high small voice of the Queen with his huge, deep, rolling bass. Lablache was endlessly good natured. Victoria recorded her appreciation: 'He is so good-humoured, and though tired, or bored (as I should think he must often be, by teaching a person like me, all the lovely songs &c, which he hears Grisi, Rubini &c. sing) he is always even-tempered, merry and most obliging . . . I liked my lesson extremely.' He had parts transposed to suit Victoria's voice, and patiently took her and Mama through the great arias. Victoria discussed music earnestly with him; she felt unable to agree about Mozart's supreme superiority. 'I am a terribly modern person', she wrote, 'and I must say I prefer Bellini, Rossini, Donizetti, etc, to anything else; but Lablache, who *understands* music thoroughly, said, "C'est le Papa de tous".' To her astonishment, Victoria discovered that her

*Right: Though Lablache tried to teach Victoria otherwise, she found Mozart a little old-fashioned and prided herself on her taste for contemporary music. Nevertheless, at the age of thirteen she made this very pretty drawing of Rosina in* The Barber of Seville.

P. V. f. Oct: 1832.

Lablache.

P.V. del:—  from recollection.
Kensington
Palace Aug: 1836.

*In 1836 Lablache began visiting Kensington Palace regularly to give Victoria singing lessons.*

hero — with whom she spoke French — was half Irish. His father was French and he was born in Naples, where several of his enormous family were being brought up.

She also discovered, and her report has a slightly puzzled air, that Lablache did not share her own high opinion of Grisi, but criticized the singer's way of swallowing before a roulade — 'a habit she has contracted from fear of failing . . . I do not think he quite *likes* her'. Indeed, when the mercurial impresario Alfred Bunn removed all the greatest singers from the King's Theatre to his new establishment at Covent Garden in 1847, Lablache refused to follow Grisi, Mario and the others. But even Lablache's reservations about Grisi could not dim her attraction for Victoria. Grisi remained the touchstone by which she judged all the great singers of the century, although slightly grudgingly she did admit later that Jenny Lind eclipsed her favourite.

Grisi never became the Queen's friend; perhaps her teenage idolatry made such a relationship impossible. Lablache, on the other hand, was the first of many to gain Victoria's impetuous affections, and to earn that high mark of her attachment: that she was really, though she knew she must not be, 'quite cross' when he could not come. Lord Melbourne and Prince Albert were Lablache's successors in this accolade of the young Queen's impatience.

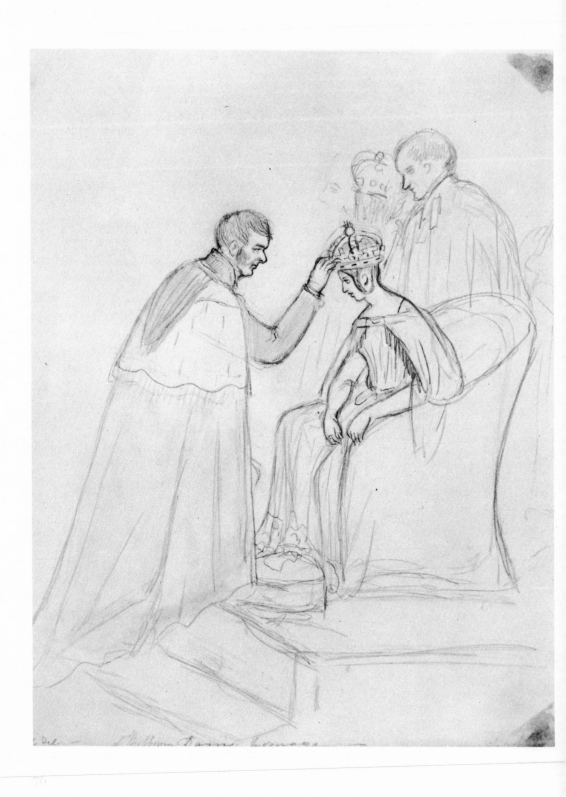

# THREE

# 'His Dear, Dear Face'

Lord Melbourne, who was Prime Minister when Victoria became Queen in 1837, did not like birdsong and could not distinguish a woodlark from a nightingale. He preferred the singing of blackbirds anyway; best of all, he liked the cawing of rooks and could watch them for hours as they circled at sunset. Victoria was surprised by this; she disliked their grating and insistent calling. 'The rooks are my delight', declared Lord Melbourne. Albert on the other hand loved the song of nightingales. Queen Victoria remembered later how he would listen for them 'in the happy peaceful walks he used to take with the Queen in the woods', and whistle to them 'in their own peculiar long note', so that they would reply in kind. On summer evenings he led her out on to the balcony at Osborne to hear them.

Rooks and nightingales: both played their part in Victoria's sensibility. She was down-to-earth, impatient of nonsense, fascinated by unembellished fact, quick to laugh 'till her gums showed', and inclined to gobble her food. But she also had a strong romantic strain, which made her less-robust, less humorous, more volatile. Melbourne was a survivor of the last century's sanguine, savoury nonchalance; his laconic wit was the epitome of aristocratic Whiggishness. Albert, whom she was to marry less than three years after she became Queen, was a blueprint of nineteenth-century German romanticism, emotional, serious, high-minded, diligent and often tormented.

*At her Coronation Victoria found the homage of all the peers 'a pretty ceremony': 'they first of all touch the Crown, and then kiss my hand.'*

77

As a young woman, Victoria was soft wax; the mixture was by nature very strong, but at the time of her accession she was ready, almost longing, to take the impress of any powerful stamp. She liked male company, and she had a gift for intimacy: she responded warmly, loved to listen, learned quickly and was flatteringly impressionable. Lord Melbourne and Prince Albert were strongly contrasted, but each, in his singular way, was a remarkable mentor.

The entry in her Journal for 20 June 1837, the day Victoria became Queen, uses the word 'alone' with defiant stress. She was *alone*, not even Mama was present, during the famous dawn encounter when the Archbishop of Canterbury and Lord Conyngham told the eighteen-year-old girl that King William IV was dead 'and consequently that I am *Queen*'.

Three hours later, Lord Melbourne came. 'I saw [him] in my room and of *course* quite *alone* as I shall *always* do all my Ministers. He kissed my hand . . . ' Victoria liked him immediately, and from then on Melbourne fills the pages of her Journal — Melbourne talking, joking, gossiping, instructing, clarifying, helping, reassuring, encouraging, enlivening; a brilliant, droll, individual mind forming that of a simple, ingenuous young woman forty years his junior. Victoria reported his conversation with the fidelity of Boswell, catching his inimitable caustic phrasing with a genuine diarist's gift of recall. The figure of Lord Melbourne crowds out all others at this time. The past is purged: Mama's bed is moved out of the Queen her daughter's room.

In 1841, Melbourne confided to Albert that when he first met the Queen he had been taken aback at how ill-equipped and immature she was and how urgently she needed guidance on all subjects. But the charm of his nature prevented any such opinion being communicated to Victoria. For the first time, she met a man steeped in the savoir-faire and culture of that most worldly-wise of societies, the London of Byron and the Prince Regent, and this man gave her his whole attention. Slowly and casually, without larding the compliments, he increased her confidence. He trusted her with stories about her rakish family, the royal uncles from

*Lord Melbourne, Queen Victoria's first Prime Minister, made the early months of her reign 'the pleasantest summer I ever passed in my life'. 'The more I see of him and the more I know of him,' she wrote, 'the more I like and appreciate his fine and honest character'.*

whom her mother had so jealously screened her. When she worried about her height, he reassured her: 'I lamented my being so short, which Lord M. smiled at and thought no misfortune.' He praised her 'fine character' when she told him she had never lied, though she was 'a passionate and naughty child'. He told her dry and wonderfully funny anecdotes about everyone from Napoleon to Robert Walpole to Queen Anne. Melbourne was the only person with whom she felt '*safe*': '*He alone* inspires me with that feeling of great confidence and I may say security . . . '

The young Queen absorbed Lord Melbourne's views on matters trivial and grave with equal interest: through her diary we know that he told her 'trees never grew so well in Ireland and were all a little bent from the wind blowing across the Atlantic', but we know too that this very experienced, subtle, discerning man took immense pains to lead Victoria to understand government, and that he was the only person to do so at the time. He undertook her first political education, a duty that he discharged in the main with wisdom, a light touch, inimitable tact and profound responsibility.

They saw each other every day, and both were the happier for it. In each case, the friendship was a sudden brightness: Lord Melbourne's rich prospects of happiness had been ruined by his marriage to the erratic Lady Caroline Lamb, who died in 1828, a year before their only son. Melbourne had no child, Victoria no father. Charles Greville, the diarist, thought their love unconsciously sexual, but realised the degree of frustrated family feeling on both sides. 'I have no doubt he is passionately fond of her as he might be of his daughter if he had one; and the more because he is a man with a capacity for loving without having anything in the world to love'. But ambiguous relations, neither blood nor contract, are always socially disturbing. The crowd booed Victoria at Ascot. 'Mrs Melbourne', they called.

When in 1839 Victoria faced the loss of Melbourne as her Prime Minister, to be replaced by Sir Robert Peel, she panicked. Then took place what has come to be known as the

*Lady Flora Hastings*

*Lady Flora Hastings, whose silhouette Victoria pasted into an album, was one of her mother's ladies-in-waiting. But she was also a friend of the Conroy family, and the Princess allowed her personal dislike of Lady Flora to colour her judgement. She suspected publicly the young woman of pregnancy (she was unmarried) and when Lady Flora died in 1839 of an internal tumour, the scandal cost Victoria her early popularity.*

Bedchamber Plot. Peel wished for the dismissal of the Whig ladies who were Melbourne's friends and surrounded Victoria; the Queen was affronted by this interference with her personal entourage. Melbourne rallied the Cabinet to support her, and remained in power.

Whether Melbourne manipulated the Queen to his own advantage or not, her terror of losing him was certainly genuine. It is written into every syllable of her letter to him at the height of the crisis, in which she plays havoc with syntax and pronouns: 'He [Peel] said he couldn't expect me to have the confidence in him I had in you (and which he never can have) . . . The Queen don't like his manner after — oh! how different, how dreadfully different, to that frank, open, natural and most kind, warm manner of Lord Melbourne . . . The Queen was very much collected, and betrayed no agitation during these two trying audiences. But afterwards again *all* gave way . . . what is worst of all is the being deprived of seeing Lord Melbourne as she used to.' She did not lose him, this time.

For most of the first three years of her reign, Victoria's watercolour box and pencils lay idle. But when she did take up her pencil, very often her subject was Lord Melbourne. His handsome, rumpled face appears again and again, on loose sheets, on blotting paper, in the margin of unfinished letters, sometimes in the scarlet and blue Windsor uniform in which Victoria specially admired him, sometimes playing with one of her dogs.

When she set down, in a thin album bound in marbled paper, a few memorial sketches of her Coronation, Melbourne was the protagonist of her imagination. The execution of other figures, and the faces of other participants (including her own) is often clumsy and lazy, but over Melbourne's features she lingered painstakingly. She wrote in her diary that she was deeply moved when, after the long process of ritual robing, the crown was placed on her head. But she proceeds immediately to her chief support: 'My excellent Lord Melbourne, who stood very close to me throughout the whole ceremony, was completely overcome

*The Queen liked dogs, and she liked people who liked dogs. Lord Melbourne qualified. Her terrier Islay, she reported, 'has a very odd trick of liking to lick and play with anything bright, and he remembers Lord M. giving him his glasses, and he sits begging before Lord M. the moment he sees them . . .'*

at this moment, and very much affected; he gave me such a kind, and I may say *fatherly* look.' Victoria drew him bowing before her, touching her crown in the act of homage; and carrying the Sword of State, a majestic figure arrayed in scarlet and ermine. Benjamin Disraeli, watching the ceremony from the Commons' pews, observed that Melbourne carried the sword like a butcher, tripped over his robes and pitched his coronet over his nose. Lord Melbourne himself was so exhausted by the long ritual that he revived himself with a glass of wine off the altar in St Edward's chapel, on which, rather to Victoria's disapproval, sandwiches were also being served. But she had no word of reproach for Lord Melbourne's need, and when he complained he found the sword 'excessively heavy', she rejoined in sympathy that 'the Crown hurt me a good deal'.

*Right: 'My kind Lord Melbourne', wrote the young Queen after her Coronation, 'was much affected in speaking of the whole ceremony.' He carried the Sword of State at the head of the solemn procession in the Abbey, and found it 'excessively heavy'.*

*Left: From her apartments in Buckingham Palace, Victoria could look across to Westminster Abbey, where her resplendent Coronation took place on 28 June 1838.*

Lord Mulhaurine bearing the Sword.

She drew herself in the same album, a tiny figure viewed from the back, swamped in a mantle, and almost toppled by a disproportionately huge crown. It had been made specially for her, set with all the historic stones, to weigh much less — just over half — the ancient Crown of England, called St Edward's. It is interesting that Victoria, trained to notice details of braid and embroidery, pattern and cut in the costumes of ballet and opera, should show such rough disregard for the different robes that marked each stage of the sovereign's investment. She mentions them by name in her diary — the Dalmatic, the Supertunica of Cloth of Gold, the Purple Velvet Kirtle and Mantle — but indistinct scribble is all they merit in her drawings. The light slippers, just like

*Wearing her circlet of diamonds, before the crowning, Victoria prayed. Her drawings of the ceremony are deeply serious — she recorded none of the mishaps and hitches and bewilderment that resulted from the lack of rehearsals.*

*Lady Fanny Cowper,
daughter of Lord
Melbourne's sister, was
one of the eight
trainbearers attending the
Queen, with wreaths of
silver corn and pink roses
in their hair, and more
roses on their silver and
white satin dresses.*

ballet shoes, embroidered with rosebuds and the royal arms
in gold, and lined with white satin reading 'All Hail Victoria'
in a wreath of rose, thistle and shamrock, are ignored; the
richly ornate, bold brocade of her golden cope, also worked
in the national symbols, is not even hinted at. She did take a
little more trouble over her own face, showing how her hair
was plaited and looped round her ears to show off their
neatness.

P.V.MLK P. 1837. Count Waldstein.
from recollection.

*Prince Esterhazy brought his 'good-looking' young compatriot Count Waldstein to visit Victoria's mother, to whom he was distantly related. Victoria enjoyed his conversation enormously, praising him as 'quiet, unassuming, sensible and highly talented'.*

In spite of her attachment to Lord Melbourne, Victoria had eyes for others, and a number of much younger men saunter through the pages of her sketchbooks in a variety of fetching costumes. Under Melbourne's influence, she assumed publicly a certain cynicism towards marriage, but this did not prevent her recording possible candidates for her favour. Count Waldstein, bearded and romantically tousled, is drawn attractively. She met him at her eighteenth birthday party; but etiquette prevented her dancing with him, for 'he could not dance quadrilles', and Victoria was forbidden the valse or the gallop with a partner not of royal blood. Later Count Waldstein's 'pretty Hungarian uniform' and his striking accomplishments in art and music met with her approval. He gave her one of his paintings, of gipsies from his own country. She stuck it, of course, in an album.

The man who fascinated her so much that while at the opera she watched him rather than the stage was someone she had known as a child but never met again since — her cousin Charles, the Duke of Brunswick. Seeing him from a distance at a ball, Victoria was struck: 'He was in a black and dark blue uniform with silver; his hair hanging wildly about his face, his countenance pale and haggard; I was very sorry I could not see him de près for once.' The Duke had been declared unfit to rule; a coup of 1830 had placed his brother on the throne instead. 'I must say I think it was well felt in him not to come near', adds Victoria, a little uncertainly. 'En revanche his gentleman came very near, and I had a full view of him; he has nothing at all fierce or tigrish about him, except his long, (but *tidy*) hair.' She was obviously gripped when 'two ladies who have seen him [the Duke] at the balls tell me that when close by, his expression is dreadful, so very fierce and desperate . . . ' This saturnine desperado, this royal Heathcliffe who so stirred Victoria's young curiosity, never regained his birthright; he became a collector of diamonds and died childless in Geneva in 1873.

*Charles, the exiled Duke of Brunswick, mesmerized the young Queen. She quizzed him from her box at the opera and out riding in the park — 'He has a very fine, dark and stern countenance', she noted — and drew him (right) 'from recollection from a distance'. She sketched as well his companion the Count d'Anglau (above), 'also very handsome and wild-looking'.*

The Queen was not entirely free to choose. Since her childhood Mama and Uncle Leopold, the shapers of her future, had planned — even schemed — that she should marry her first cousin, Prince Albert, the son of their brother Duke Ernest of Saxe-Coburg-Gotha. Both children had been brought up to expect it, but in July 1839, although Victoria remembered Albert with affection from his few days' visit in 1836, she wrote anxiously to Leopold, repudiating any idea that she had promised herself in marriage. After two years as an independent Queen Regnant, she thought she wanted to remain so.

It was therefore with feelings of hurt impatience that Prince Albert arrived at Windsor with his brother Ernest that winter. But the appearance of the man who loved music, and art and science as well as nightingales banished instantly all Victoria's reluctance and indifference. She stood at the top of the stairs at Windsor Castle to receive them, and immediately Albert stirred all her quick appreciativeness of good looks in men and all her ready, generous feelings: 'It was with some emotion that I beheld Albert — who is *beautiful*', she wrote in her diary. The next day she was enraptured by him: 'Albert really is quite charming, and so excessively handsome, such beautiful blue eyes, and exquisite nose, and such a pretty mouth with delicate moustachios and slight but very slight whiskers; a beautiful figure, broad in the shoulders and a fine waist.' She danced with him — he danced beautifully; she played Fox and Geese with him after dinner, and Tactics; they looked together at drawings by the Old Masters from her library.

The next day she told Melbourne — before she told Albert — that she had changed her mind, and wanted to marry. On 15 October, less than a week after Albert's arrival, she 'said to him, that I thought he must be aware *why* I wished them to come here — and that it would make me *too happy* if he would consent to what I wished . . . . I told him I was quite unworthy of him . . . I told him it was a great sacrifice — which he wouldn't allow . . . I feel the happiest of human beings.'

*Leopold of Saxe-Coburg-Gotha, Victoria's uncle and later King of the Belgians, was her chief adviser and 'my real father, for I have none'.*

They were both twenty, Albert the younger by just three months. The greatest difference between them was that Victoria had the unique psychological transparency that makes her diary such a compelling record of her life, while Albert was a closed character. In spite of a life of brilliant activity and splendid achievement, Albert remains a man across whom falls a shadow — the shadow of unlikeability. Yet he was a man of very fine quality, and Victoria's avowed inferiority complex beside him was well founded. In his twenties, before balding and thickening spoiled his appearance, he was indeed princely: tall, slender but strong, with the clear blue gaze of a Saxon and a romantic, well-cut profile, shapely hands, and long legs set off very well by the daring cut-away coats and tight breeches then in vogue. He was also able: well instructed, widely read, clever, filled with intellectual curiosity and the application to satisfy it. His education, devised by Leopold and the Coburg family shaman Baron Stockmar and supervised by their well-liked tutor Christoph Florschutz, took him to Brussels, Bonn and Rome and placed him in contact with such stimulating minds as Lambert Quételet the mathematician and Immanuel Fichte the philosopher.

*Sir William Ross painted a miniature of Prince Albert for the Queen in the year of their engagement; she had it set in jewels and wore it as a bracelet all her life. This pencil sketch is an early copy of it.*

Yet, for all his practical side, Albert was rather a dreamer, a man who gave way to stormy feelings at the piano or the organ (which he played well), who had a genuine collector's passion for art, not just the interest of conventional politesse. He was not easily approachable: Victoria, his elder daughters and a few intimates like Stockmar loved him, but in general he was admired and respected. The force of Victoria's love for him was such that perhaps she liked to have Albert this way, exclusively her own. But there is every indication that it did not make him happy. He was, in the double sense of the word, *étranger* — a foreigner, an outsider. He spoke excellent English, but German was his mother tongue. His combination of industry and sentiment, his persevering quest for moral improvement through art, reflected the highest philosophical ideals of German romanticism. Victoria, with her intuitive responses, saw in him this German atavism; her

favourite portrait of Albert, amongst very many that were painted, was by Robert Thorburn. At the Queen's request, he is dressed as a medieval Teutonic knight.

After the announcement of their engagement, Albert returned to Germany to say goodbye. He had a taste of his future wife's obstinacy when she appointed George Anson to be his Private Secretary, instead of someone of Albert's choice. Anson had occupied the same post on Lord Melbourne's staff, and Albert, who had pronounced ideas on the political neutrality of constitutional monarchy, did not want to be associated with Whiggery immediately he arrived in England. But Victoria would have her way, and Albert, on this occasion, acquiesced. There were other problems too. The Tories, angered by Victoria's open partisanship with the Whigs, reduced the customary grant of £50,000 a year for the Queen's husband to £30,000. But these trials became trifles when Albert returned and the couple were reunited: 'I embraced him now again, and he looked so dear and so well; seeing his *dear dear* face again put me at rest about everything!'

*Albert was such a paragon of beauty in Victoria's eyes that she seems to have hesitated to sketch him, and these watercolours are the only portraits she made.*

*The profile (right) is again after Ross's miniature, and the full face (left) captures well Albert's serious idealism. At the top of the page we can see how she tried out her colours as she worked.*

Original Sketch by
M[r] for the dress of the
Queen's 1st Brides Maid —

On 10 February 1840, in the Chapel Royal at St James's Palace, Victoria and Albert were married. She promised to obey him, though the Archbishop had asked her if she wanted the word deleted. After the ceremony, and the wedding breakfast, the couple drove to Windsor for a very short honeymoon — Victoria, robust in all things, and in defiance of Albert, wanted to get back to government as soon as possible. But all her fresh, happy, absolutely guileless immediacy is there on the pages of her diary. She describes how she had a headache after the long ordeal and retired to a sitting room, where she found Albert playing the piano. He took her on his knee and kissed her: 'I NEVER, NEVER spent such an evening!! My DEAREST DEAREST DEAR Albert sat on a footstool by my side and his excessive love and affection gave me feelings of heavenly love and happiness I never could have *hoped* to have felt before! He clasped me in his arms, and we kissed each other again and again! . . . to be called by names of tenderness, I have never heard used to me before — was bliss beyond belief! Oh! this was the happiest day of my life!'

Neither Victoria nor Albert came from a happy family. Albert's gentle and imaginative mother Louise had run away from her libertine husband and left her children when Albert was only five. He had never seen his mother again, but he bore her no grudge, indeed always spoke of her with understanding and tenderness. After his parents' divorce, his father Duke Ernest of Saxe-Coburg-Gotha married again; Albert and Victoria were both fond of Mama Marie, as they called her. Coburg had been for Albert 'a paradise', and there he had perfected his innate gift for amusing himself, hour after hour, without social stimulus except a single companion — formerly his much-loved brother Ernest, now his wife Victoria.

There began for the twenty-year-old Queen days of mutual activity and pleasure such as she had never known before. The isolation of her childhood was banished. Spicy conversations with Lord Melbourne continued, at least until he resigned in the following year; but with Albert there was

constant companionship, much less talking, and more doing. It is striking how very little Victoria quotes Albert's words. She gives his opinions, reactions, and state of mind, but his cadences are not audible, as Lord M.'s are. Yet the texture of their everyday existence, in the first year of their marriage, is palpable.

Albert, for all his goodness, was great fun to be with. On one of the first mornings she writes: 'Got up at 20 m. to 9. My dearest Albert put on my stockings for me. I went in and saw him shave; a great delight for me.' They spent their days walking, reading aloud to each other, looking at pictures, playing duets, accompanying the other singing. Albert's tastes predominated: the choice of literature was often Goethe — *Wilhelm Meister* — or Schiller, 'Das Lied von der Glocke'. The treasures of George III's collection at Windsor, hitherto largely unsorted and neglected, immediately fascinated him, and he began work on reorganizing the Royal Library. They still did the things Victoria had done before her marriage: there were dogs and horses and balls, but the

*Victoria and Albert's first home was at Windsor Castle, which had been successfully restored, remodelled and redecorated in the romantic spirit of the Gothic revival by Jeffry Wyatville for Victoria's uncle George IV.*

hours kept were earlier. In this she was pliant to him; but she did not yet let him see despatch boxes. To Victoria, Albert was a paragon, but to him Victoria was frustratingly authoritarian. 'I am only the husband, not the master', he complained.

Albert's education had been in every way more cosmopolitan and wide-ranging than Victoria's. This was true of his training in art. He drew with the intemperate earnestness that characterized so many of his enterprises: hussars, their uniforms accurately portrayed down to the last twist on the frogging, fill the pages of an album at Windsor which he completed before he was married. But his taste was formed, interesting and personal; he appreciated many painters, from Trecento Italians to contemporary masters such as the German portraitist Franz-Xavier Winterhalter, with a genuinely independent and knowledgeable eye. He was among the first to like and buy Italian primitives, and he encouraged

*Enormous sums of money were spent on improvements at Windsor, some purely decorative, others urgently necessary, such as a modern drainage system. In 1859, after the Queen drew this view from her sitting room, the buildings that crowded up to the castle walls were razed.*

Victoria, whose natural taste, as displayed after Albert's death, was much less fine. Under his influence she bought a Lucas Cranach, for instance, as a Christmas present for him in the first year of their marriage, and over the years she presented him with several masterpieces — some Cima da Conegliano panels, and Bernardo Daddi's magnificent *Marriage of the Virgin*.

Prince Albert did not reject the contemporary painters Victoria had patronized before their marriage: Edwin Landseer, whom she had commissioned to paint her favourite dogs, and George Hayter, who had painted her as a girl and whom she appointed 'my Painter of History and Portrait' four days after her accession. After her marriage both artists were invited to Court, to coach the young couple in a medium that had taken Albert's fancy, for it ideally combined science and art: etching. In the autumn of 1840, a copperplate printing press was set up in Buckingham Palace by the master-printers Richard Holdgate and Henry Graves. Victoria was expecting her first child, and she passed her days quietly, resting a great deal, listening to her husband reading, and etching — sometimes from her own work, sometimes from sketches by Albert. Often they worked together. She traced the compositions and then transferred them with a needle on to the wax, gum and pitch preparation on the plate. Etching suited her light, rapid eye, and though the early results are sometimes a little stiff and insipid, the later etchings of dogs and children are much more lively and full of charm. Underneath she always inscribed, sometimes forgetting to invert the lettering and so avoid the mirror effect of printing — *VR del. et sclt.*, *Albert del. VR sclt.*, or *VR del. et A. sclt.*

Etching relaxed her: 'We spent a delightful, peaceful morning — singing after breakfast, and etching together', she wrote after their first attempt. Hayter was present to give advice; under his supervision Victoria copied a turbaned head by Stefano della Bella, a seventeenth-century Florentine artist well represented in the Royal Collection. Amazingly, this is the only artist whom Victoria ever copied who was not a contemporary or near contemporary. She preferred

*Victoria's terrier Islay, engraved by her (above) and by her master Edwin Landseer (below).*

*Right: A copy, etched by Victoria, of a drawing by the seventeenth-century Florentine, Stefano della Bella.*

*Her Majesty Queen Victoria's first etching*

*L. Haghe*

*Augt 29. 1840.*
*Windsor Castle*

modern work, and from Hayter's own vast output she chose to copy on to a plate his profile head of her husband from the big tableau he painted of their wedding.

Victoria was not at this stage as intolerant as she became in later years. She admired Hayter's virtuosity — he was famous for producing 189 likenesses in his monumental history painting *The Trial of Queen Caroline* — and over-looked his private affairs. She told Lord Melbourne that she knew Hayter had not been elected to the Royal Academy because 'he had quarrelled with his wife, and had separated from her. "And did he get another?" said Lord M. I laughed and said I was not sure of that.' So little did Victoria mind the irregularity, she knighted him in 1842.

Landseer's art was of a different order. As a child he had kept carcasses of animals hidden under his bed so that he could study their anatomy at night. His animal painting was often vigorous and masterly, but occasionally sentimentally anthropomorphized. This appealed hugely to Victoria, as did his rough, nearly risqué sense of humour. She thought him 'certainly the cleverest artist there is', and examining his work through a magnifying glass, could not get over his

*Albert and Victoria worked side by side at their etching plates, sometimes collaborating on the same drawing. Albert corrected his wife's efforts, and encouraged her to annotate in detail. As her skill grew, she began to draw directly on to the plate, as with the washerwoman and the man in a fez in this etching of 1843.*

*In May 1842 James Planché was commissioned to dress Victoria and Albert as Edward III and Philippa for a ball to raise funds for the silk workers of Spitalfields. The Queen added these 'rough sketches' to her diary, and then asked Edwin Landseer to commemorate the costumes in a monumental portrait.*

exquisite handling of detail. They made friends, and she and Albert when out riding together in London would sometimes call on the painter in his studio to look at his latest work, or help him with an impromptu sitting for one of their numerous commissions.

In May 1842, Victoria and Albert posed for Landseer in the costumes of Queen Philippa and Edward III, which had been designed for them by the theatrical designer Planché for a special ball at Buckingham Palace. Albert, who always hoped to turn even frivolity to good, wanted to raise money for the unemployed Spitalfields weavers and therefore commanded all the guests to dress in silk. But it was a misguided gesture: his philanthropic energies needed a larger scale of operation. They were soon to receive it.

*Pussy.*

*Before going to Bed.*

By late 1842 Albert was effectively acting as the Queen's Private Secretary. He was reading state papers, commenting, drafting memoranda and guiding her. His ascendancy was achieved by a combination of diplomacy, strength of mind and chance, and his influence was healing, both to Victoria herself and to the country he had adopted.

Chance played its part because Victoria was weakened by pregnancy and childbirth. The Princess Royal was born so soon — 21 November 1840 — that she must have been conceived in the very first weeks of their marriage. This was bad luck and Victoria felt it keenly, especially after the 'good many hours suffering' she endured during the birth. Victoria and Albert both adored 'Pussy', as Vicky was first known, and Victoria filled her diary with comments and her albums with drawings and etchings of the Pussette's cleverness and beauty. But it was a terrible blow when she found that she was immediately pregnant again. This pregnancy made her

*'Pussy' was the nickname of the Princess Royal, Victoria, etched here by her mother as she is washed in the royal nursery.*

*Victoria was at her best drawing spontaneously scenes from her immediate and personal surroundings, like this sketch of Vicky on gold-crested writing paper.*

feel 'quite done up', 'very wretched', 'tired and depressed' and 'very low'. She was barely twenty-one, had been married under two years, and was having her second child. Even the birth of a longed-for Prince of Wales on 9 November 1841, within a year of Vicky, did not raise her from her lassitude. Albert was astonished to find that, while he was reading summaries of important papers to her on Parliamentary debates, she fell asleep. He had had the keys of the despatch boxes during her confinement with Vicky; after the birth of the Prince of Wales he did not have to give them back. She wrote of Bertie's birth afterwards: 'My sufferings were really very severe, and I don't know what I should have done, but for the great comfort and support my beloved Albert was to me during the whole time.'

At the side of his wife in childbirth, Albert was allowed the role of protector, colleague, minister, mentor, doctor and lover that he had desired to play from the beginning. His usefulness was now assured: at home, he had reconciled Victoria with her mother whom she had since her accession cruelly cold-shouldered, and he had finally persuaded his wife to wean herself from Lehzen, who through jealousy and insecurity had created much mischief between them since their marriage. In September 1842 the governess left for Germany, and though Victoria had seemed to cling to her, the parting was accomplished so easily that it must have been a relief. In politics, Albert had quickly forged strong links with Lord Melbourne's successor as Prime Minister, the Tory Sir Robert Peel, an active reformer after Albert's heart. In the country as a whole, Albert had won a notable mark of confidence when, during the Queen's first confinement, he was appointed sole Regent in the event of her death.

Victoria's moorings to the past were cast off: Albert filled all her present and her future. As Greville noted with his usual dyspepsia: 'He is really discharging the functions of the Sovereign. He is King to all intents and purposes.'

*Beatrice*

V, Osborn Aug. 12 1860

# FOUR

## Scenes from Family Life

Victoria did not enjoy submitting, but she accepted submission as woman's lot with a completeness that amounted to an endorsement. The early meetings for women's suffrage enraged her. She wanted 'this mad, wicked folly of "Woman's Rights"' checked immediately, and thought one of the leaders should be whipped; the whole subject made 'the Queen', she wrote, 'so furious that she cannot contain herself.' Yet she did kick against the pricks, complaining to her daughter Vicky: 'There is great happiness and great blessedness in devoting oneself to another who is worthy of one's affection; still men are very selfish and the woman's devotion is always one of submission which makes our poor sex so very unenviable.'

The aspect of womanhood that especially moved Queen Victoria's sympathy was childbearing. She herself was wonderfully strong and healthy, and gave birth, without physical complications, to nine children in seventeen years, of whom only one — the youngest son Leopold, born in 1853 — suffered from any innate ailment. (He was a haemophiliac, and died at the age of thirty-one.) Victoria's is a formidable record of maternity, and unrepresentative of the

*Beatrice was the youngest of Victoria and Albert's nine children. The Queen liked sketching her children from the back and picking out such details as the big bow and lacy washable dress-saver Beatrice is wearing over her fashionable purple frock.*

*Left: Victoria and Albert were deeply absorbed in the upbringing of their children, although of course the nursery was fully staffed with nursemaids like the one in this ink sketch.*

time, when death from puerperal fever was commonplace and infant mortality high. She was aware that she had been more fortunate than many women: 'Few were or are better than I was', she wrote, not in a tone of pride, but of compassion. But in a telling image she called maternity 'the shadow side' of life.

In a letter to Vicky soon after her daughter's marriage in 1858, she revealed some of the strain her enormous family had cost her: 'Now to reply to your observation that you find a married woman has much more liberty than an unmarried one; in one sense of the word she has, — but what I meant was — in a physical point of view — and if you have hereafter (as I had constantly for the first 2 years of my marriage) — aches — and sufferings and miseries and plagues — which you must struggle against — and enjoyments etc. to give up — constant precautions to take, you will feel the yoke of a married woman! . . . I had 9 times for 8 months to bear with those abovenamed enemies and real misery, (besides many duties) and I own it tried me sorely; one feels so pinned down — one's wings clipped . . . only half oneself . . . And therefore, I think our sex a most unenviable one.'

*Right: Vicky, the firstborn, made quick progress: at about the time of this pen and ink sketch, Vicky was reading 'before me, and so nicely'. The toy pram she is pushing was an innovation: the 'perambulator' itself was a very recent Victorian product.*

*Vicky*—

*Alfred & Alice*

Queen Victoria had all her children at home, either at Buckingham Palace or Windsor Castle. The Queen's Physician Accoucher was in attendance at each birth and the same monthly nurse, Mrs Lilly, assisted her throughout all nine confinements. The Queen trusted her: 'she is an excellent, clever, sensible woman, and still very handy and quick in what she does . . . ' Victoria was always pleased to see her go, however, because she was then 'émancipé', and 'so glad and thankful to be able now quite to resume my normal life', her old pastimes and her work. But the person who made her

*Prince Alfred — pictured here with Princess Alice, his elder by only fifteen months — was very attached to his sister, and when she married he wept bitterly.*

*Alice*
*April 25 - 1845.*

*On her second birthday Alice, garlanded in flowers and dressed in a new spring frock, came down before dinner to receive and give her presents.*

sufferings tolerable was Albert. Contrary to our prejudice about Victorian prudery, the Prince was present at Queen Victoria's side almost all the time, there remaining to lift and carry and comfort and help, to read and sing and summarize despatches and deal with visitors throughout the fortnight or more after the birth when Victoria, like all prosperous women of her time, remained in bed. He is 'so wonderfully handy and gentle', wrote Victoria gratefully. When the Archbishop of Canterbury and other dignitaries, whose presence was customary as witnesses to royal births, missed

Princess Alice's entry, Albert in his thoughtfulness took the opportunity to change this intrusive practice.

The Duchess of Kent had nursed Victoria herself, unlike her first children Feodore and Charles. Breastfeeding was considered unusual for a lady at the time. By the 1840s, however, all manuals advocated it, and the practice was spreading to the aristocracy. Victoria, who found it horribly indelicate when someone spoke of morning sickness at dinner, does not say in her diary whether she would have liked to nurse her own children. Her duties as a reigning queen would have made it difficult, but her horror of 'animal-like' biology probably made it repugnant to her anyway. Later, she advised her daughter Vicky not to breastfeed, warning her against indulging in 'Baby-worship' or overdoing 'the passion for the nursery'.

The glorious assemblies of Victoria's progeny, painted in a rich palette borrowed from High Renaissance celebrations of the blessed gathered in heaven, or of heroes and poets on Parnassus, have accustomed us to forget 'the shadow side'. Nor did Queen Victoria herself want it commemorated or recorded. The idyll of family happinesses that filled album after album, inspiring watercolours, miniatures, photographs and her own drawings, disguise it. Such a pictorial chronicle was a Victorian family obsession, and in this respect as in so many others Victoria and Albert and their children provide a microcosm of the prevailing ethic, accurately reflecting the society over which they reigned.

For in spite of Queen Victoria's disgust, it would be quite wrong to impute to her any resentment towards her children. She was a committed, conscientious and loving mother. Her overflowing sentiments of motherly attachment and her real pleasure in her children's natures, appearances, activities, progress and company typify the new parental response that developed towards the end of the eighteenth century, when the child was consecrated the symbol of goodness and purity in such influential works as Rousseau's treatise on education, *Emile,* or the novels of Dickens.

*Right: With a bold use of cross-hatching, a result of her interest in etching at this date, the Queen sketched Princess Alice with her nurse in the grounds of Buckingham Palace.*

*Overleaf: The brilliant use of colour, the assured evocation of pleasant heat, the firmly handled idyllic atmosphere in this family scene at Osborne House in 1850 show the influence of William Leighton Leitch, a master watercolourist who started teaching the Queen in 1842 and continued to visit her regularly at all her houses.*

A conversazione group, like the famous Winterhalter portrait of 1846 showing Victoria and Albert enthroned side by side, with the first five children — Vicky, Bertie, Alice and Alfred — gathered like secular seraphim attendant on the Holy Family around their parents and the newborn Princess Helena, presents a new and determined argument about the nature of domestic life. Victoria loved this picture, and copied its superb stylish composition in a quick pen and ink sketch. It was in her opinion 'one of the finest modern pictures painted . . . in the style of a Paul Veronese . . . ' Prince Albert instructed the artist to paint 'fine turquoise-blue skies' in the background, enhancing the atmosphere of sublime content breathed by the whole picture.

Although Queen Victoria herself rarely painted in a background to the portraits of her children that from 1840 onwards began to flow from her pen and her brush, her visual language is as unclouded and serene as Winterhalter's. In the thick morocco-bound volume, stamped in gold 'Sketches of the Royal Children by V.R. from 1841–59,' she pasted dozens of watercolours and drawings of her offspring, annotating them with captions such as 'Pussy with Bertie in

*Right: Both these drawings of Vicky were made when the Queen was absorbed with etching, and she later engraved them and gave prints to her friends. Eos the greyhound, pictured here with the two-year-old Vicky, was the Prince Consort's favourite dog. He brought her from Coburg, and when she died he had her statue placed on the sculpture terrace at Osborne, where it is today.*

*Vicky* —                    Claremont Jan: 15 — 43

*Vicky & Eos* —      Jan: 15 — 1843
                          Mr — Claremont

the dresses they wore on little Alice's christening day June 2 1843'. Pussy absorbed her mother more than any of the subsequent children. She is sketched crawling, being bathed by her nurse,'taking her bottle and showing the first signs of interest in the external world — in a coloured ball, in a caged bird. The other children usually graduated into the family album as toddlers, planted foursquare on sturdy legs under flounces and petticoats. Their dress — frocks were worn by the boys as well until the age of five or thereabouts — is painted with pride: the plaid silks, trimmed bonnets, gorgeous sashes, satin bows on sleeves and frills threaded with ribbon, the pleats and tucks on clothes which were, in a house where profligacy was frowned on, handed down from one child to another. Interest in costume dominates; the Queen had a preference for back views. Though she was good at likenesses, they were perhaps an effort: she often copied the faces from Sir William Ross's miniatures.

*Right: Until they were five or six, Victorian children of both sexes wore dresses, the only difference being that the girls' skirts were gored while those of the boys, like Arthur's pictured here, were pleated.*

*Below: On New Year's Day 1844, Vicky, aged three, was dressed up in a blue and white silk dress copied from a West portrait of Princess Charlotte.*

114

Arthur — Vy. d. 1ˢᵗ May 7 1853 Osborne —

Bertie
VR: del Balloch
House
Sept: 16. 185[?]

Concealment was not Queen Victoria's forte, and the
determined rhetoric of a family idyll in her album does not
hide her preferences and disappointments. Pussy is the
heroine; Bertie, the Prince of Wales, begins well, with loving
drawings of his infant progress, playing with Vicky, or with
a rabbit, or with the parrots that the Queen had always
enjoyed as pets. But after the age of ten Bertie disappears
from the album, except in family groups. She had set great
store by 'Albert junior's likeness to dearest papa', but it
seemed to fade as Bertie, unlike his clever elder sister, failed to
take to his lessons. 'There is much good in him', sighed his
mother on his ninth birthday. 'He has such affectionate
feelings, — great truthfulness and great simplicity of character'. But Mr Gibbs, the tutor engaged for the Prince of
Wales, was a typically serious choice of the Prince Consort.
His academic sobriety and his rigorous discipline were

Victoria. Albert. Alfred. Alice.

My 2d from nature.
July - 1846.

quite unsuited to the child's nature. Bertie was difficult: 'A very bad day', reported Mr Gibbs on 8 March 1852. 'The P. of W. has been like a person half silly. I could not gain his attention. He was very rude, particularly in the afternoon, throwing stones in my face. . . . He made faces and spat. . . . There was a great deal of bad words'. Prince Albert, taking up one of his pseudo-scientific hobbies, had the bumps of his elder children read by the leading phrenologist, Dr George Combe. The sage pronounced Bertie's bumps of 'combativeness' and 'destructiveness' and 'ostentativeness' very large. But Vicky's cleverness was obvious, right down to the last bump, and favouritism was one of her parents' failings. It is no wonder that Bertie, when he was informed that he would succeed to the throne, was sadly puzzled that he should take precedence over Vicky.

*Many of Victoria's paintings of her children, like the portrait of Princess Alice (above), show the influence of Sir William Ross.*

*The picture of her two elder daughters (above right), begun in May 1846, was interrupted by the birth of Princess Helena, painted (right) in the local peasant costume of Albert's Gotha homeland.*

*Alice & Vicky begun Monday & finished Nov: 1846.*
*V de.*

*Leuchin (Helena)*

Prince Arthur, the third son, was Victoria's favourite child, and inspired this rare nude study (left). He was born on 1 May 1850, the eighty-first birthday of the 'beloved hero' the Duke of Wellington, after whom he was named. He is pictured below, aged four, in the uniform of the Grenadier Guards.

*Arthur — May — 17 — 1853*

*Arthur. —*

*Prince Leopold, fourth and last of Victoria and Albert's sons, suffered from haemophilia, endemic in the next generation of the family. This sketch of him playing with Arthur is one of the very few drawings of Leopold made by his mother.*

The Queen's love of good looks influenced her attitude to her children: she hated Bertie's knock-knees and the largeness of his features, especially his long Hanoverian nose 'which begins to hang a little'. There is hardly a single drawing of Leopold on his own, though his brothers, especially the blue-eyed, graceful Arthur, inspired his mother's pen to chronicle their growth. Leopold 'is a very common-looking child, very plain in the face', wrote his mother; 'clever but an oddity — and not an engaging child though amusing.' Arthur on the other hand was 'a precious love', and though Victoria was of the opinion that 'the prettiest [child] is frightful when undressed', she painted Arthur naked, like an Italian *putto*. Beatrice, the last of all, and always affectionately called Baby, delighted her mother. She was the second child to be born under 'soothing, quieting and delightful' chloroform. Baby 'is such a pretty, plump, flourishing child . . .' wrote Victoria, 'with fine large blue eyes, marked nose, pretty little mouth and very fine skin.'

a)

b)

*Baby Beatrice was the favourite daughter, and she grew even closer to her mother after the death of Prince Albert when she was four. The Queen almost abandoned painting her family during her widowhood, but she made an exception for Beatrice's blonde-red head.*

Victoria was not alone in adoring her children; Albert led the way. In 1842, he had himself drawn in pastel by Landseer as a present for the Queen on his own birthday: he gazes down into the small round face of the Princess Royal whom he holds in his arms. The assignment of baby love to female psychology is a later social phenomenon: to the Prince Consort babies seemed a natural spur to pride and interest and love, as much in the father as in the mother. The Queen records in her diary the precious times they enjoyed with Vicky in the morning and afternoon, how they would visit the nursery twice a day or how Vicky would be brought down to see them. Albert is always very much in evidence in these diary entries, especially about Vicky. She was the firstborn, beloved for that alone, but she remained her father's favourite always on account of her aptitude, quickness, forwardness and talents. Albert's joy in her leaps from his wife's pages: the young father trundling his daughter about in 'that basket, or go-cart, which came from Paris', or setting her on his knee to 'touch the keys of the piano, which delighted her'.

*In 1849 James Izzard, Turner in Ordinary to Her Majesty and the Royal Family, charged the nursery 12/6 for repairing a 'Skin Horse' and providing a new mane and tail and bridle and saddle.*

*Helena, Alfred & Alice.*
*My Dr Osborn Dec 10 1847.*

Albert also took on more serious responsibilities for his children's upbringing. He had a broad sense of family life, and he became the architect for the royal household's totally novel style. From 1842 onwards, he purged the staff: Lehzen was not the only person to go. Mrs Southey, sister-in-law of the poet, was dismissed from her post as Superintendent of the Nursery and was replaced, until 1851, by 'Laddle', the efficient Lady Lyttelton. A heavy 'Plan' of lessons was devised for the children and their tutors. Queen Victoria herself undertook Vicky's religious instruction, in the evenings, a privilege that made the excluded Bertie somewhat wistful. As the children grew up, Papa spent an hour a day instructing them himself, adding this duty to his already crammed timetable. For all his commitment to improving pursuits, Albert was an inventive father, and liked having 'our tribe' about him. He took them to the theatre, to see the waxworks at Madame Tussaud's, and to visit the new animals at the Zoo, a recently founded institution that much appealed to the Prince Consort's scientific bent. But the greatest monument to Albert and Victoria's pioneering of the modern nuclear family was the building of Osborne House, the royal retreat on the Isle of Wight.

*Osborne House, which Victoria and Albert made their family home for the summers, was set in extensive acres of good farmland. The annual haymaking was always a great event: Albert turned somersaults in the stacks to show Bertie how to do them. But the Prince Consort's farming interests were also more serious: he built model workers' cottages on the estate and designed a complex and innovatory drainage system.*

The accommodation at all the royal houses, their lack of comforts, hygiene and conveniences, and the appalling cumbrousness of their administrative structure, horrified the young Prince when he first came to live at Windsor and at Buckingham Palace. When the Queen was lying in after the birth of the Princess Royal, Mrs Lilly heard a sound in her room. Under the sofa, a small boy was found: he had visited the royal apartments, he admitted, secretly and without hindrance on a number of occasions, had sat on the Queen's throne and heard the new-born princess squall. Such slackness affronted the deepest parts of Albert's clear and organized mind. He prised retainers out of ancient sinecures and streamlined the staff, offending many but achieving order.

Even so Albert had an urgent need for home life, deriving from Coburg well-being, that was hitherto unknown in the house of the English royal family, and it was soon clear that neither Windsor nor Buckingham Palace, let alone the exotic Brighton Pavilion, provided the fast increasing family with a home.

The Isle of Wight was easy of access from the capital, yet distant enough to give the needed sense of release from state affairs. Victoria had liked it when she stayed at Norris Castle as a girl in 1833. In 1845 she bought, out of her own income (she was much more thrifty than her uncles), Osborne House, set in good farmland on a rise above the Solent, cradled by slopes and rolling hay fields, yet on a sufficient crest to give breathtakingly beautiful views over the Solent. The pleased Queen wrote to her uncle: 'It sounds so snug and nice to have a place of *one's own*, quiet and retired, and free from all . . . other charming Departments who really are the plague of one's life.'

*When the Queen was at Osborne, she relaxed. The splendid situation above the Solent created a peaceful, holiday atmosphere, and the weather, judging from her Journal and her watercolours, seems always to have been fine.*

Prince Albert, masterful and energetic as ever, immediately laid plans: the old house was to be pulled down and a new house, built with every contemporary invention, to rise in its place. With characteristic independence of spirit, he overlooked all architects and chose instead the master builder whose sweeping reconstruction of Belgravia had much impressed him: Thomas Cubitt, who liked and understood up to date methods as much as the Prince.

Together, they designed Osborne House. On a series of massive ornamental terraces facing the sea, a stucco'd villa began to take form, with an Italian campanile-style flag tower on one wing — the Pavilion — and another, differently scaled clock tower standing at an angle to it over the Household quarters. The asymmetrical profile and determined vernacular rather than palatial appearance of the building was bold and successful, and very attractive. Above

*One of the delights of the Isle of Wight was sea-bathing. From a bathing-house such as this, on the beach below Norris Castle close to Osborne, Victoria would step into a bathing machine which was then drawn down into the sea by a horse.*

*This painting of the new Pavilion wing at Osborne shows Edward Lear's influence in the strongly inked outlines, the fluidity of the strokes, the attention to architectural detail. With a touch of pride, Victoria adds to the watercolour that it was only* partly *copied from Lear.*

all, Osborne was a superbly conceived home, which is what Albert wanted for his wife and his children. In the Pavilion wing, he and Victoria had a set of rooms, ample yet enfolding, with magnificent bow windows giving flowing views of the sea. Their rooms are arranged *en suite*, in a horseshoe shape with no corridor, so conveniently intimate; the technology of the 1840s assured them the hitherto unknown luxury of running hot water in baths that were plumbed in to drain as well. Above these private rooms was situated the nursery, so that the parents could make their cherished visits to the children with ease; below were the official audience and reception rooms. Even these have a cosy Biedermeier-like atmosphere, with the statues by Mary Thornycroft of the children dressed as Thomson's The Seasons, the deeply cushioned sofas, and the drapes.

As the children grew up, they moved away from their parents and across to another wing, nearer to the staff Household wing. This was connected to the Pavilion by an open arcaded passageway that was not only decorative and original, but effectively cut off both geographically and psychologically the staff from the family and sealed the latter's domestic happiness together more completely.

Albert planted drifts of dark-leaved bushes against the brightness of the wide lawns, and rare trees in groups about the grounds; he designed alcoves, much loved by Victoria, to provide shelter in which to draw and read and write, amongst formal terraces of flowerbeds set off by statues. In the house itself, the royal collection of contemporary painting and furniture — few pieces at Osborne were made earlier than 1826 — created an opulent, but utterly unforbidding interior. Albert and Victoria's taste was remarkably voluptuous: *Florinda*, which used to hang in Victoria's sitting room opposite the two desks at which she and Albert worked side by side, abounds with glabrous nudes rendered by Winterhalter in his most lacquered yet luscious manner. Victoria gave it to Albert for his birthday in 1852, and they both remarked how like a German relation of theirs was one of the frolicking nymphs.

*Thomas Cubitt's bold and original plan of two dissimilar but balancing towers gave Osborne House a famous profile, copied in holiday houses from England to the United States. Victoria's sweeping watercolour shows how her handling of shadows was being developed by her teachers, but perspective still caused her problems.*

The children were not forgotten. In 1853, Albert imported a Swiss chalet, one of the first prefabricated buildings to be assembled in England, and equipped it with a kitchen for the children to learn cooking, allotments for each of them to learn gardening, and a most contemporary model of a fort — no crusader romance or sandcastle nostalgia here — for the royal war games. They went on boating expeditions with their parents, and the family's deep content colours many pages of the Queen's diary. In August 1857, she described a typical day: 'Very hot and perfectly still . . . in the afternoon embarked in the Fairy with the 6 eldest children, Ladies &c and steamed to Sconie[?] Point and back. Beautiful calm evening and the sea like oil. Home late. We dined alone with Vicky, and afterwards went out on the Terrace and watched falling stars. Splendid reflection of the moon in the sea. Reading and playing.'

*In July 1849 a 'rustic fête' was held at Barton Farm, one of Osborne's dependencies, to celebrate the hay harvest. Victoria painted the gay tents, where after a hands' dinner, sailors and neighbours joined in to play 'Blindman's Buff, Leapfrog, Cricket...' and dance the Hornpipe.*

*Bertie & Lenchen – Jan: 1 · 1851 —*  *Alfred & Louise*

*Victoria's love of dressing up inspired all her children. Bertie and Alfred, in costumes 'of the time of the Pretender', were joined (left) on New Year's Day 1851 by their two younger sisters, Lenchen and Louise, then aged four and three respectively, as 'Marquises' in a ballet. Princess Helena (below), aged three, is dressed as Minerva, Goddess of Peace.*

Each of their birthdays, and important anniversaries like that of their parents' wedding, were ritually celebrated: birthday tables decorated with swags and wreaths were laden with presents, plays were performed, concerts were given, fancy dresses made and worn. At Victoria's thirty-fifth birthday party, all the children contributed, Princess Louise, then aged six, ending the evening with a grand solo performance of a 'Scale in C'. There was an edifying side: part of Racine's *Athalie* was acted in French; plays like A.F.F. von Kotzebue's *Das Hahnenschlag* (The Cockshy), a gentle bucolic piece, gave a polish to their German.

This harmony is the substance of Victoria's drawings of her growing family during her twenties and thirties. What astonishes the spectator today is that its motive force and inspiration, Prince Albert, is invisible. The Queen never drew or painted her husband with her children. He is absent. The unflagging work he undertook, both on his own account and on the Queen's, passes unrecorded. Victoria's subject matter, it is true, did not encompass politics, but it is very surprising not to find Albert the paterfamilias at all in her albums. It is equally conspicuous that after Albert's death

*Minerva*

Bertie — Vicky Alice Lenchen Alfred.

*The first five children wear the costume of Thuringian peasants to mark an occasion — but in an unusual oversight, the Queen did not date this lively sketch.*

Victoria's interest in the family lost its liveliness. The album of 'Sketches of the Royal Children' is stamped Volume One, but the entries end in 1861, when the Prince Consort died; blank pages only remain, with here and there a loose sketch thrown in, but not pasted down. There is no second volume. Yet the much-loved Beatrice was still only four years old. The camera was of course replacing the pencil, and Victoria was an avid collector of photographs. It seems nevertheless that Albert gave her the incentive to paint her children — that she did this, as she did so much else, because he liked it. The imagery of family pleasure was not exactly hollow for her, but it was borrowed, and she needed Albert beside her to mastermind it. On one of their rare separations, in 1857, when Albert went to Belgium for the wedding of King Leopold's daughter, Charlotte, Victoria wrote to her uncle to congratulate him, and in a revealing passage added: 'you

133

cannot think *combien cela me coûte* or how completely *déroutée* I am and *feel* when he is away, or how I count the hours till he returns. *All* the numerous children are as *nothing* to me when *he is away*; it seems as if the whole life of the house and home were gone, when he is away!'

The interplay of personal inclination and social ethos is always very complex. Queen Victoria mirrored her times' discovery of the family as the fountainhead of happiness and the microcosm of a happy society, she reflected its concern with material comforts and prosperity as the reward of virtue and endeavour. She herself was very proud of her family in this respect: as early as 1844, then the mother of only three children, she wrote: 'They say no Sovereign was ever more loved than I am (I am bold enough to say), & *this* because of our domestic home, the good example it presents.' But her satisfaction with the children was derived from Albert: the

*Right: When she was thirteen, the Princess Royal came down to a formal dinner with her parents for the first time.*

*Below: A small theatre was specially built at Windsor for the frequent family theatricals. The Queen painted this scene from a German play,* Die Tafelbirnen, *put on for Victoria and Albert's thirteenth wedding anniversary.*

*Feb:10 - 1853 —*

Helena — Alice — Alfred Scene from The Play of Die Tafel Birnen.
Louise Bertie. Vicky —

IK del May 21—

Vicky in her 1st Drawingroom dress
May 20 - 1854.

*Just before her twenty-sixth birthday, Victoria drew this image of unflinching self-scrutiny. After eight years of ruling, the face in the mirror is that of a serious, obstinate young woman, a little overwhelmed at the speed and weight of events, and determined not to show it, not to yield.*

pleasure he took in fatherhood, and the moral and philo-sophical stress he laid upon it.

The matriarchal image posterity has made of the Queen, though it accurately reflects her strength, her imperiousness and her will, distorts the truth of her own idea of herself and her absolute adherence to the idea of patriarchy. For in her own eyes, her position as Queen Regnant was 'anomalous': 'It is a reversal of the right order of things which distressed me much and which no one, but such a perfection, such an angel as [Albert] is — could bear and carry through.' Fortunately, however hard she schooled herself in adoration and abneg-ation, her natural spirit did not bend altogether, and some of the family pleasure — and pain — originated with her.

Woman & Child—
Cherbourg—
(from
recollection) Aug.st 18. 1857.

Woman at Bricquebec
Normandy
Aug.st 18. 1857

# FIVE

# Travels Abroad

Queen Victoria, ruling over the Empire at the time of its greatest expansion, never saw any of her dominions beyond the British Isles. Yet ever since she had glimpsed at St Leonards sailors from Spain lounging on the quay, and young fisher boys in clogs from Normandy, anything and especially anyone foreign seemed to her captivatingly exotic. At a time when the art of engraving was bringing before people's eyes for the first time the beauties and wonders of 'abroad', Victoria was an eager consumer of travellers' tales. The splendours of the Alhambra described by Washington Irving, the Oriental Tableaux drawn by Lady Wilhelmina Stanhope — a friend and one of her trainbearers at the Coronation — *Sketches of Persia* by an anonymous 'Traveller', all these excited her, even though she felt such 'Arabian-like tales' were not quite respectable. She had come across Edward Lear, not as a composer of nonsense songs but as a recorder of delightful excursions in Italy and elsewhere.

*'All the women', noted the Queen on a trip to Cherbourg in the summer of 1857, 'wear caps, many the regular Cauchaine ones, and full woollen skirts, with aprons and fichus ...' She took with enthusiasm to travelling, relishing different, unfamiliar customs.*

139

It was not the custom for the monarch to go abroad. Of her immediate predecessors, only George IV had done so, to visit his own kingdom of Hanover. The last English ruler to see Paris was Henry VI, when he was crowned King of France in Notre Dame in 1431; the last to set foot in France had been Henry VIII, on the Field of the Cloth of Gold. But faster communications made it possible for the monarch to leave the country and yet remain in contact, and Victoria was delighted that she did not have to appoint a Regent in her absence, as had been the practice until then. She thus pioneered both the regal tradition of grand diplomatic travel, and incognito royal holidays.

Victoria was twenty-four before she left the British Isles. The nation had presented her with a superb yacht, the *Victoria and Albert*, a paddle steamer carrying sail as well, so large and luxurious that even the Emperor Napoleon III, no stinter himself, observed when he saw it that he should like

*This view of Portland, painted from the deck of the* Victoria and Albert *on one of the family's sailing trips from the Isle of Wight, shows again in its deft penmanship the inspiring influence of Edward Lear, who had tutored Victoria the month before.*

one like it, but smaller. In 1843 the Queen and Prince Albert, leaving behind Vicky and Bertie as well as the new baby Alice, sailed across the Channel; breaking the coldness of centuries, they were to visit the King of the French, Louis Philippe, *en famille* in his castle of Eu in Normandy.

The *Victoria and Albert* outdistanced the naval escort, and her passengers were soon 'horrified not to know *where* we were'. But the Prince de Joinville, one of Louis Philippe's sons, found them and came on board to greet them, so early that Victoria was not even dressed They proceeded along the Normandy coast, and the Queen became very nervous as the moment of arrival in France drew near: 'at length Joinville discerned the King's barge approaching and as it came nearer and nearer, I felt still more agitated.' She nearly cried, she wrote, when Louis Philippe, all impatience, clambered on board and kissed her warmly.

The Queen found the French countryside pretty, 'enhanced by the setting sun', but was particularly delighted to note the 'crowds of people (all so different to ours)' and the 'number of Troops (also so different to our Troops)'. The strangeness continued to fill her with enthusiasm: the gardeners working beneath her windows — on a Sunday; the

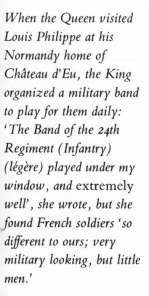

*When the Queen visited Louis Philippe at his Normandy home of Château d'Eu, the King organized a military band to play for them daily: 'The Band of the 24th Regiment (Infantry) (légère) played under my window, and extremely well', she wrote, but she found French soldiers 'so different to ours; very military looking, but little men.'*

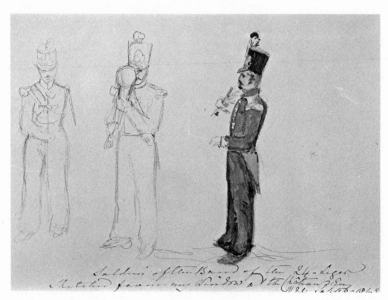

'faces, dress, manners, everything . . . so extremely different';
the swaddled babies and the tall white caps of the women; the
Catholic paraphernalia of wayside crucifixions and 'bijou'
chapels; and the French King and Queen's private chara-
bancs, which transported the huge royal party on *fêtes
champêtres* in the grounds, and which Albert later copied to
accommodate his growing family at Osborne. 'I felt as
though it were a dream', sighed Victoria, 'that I was at Eu,
and that my favourite Air Castle of so *many* years should at
length be realised.'

Though Eu was palatial, the style of the Citizen King had
the same personal, family quality so prized by Victoria and
Albert. Louis Philippe and his Queen, the Bourbon Marie-
Amélie, were surrounded by their children and their
children's children, and Victoria was radiant at the huge long
family breakfasts. The King's 'liveliness & vivacity & little
*impatiences* are my great delight and amusement . . . ' she
wrote. The Orléans and the Coburgs were intertwined by
any number of marriages — Louis Philippe's daughter Louise
was Uncle Leopold's wife, who gave Victoria motherly
advice as well as gowns in the latest Parisian fashion; his son
the Duke of Nemours was married to Victoire, daughter of
Victoria and Albert's uncle Ferdinand of Saxe-Coburg-
Gotha, and the beautiful childhood playmate of Albert,
whom he at one time thought of marrying. In spite of this,
Victoire de Nemours was one of Queen Victoria's beloved
friends. Though she was not at Eu during the visit, she
inspired part of Victoria's bubbling feeling of happiness at
belonging for a time to this huge rambling household: 'I felt
at home with them all', she wrote, 'as if I were one of them';
and again, 'I love them all so much, I feel so gay and happy
with these dear people.' But her steely side was to show itself.

The motive underlying the stay — the gay picnics, the
informal breakfasts, the uproarious theatricals — was to
obtain Louis Philippe's undertaking that his dynastic in-
trigues would cease, that he would not marry his son off to
the teenage Queen of Spain or her sister, in return for the
British promise that the young Queen would not marry a

*Clémentine, the daughter
of King Louis Philippe of
France, was married to
Augustus of Saxe-
Coburg-Gotha, cousin to
Victoria and Albert. On
12 May 1849 they came to
stay at Buckingham
Palace, with their
daughter Clotilde.
'Clotilde is a great
beauty', wrote the Queen.
She immediately painted
the two-year-old child and
commissioned a portrait
from Ross.*

*Clotilde Coburg.*  VR del May 16 1849.

Coburg prince either. Louis Philippe gave his word. When he reneged in 1846, after a misunderstanding caused by an indiscretion of Lord Palmerston, the Foreign Secretary, Victoria hardened towards him. The mistrust inspired by the 'Spanish marriages' turned to hardly disguised contempt on his docile abdication and flight after the revolution of 1848. For although Victoria appreciated the bourgeois home life of the King, her ideas about a monarch's right to rule were less democratic.

The Orléans exiles, smuggled out of their hostile country in a series of Pimpernel-like adventures, were given shelter in England. Victoria shuddered to hear that the clothes of her dearest Vecto (Victoire) were being worn 'by the worst women', and was appalled at the financial straits of the whole family. But she was smug that the typhoon of 1848, which ravaged Continental Europe, hardly stirred the leaves in England.

On the eve of the huge Chartist demonstration on Kennington Common in April, the worst threat to British stability that year, she left London quietly for the safety of Osborne with her three-week-old daughter, Princess Louise. But the Chartists did not rouse the variety of support they needed and the meeting passed with a minimum of incident. The most severe trial undergone by Victoria and Albert during that turbulent year was the news — by anonymous letter — that prints of their etchings, the private record of their home life, had been surreptitiously made and were to be published and sold to the public. In one of the few cases ever brought by a member of the royal family as a private citizen against another, the Prince Consort took out an injunction against William Strange the publisher. When Strange appealed, in February 1849, the injunction was upheld, establishing a legal precedent that a work of art cannot be published without the artist's consent. *The Times* cooed complacently: 'We rejoice that Her Majesty and her husband should have stepped down from their altitude thus to defend their personal rights. . . . While other Sovereigns of Europe are fugitive or trembling on their thrones, the chief anxiety

*When Victoire de Nemours, Victoria's cousin, died in 1857 at the age of thirty-five, the Queen was grief-stricken. She made an album in her memory, with copies after all the many painters for whom Victoire sat, and this delicate profile she had painted herself.*

of the Queen of England . . . is to protect herself against the annoyance . . . of having her drawings . . . published.'

Drawing served to remind: the Queen used her skill as a memory bank. This function of the pad and pencil was to some extent usurped by photography by the 1860s, but as the manageable amateur's camera had not yet been developed, sketching remained the prime method for travellers wishing to capture the sights for themselves. On all her trips Victoria took with her little albums made by firms still famous today for artists' materials, entitled 'Combination of Pocket Book Sketch Book and Palette . . . in the most convenient and portable form, particularly adapted for Tourists'. She had declared on her sixteenth birthday, 'I *love* to be *employed*: I *hate* to be *idle*', and whenever she was on board the *Victoria and Albert*, or riding in a carriage, or stopping for refreshments *en route*, she would busy herself drawing the scenery about her, or quickly noting down particulars of dress in the local people.

*In 1844 Victoria drew the first Chinese boy she had ever seen. The policies of her reign towards the Celestial Empire were never as sensitive or observant of Chinese individuality as this fine sketch.*

Ro Juley 31.
after a Sketch July
? 0 — 185?

Napoleon III<sup>d</sup>.
may 4 - 1855 from a Medallion

Except for a brief visit in 1845, the Queen did not return to France for twelve years. When she did, it was to pay a state visit to Napoleon III in 1855, to cement the alliance of France and England against Russia in the Crimean War. Napoleon and Eugénie had visited Windsor in April that year (the Waterloo Room in the castle was speedily rechristened the 'Picture Gallery'). In August, Victoria and Albert returned the honour. Albert's birthday, 'the *dearest* of days', was spent in Paris, and Victoria gave him a set of studs with one button left blank: 'I hope for Sevastopol'. Victoria found the Emperor scarily compelling, Eugénie beautiful and well dressed, and the imperial style very rich indeed. She felt better when she had told Napoleon how much she felt for her friends the Orléans refugees and deplored the confiscation of all their goods. She was incredulous when he assured her they were dangerous enemies to him. 'The Emperor said . . . that their agents were in constant communication with his enemies, even "avec ceux qui prêchent l'assassinat." I said I could hardly credit this; they were incapable of any such act, I was sure.'

*Previous page : This fine watercolour, showing how the Queen could sometimes use her linear assurance to greater advantage with subtle colour wash, was made aboard the* Victoria and Albert *while she lay at anchor off Torquay. 'The situation is beautiful', wrote the Queen, and thought the port 'quite like a foreign town'.*

The Empress Eugénie
from a bust & p. collection
T del May. 14. 1855

The shiningly clean air of Paris made the Queen of smoky London wistful; she made several drawings of the bright gardens of St Cloud, and at Le Petit Trianon where she enjoyed the model mill and dairy of 'the poor unhappy Queen', Marie Antoinette. But the most powerful *frisson* came at a state ball given in the glittering Galerie des Glaces at Versailles, for the first time since the Ancien Régime, with fireworks, devised by the Empress, and including a tableau of Windsor, and décor modelled on a print of a *fête* given by Louis XV. There Victoria 'valsed very quietly' with Napoleon III and was yet again awed, as she had been at Windsor earlier in the spring, 'to think that I, the granddaughter of George III, should dance with the Emperor Napoleon, nephew to our great enemy, now my nearest and most intimate ally'.

Queen Victoria had written to Uncle Leopold at the height of the ferment in 1848: '*Great* events make me quiet and calm; it is only trifles that irritate my nerves.' This was true, and not entirely creditable. Similarly, she found greater

The palace of Saint-Cloud, where Victoria and Albert stayed in 1855, was 'like a fairy tale and everything so beautiful . . . the air so light and so very clear and sharp against the horizon. The absence of smoke helps to make everything white and bright', wrote Victoria on 20 August. This view of Paris was painted from her window.

*On the same occasion, Victoria 'sat drawing on the balcony, and took a little sketch of the avenue looking towards the town of St-Cloud, all so pretty.' She had received a few lessons in perspective as a child from an English watercolourist, John Foulon, but this avenue of trees is a rare attempt at a painting with a vanishing point.*

excitement in modest pleasures. Her imagination did not engage with the epic: she preferred the cameo. Her enjoyment of her next visit to France, a private and unofficial sailing trip to Normandy in August 1857, inspired paeans of praise. It was made at the height of the Indian mutiny, during the bitter siege of Lucknow. But not a mention of this shadows Victoria's gaiety. Her priorities were different. On her previous trip to France Vicky and Bertie had come with her, and she had received cables daily about the other children left behind. In 1857 the whole family, with the exception of the baby Leopold, embarked on the *Victoria and Albert*, and on arrival at Cherbourg boarded a rickety coach

for a day's outing to the village of Bricquebec, 22 kilometres along the coast. The Queen was in raptures at roughing it: 'It was the regular French Poste driven by one postillion on the wheel horse; the horses harnessed with ropes — no springs to the carriage, so that we bumped along the paved roads, pretty hard... The Postboys made such a noise, clacking and flourishing their whips...' When they went downhill 'a sort of drag had constantly to be let down on both sides to keep back the wheels... Intensely hot and dusty, but all, too

*At the Normandy village of Bricquebec, which Victoria and the family visited incognito in August 1857, the Queen made these sketches of local costume, noting in particular the starched white caps of the women.*

*Charlotte of Belgium, daughter of Uncle Leopold and later the tragic Empress of Mexico, drawn by Victoria in her first beauty at the age of fifteen.*

delightfully interesting . . . '

There was 'no end to the picturesque groups' that she and Vicky sketched, making the conventional nineteenth-century equivalence between the primitive and the pleasing. In the village itself, the mayor was 'tipsy'; the crowd eventually recognized the party, calling out, *'laquelle est donc la reine?'* They took refuge in a smoky upstairs room, and only managed to escape so late that dinner, in that most regular of households, took place 'at a quarter to ten!'

*Left: The Queen was quick at capturing a likeness: this frankly admiring study is of Robert Brison, a sailor on the royal yacht.*

*Below: This serene and glowing treatment of an English headland at twilight is one of Victoria's most richly coloured and finished watercolours.*

The following year, the *Victoria and Albert* made the channel crossing again. Twelve ships escorted them, nine ships of the line received them, and the House of Commons chartered a boat for a hundred of its members. The full royal salute thundered in Cherbourg harbour 'repeated I think five times — really magnificent . . . ' while scores of small craft, bright pennants fluttering, welcomed the English Queen. Napoleon sailed over to greet them in a burnished barge, and seventy people sat down to dinner on deck. But Victoria noticed that Napoleon was not in good spirits 'and seems sensitive about all that has been said of him in England and elsewhere'.

The next day, the Queen and the Prince returned to Osborne, found all their children waiting at the door, and in honour of Alfred's birthday joined in a country dance on the terrace. As the shadows lengthened in the summer evening, their weaving figures amid the parterres and the statuary of Osborne danced for Alfred's birthday; but they celebrate for

us now the untroubled certainties of Victoria's rule. She had been introduced to Count Bismarck at the Versailles ball in 1855; only twelve years after her last meeting with Napoleon and Eugénie at Cherbourg, Bismarck's Prussian might destroyed the Second Empire, and the Imperial family, following the Orléans, took refuge in England. Hearing of the siege of Paris, the unimpeachable Victoria exclaimed to Gladstone: 'It is a great *moral*!' Her throne, it seemed, was set fast in granite.

The day trip to Bricquebec had been 'altogether charming' except that it was 'poor dear Vicky's last one with us, which is very sad.' Although childhood had been consecrated as inviolable, adolescence had not yet received its twentieth-century status, and the Princess Royal, at the age of fourteen, was engaged to Prince Frederick William of Prussia, 'Fritz'. The marriage had been planned by both sides when the couple were babies; it had been formally broached by Fritz and consented to in 1855, though then, as Victoria wrote to Leopold, 'the child herself is to know nothing'. On a visit to Windsor the following year, Fritz wooed Vicky and to the satisfaction of everyone the sixteen-year-old Princess and the young Prince fell in love. 'Every spare moment Vicky has (and *I* have, for I must chaperon this loving couple . . . ) is devoted to her bridegroom, who is *so* much in love, that even if he is out driving and walking with her, he is not satisfied, and says he has not seen her . . . '

Vicky and Fritz were married on 25 January 1858 with 'amazing éclat', wrote Greville, in the Chapel Royal St James's — her mother had huffed indignantly at the suggestion that the wedding should take place in Prussia. It was 'the second most eventful day of my life as regards feeling. I felt as if I were being married over again myself . . . ' The parting afterwards was terrible, for both parents and child. 'I am not of a demonstrative nature', wrote Albert to his adored daughter, 'and therefore you can hardly know how dear you have always been to me and what a void you have left . . . ' 'I thought my heart was going to break . . . I miss you so dreadfully my dear Papa, more than I can say',

*Ada, the Queen's niece, fifth child of her beloved sister Feodore, was one of Victoria's favourite subjects, and drawings of her were transferred on to engraving plates.*

she answered. Then began the feverish, impassioned correspondence of mother and daughter that was to go back and forth between Germany and England for the next forty-two years — over 7000 letters altogether.

However painful this early fledging, it realized a long and potent dream of Albert and his Queen: to ally Germany with England by a dynastic marriage, and through the Princess Royal, acolyte in Albert's school of political theory, to educate Prussia in the constitutional and liberal forms of government and divert it from the 'blood and iron' imperialism advocated by Bismarck and later the Junkers of the Kreuzzeitung party. Vicky would become Empress, and her children the future rulers of a progressive Germany in the English mould.

Seven months after the wedding, Victoria and Albert visited their 'beloved Child'. The Prussians exacted a meeting on their home ground. Coburg or the Rhine, where the Queen wanted to meet her daughter, were turned down as unsuitable, and so Victoria was forced to make the long journey to Potsdam and Berlin, site of innumerable Prussian palaces. She sailed on the *Victoria and Albert* up the Scheld from Gravesend, and then took the train from Antwerp via Dusseldorf and Cologne. At each stage of the fatiguing route, the Queen was met by elaborate ceremonial and royal relations. It was 'blazingly hot, and there was such a haze'. The heatwave persisted, and Victoria, who thrived on draughts and frost, suffered from 'racking' headaches and bouts of short-temperedness. At the same time, they heard that Albert's valet Cart, who had come with him from Coburg in 1840 and along with his greyhound Eos had been Albert's only links with his youth, had died; the royal couple's spirits were very low.

Victoria cheered up at the illuminations in Dusseldorf, where she was received by Prince Hohenzollern. The 'transparent paper lamps, and some like baskets of flowers, also splendid red and blue lights . . . All was the spontaneous act of the Artists and the inhabitants'. And they both rallied when Fritz boarded the train and rode with them to the

*Vicky at her Marriage.*
*Chapel Royal Jan 25: 1858*

*V. del from recollection 1858*

Wildpark station at Brandenburg, where Vicky — 'our darling child, with a nosegay in her hand' — awaited them. At Babelsberg, a summer palace built above water in the countryside near Potsdam, Vicky and her mother talked and kissed each other goodnight, and it was 'very pleasant' and the Queen felt 'as if she were my own again . . . '

But the round of functions and sightseeing, one imposing palace after another, was arduous. Victoria made dutiful notes on the possessions and décor of each princely seat; in view of the later destruction of so many of them, it is a shame how imprecise her jottings are. She was most affected by the mourning customs of Prussia: the chair in which Frederick the Great had died, still stained with his blood, and the 'unfinished work' of the last Queen, preserved untouched in her apartments in the Palace of Charlottenburg, Berlin. She,

*On 25 January 1858, in the Chapel Royal, St James's, the Princess Royal married Prince Frederick William of Prussia. This watercolour, made by her mother from memory, shows Vicky in a dress of white moiré antique, with three tiers and a veil of Honiton lace, caught up and wreathed with myrtle and orange blossom.*

who was to emulate this reverence so morbidly herself, found it 'melancholy'. Always with a keen eye for military turn-out — in Paris she had remarked the superior tailoring of the men's uniforms — Victoria observed how everyone in Germany seemed to be in uniform all day long, and that Prussian drill excelled English, 'though the men only serve three years'. Prophetically, she recoiled from the goose-step: at a parade of 4000 troops in Potsdam, she watched as they 'marched past in very quick time, with that peculiar step, throwing the leg out and stamping . . . '

Only in the shade of the beautiful gardens at Babelsberg and Charlottenburg, and in the evening boat rides and picnics at the Neue Palais, did the Queen escape from the unrelenting heat and the political tensions of the Prussian court. She sat out and drew with Vicky watercolour pictures of the temples and follies and lakes, blotting from her mind the dangerousness of her daughter's position. For Vicky, a foreign Princess still fiercely loyal to the country she thought of — and more tactlessly spoke of — as 'home', was surrounded by a faction-ridden court. King Frederick William IV had had a stroke and become senile, and the Regent, his brother Prince William, Fritz's father, was anti-constitutional, Bismarckian and pro-Russian. Vicky had few

*All around Potsdam, Frederick the Great and his successors had built themselves summer palaces which Victoria visited in the summer of 1858, making these attractive watercolour studies of the Marmorpalais and the bridge at Klein-Glienicke, another beautifully laid out park, painted as the light changed between afternoon and sunset.*

friends. Even the choice of an English nurse made her the object of suspicion from the surrounding Germans. Neither Victoria nor Albert wished to see this; they dreamt of subduing Prussian despotism in a united German empire.

Their hopes centred on Fritz, who would succeed his father, and on the child whom Vicky was expecting in that summer of 1858. In fact, Fritz survived his father only a few months when he died in 1888, and the child Vicky bore was to take the imperialist road of his grandfather and, as the Kaiser, to cut the fragile thread bound by Victoria and Albert

about the two great powers of Europe. But in 1858 none of this disturbed them. Victoria minded above all else that she could not stay with Vicky for the birth: 'I feel it bitterly that I have to forgo my natural right and duty to be with my dear Child in her hour of trial, as every other mother does.' She hoped to be able to attend the christening, but in the end only managed to see her first grandchild in the autumn of 1860, when she returned to Germany for a much more pleasant three-week stay in Albert's ancestral home at Coburg, where Vicky and Fritz and 'little William' awaited them.

*When 'little William', Vicky's first child, was born the 'children were in extacies', wrote the Queen, 'at Uncle and Aunt-ship, Arthur shouting out: "I'M an uncle".'*

*The future Kaiser's military bearing already shows in the Queen's pencil drawing of him (right), but she also caught his childlike sweetness in the exquisite sketch of him (left), in the arms of her youngest child, Beatrice, only two years older than her nephew.*

*The countryside around the Rosenau, Albert's birthplace, became so familiar to Victoria on their two happy and leisurely visits that she was able to plan her compositions with forethought, as in this romantic view of the gabled Gothic schloss.*

Victoria had first visited Coburg in the summer of 1845, when she was flush with love for Albert, and every tree in whose shade he had strolled, every building he had lived in or known, every detail of the modest yet beautifully furnished rooms of the castle of Rosenau, every item in the museum of specimens that he and Ernest had collected, had been a source of intensified passion for her husband. Since then Albert's realization that his wife's grasp of affairs, though quick, was so much more frivolous and superficial than his own had led him to take on more and more work, until the Queen became jealous of it — not because Albert usurped her role, but because she did not have him to herself. Her passionate nature erupted in tantrums, met by meticulously argued and patient letters in reply from Albert, to whom in real life *sturm und drang* was torment. On top of this he was a sick man, suffering from rheumatism in the shoulder which prevented him shooting, from stomach pains, and from frequent undiagnosed disturbances which enfeebled him and which Victoria's iron health and intolerance of weakness only exacerbated.

Victoria was happy to be back in Coburg, to be out tranquilly with Vicky, with their sketchbooks and their new-

*Market day in Coburg fascinated her, and she made many studies of the people, their distinctive costumes and the scene, including this ambitiously constructed and fully realised view of the stalls set up in the square beneath her sitting room window in the Ehrenburg Palace.*

found bond of motherhood, but Albert's presence does not cast the peachy glow over her diary that it had in 1845. Nevertheless they were in a holiday mood until, in the third week of their visit, the horses drawing the Prince's open carriage bolted at a level crossing. The bar was down, a waggon stood in the way. Albert threw himself to the ground; the carriage crashed through, the coachman was badly injured and one horse killed. Albert escaped with bad bruising, but he was a man under strain, and the accident drained his resources. Only Baron Stockmar, ever the percipient observer, saw the whole gravity of the case: 'God have mercy on us!' he wrote. 'If anything serious should ever happen to him, he will die.' Albert, visited by his brother, broke down. In tears he told him that he knew he would never see Coburg again.

For the first time since 1835 Victoria fell very ill herself; but though her body may have been warning her of the seriousness of the Prince's condition, her mind, always determined to outface disaster, firmly pushed it aside. On their return to England Albert had resumed his self-imposed punishing routine, snatching moments between matters political, domestic and artistic to play duets with Victoria and read aloud to her the 'last new book' of George Eliot, *Silas Marner*.

In August 1861, they travelled together for the last time, to Ireland. It was the Queen's second visit: in 1849 she was the first British monarch ever to set foot in Cork, and though guarded in her political comments, had been pleased at the people's 'enthusiasm' and very struck by their handsomeness — 'almost every third woman is pretty, and some remarkably so'. In 1861, Victoria took Alfred, Alice and Lenchen with her, and her main purpose was to see Bertie, the Prince of Wales, who was with the Guards at their camp in Curragh; Albert also hoped that the beautiful surroundings of Killarney would coax his wife out of her rage and grief at the death of her mother that March. But Victoria was never more obstinate than in her attachment to mourning. 'I *derive* benefit and *relief* both to my body and soul in *dwelling*

*In the last month's of his life, Albert was utterly crushed by the news that his Portuguese cousins, King Pedro V and two of his brothers, had all been carried off by typhoid. Louis, the last remaining brother, succeeded to the throne of Portugal, and reigned until 1889.*

on the sad object which is *the* one which fills my heart!' she wrote, on the death of her half-brother Charles in 1856. So Albert's increasing debilitation passed unobserved by his wife, except that in a tone of sympathy that scarcely conceals her frustration, she records continually that dearest Albert was 'fagged'.

On 25 November, with that attention to hopeful details that accompanies all efforts to placate implacable furies, Victoria began to record the onslaught of his final illness. He was sleepless, restless, in pain, unable to eat and hardly to drink; the ignorance of his medical staff and the heroic optimism of his family prevented him being nursed or rested with any proper care. He could hardly smile, though he managed to enjoy Baby reciting some French verse for her lessons. He often greeted his wife with a blind, strange look that scared her. On 8 December he asked to hear music, and Princess Alice played his favourites chorales on the piano next door; on 13 December the Queen's diary ends with the sentence that had appeared again and again, that the doctors 'said there was no reason to anticipate anything worse'. There were no more entries after that. Albert died the next day, perhaps of typhoid, perhaps of a long cancer, but most certainly of overwork.

Albert had always struggled to make Victoria, to whom he had devoted his life, understand the ugliness of excess; like so many of the lessons he had repeated with such thought and justification it was a waste of time, and never more so than after his death. 'My *life* as a *happy* one is *ended*!' she wrote; 'the world is gone for *me*! . . . Oh! to be cut off in the prime of life — to see our pure, happy, quiet, domestic life, which *alone* enabled me to bear my *much* disliked position, *cut off* at forty-two . . . is *too awful*, too cruel!'

# The Highland Haven

Prince Albert's memory was not well served by his widow's cult. The spires, institutions, plinths and platforms that bore his statue or his name pressed his perfections too hard on a nation that is suspicious of paragons, preferring Falstaff in his cups to Thomas More or adulterous Lancelot to pure Percival. It infuriated the Queen that Albert should not be loved while the Prince of Wales, indolent, pleasure-loving, ignorant and even immoral, should win effortlessly the popularity that had eluded her beloved husband. Through-out her long widowhood — she lived almost exactly twice as long as Albert — and especially during its first two decades she drove herself to lead her life as a living memorial to his values and his teaching. 'I am (also) anxious to repeat one thing, and *that one* is my firm resolve, my *irrevocable decision*, viz. that *his* wishes — *his* plans — about everything, *his* views about *every* thing are to me *my law*! . . . ' Like many a disciple before her, the Queen chose to interpret her master's law according to her own lights.

She was broken by his death, through sincere love and re-morse at her shortcomings — the tantrums, the nagging, the intolerance of weakness with which she had plagued him — and through sheer helplessness, for together they had contrived to make her exaggeratedly dependent on him. She retreated, and squirrel-like hid herself away during the winter of her bereavement in the place where Albert had been happiest, 'my dear Albert's *own* creation, own work,

own building, own laying out' — Balmoral Castle in the Highlands.

In 1842, during her post-natal exhaustion after Vicky and Bertie's births, the Queen had made her first journey to Scotland, sailing up to the West Coast on the recommendation of her doctor. She and the Prince stayed in Lord Breadalbane's castle at Taymouth; two years later, Lord and Lady Glenlyon lent them Blair Atholl. Victoria's artistic eye was captivated. 'Every turn you have a picture', she wrote. She agreed with Albert that 'the chief beauty of mountain scenery consisted in its frequent changes', and she began to chronicle the effects of weather and season and light on the glens and lochs that unfolded themselves before her entranced vision as Albert drove her, often for more than two hours at a stretch, along the Highland roads.

One of the Queen's ladies-in-waiting during this visit was Charlotte Canning, later Vicereine of India, and together they sat down on the hillside, on plaids spread out for them, to sketch and paint. Lady Canning was one of the celebrated Stuart daughters — her sister was the remarkable beauty and gifted artist Lady Waterford — and she too had a developed artistic gift. One of the reasons for the paucity of water-colours painted by Victoria on her first visit to Coburg may be that Charlotte Canning accompanied her and made some very graceful, finished and keen-eyed paintings of the sights, which the Queen later kept in her souvenir albums. But in Scotland Victoria was not cramped by Lady Canning's skills. In 1844, and again in 1847 when she and Albert stayed at Lord

*1862*

*1st year of my misery.*

Abercorn's shooting lodge of Ardverickie, she was painting with a fresh, bold use of colour, her powers of observation sharpened by the magnificent views and the tonic romance of scenery far wilder and grander than anything she had seen hitherto. After a ride in the hills, she surpassed herself in sensuous description: 'As the sun went down the scenery became more and more beautiful, the sky crimson, golden-red and blue, and the hills becoming purple and lilac, most exquisite, till at length it set, and the hues grew softer in the sky and the outlines of the hills sharper. I never saw anything so fine.'

Victoria's growing skills were also the result of excellent tuition. In July 1846 Edward Lear, whose *Excursions in Italy* had just been published, came to Osborne and coached the Queen in draughtsmanship. She was also receiving regular lessons from William Leighton Leitch. 'Good old Leitch' as

*These two studies of the same view from Victoria's window at Balmoral, on successive days in September and October 1848, show how conscientiously Victoria applied herself to capturing the beauty she and Albert found in the Highland scenery. The first, showing rain clouds blurring the outline of the mountains, has great attack and softness.*

*In this brighter second attempt, her effort made on a rougher cartridge paper is more self-consciously artistic, and less fresh.*

the Queen called him was a marvellously sensitive draughts-man and a glowing painter who exploited to the full the breadth of a watercolour palette, from sombre tones in the depths of foliage to a hard brilliance for flowers and sunlight. Leitch was introduced to Court by Lady Canning, having been recommended by the Duchess of Sutherland, Victoria's great friend and her Mistress of the Robes. Her cousin, Richard Cavendish, had been instructed by Leitch during his travels in Italy. Leitch gave the Queen a basic technical knowledge of the potential of watercolour that Westall had failed to do: 'I showed how light, that is, brilliancy, was produced by yellow ochre, pink madder, and cobalt blue, and darkness, deeper than black, by sepia, purple lake, and indigo — also primitive colours. Using these two classes of colours with their compounds, I then did skies, distance, middle-ground, foreground, white clouds, and their shadows, no whiter than a lady's satin dress; and then with the same colours, a black dress full of colour and shadow, but with no *black* in it; and then a great many varieties of green colours. After attending to this part of the lesson with great earnestness . . . the Queen turned to Lady Canning and said, "This is very wonderful . . ."'

Leitch was a native of Glasgow, and after scraping a living in Scotland as a scene-painter and snuff box decorator, he came south to improve his fortunes. He became a favourite instructor in aristocratic circles; he was a good raconteur and an entertaining mimic, and he soon found that he had a 'great relish for society'. One of his pupils, Sir Coutts Lindsay, later the owner of the Grosvenor Gallery, thought 'he was often held away from the more ardent pursuit of his art by the insistence of those who would by no means allow themselves to be deprived of his teaching and his gaiety'. Leitch attended Victoria over a period of twenty-two years, accompanying her to Osborne and Windsor as well as Balmoral, until the excruciating migraines from which he suffered forced him to give up teaching.

*On Victoria and Albert's first visit to Scotland they sailed up the West Coast, past such striking landmarks as Dunollie Castle, guarding the mouth of the Sound of Kerrera.*

*Landseer F[illegible] on the B[illegible] at A[illegible]*
*[illegible] Sept. 5. 1847.*

'Who does not glory in the death of a fine stag?' wrote Landseer. The stag at bay symbolized for the Victorians the nobility of nature and man's primacy in the created world.

Overleaf: This detailed study of Ardverickie Lodge pays homage to the dramatic scenery that intoxicated Victoria and brought her back to Scotland almost annually.

At Ardverickie, Victoria admired particularly the walls 'ornamented with beautiful drawings of stags by Landseer'. Landseer was so inspired by the scenery and the life of the Highlands that it is sometimes difficult to remember he was not Scots by birth. He was at his best when working spontaneously and prevented from reworking and over-painting, and the frescoes at Ardverickie, drawn straight on to the wet wall with a burnt stick and red brick, were probably amongst the most vivid and fresh examples of his work. But they were destroyed by fire in 1873, and Victoria's copies, together with a single photograph taken by a workman at the lodge, remain the only record of them. Like Leitch, Landseer took to high company with relish. He too taught the Queen on her Highland visits, adding highlights and touches of definition to her many drawings of stags 'dear Albert shot', and helping her to draw in pastel.

173

'There was a quiet, a retirement, a wildness, a liberty and a solitude', wrote Queen Victoria, who felt as intensely about the Highlands as Wordsworth about the Lakes, identifying

> *Not with the mean and vulgar works of man,*
> *But with high objects, with enduring things,*
> *With life and nature . . .*

Victoria and Albert were determined to return, and not only for the 'beautiful scenery', but for the Scots themselves: 'such a chivalrous, fine, active people'. By extraordinary fortune a miser and eccentric, John Camden Nield, died in 1852 and left the Queen half a million pounds. Not long after this, she and Albert first leased, and then bought, the estate of Balmoral on Deeside near Aberdeen, where the weather was more clement than on the rugged and rain-swept West Coast.

*Right: Albert built at Balmoral a model farm and dairy on the lines he had already begun at Windsor, and Victoria made these delicate sketches of cattle there.*

*Below: This spirited evocation of one of the Queen's favourite haunts below Balloch Buie was spread over two pages in one of her small travelling sketchbooks.*

Once again the old house was thrown down, and a new one raised in its place. Albert was again the architect, collaborating with William Smith, the City Architect of Aberdeen. The conception sprang even more directly from his imagination than Osborne had: the Dee's pretty run at the foot of the castle's site became visible from the windows, and the white granite walls, the crow-stepped gables, pepperpot turrets, finials and castellated parapets recalled the silhouettes of the Rosenau and the Ehrenburg Palace of Coburg. The foundation stone was laid by the Queen on 28 September 1853, with much dancing of reels and even sips of whisky at the gillies' ball that evening.

Following Albert's example, Victoria threw herself with unconditional enthusiasm into the life of the Highlands, and thus hallowed the Scottish mystique that Sir Walter Scott's writings had recently brought before English eyes. The

*This painting by Victoria of the new Balmoral, designed by Albert to resemble his native German castles, was made in 1854 while it was being built.*

*Alfred & Bertie* —

*The Prince of Wales and Prince Alfred dressed in full Highland costume: the idealized faces and poetic suggestion of the Scottish landscape behind them shows some influence of Robert Thorburn, whom the Queen commissioned to paint portraits of the family.*

autumn round of deer-stalking, rambles, hikes, climbs and picnics in scenic spots was carried out with vigour and maximum authenticity. Haggis was sampled. A Balmoral tartan was designed, and added to those already decorating the antlered halls of the castle. Prince Albert, the Prince of Wales and all the royal children set the fashion for kilts that has proved one of the most durable of all, in children's dress in particular. Silk tartans were made up into dresses for the Princesses, and the Queen's adoption of the plaid spread its wearing throughout English society.

The first novel Victoria had ever read was Scott's *Bride of Lammermoor*; for the rest of her life she recorded her delight in the picturesque people of Scotland and their customs, in the sword dances by torchlight and the bagpipes — a piper or

The Shiel of Allt-na-Guithasach.
Loch-Muick.

B. del. Aug. 31. 1849.

'It had a very pretty effect', wrote the Queen after watching Albert and the tenants at Balmoral 'leistering' (spearing) salmon in the Dee. 'I wished for Landseer's pencil . . . ' Landseer absent, the Queen tried — one of her few attempts at a group scene.

two always accompanied their excursions. She took down carefully the place names, revelling in the strange, tongue-twisting sounds: the Pass of Killiecrankie, the Shiel of Alt-na-Giuthasach, the mountains of Loch-na-Gar and Ben Muich Dhui; she tried to pick up a word or two of Gaelic, and admired Albert's quicker tongue. She followed patiently on ponies, or on foot — it is remarkable how much scrambling she did, crinolines regardless, on Scottish hillsides — as Albert fished for salmon, or manfully stalked the valleys. The Prince Consort's sportsmanship was derided; he was reputed — and still is in Scotland — a very bad shot, and reports that his gillies and keepers constantly covered up for him filled the pages of *Punch* with gleeful and very xenophobic ribaldry. On their visit to Coburg in 1845 a *battue* had been organized for the Queen's entertainment: the animals were driven into a ring where they could be picked off by the huntsmen from a pavilion — a practice considered by the English un-sportsmanlike and ungentlemanly. Albert never really re-covered from the huge unpopularity the *battue* caused him. But Victoria remained aloof, perhaps even deaf, to the taunts. She referred constantly and tactlessly to the Prince's home-sickness, writing how he loved the Scottish landscape because it reminded him of Thuringia, and how he said that 'many of the people look like Germans'. She was thrilled when, after a good day's sport for Albert, the huntsmen told her she had 'a lucky foot', and with wifely devotion noted over two pages of a sketchbook the exact weights of six deer 'killed with 6 shots, out stalking in the Muichle Pass'.

Together they pursued the simple life. To escape Balmoral's middle-class comforts they built austere shiels in picturesque spots at Alt-na-Giuthasach and Glen Gelder, where they could stay, virtually unattended in a few humble rooms, like the crofters who were their tenants. Together they explored the countryside, enjoying the thrills of being incognito. After a picnic lunch 'on a very precipitous place' above Glen Isla, Albert scribbled on a bit of paper that he had lunched 'at this spot'. He then stuck the note in the ground, 'in a seltzer water bottle' for the wonder of later travellers.

Victoria and Albert first stayed in the simplicity of the shiel at Alt-na-Giuthasach in August 1849, and it remained a favourite experience of the Queen's, frequently repeated.

Victoria was inspired to experiment with different media and in the fifties briefly took up oils: she painted her children performing *Athalie*, and set their interpretation of *Das Hahnenschlag* in a realistic rather than theatrical bucolic setting. She also painted portraits of Annie and Archie MacDonald, which she later hung in her bathroom at Osborne. They were the children of Albert's gillie from the west of Scotland, 'a remarkably tall and handsome' man, in the Queen's opinion. Archie became *Jäger* to the Prince of Wales; Annie died of tuberculosis in 1866.

Landseer tutored the Queen's efforts in oil, and introduced her to pastel, a medium he favoured. In 1851 and 1852 the Queen made dozens of bold, garishly coloured portraits of retainers and tenants and neighbours at Balmoral — the Grants and the Flemmings and Jane MacKenzie at her tub,

*Archie and Annie MacDonald, painted here in the model kennels at Balmoral, were the children of Archibald MacDonald, the Prince Consort's gillie, and his wife Anne.*

Maggie Gow.                                    ... ... Sept. 14. 1849.

*Maggie Gow, daughter of the Balmoral tenant James Gow, was one of the many 'Highland lassies' whom the Queen visited regularly and painted.*

and other 'Highland lads and lassies' whose simplicity and goodness of heart touched her so deeply. She dispensed warm socks and red pinafores when she went visiting, but was the first to admit that her attempts at portraiture were not altogether a success: Landseer had shown her 'how to draw in chalks', she wrote, 'but I never could manage that well.'

The faithful Scottishness of Victoria and Albert's style was painted by Landseer, and also by Carl Haag, a Bavarian specialist in sporting and mountain scenes who came to England via Brussels and commemorated in the fifties the strenuous riding excursions and shooting exploits of Albert and the Queen. In their embrace of the Scottish cult, Victoria and her husband embody the contemporary spirit of their times. Wordsworth and Coleridge and Keats had raised them, however indirectly, to know that nature in her wild

183

state is the great teacher and the supreme uplifting mystery, while Scotland and its customs represented an ancient culture that was independent of classicism; its rediscovery constituted a romantic rejection of Greek and Roman formalism in favour of a distinguished barbarism — poetic, primitive, simple and autonomous. Victoria and Albert's eager identification with it, which seems to us now comical and rather absurd in two 'foreigners', reflects the lively confidence of their age in all things British and homegrown. In their lifetime its antiquarian side was not fustian, but energetically modern.

Prince Albert's interest in the Highlands reflected his progressive innovatory character as surely as his inspired organization of the Great Exhibition in 1851, and Victoria returned there after his death to recreate, as a living testimonial to his superior judgement in all things, the life they had led together. At the peak of her seclusion, in 1868, when murmurings against her prolonged withdrawal from public life were becoming louder, she published *Leaves from*

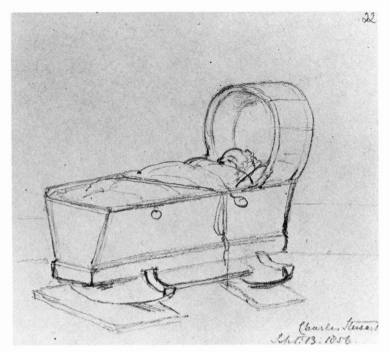

*Victoria often visited the workers on the Balmoral estate; this baby asleep in a wooden cradle is the newborn son of Donald Stewart, one of the keepers.*

the *Journal of Our Life in the Highlands*, extracts from her diary, with illustrations of her life in Scotland with the Prince and the happy excursions they had made together. Her children and some members of her household disliked its publication. The book gave the impression that the Queen's life was all play and no work, and during her long absences from England, either in Scotland or on the Isle of Wight, such an impression seemed inadvisable.

William Gladstone, Prime Minister during much of the period of Victoria's determined retreat, was compassionate and understanding, and travelled to Balmoral frequently to despatch state business. In 1869, after much pressure gently but firmly applied, he prevailed upon the Queen to show herself again in her capital and open Blackfriars Bridge and Holborn Viaduct, both high examples of the Age of Iron. In 1871, the Prince of Wales had been very ill indeed with typhoid, and a national day of thanksgiving for his delivery was proclaimed. Victoria, in spite of her disclaimers that life, especially as a Queen, held any pleasure for her, found that she thoroughly enjoyed herself: ' . . . a day of triùmph', she wrote to Vicky. 'Really most marvellous! Such touching affection and loyalty cannot be seen anywhere I think . . . Millions must have been out and the decorations were really beautiful — the cheering deafening . . . when we were stopping at Temple Bar amid deafening cheers I took dear Bertie's hand and pressed it — people cried.'

On that occasion, John Brown 'in his very fullest and very handsome full dress' rode on the box, and it was in some good part his achievement that the Queen felt strong enough to return to public life. Her first volume of *Leaves* was dedicated to the memory of Albert, her second, *More Leaves*, published in 1884, to that of John Brown. Her nature demanded support from someone whom she had created in her mind's eye as a source of strength, wisdom and truth, serving her as exclusive priestess. Although it annoyed her that others did not share her view of Albert's or Brown's perfections, she certainly thrived on her undivided possession of them.

*Left: From the small albums Victoria kept when she was in Scotland, she chose her most successful attempts and pasted them in to beautifully bound books on large pages (left).*

*Her range of colour had become more sophisticated since her earliest days: she took the bluest of the blues to capture the eyes of John Brown (above) at the age of 23.*

But it would be wrong to equate Albert and Brown in any other respect. She admired 'Johnnie Brown' because Albert had; as a young man he had been picked by the Prince Consort to be the Queen's servant, to lead her horse, to wade through streams holding her above the water wrapped in a plaid, to sit on the box of her carriage and oversee the coachman. He was a magnificent specimen of the Highlander so venerated by Albert: 'marked by that honesty and sympathy, which always distinguish the inhabitants of mountainous countries. . . . ' His blond good looks and blue blue eyes, his 'vigorous, light, elastic tread' which the Queen found 'quite astonishing', added to the picture of Celtic purity in an era before Nazi ideology had made such attitudes suspect. He was courageous and quick, and above all 'handy' — high praise in Victoria's lexicon. He twice saved the

Queen from nasty coach accidents by his presence of mind, and when she was threatened by a pistol-brandishing Fenian in 1872, it was Brown 'alone' who noticed the danger and seized the assailant 'by the throat'. In 1865 she appointed him to the special post of 'The Queen's Highland Servant', 'to attend me *always* and everywhere out of doors, . . . and it is a *real* comfort, for he is *so* devoted to me — so simple, so intelligent, so *unlike* an *ordinary* servant, and so cheerful and attentive . . . ' Queen Victoria had a special feeling for her servants' friendship. She warned Vicky against changing hers often, for then 'there can be no mutual attachment . . . But I think you don't care much for the inestimable comfort and value of a truly devoted and attached and trustworthy servant.'

Initial enthusiasm in Court circles for John Brown's reviving influence on the widowed Queen soon waned: the informality of his manners, so relished by Victoria, seemed insolent to many around her; his drunkenness, his privileges, his prejudices and his unspoken but very real prerogatives infuriated almost everyone — the Prince of Wales in particular — and gave rise to angry and malicious comment in the press. But in spite of his attaining the rank of Esquire when the Queen moved him to serve her indoors as well as

*In spite of her assiduous widowhood Queen Victoria never lost her sense of fun, as is shown by this lively picture of her taking 'tea in a snow storm' up in the Cairngorms.*

J. Coutts & C. Campbell watching the deer.
VR. 24th Sept. 1857

out, and gaining considerable increases in revenue, he remained a servant. On his death he was commemorated by an astonishing tribute: 'the faithful and devoted personal attendant and friend' is immortalized in copperplate engraving at the base of a column in the personal pantheon of Victoria, the mausoleum at Frogmore.

Benjamin Disraeli, who became Prime Minister for most of 1868 and again from 1874 to 1880, fascinated and flattered the Queen into renewed interest in her ever more splendid realm. Both he and John Brown, at the same period of the Queen's life, knew how to handle her, how to reassure and complete her when she was stalked by Albert's ghost, which made her feel bereft and hesitant and inadequate. John Brown called her 'wumman' and Disraeli 'the Faery'; John Brown told her it was 'very pleasant to walk with a person who is always content'; Disraeli in conversation would say 'we authors, ma'am'. Her zest, her wit, her liveliness returned in the decade of the seventies. 'She was wreathed in smiles', wrote Disraeli after one of their many long audiences, 'and, as she tattled, she glided about the room like a bird.' She did not paint Dizzy's seamed, compelling, bony and ironic face, but among her sketches made at this date appears one watercolour of a primrose. Victoria never painted flowers, except as flashes of colour in a landscape. But she sent by train to Disraeli in London nosegays of flowers she had picked herself at Osborne. His favourites, he told her, were the primroses, 'the ambassadors of Spring . . . the gems and jewels of Nature'. His gallantry knew no bounds: 'They show', he wrote, 'that your Majesty's sceptre has touched the enchanted isle'.

Victoria chose a primrose, rather than the man. After Albert died, people recede from the pages of her sketchbooks. The two folio albums, bound in soft suede with blue spine and corners, into which she stuck the best work from her smaller sketchpads after his death, begin with a watercolour view of the mausoleum at Frogmore where the Prince lay buried and where she was to join him. She painted it from her window at Windsor Castle, and it sounds the quiet, melancholy note of the sequence that follows. There is view after view of the places they enjoyed together — Glen

*Nosegays were part of the important Victorian ritual of celebrating a birthday or a feeling, and this bunch of primroses is perhaps a tribute to Disraeli, whose favourite flowers they were.*

The different techniques used by Victoria are clearly shown on this first page of her album of views (right) after the Prince Consort's death.

With considerable skill, the Queen used the background of the untouched white paper to create the impression of the snow-covered slopes outside the castle (below).

Balmoral
Dec: 1865 —

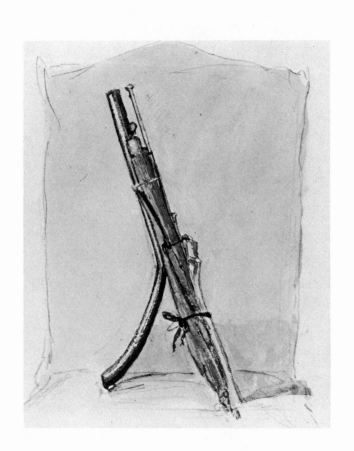

Muich, Balloch Buie, Craig Gowan — but they rarely feature the active figures stalking and shooting and fishing, the healthy Highlanders and local friends who appear in the earlier drawings. The landscape itself has been widowed. The watercolours are not in themselves melancholy, but their emptiness contrasts bleakly with her previous vitality. She continues to observe with a keen eye, but that eye is turned on the changing colours of the heather, the profiles of the mountains, and the tones and movements in the sky. A true inheritor of romanticism, she found in the Highland landscape, uncultivated, wild, majestic, almost untouched by man's influence, an uplifting and tranquil solace in her long bereavement.

In 1862 she had spoken to Gladstone of her loss: he recorded how it 'continually returned upon her and met her at every turn — how in every thing great and small his [Albert's] ready, watchful mind, his taste, his affection, undertook all and effected all — for her business, her children, her very ornaments which all passed under the ordeal of his taste.' She told Gladstone that 'All this was gone from her, and the sun and light of her life was gone with it.' The Scottish views commemorate what Albert loved, what Albert left.

*Moritzkirchen April 1816 ...*

# SEVEN

# Family
# and Empire

In 1887, when Queen Victoria celebrated her Golden Jubilee, the *Graphic* magazine was serializing Rider Haggard's classic empire adventure, *She*. Though Victoria's unrelenting weeds and sad widow's cap, the famous asperity of her tongue and the austerity of her household lessen the visual exoticism of her last decades, she herself was as much a part of the highly coloured romance of her times as Rider Haggard's imperishable heroine. When 'Fritz' Ponsonby, son of Victoria's private secretary, became an equerry at Court in the nineties, he was struck by the picture she presented at breakfast: 'Everything on the table was gold . . . and she was eating a boiled egg in a gold egg-cup with a gold spoon. Two Indian Khitmagars in scarlet and gold remained motionless behind her chair, while outside a page and a Scotchman in a kilt waited till she rang.' She was indeed the queen who held, in the words of Kipling's Jubilee hymn, 'dominion over palm and pine'.

Disraeli had made Victoria Empress of India in 1876, but only because she wanted it. The Commons and the Cabinet were against this change of the royal title, but the Queen, spellbound by its glamour, insisted. India was her last

*Prince Alfred, Duke of Edinburgh, was in direct succession to the Dukedom of Saxe-Coburg-Gotha as well, and he had a house in the main square of Coburg, where his mother stayed in 1876. Luther had preached in the Moritzkirche, with its distinctive late Gothic spire, which also stood on the square.*

The Greece cutter of Dragon funnels — in Portsmouth Harbour Aug: 9, 1882

enthusiasm in a lifetime of enthusiasms, and in this as in others she showed herself sovereign and impervious to criticism or dissent. In the case of John Brown, or of prolonged Highland visits, her tenacity was not so remarkable, for she was fighting a largely personal battle, but over India and the Indians she was uniquely free of the common prejudice prevalent all over England and in her own household. In 1857, when the Crown took over the government of India from the East India Company after the civil war and mutiny, the Queen and Prince Albert had tempered the proclamation with phrases much more tolerant and less imperialist than the original. She had objected to the document's missionary tone, for instance, and amended it to read: 'The deep attachment the Queen feels to her own religion and the comfort and happiness which she derives from its con-solations will preclude her from any attempt to interfere with the native religions . . . ' In the 1890s, having employed Indians as servants in her households at Osborne and Balmoral, she stopped her ears to the campaign of complaint raised by other members of the Court who, already disgruntled at the bands of Highland attendants, found

*This watercolour of 1882, in which one can see the Queen's shakier grasp on her paintbrush, is one of the very few subjects she chose with an immediate political content. The Greece was a troop ship transporting cavalry to Egypt, to support the Khedive against rebels who had been crushed by British intervention in June.*

Moslem customs as well too much to bear.

Victoria's attraction to the picturesque was deep-seated and instinctive, and she defended it against her attackers with loyal ferocity. In her youth the exotic settings of the ballet had seized her imagination; as early as 1833, she commented in fascination on the visit of a Captain Burnes, 'who had travelled over N.E. India' and brought 'some very interesting accounts' to Kensington Palace, as well as 'his servant, a native of Cabul, dressed in his native dress. He . . . is of a dark olive complexion and had a dress of real Cashmere made in the beautiful valley of Cashmere.' At a concert in the same year, she mentioned 'the oriental attire' of 'Prince Jame o deen, son of the famous Tippo Saib' (*sic*). But her account does not bristle with horror at the man whose father was a byword for cruelty; his life-size model of a carving of a tiger devouring an Englishman, complete with clockwork mechanical groans and moans, was found in his palace after its destruction and is now — perhaps inappropriately — in the Victoria and Albert Museum. In 1854 Victoria welcomed Dhuleep Singh, son of the Chief of the Sikhs, who had been removed from his throne as a child by the British. When she learned that the boy was showing no sympathy with British victims of the mutiny and its aftermath, the Queen defended him, pointing out that he was hardly in a position to delight in British victories, 'or be expected to *like* to hear his country-people called *fiends* and *monsters*, and to see them brought in hundreds, if not thousands, to be executed' and ending, 'It is a great mercy that he, poor boy, is not there.' She was convinced of his Eastern gentleness and touched by his 'striking good looks'; she painted him in watercolour at Osborne as, covered in jewels, he played with her children.

To be Empress of these beautiful, dazzling creatures was pure romance. At the reception of the Indian deputations for the Golden Jubilee Victoria retrieved from her past stock of images a word she had hardly used since the happy days of her marriage: the Princes' appearance was 'like a dream'. They had 'wonderful jewels on'; they lavished magnificent gifts on her; Sir Partab Singh placed his sword at her feet, and

told her everything he possessed was hers to use. After the Colonial and Indian Exhibition, forty-three Indian craftsmen paraded before Victoria and 'knelt down and kissed and stroked my feet and knees, some prostrating themselves more than others.' The Empress of India was not displeased.

She would like to have seen for herself her sub-continent, and her remarks to Vicky during the Prince of Wales's resplendent tour of 1876 have a touch of jealousy to them: 'Bertie's progresses lose a little interest and are very wearing — as there is such a constant repetition of elephants — trappings — jewels — illuminations and fireworks.' But if she could not experience India in person, she would create the atmosphere of the civilized, paternalist Orient at home; she would bring, incongruous as it may seem, the majesty of the Raj to the homely Isle of Wight.

The Queen's first two Indian servants, whose photographs still hang in her dressing room just beneath one of John Brown and his brothers, were Mohammed Buxsh and Abdul Karim. They entered her service three days after the Golden Jubilee. The former was large, bearded and genial, but little else is known of him, for he never climbed higher than the

rank of bearer. But the latter became more loathed even than John Brown. On the day they kissed her feet and began to wait on her at Windsor, the Queen wrote that Abdul Karim was 'much younger [he was twenty-four], much lighter, tall, and with a fine serious countenance.' She knew that the father of the Munshi ('Teacher') was a native doctor in Agra. Her courtiers, suspicious that the Munshi was working for his own Moslem ends and endangering the Queen's impartiality in the agonising religious problems of India, worked to discredit him. When they found that his father was only a hospital attendant in the Indian medical department, they pounced. But Abdul was clever and quick-witted and charming, and the Queen cried fiddlesticks at her household, issued terse reprimands about 'red-tapist' narrowminded-ness, and thought the inlaid marble chess table sent to her by Abdul's father worthy of a place at Osborne beside the famous Renaissance-style billiard table Albert himself had designed, and a painted *guéridon* from the Vatican.

Shortly after the Munshi's arrival, the Queen recorded in her journal: 'Am learning a few words of Hindustani to speak to my servants. It is a great interest to me, for both the language and the people.' The Munshi soon explained to the Queen that waiting was beneath him, since at home he had been a clerk. Photographs in which he appeared as a menial were speedily destroyed, and his advancement began. Before the eyes of attendants who could hardly bring themselves to speak to an Indian, the Munshi was given Karim Cottage at Balmoral, Frogmore Cottage at Windsor, and Arthur Cottage at Osborne. Despatch boxes about Indian affairs were shown to him, his advice was solicited, and he was taking part in the holy privacy of family theatricals, as a figure in the 'tableau vivant' of an Indian bazaar.

The last full-scale paintings Victoria attempted are copies of portraits, one of the Munshi in 1889, the other of Mohammed Burhsh in 1892. The originals were painted by Rudolph Swoboda, a Viennese and the nephew of L. K. Müller, who was not only gifted at exotic foreign genre scenes but also won high favour as a portrait painter to the aristocracy. Swoboda was the last artist to receive full patronage from the Queen. He came to London via Egypt, where he had specialized in bazaar vignettes. The Queen chose him to be her eyes on India, commissioning him first to paint the craftsmen at the Colonial Exhibition, and then sending him on a journey to India itself to record for her the typical features of her new subjects, their everyday life and activities.

Swoboda's enormous collection of small oil sketches, vivid, colourful and wrongly neglected, hangs in the Indian Corridor at Osborne, alongside portraits of Indian loyalists such as Sir Partab Singh and Maharajah Dhuleep Singh by Winterhalter. The Corridor leads to the largest building undertaken by Victoria after Albert's death, and, in its flash display — just as the bleak bothy of Glassalt Shiel is in its humility — it is entirely characteristic of the Queen who had loved dressing up as a child. The Durbar Room occupies a whole wing, opposite the earlier Household Wing at Osborne. It is an enormous, single reception room, lit by tall, rather un-Indian, sash windows overlooking the lawn, and decorated throughout in the elaborate plasterwork of peacocks, rosettes, arabesques and scrolls characteristic of Mudejar work in Spain. It was designed by John Lockwood Kipling, father of Rudyard and keeper of the museum at Lahore, with the help of a master of Indian stucco technique, Bhai Ram Singh, and it was used throughout the nineties as a banqueting hall in which the Empress of India and the 'Mother of Europe', a tiny, stout, dazzling figure, would appear, laden with the enormous gems and cabochons presented to her by the subjects of the Raj.

By 1897 and the Diamond Jubilee, the Queen and Empress was a living icon. In New Guinea, some of the most distant tribes under British rule failed to make the distinction between monarchy and divinity, and worshipped the Queen as their holy Mother. Photogravure had made her face familiar to everyone: her famous profile, of which even the sloping chin cannot efface the determination, was discerned in the silhouettes of American mountains; her bell-like figure,

Osborne
July – 1860 –

Little Charlotte of Prussia (our
granddaughter!)

stiff in its mourning crape and surmounted by her widow's cap (which she would not even put off for the Jubilee processions), became in the eyes of the world the image of the archetypal mother.

Family trees, with medallions of her progeny hanging like fruit from the branches, were published in newspapers and magazines all over the Empire for her Jubilees. Victoria was the sturdiest vine the English royal house had ever known. By 1879 she was already a great-grandmother: Vicky's eldest daughter, Charlotte of Prussia, gave birth to a girl, Princess Feodora of Saxe Meiningen. 'Quite an event', commented the sixty-year old Queen. Victoria's children were vigorously fertile: Vicky bore eight children in all, in fourteen years — two died in childhood; Alice had seven children in eleven years, lost one aged three, and, while nursing her last-born, 'May', caught diphtheria and died in 1878, by some freak of destiny on the same day — 'the terrible day come round again' — as her father, 14 December. She was buried at Darmstadt, the home of her marriage, but her effigy, with May in her arms, carved in marble by Boehm, lies in the mausoleum at Frogmore beside her father.

All the children's birthdays, and all the children's children's birthdays, were remembered by the Queen with a card; even her fortune could not extend to gifts for the fifty or so offspring. When Alice died, she visited her Hesse home and took special care of the orphans, including red-haired Alix. In 1894, when Alix married the Tsar, the Queen wrote wonderingly: 'How I thought of darling Alicky, and how impossible it seemed that that gentle little simple Alicky should be the great Empress of Russia.' But Victoria began to lose interest as the numbers grew. To Vicky, on the birth of Margaret in 1872, she expressed her weariness: 'I don't dislike babies, though I find very young ones rather disgusting, and I take interest in those of my children when there are two or three . . . But when they come at the rate of three a year it becomes a cause of mere anxiety for my own children and of not great interest. What name is this fourth daughter to have?'

The Princess of Wales bore Bertie five children in five years, but the last baby died at birth; Alfred's wife Marie, Grand Duchess of Russia, had five children; Lenchen, who became Princess Christian of Schleswig-Holstein, had five; Louise of Prussia, Arthur's wife, had a modest three; Beatrice, before her husband Henry of Battenberg died of fever in 1896 on the Ashanti expedition, had four; only Louise, Duchess of Argyll, had none. Leopold, when he died in 1884, left two children, of whom the young Princess Alice, Countess of Athlone, is still alive. Victoria's father, the Duke of Kent, had been born in 1767. Four generations only, in two hundred odd years: the span is astonishing.

Victoria became the ancestor of kings and queens, and emperors and empresses in the last throw of dynastic optimism in Europe. Her grandchildren before the upheaval of the First World War sat on the thrones of Russia, Norway, Spain, Germany, Greece, Roumania and Great Britain. Through the Coburgs, her descendants ruled in Belgium and Portugal. Of these only the thrones of Elizabeth II, Baudouin I, Olav V of Norway, Gustav VI of Sweden and the restored Juan Carlos of Spain have survived. The addresses of other descendants bear witness to their widespread dispossession and exile: they live in apartments in Lausanne and Rome and Madrid. But Victoria's pencil, in the seventies and eighties, knew nothing of their future glory or their future diminution. When children were gathered around her for holidays in Scotland or the Isle of Wight, she still delighted in their merriment and play. 'Baby' Margaret, eldest daughter of the favourite son Arthur, had 'her likeness' drawn when she visited her grandmother at Balmoral in the first year of her life. The many different 'Babies' who processed through the drawing rooms of Balmoral and Osborne before their awesome but ever indulgent 'Gangan' were committed to paper, often on sheets banded with mourning black. The Queen still favoured back views and details of big bows and sashes. She usually ignored the adults, especially if the visit were formal, like her grandson the Kaiser's ostentatiously grand descents on Osborne.

*Above: One of Victoria's chief preoccupations after Albert's death was to find her eldest son, Bertie, the future King, a suitable bride. The lovely Princess Alexandra of Denmark was suggested by Vicky; the Queen was won over completely by the gentleness and charm of 'Alix', and made this profile drawing of her.*

*Right: On a sheet of writing paper heavily bordered in black, 'Gangan', then aged sixty-nine, drew the flounces and bow on her granddaughter Margaret, eldest child of Arthur, Duke of Connaught.*

Her eyesight was dimming and her hand was shakier, but she still drew with pleasure. As in the early years of mourning, people occupied her less than scenery. The final sketchpads record mostly the views from the villas in which she stayed on her last years' annual holidays abroad, and, as always, scenes from the windows of the railway carriage. Queen Victoria's curiosity and gaiety did not diminish with age (the principal reason we have for thinking her severe and mirthless is that photographs in the eighties and nineties had to be exposed too long to capture a smile): excursions were still a source of delight, and she became more adventurous as she grew older, visiting Switzerland for the first time in 1868, Italy in 1879, the South of France in 1882, Spain in 1889. Her travelling style reflects her roots in the eighteenth century and its traditions of the Grand Tour. She was almost always incognito. In 1868 in Switzerland she was known as the Countess of Kent; in 1879 in Italy as the Countess of Balmoral. But the magnificent special trains, the immense suites, entire hotels and great villas made over to accommodate them did not disguise her for long. Yet in the midst of her extravagant ways, the girlish gush of pleasure at new

*This impression of the built-up skyline looking towards Whitehall was painted by Victoria from the Little Pavilion, designed by Prince Albert.*

*In the last decades of her painting life, the seventies and eighties, Queen Victoria's eyesight was weakening, but she was still sensitive to transformations in the light, colour and atmosphere of familiar and much painted places, like Loch Callater and the harbour fort of Cherbourg.*

sights and new experiences remained. An ostrich egg omelette given to her by a dubious French countess at Cimiez in 1899 prompted the question: 'Why cannot we have ostrich eggs at Windsor? We *have* an ostrich.' 'Yes, mama', replied Princess Beatrice. 'A male one.' In the South of France, Sarah Bernhardt was invited to perform before her; in Switzerland she visited the birthplace of William Tell, hero of the opera in which, so many years before, she had loved to watch the dance of La Tyrolienne.

Up to 1890, she was still busy painting throughout her holidays, seeking out splendid views with the help of local guides, sometimes ambitiously covering a double sheet with an Alpine range 'glowing in the setting sun, what is called here "Alpenglühen". It was glorious . . . ' After 1890, her eyesight worsened, and her aides were commanded to write larger and larger in blacker and blacker ink on paper so thick that it could not be folded into the despatch boxes.

The last sketchbook of her life is dated 1885–88. It contains a tentative portrait of one of the dogs who always kept her company; the trembling outline of poplars, turning gold in autumn, and the blue haze lying over the view from her window at Aix-les-Bains; the crest of Mont Blanc, 'seen from the railway'; and, last of all, a skilful quick drawing of her Indian cavalry, turbanned and carrying banners. With the exception of the second Baby Beatrice, youngest daughter of Alfred, whom the Queen sketched in June 1890 when she was six, these Sikh horsemen fittingly provided the last, admiring image from the pen of their Empress.

# Epilogue

In an undated memorandum, written towards the end of her life, the Queen listed her sketchbooks and the albums of paintings and photographs in her collection and left them 'to be considered heirlooms of the Crown'. She included Albert's drawings, commissioned views of places she had visited and houses she had lived in, and her own work: the portraits of the children as well as 'all my sketchbooks from nature'. She prized them; she did not make great claims for her talents, but she believed in good husbandry in all things, and she knew that her gifts, in art as in music as in letters, had been nurtured with care and fruitfulness. She was much more vain about her writing than her painting, amusing her courtiers with a sudden literary turn in her conversation after the publication of *Leaves*. But her regard for her albums was justified. She for whom preservation was a sacred duty, preserved in her sketches the fugitive images of her life and character, of her curiosity and her affections, her immediacy and gusto, her extraordinary simplicity in the midst of grandeur, her private values, so well defended in the course of the greatest public office and the closest public scrutiny. She stands in the centre of her accessible, coherent world, responding, not projecting, dissolving the formal barriers of majesty so that what she puts down on paper is not the pomp but the pastimes — not the relation of hierarchy, but of intimacy. She is never profound, but because she is always personal, she is not trivial either, always alert to the straightforward quiddity of her subjects: mountains are grand, the sea in summer is blue, the flounces on her children's petticoats are gay. The same absence of obliqueness that made her peremptory and sometimes wrong-headed as a queen, that led her to declare her likes and her dislikes so imperiously, gives her assurance and freshness as a draughtsman.

Her art is an exclamation at life, like the punctuation in her journal and the underlinings in her letters; through it we see her round eyes widen, her small mouth part, her brow wrinkle at the effort to take down the images as they passed by all too quickly in a life in which increasingly it seemed that she was the only fixed star while so many others fell, as the shooting stars she had watched with Albert on the balcony at Osborne had fallen into the sea. Her painting commands us to participate in her uncomplicated vitality — though the gift for enjoyment, when possessed as fully as she possessed it, is no uncomplicated thing.

Without apology, without irony, without hyperbole, she took down life's pleasures as they had been granted to her in abundance, and disregarded majesty and state; few crowns, few sceptres, or obeisances of subjects, few moments of high seriousness or glory solemnize her pages. Little William urges on the toy coach from the box; William, Emperor of Prussia, is absent. The crystal vault of the Great Exhibition is not here, but the pure regularity of Albert's face at twenty. Her Indian dominions pass unmentioned, except for the soft olive sheen of Abdul Karim's cheek. The battles, imperial and splendid, fought during her reign are missing, but Arthur and Alfred, soldier and sailor, do duty in fancy dress. Lord M. is there, unruly hair and blue-grey eyes, with Islay playing on his

*Little William of Prussia gave his grandmother warning of his mettle early on. She wrote that her daughter Beatrice was 'rather afraid' of him 'as he is so violent', and she caught his determination in this drawing of William playing coachman to his sister Charlotte.*

knees; the political changes and reforms of the century inspire not a brushstroke. Heather dyes the mountain slopes mauve and grey and emerald. Broom turns golden at Balmoral and zinnias flame on the terraces at Osborne; Albert's Rosenau stands white amongst the trees; the tribe plays on the lawn. The stags fall under Albert's gun; Baby has stiff red hair and Daisy's bow is well puffed up; Annie MacDonald draws her plaid over her head; Bertie is in armour for the play; the poor ex-Duke of Brunswick has dangerous dark eyes; Grisi wrings her tragic hands; Lehzen looks coolly down her nose; the gipsies are outside with bundles of kindling; the horses of her girlhood break into a gallop; and on stage Taglioni is dancing with a smile.

# Bibliography

## Principal Sources

Queen Victoria's Sketchbooks at Windsor Castle.
Queen Victoria's Sketchbook belonging to H.R.H. The Duke of Kent.
Queen Victoria's Journal, in the Royal Archives (referred to in References as RA QVJ).

Victoria, Queen, *Dearest Child, Private Correspondence of Queen Victoria and the Princess Royal, 1858–61*, edited by Roger Fulford (London, 1964). (Referred to as *Dearest Child*.)
*Darling Child, Letters between Queen Victoria and the Crown Princess of Prussia, 1871–78*, edited by Roger Fulford (London, 1976). (Referred to as *Darling Child*.)
*The Girlhood of Queen Victoria, A Selection from Her Majesty's Diaries between the Years 1832 and 1840*, edited by Viscount Esher, 3 vols. (London, 1907). (Referred to as *Girlhood*.)
*Leaves from a Journal*. With introduction by Raymond Mortimer (London, 1961). (Referred to as *Leaves 1855*.)
*Leaves from the Journal of Our Life in the Highlands from 1848 to 1861*, edited by Arthur Helps (London, 1868). (Referred to as *Leaves*.)
*More Leaves from the Journal of a Life in the Highlands* (London, 1884). (Referred to as *More Leaves*.)
*The Letters of Queen Victoria, A Selection from Her Majesty's Correspondence*, First Series, 1837–61, edited by A.C. Benson and Viscount Esher, 3 vols. (London, 1907). Second Series, 1862–85, edited by G.E. Buckle, 3 vols (London, 1926). Third Series, 1886–1901, edited by G.E. Buckle, 3 vols. (London, 1930). (Referred to as *Letters*.)

## Select Bibliography

Ames, Winslow, *Prince Albert and the Victorian Taste* (London, 1967).
Bennett, Daphne, *King without a Crown: Albert, Prince Consort of England 1819–61* (London, 1977).

Fulford, Roger, *Hanover to Windsor* (London, 1960).

Hobhouse, Hermione, *Thomas Cubitt, Master Builder* (London, 1971).

Lehmann, John, *Edward Lear and His World* (London, 1977).

Lennie, Campbell, *Landseer, the Victorian Paragon* (London, 1976).

Longford, Elizabeth, *Victoria R.I.* (London, 1964).

MacGeorge, A., *W.L. Leitch, Landscape Painter: A Memoir* (London, 1884).

Mallet, Victor (ed.), *Life with Queen Victoria: Marie Mallet's Letters from Court 1887–1901* (London, 1968).

Matson, John, *Dear Osborne* (London, 1978).

Ponsonby, Sir Frederick, *Recollections of Three Reigns* (London, date not known).

Rowell, George, *Queen Victoria Goes to the Theatre* (London, 1978).

Scheele, Godfrey and Margaret, *The Prince Consort* (London, 1977).

Strachey, Lytton, *Queen Victoria* (London, reprinted 1971).

Wood, Christopher, *A Dictionary of Victorian Painters* (London, 1972).

Woodham-Smith, Cecil, *Queen Victoria: Her Life and Times*, vol. i, 1819–61 (London, 1972).

Young, G.M., *Portrait of an Age: Victorian England* (Oxford, reprinted 1973).

# References

*See bibliography for full titles of sources.*

## Chapter 1

| p.11 | Not fond of learning | *Letters*, I, vol. i, p.15 |
| p.13 | Fanny Kemble | RA QVJ 20 Aug 1835 |
| p.13 | Elizabeth I's Latin | RA QVJ 8 Nov 1832 |
| p.14 | Daily routine | RA QVJ 9 Feb 1833 |
| p.14 | Westall's praise | RA QVJ 19 Nov 1832 |
| p.14 | Westall's work | RA QVJ 4 Nov 1832 |
| p.17 | Westall's death | RA QVJ 6 Dec 1836 |
| p.20 | Westall's penury | RA QVJ 13 Dec 1836 |
| p.23 | Unhappiness | *Dearest Child*, 9 June 1858 |
| p.24 | Feodore's unhappiness | *Letters* I, i, p.24 |
| p.26 | Feodore's charm | *Letters* I, i, p.17 |
| p.26 | Eliza's departure | RA QVJ 25–6 July 1834 |
| p.27 | Eliza's character | RA QVJ 2 Mar 1851 |
| p.28 | Victoire stays | RA QVJ 23 Dec 1832 |
| p.28 | Victoire dines | RA QVJ 16 Dec 1832 |
| p.28 | Victoire rides | RA QVJ 17 May 1832 |
| p.31 | Victoria's progresses | RA QVJ 13 Oct 1832 |
| p.36 | How Queens ought to be | *Letters* I, i, 19 Nov 1834 |
| p.36 | Other Queens | RA QVJ 16 Sep 1833 |
| p.37 | Donna Maria's education | *Letters* I, i, p.76 |
| p.39 | Widows at St Leonards | RA QVJ 7 Jan 1835 |
| p.45 | Gipsies wronged | RA QVJ 5 Jan 1837 |

## Chapter 2

| p.51 | La Sylphide doll | RA QVJ 18 Aug 1832 |
| p.51 | Taglioni flying | RA QVJ 5 June 1834 |
| p.51 | Taglioni fawn–like | RA QVJ 2 June 1835 |
| p.51 | Taglioni sylph–like | RA QVJ 27 June 1835 |
| p.52 | Thackeray and Taglioni | 18 July 1829: *Letters and Private Papers of W.M. Thackeray*, ed. G.N. Ray, vol i (Oxford, 1945) |
| p.52 | Victoria as Taglioni | RA QVJ 6 Jan 1833 |
| p.54 | Revolt of the Naiades | RA QVJ 24 Jan 1834 |
| p.55 | The 'Unknown' man | RA QVJ 9 Mar 1832 |
| p.57 | Melbourne and actresses | RA QVJ 2 Jan 1839 |
| p.59 | Cooper in *The King's Seal* | RA QVJ 19 Mar 1835 |
| p.60 | *The Miller and His Men* | RA QVJ 18 Feb 1835 |
| p.63 | Albert likes the music | RA QVJ 17 July 1845 |
| p.63 | Terpsichorean feelings | *Letters* I, i, pp.78–9 |
| p.63 | Prefers opera to ballet | RA QVJ 2 June 1835 |
| p.66 | Prefers Grisi to Malibran | RA QVJ 18 May 1835 |
| p.68 | Grisi in person | RA QVJ 11 May 1835 |
| p.68 | Grisi as Elena | RA QVJ 14 May 1835 |
| p.69 | Grisi at her birthday concert | RA QVJ 18 May 1835 |
| p.69 | White roses like Grisi | RA QVJ 11 Sep 1835 |
| p.71 | Lablache in *Prova di una Opera Seria* | RA QVJ 2 June 1835 |
| p.72 | Lablache's lessons | RA QVJ 28 June 1836 |
| p.72 | Mozart | RA QVJ 18 Apr 1837 |
| p.75 | Grisi's fear of failing | RA QVJ 18 Apr 1837 |
| p.75 | Victoria quite cross | RA QVJ 6 June 1837 |

## Chapter 3

| p.78 | Victoria alone | RA QVJ 20 June 1837 |
| p.80 | Her height | RA QVJ 23 Feb 1838 |
| p.80 | Her fine character | RA QVJ 12 Feb 1838 |
| p.80 | Confidence in Melbourne | RA QVJ 9 Jan 1838 |
| p.81 | Fear of losing Melbourne | RA QVJ 8 May 1839; *Letters* I, i, pp.200–201 |

# Index

223

AD

SMART01

# INSIDE SMARTGEOMETRY

**Expanding the Architectural Possibilities
of Computational Design**

WILEY

wiley.com

Brady Peters & Terri Peters

# CONTENTS

# FOREWORD
## BRETT STEELE
### ARCHITECTURE & INTELLIGENCE:
### INSIDE SMARTGEOMETRY

*'Everyone designs who devises courses of action aimed
at changing existing situations into preferred ones.'*

*'What information consumes is rather obvious: it
consumes the attention of its recipients. Hence a world
of information creates a poverty of attention.'*
*Herbert Simon*, Sciences of the Artificial

The Nobel Prize-winning polymath Herbert Simon wrote the above
observations more than half a century ago at the time  the world's
first CAD systems arrived. His freakishly prescient declaration of
the extreme consequences of modern, cognitive models captures
both the potential as well as the challenge of a) design worlds
conceived (enthusiastically) in terms of information-based problem
solving; and b) the unexpected consequences (somewhat more
tentatively) to time, and not only space, in an era dominated by
the production of information.

Long after Simon's foresight we all know now that the construction
of attention is amongst the most difficult of all architectural
undertakings, in a world of relentless media, information and
access. Surely one of many remarkable accomplishments of
Smartgeometry is its least obvious feature: its genuinely sustained,
focused attention to a bounded set of architectural, geometric
and linked questions, from which immense knowledge has
been advanced. Like other computational cultures and not only
digital design technologies, Smartgeometry is now a truly global
enterprise; a regularly convened, creative space of like-minded
architects and others interested in an open experimentation,
exploration and invention of new design systems alongside the
projects for which these associative systems have been developed.

Conceived a little more than a decade ago by Hugh Whitehead,
Lars Hesselgren and J Parrish as a cross-disciplinary series of
design workshops, presentations and discussions, and soon
joined by Robert Aish and other key collaborators giving from its
earliest days both breadth and depth (in an architectural world too
frequently describable by means of a surface), Smartgeometry has
by now come of age. This fact is the first of many demonstrated in
the wonderful volume that follows; a book that is both a document
and proposition, not only for recent (rapidly evolving) concepts,
tools and techniques, but also for future ones. This is an interest
Smartgeometry's founders share with a cast of thousands that by
now have participated (myself included) as presenters, workshop
leaders, design gurus, students, teachers and curious observers at
the group's annual gatherings.

1

2

1 Sean Ahlquist, Bum Suk Ko and Achim
Menges, *Material Equilibria: Variegated surface
structures*, ggggallery, Copenhagen, 2012.
Material Equilibria is a part of a larger body of
research done by Sean Ahlquist, a professor
at the University of Michigan and a tutor for
the 2010 Smartgeometry workshop cluster
'Deep Surfaces'. The project focuses on
the development of computational design
methodologies and techniques which enable
the generation of self-structured spatial forms
through the generation of informed material
behaviours.

The following volume provides an in-depth record of these gatherings, and has been wonderfully edited by Brady Peters and Terri Peters as two dozen chapters containing insightful accounts of both the history of these events and highlights from their various undertakings. What follows is part post-post-modern super-nerd primer (filled with fascinating weird things like 'augmented composites', 'shape grammars', 'swarm algorithms', 'parametric acoustic surfaces', or 'particle spring solvers', amongst many other things), while also being a remarkably accessible, straightforward demonstration of how contemporary design tools are at work in unexpected ways. They are reconfiguring the concepts emerging alongside the various forms of machinic, digital and physical modelling, prototyping and testing that provide the more visible outcome of Smartgeometry's remarkably robust, sustained attention. It's an approach that, like the impetus of contemporary 'object-oriented' programming cultures, crucially prefigures as well as continues to inform the generative model-making activities surrounding Smartgeometry. What we see above all else in this book is how contemporary experimentation wrestles ultimately with the most complex architectural projects of all – the cognitive architecture of the architect's own mind.

What follows is far more than a demonstration of just how far and fast contemporary experimentation has pushed architecture's millennial reliance on geometry and advanced mathematics. Writing half a century ago Herbert Simon understood the figure of the modern architect as a perfect demonstration of what it means to design today. 'The modern architect', Simon wrote, 'is the maker of instructions'. The architect's job isn't the 'making' of things in a conventional sense – it is the recording of design intentions, ideas and ambitions in the form of documents (drawings, sketches, models etc.) whose real purpose is to tell others what to do. Architects, in Simon's view, 'make instructions'. In this sense, the artefacts produced in the architect's studio are hardly anything other than memory structures. In this sense, we can grasp the real values of Smartgeometry's remarkable, collective, collaborative and sustained focus: not only on the role of information-based approaches to architectural design, but also on the making of the most difficult of all architectures, the architect's own cognitive structure. It's a memory structure of a very different sort than most kinds of architecture, and in the hands of the protagonists whose examples follow it is proven no less elastic, and intelligent, than other forms of building.

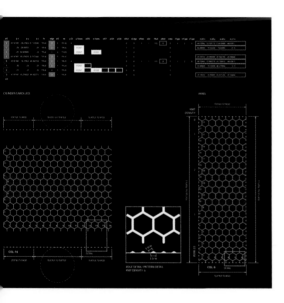

2 Sean Ahlquist, Bum Suk Ko and Achim Menges, *Material Equilibria: Variegated surface structures*, ggggallery, Copenhagen, 2012. The parametric model shown here controls the knit of shifting patterns and densities, influencing the structure of the tensile spatial surface. Through computation, the micro-structure of the textile is varied to create particular organisational and structural behaviours. The accumulated material phenomena are calibrated to derive an equilibrium which works with the resistance of an actively bended glass-fibre structure at the boundary.

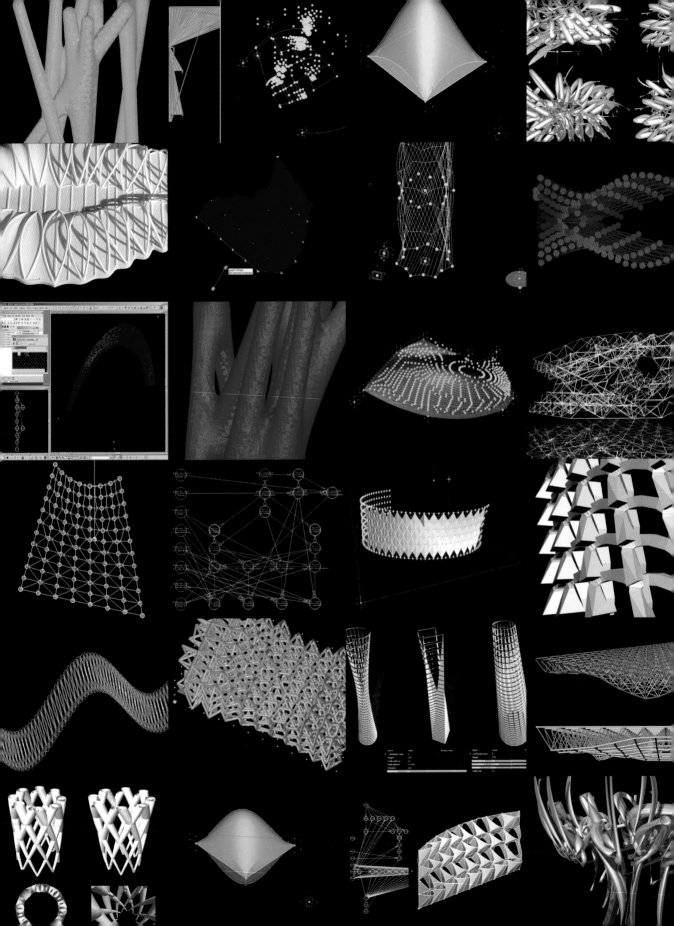

# INTRODUCTION BRADY PETERS
## TERRI PETERS

Smartgeometry (SG) was founded in 2001 as an informal network of designers interested in harnessing the powers of computation for architectural design. Friends and former colleagues Hugh Whitehead, Lars Hesselgren and J Parrish felt frustrated by the lack of resources and network surrounding computation and architecture and sought to redefine ways that architects could use digital tools. At first, the trio of architects drew on their network of friends and collaborators such as computer scientist Robert Aish, academics Robert Woodbury and Axel Kilian, and experimental practitioners architect Mark Burry and engineer Chris Williams to put together a few modest conferences and workshops. These began with a lecture and workshop in 2003 in Cambridge, UK, then in 2004 at the University of Waterloo, Ontario, Canada, where the focus was on software development, new tools for architects and engaging with ideas outside the boundaries of 'architecture'. These early workshops provided inspiration and a testing ground for the creation of new parametric software GenerativeComponents (GC) that was introduced to the group by Robert Aish and Bentley Systems. Rather than being concerned solely with software or form-making, SG focuses on the creation and application of digital tools and technologies, and in cross-disciplinary fertilisation of emerging ideas in practice. In workshop groups, designers are able to work on projects 'off the books', away from their offices or university settings, creating pure explorations of technique beyond the confines of the design project. SG embodied new ideas and new ways of thinking. The event now spans six days, with a four-day curated workshop and two-day public conference, and attracts more than 300 international participants and attendees each year.

## WHY GEOMETRY?

Architectural design software at the time SG was founded was created by software developers using object-oriented programming that almost literally translated software 'objects' as building 'objects'. SG co-founder Lars Hesselgren has written that they wanted to build new design tools and founded SG as a rejection of these conservative influences that promoted computer-aided design (CAD) solely as the organisation of building components.[1] In order to be free of these predefined tools and have a higher-level discussion of building form in terms of first principles, this led to a discussion of geometry and mathematics. As this is a more generic approach, thinking of architecture and form in this way allowed them to share computational tools between disciplines. It allowed architects to design conceptually and create their own custom 'objects' rather than use the specified objects provided by their CAD software.

As Robert Aish explains in his chapter, SG explores the ideas of design computation, with the notion that there is a distinction

1 Design explorations at SG 2006, Cambridge, UK.
Conceptual geometric design explorations using GenerativeComponents.

2 'Responsive Acoustic Surfaces' workshop
cluster at SG 2011, Copenhagen, Denmark.
Participants engage in a design discussion.

Digital models from the 'Responsive Acoustic
Surfaces' workshop cluster at SG 2011,
Copenhagen, Denmark.
Participants work on digital models of
hyperboloid geometry using a variety
of software.

'Use the Force' workshop cluster at SG 2011,
Copenhagen, Denmark.
Participants discuss design and computation.

between the generative description of the building, and the resulting generated model of the building. Therefore SG is more about the exploration of design intent and how this is inscribed in the design tools and the design environment, rather than specific technology for the integrated delivery of building projects. It is about designing a system, rather than working on a more detailed 3D model.

SG is an agile network. It is purposely structured to be able to react to and reflect ideas in contemporary practice; there is no overriding goal or charter. The idea is to engage with current issues and debates in a collaborative and non-competitive environment. Digital design leads logically to digital fabrication. Over several years, but culminating in 2010 where it was a central feature, the event embraced digital fabrication, interaction and simulation with 'workshops' that more equally split experimentation in digital and physical realms. As Xavier De Kestelier and Shane Burger explain in their chapter, the evolving workshop structure is due to shifts in participants and leadership. The earlier events attracted lower numbers of workshop participants and leaders and these were almost exclusively from professional practice. Recent SG events have had multi-day programs with larger audiences and an increased focus on academic and research questions. This shift is discussed in the chapter by CASE, where they identify the move away from the pragmatics of designing for construction of buildings, towards workshops based not only on research and experimentation, which does not necessarily rule out the practical building issues, but also on creative explorations using these same methods. The five current SG Directors are all from architectural practice, but each year attendees and workshop leaders come increasingly from research and academia.

### TALKING ABOUT COMPUTATION

'The most profound technologies are those that disappear. They weave themselves into the fabric of everyday life until they are indistinguishable from them.'[2] This statement from computational pioneer Mark Weiser in 1991 is relevant to architectural practice today. Computation is everywhere; should it really be the medium and not the message? Architects desperately need to talk about computation, and over the past decade SG has provided the only experimental workshop-based discussion forum on this topic. It is not enough to say computation is ubiquitous in our field; it is not 'just' a tool – there can be no doubt that it is fundamentally changing architecture. Computation is not what architecture is, but if architecture can be understood as a practice, concerned with technique, then computation is a technique intricately connected to designing for meaning and experience in architecture. Even architecture as edifice, separated from any discussion of technique, reveals the tool of the maker. While meaning in architecture can come from symbols and symbolism in the building itself, it also comes from the experience of that building.[3] Therefore the better we can simulate the experience of architecture, the better we can design for it. The technologies explored and discussed at SG are still quite visible. However, one hopes they will be customised,

2

3

3 Prototypes and analysis from the 'Responsive Acoustic Surfaces' workshop cluster at SG 2011, Copenhagen, Denmark.
1:10 scale prototypes were tested for their acoustic performance and this data was used to inform the design of the full-scale prototype wall.

4 Workshops at SG 2011, Copenhagen, Denmark.
View of participants and workshop clusters.

4

tested and engaged with by architects even as they continue to be woven into the fabric of the design environment.

Of course, the mere fact of using a particular computational technique does not guarantee good architecture, the same way that using the same pen as Norman Foster will not guarantee a great building. But why shouldn't architects share techniques and tools? It would be pretty silly if architects each had to invent our own pens, drafting boards and drawing conventions. So while it is the building that matters most, rather than focusing on the process of design and making, in the context of design it is critical to acknowledge that design processes are changing, and SG is at the forefront of this change.

## CREATING KNOWLEDGE AND TECHNIQUE

The ways that computation and architectural design are explored at SG are unique. The idea is to nourish a collaborative environment where participants feel as though anything can happen. The theme of the event is set in advance and then workshop leaders apply to lead a cluster based on their own research: for example, in 2012, 40 detailed applications were submitted for 10 positions. Participants also apply to join workshops, submitting portfolios and statements of interest, with only 100 selected. Carefully curated by the SG community and directors, the selected workshop themes are developed and in the four days, focused questions of design, digital technique and physical making can be explored. In contrast to many other design workshops with traditional student–teacher dynamics, workshop leaders do not bring work they have done earlier to get 'students' to build, participants do not come to learn something they know nothing about, and experts do not arrive with 'answers' to disseminate. Research and knowledge is created during the workshops. The challenge is not to construct a research question that can be 'answered' in four days but rather to construct a line of thinking that can be investigated intelligently and discussed through experimentation. The SG environment is part research and part professionally focused, which seems to inspire productivity, as participants work long into the night to actually *do* something as a group within the given time, to produce some results to share with the wider group by the end of the workshop, and to work together. In Robert Woodbury's chapter, he calls this the 'flow' of design computation. There is of course a healthy fear of failure and underlying pressure to make it perfect, or at least beautiful. This is architecture after all.

SG makes no claims to produce 'architecture'. It is not about form, it is about how we arrive at form. SG is about technique. There are, of course, many valid ways to design and SG celebrates this plurality of concept. It is not the place for design crits. In the four-day workshops, there simply is not time. Instead, techniques and tools are developed and tested. Participants find where a tool hits the wall, then how to mash it up with other tools and make it work better. It is like building a racing car – how fast and how hard can we push this machine – not how nicely can we drive it.

5 Aggregate module structure from the 'Agent Construction' workshop cluster at SG 2011, Copenhagen, Denmark.
The participants operate as 'agents', building and altering the structure without pre-made drawings or plans, instead being guided by rules responding to local conditions – 'here and now'.

6 Virtual agent model from the 'Agent Construction' workshop cluster at SG 2011, Copenhagen, Denmark.
In the computer model, a swarm of virtual agents gradually and collectively build up a structure. Different agents are guided by different rule-sets, and the only communication between them is through the environment which they manipulate and which in turn affects their behaviour.

7 Visualisation of scan data from the 'Agent Construction' workshop cluster at SG 2011, Copenhagen, Denmark.
The emerging physical structure is continuously scanned, and the data imported into virtual formats for analysis and further processing. In this format it can be directly analysed beside the virtual agent models, or used as an input in these.

8 Airflow simulation from the 'Agent Construction' workshop cluster at SG 2011, Copenhagen, Denmark.
The scan data allows for simulation of the structure's performance, here through a fluid dynamic simulation in X-Flow.

5

## CODING

*'The ability to 'read' a medium means you can access materials and tools generated by others. The ability to 'write' in a medium means you can generate materials and tools for others. You must have both to be literate. In print writing, the tools you generate are rhetorical; they demonstrate and convince. In computer writing, the tools you generate are processes; they simulate and decide.' Alan Kay*[4]

When a designer writes a script to solve a problem, the algorithm becomes part of the design and may then be explored in a creative way. But, as Fabian Scheurer explains in his chapter, algorithms are both a description of the problem and the solution. They define the solution space and they are built around the definition of the problem. He argues that design is all about decisions and that delegating these to an algorithm always means following predefined paths. Often the use of existing tools leads to existing solutions. Through the creation of new tools, new ways of thinking and new solutions can be found. Algorithmic thinking means taking on an interpretive role to understand the results of the generating code, and understand how to then modify the code to explore new options, and to speculate on further design potentials. As designers, we are influenced by the tools and techniques that allow us to realise our visions. It has been said that the tools determine the boundaries of art, and that it is the use of the right tools for the thing that one is making, and a deep relationship between the use of the tool and its formal results, that establishes the potentials of what can be made.[5] With computation, the boundaries of what can be made just got a lot bigger. Parametric systems and computational tools have enabled the realisation of projects that were previously inconceivable.

Nicholas Negroponte introduced the concept of bits and atoms, arguing that atoms make up physical, tangible objects around us – the architecture that we inhabit – while our design environment and our digital models inhabit the space of the bits – the information that is contained within the computer that we use to design.[6] So, how does this relationship affect the architecture we design? This relationship between bits and atoms is becoming blurred. Not only do the experiments undertaken at SG work in between physical and digital realms, but design tools are increasingly used that simulate real-world performance and provide feedback on designs. Computational tools become co-creators in design, extending the intellect of the designer, and so the role of the designer becomes one of tool builder, of interpreter of results, and of a guide through solution spaces. In his chapter, practitioner Neil Katz explains that the technology needs to disappear: it is the design intent and process that is more important than the tool itself.

*'Software modified by the designer through scripting, however, provides a range of possibilities for creative speculation that is simply not possible using the software only as the manufacturers intended it to be used.*

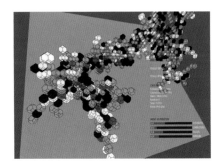

6

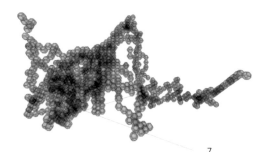

7

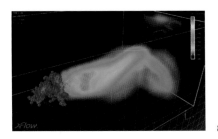

8

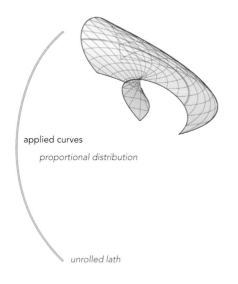

applied curves

*proportional distribution*

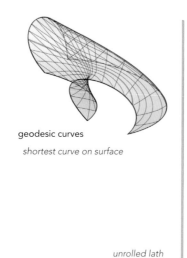

geodesic curves

*shortest curve on surface*

*unrolled lath*

*unrolled lath*

9

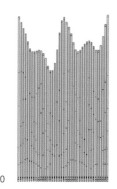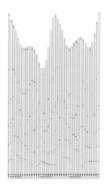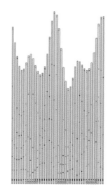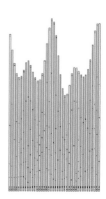

10

9 Geodesic curves from the 'Gridshell Digital Tectonics' workshop cluster at SG 2012, Rensselaer Polytechnic Institute, Troy, New York, USA.
Geodesic curves allow for complex curvature from straight segments.

10 Fabrication layout of laths from the 'Gridshell Digital Tectonics' workshop cluster at SG 2012, Rensselaer Polytechnic Institute, Troy, New York, USA.
Geodesic laths are unrolled with precise lengths and spacing of nodes for pin joints.

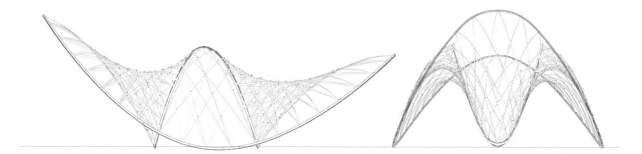

11

11 Elevation from the 'Gridshell Digital
Tectonics' workshop cluster at SG 2012,
Rensselaer Polytechnic Institute, Troy, New
York, USA.
Diagrams of the lattice gridshell identified the
location of each piece in the four-layer lath
system.

*Because scripting is effectively a computing program
overlay, the tool user (designer) becomes the new
toolmaker (software engineer).' Mark Burry*[7]

**SIMULATING EXPERIENCE**

Architecture can be thought of as drawing, but should be thought
of as simulation. Architecture is the act of imagining a building
at a remove from its construction, and then communicating
this concept for others to build. To date, the imagining and
communicating has been largely through drawing. However, it is
not necessarily drawing that defines architecture, but this ability
to create an abstraction of the building through some means.
Through the drawing, the architect is able to imagine how light
and space and material relate in the creation of architecture.
Although largely within the mind of the architect, this simulation
of effect and experience is a necessary part of architectural
design. The pragmatic aspects of performance can be simulated
as well. The digital design environment can be a design partner
for this simulation of architecture. Through the adoption of new
technologies, the creation of design techniques, the coding
of custom design tools and the gaining of critical performance
feedback, the abilities of the architect are extended.

SG was founded on the premise that a first-principles exploration
of geometry in relation to design intent could benefit architectural
design. The development, discussion and dissemination of these
explorations of technique have been central to the SG workshops and
conferences. The SG community explores these through parametric
design, computer programming, digital fabrication, interactive
design, simulation and optimisation. The scope of these approaches
is enlarged at each yearly event. SG has been, and continues to be,
a place where these concepts are not only discussed, tested and
critically reflected upon, but critically, a place where this knowledge is
created. A place for designing, coding and building.

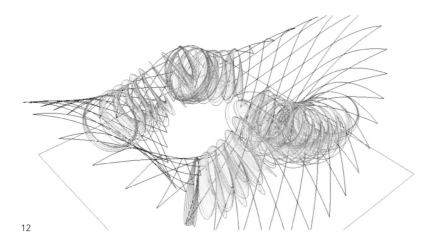

12

12 Curvature analysis from the 'Gridshell
Digital Tectonics' workshop cluster at SG 2012,
Rensselaer Polytechnic Institute, Troy, New
York, USA.
Curvature analysis determines radii of curvature
to verify the minimum radius allowable for the
bending of lath segments.

13 Completed gridshell from the 'Gridshell
Digital Tectonics' workshop cluster at SG 2012,
Rensselaer Polytechnic Institute, Troy, New
York, USA.

13

REFERENCES
1 Lars Hesselgren, 'Smooth Is Not Enough', 18 January
2009, http://www.core.form-ula.com/2009/01/18/smooth-is-
not-enough/ [accessed 12/09/2012].
2 Mark Weiser, 'The Computer for the 21st Century', in
*Scientific American*, September 1991, pp 94–104.
3 Stan Allen, 'Introduction: Practice vs Project', in *Practice:
Architecture, Technique and Representation*, G+B Arts
International (Amsterdam), 2000, page XIV.
4 Alan Kay, 'User Interface: A Personal View', in Brenda
Laurel (ed), *The Art of Human–Computer Interface Design*,
Addison-Wesley (Reading), 1990, p 125.
5 Jose-Manuel Berenguer, 'Interview with Jose Manuel
Berenguer' in *Mosaic*, 2005, http://mosaic.uoc.
edu/2005/09/09/jose-manuel-berenguer/ [accessed
10/02/2010].
6 Nicholas Negroponte, *Being Digital*, Vintage Books
(New York), 1995.
7 Mark Burry, *Scripting Cultures*, John Wiley & Sons
(Chichester), 2011, p 9.

IMAGES
Figure 1 © Smartgeometry Ltd; Figures 2, 3, 4, 5 ©
Smartgeometry Ltd, photos by Anders Ingvartsen; Figure
6 © Peter Suen; Figures 7, 8 © Samuel Wilkinson; Figures
10, 11, 12 © Andrew Kudless with the Gridshell Digital
Tectonics Cluster; Figures 9, 13 © Mark Cabrinha, PhD

# THE ORIGINS OF SMARTGEOMETRY

## HUGH WHITEHEAD, LARS HESSELGREN J PARRISH

Smartgeometry (SG) was founded in 2001 by former colleagues and friends Hugh Whitehead, Lars Hesselgren and J Parrish as a way to recapture parametric and computational design for architecture. At the time of founding SG they were leaders in the London-based architectural practices Foster + Partners, Kohn Pedersen Fox (KPF) and ArupSport respectively, and were strong proponents of digital design. Each was striving to create architecture through the use of parametric tools and computational methods. Through SG they hoped not only to create new digital tools, but to foster a community that would develop, test and disseminate these ideas of architecture and design to a wider audience. Whitehead founded the Specialist Modelling Group at Foster + Partners in 1998 which has been responsible for a host of innovative buildings and consistently pioneers computational design methods in architectural practice. After years at KPF in London, architect Lars Hesselgren is now the Director of the Computational Design Research Group at PLP Architects. J Parrish is a globally renowned sports stadium designer leading teams to design some of the most iconic stadium projects in the world. After many years at ArupSport, he moved to AECOM where he is currently working on the venues for the Rio Olympic Park. Here each tells their story of the origins of SG, now an international multidisciplinary community of professionals, academics and students in the fields of architecture and engineering.

1

# HUGH WHITEHEAD

### BACK TO THE FUTURE

Four people were sitting in a car travelling to a Bentley conference. Robert Aish, in the front, was due to host a research seminar; and architects Lars Hesselgren, J Parrish and Hugh Whitehead, in the back, were enjoying the opportunity to tease a captive software developer. It was a familiar formation: we had all worked together with YRM back in the 1980s. So we began the light-hearted banter with a searching question: 'Why is it that ten years have passed, and we still cannot even get close to the kind of capability that we had then?'

At the end of the 1980s boom, YRM had grown to an international multidisciplinary design consultancy of 600 people, and took the strategic opportunity to acquire Anthony Hunt Associates, the engineering firm of choice for Norman Foster, Richard Rogers, Nicholas Grimshaw and many other leading architects. What Anthony Hunt Associates needed was access to computer modelling expertise, which was already well advanced at YRM. The dialogue between architect and engineer was shifting rapidly from back-of-envelope sketches to digital representations, where 3D geometry became the input to analysis routines and setup cycles of design iterations.

1 Hugh Whitehead, Lars Hesselgren and J Parrish, the original SG founders, at SG 2011, Copenhagen, Denmark.

2 Foster + Partners (architects), Anthony
Hunt Associates (engineers), Faculty of Law,
University of Cambridge, UK, 1995.
The geometry of the diagonal panels and
offset supporting structure was formed by
proportional subdivision of a cylindrical vault.
A parametric model was developed by Hugh
Whitehead so that changes to the radius of the
vault caused the geometry to regenerate the
data needed for structural analysis.

2

The acquisition of Anthony Hunt Associates brought exposure to a whole new world of adventurous designers, who were expecting us to provide them with new design technology. Where would we find it? Engineers and product designers always seemed to have far better tools than architects, and we realised that we were looking for something that was generic rather than discipline-specific.

Around this time we saw a presentation by Robert Patience who led the development of the new Intergraph Vehicle Design System (I/VDS). It was a revelation. That rare kind of presentation that seems to come from another time or another place and brings you out in a cold sweat! There, back in the 1980s, we saw a first glimpse of the power of parametrics, associative geometry and relationship modelling, all in full 3D, at a time when leading computer-aided design (CAD) systems of the day were still only trying to mimic and crudely automate flat drawing-board technology. Robert Patience ended his presentation with the throwaway line, 'Last weekend I did HVAC [heating, ventilation and air conditioning], with automated duct sizing and routing just from a rule-based schematic, all in full 3D with clash detection!'

We invited Robert Patience to visit YRM to discuss the potential for developing his ideas in an architectural context. He brought with him Robert Aish, who was working with him in Paris, helping to implement the new technology for the Gdansk shipyard, where the aim was to directly flame-cut steel from a rule-based 3D design model. Design-to-fabrication was already happening.

The show-and-tell session lasted far into the night, while we explained the design challenges we were facing and the two Roberts talked about the potential of associative systems. At the end we asked, 'Why label the product as a Vehicle Design System (VDS), when it clearly has the potential to provide generic solutions which could support a far more integrated approach to design?' Robert Patience replied, 'I always think in generic terms, but as a software developer I can only get funding from the Marketing Department by pretending to be discipline-specific, so I chose vehicles because at least they include cars, ships and aircraft. All have structure, services, form, space and aesthetic requirements, just like buildings! Perhaps we could describe buildings as very slow-moving vehicles, almost tending to the limit!' At this moment an idea was born, and we convinced Intergraph to develop an architectural application based on VDS technology. The result was a specification for a product called 'Master Architect'. Robert Aish joined us at YRM to help develop the brief and explore concepts based on the challenges of live projects. With Robert's help, Lars Hesselgren produced a fully associative 3D model of London's Waterloo Station for Grimshaw while Hugh did a similar exercise on the University of Cambridge Faculty of Law for Foster + Partners. We all worked with J Parrish on a modular concept design called 'Stadium for the '90s'. The stadium roof was a tensile membrane structure supported on cantilever beams with a retractable centre section.

3 Antoni Gaudí, Sagrada Família Basilica,
Barcelona, Spain, 1883–, central crossing of
the nave.
The progression from constructive geometry
to parametrics and then to scripting and
computational design was already mapped out
by designers like Gaudí, who worked only with
models and raw intellect.

3

4

$$\frac{z}{h} = \frac{\left(1 - \dfrac{x}{b}\right)\left(1 + \dfrac{x}{b}\right)\left(1 - \dfrac{y}{c}\right)\left(1 + \dfrac{y}{d}\right)}{\left(1 - \dfrac{ax}{rb}\right)\left(1 + \dfrac{ax}{rb}\right)\left(1 - \dfrac{ay}{rc}\right)\left(1 + \dfrac{ay}{rd}\right)} \tag{1}$$

where $r = \sqrt{x^2 + y^2}$

$$\frac{z}{H} = \left(1 - \frac{x}{b}\right)\left(1 + \frac{x}{b}\right)\left(1 - \frac{y}{c}\right)\left(1 + \frac{y}{d}\right)\left(\frac{r}{a} - 1\right) \tag{2}$$

$$\frac{z}{\lambda} = \frac{\left(\dfrac{r}{a} - 1\right)}{\dfrac{\sqrt{(b-x)^2 + (c-y)^2}}{(b-x)(c-y)} + \dfrac{\sqrt{(b+x)^2 + (c-y)^2}}{(b+x)(c-y)} + \dfrac{\sqrt{(b-x)^2 + (d+y)^2}}{(b-x)(d+y)} + \dfrac{\sqrt{(b+x)^2 + (d+y)^2}}{(b+x)(d+y)}} \tag{3}$$

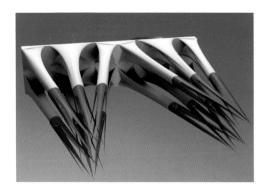

5

So what happened in that decade between the introduction of VDS to YRM and the car ride to Exton? How was parametric design lost to architecture in those 10 years? The1980s bubble burst: YRM went down, Intergraph went down, Lars moved to KPF, J moved to ArupSport, Hugh to Foster + Partners, and Robert to Bentley Systems, but the friendship and the shared experience remained. In the car that day, the response from Robert was this: 'Sometimes I feel as though I have been to the future. I have seen it and I know that it works!'

But the question was, how could we get back to the future?

We held a conference in Cambridge, UK in 2003. The event attracted strong interest with many presentations. Two were particularly inspirational. Mark Burry described 15 years of decoding the designs of Antoni Gaudí (1852–1926) which enabled the completion of the Sagrada Família in Barcelona, and Chris Williams explained the generation of the geometry for the Great Court roof at the British Museum in London. Here were two people who had already delivered the kind of projects that we aspired to. They both combined a background in architecture and engineering with fluency in mathematics and scripting. This expertise was used to give expression to design ideas by developing custom workflows, which engaged a variety of applications. Mark described how he used Excel as a kind of blind CAD system to process data before exporting to graphics. Chris gave a live demonstration in which he showed how to 'sketch with code'.

We were delighted when Mark and Chris agreed to join us as tutors at the next SG workshop at the University of Waterloo, Ontario, Canada in 2004. With the addition of Axel Kilian from the Massachusetts Institute of Technology (MIT) and Robert Woodbury from Simon Fraser University (SFU), British Columbia, we had an international all-star team. The significance would only appear in retrospect as the community reached critical mass and gained momentum. So we approached the first workshop as a 'learn by doing' experiment, not just in design technology but also in design sociology, and this spirit continues.

If the future lay in integrated design then we needed a comprehensive platform that would support disparate activities

4 Foster + Partners (architects), Buro Happold and Waagner-Biro (engineers), Great Court at the British Museum, London, UK, 2000.
The elegant resolution of complex aesthetic and structural requirements is reflected in the elegance of the mathematics derived by Chris Williams. Three functions describe the transformation from rectangle to circular boundary, maintaining singularity of curvature. The triangulated pattern floats on this surface using dynamic relaxation to achieve continuity of geodesic curvature.

5 Digital model by Mark Burry of the Sagrada Família Basilica, Barcelona, Spain, 1995.
The work of architect Mark Burry helped to decode Gaudí in terms of a language of intersecting helicoid, hyperbolic paraboloid and hyperboloid surfaces. This enabled contemporary design technology to engage with traditional craftsmanship and so to realise a vision that had never been fully described.

6

7

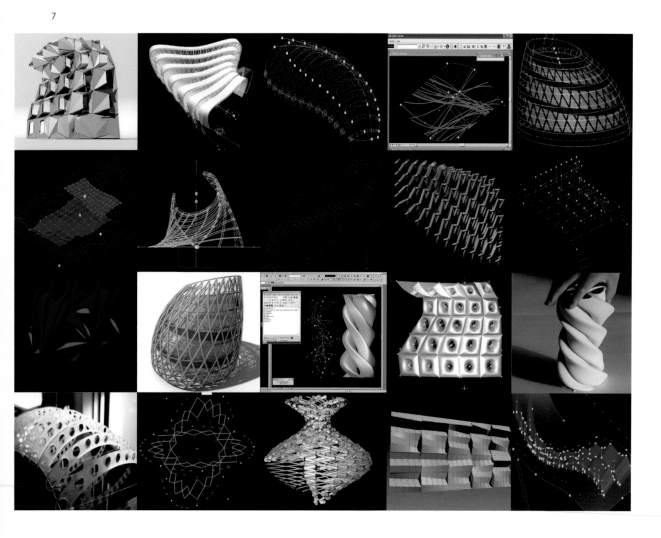

and promote collaboration between different specialists. To give the workshop an experimental focus, we then invited Robert Aish to join and asked Bentley Systems if they would agree to let us trial their new object-based system, GenerativeComponents (GC). Never before had a group of designers experienced a raw development platform in the early stages of specification while the author of the software looked over their shoulders. It was a rough and bumpy ride, but a rare privilege and everyone was captivated by Robert's tireless enthusiasm. Often he would work through the night to address issues that arose and emerge in the morning with a 'crisis build' which he distributed on a memory stick.

Almost by accident, SG became a design process laboratory with a unique characteristic. It became a community of people drawn from competing organisations, but the bonds that were formed crossed all known boundaries. Instinctively the tutors led from the front and the participants followed their example and competed to share knowledge, ideas and experience, and even tools, techniques and concepts. This special synergy was well appreciated by Bentley, who gave Robert the opportunity to pursue his vision. They have continued to support SG in what became a series of annual events that have spanned the last 10 years. But those early workshops were all high-risk ventures with an edgy quality, and so we would treat each one as if it might be the last.

Not everything went according to plan and 'the great pizza disaster' has now passed into SG folklore. We had no experience of event management on this scale and there was so much to organise – tutors, participants, admission, registration, venues, accommodation, travel, facilities, equipment etc. We forgot about food! At the end of a totally exhausting first day we suddenly realised that we had 40 starving people out on a university campus miles away from civilisation. If everyone just left in search of sustenance the event would lose all momentum and we would lose their goodwill. At an emergency meeting the SG Directors agreed to put their hands in their pockets and send out for a pizza delivery, but could we afford a few beers? Fortunately we could, because the pizza was late and cold, but at the sound of popping cans the spirits revived and the intense discussions flowed again.

When we related the story of this near-disaster to Greg Bentley the next day, he kindly offered to pick up the tab and bail us out, but added a stern warning that we had to become more businesslike because 'altruism is not commercially viable'. However, it could be said that Bentley have spent the last 10 years proving that with the right community it can be. During this period the SG workshops helped to specify and test four different versions of GC, which demanded extreme patience and perseverance from all concerned. The concepts that were being prototyped proved to require a new type of development language with advanced capabilities. Perhaps, if the SG Directors had not sent out for the pizza, GC might never have happened!

6 The SG 2004 workshop briefing at the University of Waterloo, Ontario, Canada. Tutors gave a brief description of their background and special interests. Participants then formed groups around their chosen tutor to discuss their projects before moving off to rooms to begin the workshop. We became a self-organising community.

7 Design explorations at SG 2004, University of Waterloo, Ontario, Canada.

8

9

Some participants look back on those early workshops as a life-changing experience, which launched a whole new career – and it is comments like these that provide our motivation. Now, with the addition of a ShopTalk day and a public conference, SG provides not just a forum but also a stage, which many people regard as a window on the future. The original founders can only look back and marvel at the culture that grew from a cold pizza in Cambridge!

# LARS HESSELGREN

### APPLIED PARAMETRIC DESIGN

In 1982 I was a fully-fledged computer addict with an early-generation Sinclair computer to my name. I was working at Halcrow where we were trying to convince them that CAD was the future. At the time, we spent a lot of time stencilling notes onto contract drawings. I was a port architect and Halcrow was designing all the new ports during this first Middle Eastern building boom: Jubail, Jeddah, Dubai, and Jebel Ali. I made a change after seeing a lecture at the RIBA where YRM showed off its new technology, the fabulous Intergraph system. I joined YRM to play with the new toy; it was so fabulously expensive we worked the machines in shifts. Hugh Whitehead joined YRM soon after as we graduated from 2D in black and white to 3D in colour.

Hugh and I were both sent to the conference in Huntsville, Alabama every year and here we got to know the cutting-edge CAD scene. As a result of connections made there, we had the opportunity to alpha test Intergraph's 'Master Architect' software and one of the developers was Robert Aish. Master Architect was sitting on top of a mechanical modelling system that was very advanced and had parametric modules. When Master Architect was cancelled, Hugh and I persuaded YRM to employ Robert to continue with our parametric work. One summer Grimshaw came along with the Waterloo Station International Terminal project. I grabbed the model, cross-examined the project architect on the setting-out principles behind the design and built a parametric model of it.

A contemporary example of the need for 3D parametric technology in practice was the Pinnacle Tower by KPF. This tower at Bishopsgate in London has a unique cascading rooftop with a viewing gallery and restaurant, and was designed to be the tallest building in London, exactly in line with the Shard. The design team were hard at work but found it difficult to come up with a rational geometry to realise their design goals. The geometry of the tower is based on inclined planes in 3D, and on plan, circular arcs which get smaller to form a sheared cone. The top is mapped as a curve. This is then remapped back onto the inclined planes and sheared cones. The design of the project was carried out on the new GC software developed by Bentley and used at SG.

### THE FUTURE OF SOFTWARE

SG emerged at a time of great opportunities in computational

10

8 Architect: Grimshaw (architects), YRM Anthony Hunt Associates (engineers), International Terminal, Waterloo Station, London, UK, 1993.

9 Parametric model by Lars Hesselgren of the International Terminal, Waterloo Station, London, UK, 1980s.
The original parametric model of Waterloo Station by Lars Hesselgren while at YRM Anthony Hunt Associates for Grimshaw using I/EMS mechanical modelling software.

10 Parametric model by Lars Hesselgren of the International Terminal, Waterloo Station, London, UK, 1980s.
Rebuilt parametric model of the Waterloo Station arches, architects Grimshaw, structural engineers YRM Anthony Hunt Associates. The original model used Intergraph I/EMS software, the rebuild is done with Bentley GC software.

11

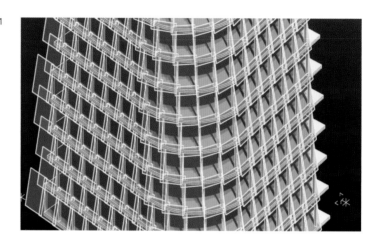

12

tools and developments in computer hardware. This has meant that, far from being an elitist pursuit, anybody could join in. A new product category in architecture, 'parametric design', was born. It seems likely that this will soon disappear as it is increasingly clear that parametric design will become embedded into mainstream CAD software, just as it has in the mechanical arena. In order to use parametric software well, a user needs to have an underlying mental model of a process. This is often geometric in nature, but it increasingly encompasses other aspects such as performance, cost and end-user enjoyment. The digital age is changing our perceptions as designers and for myself this is where the future of architectural design lies. How do we use digital technology to inform, survive and entertain ourselves?

# J PARRISH

### THE FUTURE SEEMED SO CLEAR
The late 1960s and early 1970s were exciting times – as students we felt we could do anything, and Concorde and the Jumbo's first flights and the first moon landing helped convince us even the sky wasn't the limit!

My 'eureka moment' came with a final-year visit to architect John Lansdown of Turner, Lansdown & Holt. We'd already been introduced to CAD by our Systematic Design department at Bristol University, but in his dimly lit London office we were amazed by parametric design tools that calculated, designed, modelled and documented stairs, lifts and other building elements in 2D and 3D and provided neatly tabulated performance data. John had even written a program for specifying planting for different climates and locations with an interface that responded to questions typed as normal English sentences, just because it was an interesting challenge.

### I'D SEEN THE FUTURE OF ARCHITECTURAL DESIGN!
1975 was not a good year for Part II architectural students entering the job market, and I was extremely lucky when the RIBA's Appointment Service directed me to a successful interview with Howard V Lobb & Partners in London's Tottenham Court Road. Two years later I found myself with the plum job of project architect working for leading UK expert Jim Cutlack on the redevelopment of Cheltenham Racecourse. I didn't realise at the time, but the direction of my architectural career and the roles to be played by sport and computational design were set.

*In 1975 most architects had not even heard of parametric design. Even thirty years later few understood its potential and would have considered it the future of their profession.*

### JIM'S RULE OF THUMB
Developing a new masterplan and designing the first section of a new grandstand for the Racecourse in a short time and to a

11 GC model of Kohn Pedersen Fox (architects), The Pinnacle, London, UK, under construction.
The sheared cones concept was used in the Pinnacle building designed by the current PLP partners while at KPF. This image, which illustrates the sheared cones and the overlapping sets of inclined snakeskin facade components, is drawn from a new GC model built by Lars Hesselgren in 2012 while at PLP.

12 Kohn Pedersen Fox (architects), The Pinnacle, London, UK, under construction.
The Pinnacle in Bishopsgate, located between Tower 42 and St Mary Axe, will form a prominent landmark on the London skyline when completed. It is a project of Kohn Pedersen Fox (International) PA in which the following people at PLP Architecture were involved: Lee Polisano was Partner-in-Charge; Karen Cook, Design Partner; Lars Hesselgren, Head – Computational Geometry. (Lee Polisano and Karen Cook are partners of PLP Architecture.)

very tight budget was challenging and we relied heavily on Jim's knowledge and experience. To create the section through the grandstand, we needed to know the height of the steps in the lower and upper tiers that would give each spectator a good view over the heads of spectators in front. As usual, I asked Jim.

He examined the sketch drawings and dimensions closely and, after checking a few key distances with a scale rule, recommended an appropriate constant riser height for each tier. When asked how he determined the required riser heights, he admitted it was basically a rule of thumb and, yes, he did get a bit nervous when making the first site visit after the steppings had been installed. He explained his routine was to 'have a nice lunch and a couple of glasses of wine before attending the key site meeting and it has always worked so far'!

> As a young architect who believed in computational design, I knew there had to be a better way to design spectator seating tiers.

## ARCHITECTS DON'T INVEST IN RESEARCH

The project structural engineers, Jan Bobrowski & Partners, clearly did understand sightlines, and an article they'd written for *New Civil Engineer* set out the principles clearly and succinctly. It revealed that sightlines were not rocket science. The only slight complication was that for a properly optimised viewing tier, the riser for each row needed to be calculated from the preceding row – a simple iterative process for a computer. The practice needed a computer; or, more accurately, J Parrish wanted a computer so he could develop a program for working out sightlines, and he thought it only reasonable the practice should pay for it.

Mini computers were unfortunately far too expensive in 1976, and the Apple II (1978) and IBM PC (1982) had yet to be developed, but the Texas Instruments TI-52 (1976) card programmable scientific calculator was available and, although expensive, just about affordable. My pitch to the partners for a TI-52 was turned down – investment in technology has never been a construction industry strong point – so I bought one myself and started programming. The result appears to have been the world's first sightlines program. The highly unreliable TI-52 was eventually replaced by the excellent TI-59 which was used for all the subsequent Lobb sports projects for the next five or six years including Goodwood Racecourse's main grandstand, Cheltenham's new parade ring and Twickenham's South Stand.

> Others often don't understand or appreciate the potential benefits of developing software – ignore them and develop your own in your own time, based on your own expertise.

## DESIGNING IN 3D FROM FIRST PRINCIPLES FROM DAY ONE

After a hiatus from sports architecture I moved back to Lobb in 1989, tempted in part by the offer of a proper CAD system. The architectural world was waking up to CAD at long last. Pioneers, led by YRM, were investing heavily in sophisticated multi-user systems and developing highly skilled user teams. Our investment was much more modest, a basic version of the gold-standard Intergraph system, plotter and software but still nearly £25,000, probably equivalent to 10 far more powerful workstations today. While other practices developed plans for implementation, we adopted a much simpler approach – start immediately on live work and learn on the job. It worked; and we also avoided falling into the trap of giving the expensive computers to technicians, or to architects who were then treated like technicians, with inevitable consequences. Instead, we gave each new machine we bought to the next most skilled architect. Our team embraced computers with enthusiasm and never looked back.

*Always give the most powerful tools to the most able.*

After a brief but intense dabble with 'Project Architect', which repaid me by deleting every element in a highly complex ground-floor plan for a large hotel on the eve of the first site meeting, I was convinced the best way to design great buildings was to design as many aspects as possible from first principles and in 3D. I learned complex, underdeveloped software should be avoided.

*Microstation became my working environment. All my projects from then on were designed from first principles, in three dimensions, from day one.*

### SIGHTLINES MARK II

Microstation's User Commands provided a platform for computational design with direct CAD output, and the development of tools for creating complete seating bowl sections was straightforward. Anyone in the office could use my simple User Command to create a properly calculated multi-tier seating bowl section for any stadium from local club to Olympic venue. It soon became clear there were potential problems with releasing software for general use.

*Providing system-wide software tools for use by any designer carries risks – garbage in and garbage out is just as relevant to architects and engineers as to any other computer users. Automated systems can be appropriate for tasks requiring minimal designer involvement; but designing major spectator venues well, even with the most sophisticated computational design tools, still requires great skills and experience. Using software based on expert knowledge does not in itself create a great design or an expert designer.*

### STADIUM FOR THE '90S

The stadiums being developed for the Italia 90 World Cup were a revelation to UK sports architects used to a diet of tight budgets and low aspirations. Stadiums really could be fun, adventurous, dramatic and iconic. My Lobb colleague Rod Sheard and Geraint John of the Sports Council were determined England should

13 J Parrish for Lobb Partnership (architects),
YRM Anthony Hunt Associates (engineers),
Stadium for the '90s, concept design shown at
Interbuild, Birmingham, UK, 1990.
The stadium roof was modelled in I/VDS by
Hugh Whitehead for J Parrish and YRM Anthony
Hunt Associates. The technique of populating
a structure with rule-based variational
geometry was to become a prototype for
GenerativeComponents.

13

compete in stadium design as well as on the football pitch, and hatched a plan. We'd develop a prototype of an affordable 25,000-seat English stadium that could be constructed in stages, would provide excellent views, comfortable seats with safe access and egress, excellent revenue-generating facilities and be fun, adventurous, dramatic and iconic. And for good measure it could also be built with a closing roof.

An ultra-efficient stadium clearly warranted an ultra-efficient (minimal-cost) architectural design team of one. We also needed a highly talented structural engineer and, at Geraint John's suggestion, Stephen Morley of YRM Anthony Hunt Associates joined the team. It was my ideal project: to design a stadium for the future with a multidisciplinary team, from first principles, in three dimensions, from day one. The design process proved a great success and the stadium was developed in record time. We worked directly on computer in 3D, with the architect and engineer communicating by phone and exchanging drawing files, albeit frustratingly slowly, using dial-up modem links. Just five sheets of paper were used and only because affordable computer projectors had yet to be invented. Having a great design is one thing, but we needed to show our creation to the world. We needed computer renders and a state-of-the-art animation and we needed them in time for the Interbuild exhibition. Stadium for the '90s was shown at Interbuild 1990 in Birmingham. It attracted much attention and was a great success. In developed form it became the McAlpine Stadium in Huddersfield and was awarded the UK's highest architectural prize, the RIBA Building of the Year award, in 1995.

*We turned again to YRM Anthony Hunt Associates and to Hugh Whitehead, Lars Hesselgren and Robert Aish. It had taken 15 years to find colleagues and friends that shared my vision of the future.*

**TEXT**

**IMAGES**

# FIRST BUILD YOUR TOOLS

### ROBERT AISH

One of the original members and former Director of Smartgeometry (SG), designer and software developer Robert Aish created software that responded to the vision of the SG community. In this chapter, Aish contextualises the history of SG within the development of computational design software. He explains that the contribution of SG has been to refocus the use of the computer towards design exploration rather than on production and downstream data management.

1

The objective of the Smartgeometry (SG) initiative is to cultivate a thoughtful approach to design which combines advanced geometry and computation. Geometry and algorithms can exist in the abstract, but to be of any practical significance, to become a design tool which can be used by designers, then these have to be encapsulated in an executable form, as working software, hence the title of this chapter: 'First build your tools.' Tools do not exist in isolation. Tools require complementary skills to be effectively used. A computational tool requires cognitive skills. With this in mind we might summarise the mission of SG: to encourage the development of those cognitive and creative skills that matched the geometric and computational possibilities of a new generation of design software.

Much of the SG book will focus (correctly) on how designers are able to harness the ideas encapsulated in this software and express design concepts that otherwise would be difficult, if not impossible, to express. But occasionally (and this is one of those occasions) it may be interesting to go 'behind the facade', and understand some of the key ideas that contributed to the development of that software. We are going to focus on three ideas: Sketchpad, formal design methods and object-oriented software.

## SKETCHPAD

The original computer-aided design (CAD) system was Sketchpad, developed by Ivan Sutherland in 1963.[1] The key features of Sketchpad are: an interactive real-time graphics display; an interactive input device (in this case a light pen); and an underlying model (in this case a constraint model). When the display and light pen are combined, they provide a complete interaction loop between the computer and the designer. The geometry displayed on the screen is a representation, not just of the apparent graphics (points, lines, etc), but also the underlying constraint model, which includes the symbolic representations of constraints (anchor points, parallel and orthogonal constraints between lines, etc). The manipulation of one geometric element by the user triggers a new resolution of the constraint model, which in turn propagates changes to the other geometric elements.

Sketchpad is a very early example of the model–view–controller (MVC) paradigm. The constraint system is the model, the display system is the view, and the light pen is the controller.[2] What is important is that the model, the view and the controller form a complete system and this is matched to the cognitive skills of the user, which taken together forms a man–machine system. In 1967, I had the unique opportunity of using a direct successor to Sketchpad, the DEC PDP-7 at Imperial College, London.

This was a career-changing experience. The idea of a CAD as a man–machine system, with an intelligent model linked by views and controllers to a designer, was fully established in the early 1960s. It would take a further 20 years to make this technology affordable and accessible to a wider audience.

2

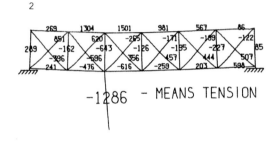

−1286 – MEANS TENSION

1 Ivan Sutherland's Sketchpad, 1963.
Real-time computation, graphical display, light pen interactions.

2 Ivan Sutherland's Sketchpad, 1963.
An example CAD model showing a truss under load.

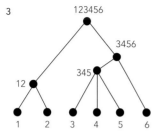

3

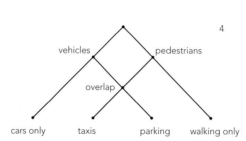

4

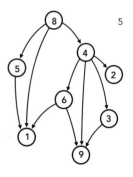

5

3 Christopher Alexander, tree diagram, from Alexander's 'A City is Not a Tree', first published and printed in two parts in the American journal *Architectural Forum* in April and May 1965.
The nodes of the graph represent components and assemblies and the arcs of the graph represent the 'contained in' relationship. The strict hierarchical decomposition of the tree structure only allows each subcomponent to be a member of a single higher-level (parent) assembly.

4 Christopher Alexander, illustration of a vehicular traffic system and a system of pedestrian circulation that overlap, from Alexander's 'A City is Not a Tree', first published and printed in two parts in the American journal *Architectural Forum* in April and May 1965.
The semi-lattice allows for overlaps, so that the same subcomponent can belong to multiple higher-level assemblies or subsystems.

5 A directed acyclic graph (DAG).

## FORMAL DESIGN METHODS

Christopher Alexander is recognised as a pioneering design methodologist. Alexander's two main contributions to formal design methods are his book *Notes on the Synthesis of Form*[3] and his essay 'The City is not a Tree'[4]. Alexander was quite probably the first design theorist to propose that a hierarchical decomposition (as a formal *tree* structure) could be a useful way to understand a design problem or to describe a product. In his essay 'The City is not a Tree', Alexander rejected his initial use of the tree structure as being too restrictive because it failed to correctly represent the true complexity of relationships such as those he observed in the organisation of a city. He proposed the slightly more complex formalism of the *semi-lattice*.

Alexander proposed using formal graph methods mainly as a descriptive technique to help designers understand the structure of resulting products or systems. Further research in the mid-1970s explored the use of the more general *directed acyclic graph* (DAG) to model design decision-making.[5] Here the nodes are the decisions and the arcs represent the directed relationships of a superior decision influencing or providing the context for a subsidiary decision.

The idea of representing a design problem as a direct graph is very general. It could be used to represent the *dependencies* between geometry, or between components, or even between more abstract ideas such as design decisions. The concept of graph-based dependency is quite understandable on a small scale. But for the designer (without any supporting software) it is difficult to apply on a scale that is appropriate to real-world problem solving. On the other hand, graph dependency is easily implemented as a program and can be applied to complex real-world tasks. Therefore graph dependency provides a common abstraction that can be shared between man and machine, with each playing a complementary role: one to define and the other to execute the graph. The idea of using a graph to present design dependencies was already established in the mid-1970s.

## OBJECT-ORIENTED SOFTWARE

Object-oriented software emerged in the 1980s, pioneered by the development of the Smalltalk language at Xerox PARC in Palo Alto, California[6] and by researchers such as Alan Borning,[7] who used Smalltalk to develop ThingLab.

It is beyond the scope of this chapter to discuss the full range of concepts that are included in object-oriented (OO) programming (type system, inheritance, extensibility, encapsulation, polymorphism, method overloading, etc). The key aspect of OO programming which is relevant here is the idea that the organisation of a program could more directly reflect the mental model of those involved. But this raises the questions: Whose mental model? That of the software developer or that of the program user? As I explained at the Object-Oriented Software Engineering Conference in London in 1990:

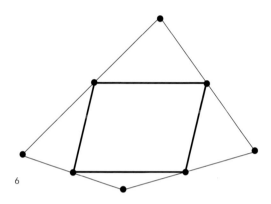

6

6 A constraint model (after Alan Borning). For any given quadrilateral, joining the mid points of the side yields a parallelogram. Redrawn by the author, with permission, from Alan Borning, 'The Programming Language Aspects of ThingLab, a Constraint-Oriented Simulation Laboratory', *ACM Transactions on Programming Languages and Systems*, Vol 3, No 4, October 1981, pp 353–87.

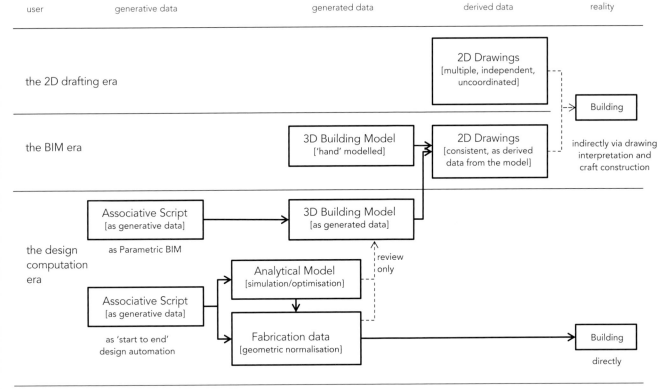

| user | generative data | generated data | derived data | reality |
|---|---|---|---|---|

**the 2D drafting era**

2D Drawings
[multiple, independent, uncoordinated]

Building

**the BIM era**

3D Building Model
['hand' modelled]

2D Drawings
[consistent, as derived data from the model]

indirectly via drawing interpretation and craft construction

**the design computation era**

Associative Script
[as generative data]

as Parametric BIM

3D Building Model
[as generated data]

Associative Script
[as generative data]

as 'start to end' design automation

Analytical Model
[simulation/optimisation]

review only

Fabrication data
[geometric normalisation]

Building

directly

*Object oriented software is based on a metaphor between real-world objects and computational objects. A specific assumption is made that a convenient 'user model' for software developers is one which mimics some of the attributes and behaviour of real-world objects. A CAD system is based on the inverse metaphor, that a convenient 'user model' for architects and designers is one where real-world objects (such as buildings) are represented as a computational system. An object-oriented CAD system is therefore a circular metaphor in which OO software concepts, derived from the real world, are re-applied to the design of further real world objects.[8]*

Therefore, when the OO software engineering principles are applied to the design of a CAD system, the inherent flexibility and extensibility that object orientation provides should be harnessed to benefit the designer. The use of OO software as the basis for computational design applications was already established in the early 1980s.

### REVIEW OF SOFTWARE

In the diagram opposite, we can summarise the history of practical CAD in terms of three eras: the 2D drafting era, the building information modelling (BIM) era and the design computation era. These eras are recognisable but overlap in practice.

### THE 2D DRAFTING ERA

Starting in the early 1980s, 2D drafting continued the practice of representing buildings as multiple 2D drawings. 2D drafting technology could be retrofitted to existing design practice using existing skills without challenging established professional methods and conventions. 2D drafting looks very much like Sketchpad but with the constraint model left out. But the constraints were the whole purpose of Sketchpad. In retrospect, 2D drafting is really a travesty of Sutherland's original intentions. The spectacular flaw of 2D drafting is that it failed to harness the potential of the computer as a creative design tool.

There are conflicting opinions about 2D drafting. Some have criticised 2D drafting systems as having a conservative influence on architecture because it perpetuated the use of drawings long after more advanced modelling technologies were available. Others have commented that the widespread adoption of 2D drafting could be claimed to be the 'democratisation' of technology. But the challenge is not how to 'democratise' the superficial aspects of a technology (in this case the graphic display and the input devices of Sketchpad), but how to 'democratise' the underlying concepts (in this case the constraint system): indeed the real challenge is how to 'democratise' thoughtfulness.

In fact it takes a real effort to re-establish the vision of the original innovators (such as Sutherland), that CAD is not a better way to draw, but a deeper way to think. The contribution of SG can be

**7 The three eras of CAD.**
The flow of information from the designer to the realisation of that data as a constructed building is tracked from left to right.

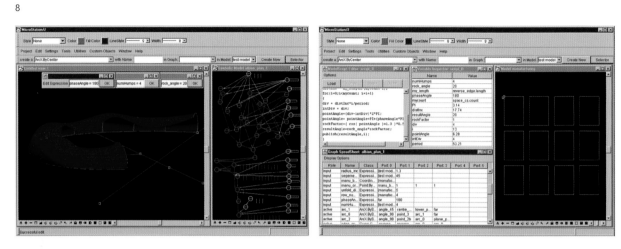

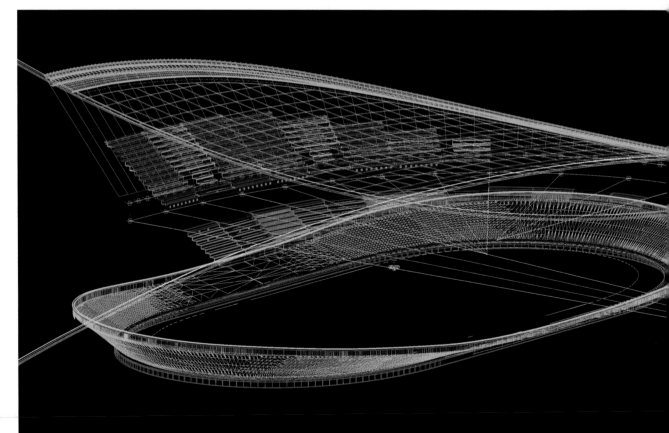

viewed as part of a movement to put 'thoughtfulness' back into the use of computers in design.

## THE BIM ERA

It may be surprising that the BIM era started before the 2D drafting era in the 1980s. One of the objectives of BIM is to overcome the limitations of 2D drafting that the description of the building is spread over multiple independent representations and there is no automated way to enforce consistency between these representations. BIM is based on the idea of creating a single 3D building model with drawings extracted from the model considered as derived data. BIM applies the principle of data normalisations to architectural modelling.[9] It is inherently a much more systematic approach to the application of computing to design. The BIM principles were already established in the mid-1980s: that is more than a quarter of a century ago.[10]

BIM assumes that buildings are assemblies of components, but that does not necessarily imply that a designer conceives of a building in terms of such assemblies. This 'component' assumption forces the designer to think about micro-ideas (the components) before macro-ideas (the building form). Some of the early 'proto' BIM systems – for example, MasterArchitect[11] – introduced a network of relationships between the components and used a special adaptive behaviour to make the editing of the architectural models more 'intuitive'. Again these rules presuppose not just a particular form of construction, but a particular way of design thinking. BIM has sometimes been criticised because it is extremely easy to create the obvious, but it is much harder to develop modelling innovations that do not follow the assumptions and hardcoded behaviour. BIM is a *technology*, combining data normalisation with geometric projection. BIM is a *methodology* which supports efficient integrated project delivery. But BIM should not be construed as a *philosophy* of design. It is not the reason for designing a building in a particular way.

The contribution of SG has been to refocus the use of the computer towards design exploration rather than on production and downstream data management.

## THE DESIGN COMPUTATION ERA

Design computation introduced the distinction between a *generative* description of a building (as a graph or script) and the resulting *generated* model. The designer is no longer directly modelling the building: instead he develops a graph or script whose execution generates the model. This enables a completely different kind of architecture to be created. The design process also changes. An apparently minor edit to the graph or script could have a profound effect on the generated building, enabling the exploration of a vast array of alternatives. The objectives of design computation are to overcome many of the limitations of BIM: first, to move away from the manual model building and instead to directly harness program execution as a generative design tool; and second, to move away from hardcoded building semantics and allow the

8 CustomObjects.
This was an important precursor to GenerativeComponents where the core ideas such as graph-based dependency and replication were originally developed. The model illustrated is the roof of Albion Wharf, designed by Foster + Partners, based on a parametric cosine curve. This CustomObjects model was a 'calibration' study to see how it could emulate the existing programmatic methods previously developed by Francis Aish and Hugh Whitehead at Foster + Partners.

9

9 Associative parametric model created using GenerativeComponents.

(a) Starting with a solid primitive

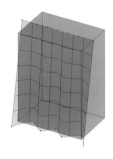

(b) Define a trimming surface

(c) Trim the solid with the surface to create the manifold building envelope

(d) Edges of the manifold building envelope as geometric supports for structural members

(e) Create horizontal, vertical and lateral 'slicing' planes

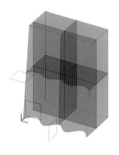

(f) Slice the manifold spatial building envelope to create a non-manifold spatial building model

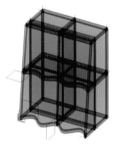

(g) Edges of the non-manifold spatial building model as the geometric supports for curvilinear structural members

(h) Hide the non-manifold spatial building model to show the structural members

(i) Create a cone primitive to represent an atrium and use the 'impose' operation on the spatial building model

(j) Move the atrium so that it intersects with the spatial building model. New cells and edges are created

(k) As the atrium moves through the spatial model, new edges create related structural members

(l) Finally, the atrium is moved out of the spatial building model and adges and structural members adjust accordingly

designer to create his own components and, more importantly, to define his own inter-component modelling behaviour.

A further motivation for developing the first generation of design computation applications (such as CustomObjects[12] and later GenerativeComponents (GC)[13]) was to combine the ideas from Sketchpad, formal design methods and object-oriented software concepts into a single system and to allow designers direct access to these ideas. During the first part of the design computation era, a number of related geometric concepts were also introduced: first, the use of the parameter space of curves and surfaces as a modelling context; second, providing the user with full access to transformation operations (shearing, scaling, rotation, translation); and third, the use of multiple model spaces, so that the same design could be represented in multiple configurations – for example, unfolded (for fabrication) and then folded (in situ).

The design computation era overlaps with the BIM era. Some design computation applications are used to generate BIM models (could we call this parametric BIM?).[14] The design computation era also saw the introduction of simulation and optimisation tools and the adoption of digital fabrication. It was apparent that analysis and simulation tools only required an idealised model of the building, and the data required to drive digital fabrication could be reduced, for example, to a tool-cutter path. The idea of 'geometric normalisation' was introduced.[15] Essentially, how could the designer build the lightest possible model, with the least effort, which would provide him with the most feedback, earliest in the design process? Why build a detailed BIM model (with all the extra effort and resistance to change) when an idealised, geometrically normalised model would be more appropriate?

The original tools of the design computation era (GC and Rhino Grasshopper) were directly based on a graph representation: indeed the graph was also the user interface. The visual graph approach is an excellent training device especially for novice users to construct simple associative models. Indeed, one of the major benefits of the graph as the user interface is that it has successfully attracted designers with little or no traditional interest or experience in programming. Only subsequently was the limitation of this approach appreciated when it was found that the visual graph approach does not scale to real-world complexity. We may convince ourselves that a picture is worth a thousand words, but after a while a graph diagram of hundreds of nodes becomes intractable. The architectural results may be geometric, but as we become more familiar with the programming concepts then a more compact description as algebra (or program notation) eventually trumps node-based diagramming. Although the associative graph approach is well suited to the capture (and re-execution) of some geometric modelling operations, it is outside the mainstream of computing, which is dominated by imperative scripting and programming languages. Indeed many of the familiar concepts of imperative programming, such as iteration, cannot be expressed with a directed graph.

10 The modelling sequence to construct a non-manifold spatial model of a building and the use of the edges of this model to construct a structural model.

11

```
DesignScript Editor
File

nested_programming_block...  ×
 1 import("ProtoGeometry.dll");
 2
 3 WCS = CoordinateSystem.WCS; // setup world coordinatesystem
 4
 5 controlPoint = Point.ByCartesianCoordinates(WCS,0, 7.5, 0);
 6
 7 internalLine : Line  = null; // define some variables
 8 pointOnCurve : Point = null;
 9 testLine     : Line  = null;
10 totalLength = 0;
11 i = 5;
12
13 [Imperative]
14 {
15     while (totalLength < 30) // create a simple outer loop
16     {
17         [Associative] // within that loop build an associative model
18         {
19             startPoint  = Point.ByCartesianCoordinates(WCS,i, 5, 0);
20             endPoint    = Point.ByCartesianCoordinates(WCS,5, 10, 0);
21             internalLine = Line.ByStartPointEndPoint(startPoint, endPoint);
22             pointOnCurve = internalLine.PointAtParameter(0.2..0.8..0.2);
23
24             [Imperative] // within the associative model start some imperative scripting
25             {
26                 for (j in 0..(Count(pointOnCurve)-1)) // iterate over the points
27                 {
28                     if(j%2==0) // consider every alternate point
29                     {
30                         pointOnCurve[j] = pointOnCurve[j].Translate(0,0,1); // modify by translation
31                     }
32                 }
33             }
34             // continue with more associative modelling
35
36             testLine    = Line.ByStartPointEndPoint(controlPoint, pointOnCurve);
37             totalLength = Sum(testLine.Length);
38         }
39         i = i + 1; // increment i
40     }
41 }

Output     Watch     Errors                                      Report Issue
```

11 The DesignScript IDE showing an associative graph model embedded within a user-defined imperative outer wrapper and iteratively driven, for example as an optimisation loop.

12 Hopkins Architects, London 2012
Velodrome, London, UK, 2012.

12

The objective of the second generation of design computation tools (such as DesignScript) is to overcome many of these limitations by completely integrating associative and imperative scripting and by reducing the reliance on the visual graph as the principle 'driver' interface.[16] These second-generation tools have also introduced topological and idealised representations[17] that are more suited to the geometric normalisations required for simulation and optimisation.[18]

Programming (as with exploratory design) is all about control. Different styles of programming use different approaches to *flow control*. Imperative programming is characterised by explicit 'flow control' using *for* loops (for iteration) and *if* statements (for conditionals) as found in familiar scripting and programming languages such as Processing or Python. On the other hand, associative programming uses the graph dependencies to establish 'flow control'. Changes to 'upstream' variables automatically propagate changes to downstream variables, as found in data flow systems such as GC, Rhino Grasshopper and Max/MSP. Imperative programming is appropriate for conventional scripting, while associative programming is an appropriate way to represent complex geometric modelling operations. Any serious design project is likely to require both approaches. Therefore it is highly desirable that the border between imperative and associative programming be as porous as possible. In DesignScript this is achieved by using a common programming notation for both imperative and associative programming.[16]

## CONCLUSIONS
In retrospect the history of SG appears to be a perfectly logical progression. New innovations triggered the development of successive waves of software which addressed the limitations and conceptual mismatches evident in earlier software. But there was nothing inevitable here. There were false starts. Tangents were followed. Blind alleys were explored. Software platforms were developed and cancelled. Risks were taken. Applications were written and rewritten and rewritten. The midnight oil was burnt.

The key contribution of SG was to create an environment where designers (as software users) and software developers could share ideas. The emphasis was on exploration outside of the conventional, on abstractions beyond the familiar, on deliberately embracing cognitive retooling, on intentionally searching for integration across discipline boundaries, and on focusing on the ultimate quality and thoughtfulness of design rather than on immediate productivity. Whatever the initial hesitation and however tortuous the path, the final results speak for themselves.

This leads to two important conclusions. First, computational design is now recognised as an intrinsic aspect of design creativity so that the mark of the accomplished designer is that he can move effortlessly between intuition and logic. Second, the distinction between the role of the professional software developer and the designer (as an end-user programmer) has been blurred. Now we can all create that final layer of scripting that represents our unique design logic, so that we can all say: 'Before I design I will first build my tools.'

## REFERENCES

1 Ivan Edward Sutherland, 'Sketchpad: A Man–Machine Graphical Communication System', *AFIPS Conference Proceedings*, Vol 23, 1963, pp 232–8.

2 Trygve Reenskaug, 'Models–Views–Controllers', http://heim.ifi.uio.no/~trygver/themes/mvc/mvc-index.html [accessed 5 October 2012].

3 Christopher Alexander, *Notes on the Synthesis of Form*, Harvard University Press (Cambridge, MA), 1964; Christopher Alexander, 'A City is not a Tree', *Design*, No 206, Council of Industrial Design, (London), 1966 (online at http://www.rudi.net/pages/8755 [accessed 5 October 2012]).

4 Robert Aish, *An Analytical Approach to the Design of a Man–Machine Interface*, PhD thesis, University of Essex,1974.

5 Adele Goldberg and David Robson, *Smalltalk-80: The Language and its Implementation*, Addison-Wesley (Reading, MA; London), 1982.

6 Alan Borning, 'The Programming Language Aspects of ThingLab: A Constraint-Oriented Simulation Laboratory', *ACM Transactions on Programming Languages and Systems*, Vol 3, No 4, October 1981, pp 353–87.

7 Alan Borning, 'ThingLab Demonstration Video', presented at The Computing Forum, Xerox PARC, Palo Alto, CA, 1978.

8 Robert Aish, 'A User Extensible Object-Oriented CAD System', *Proceedings of the Object-Oriented Software Engineering Conference*, British Computer Society (London), 1990.

9 Edgar Frank Codd, 'Is Your DBMS Really Relational?', *Computerworld*, 14 October, 1985.

10 Robert Aish, 'Building Modelling: The Key to Integrated Construction CAD', *Proceedings of the Fifth International Symposium on the use of Computers for Environmental Engineering related to Buildings*, CIB, 1986.

11 Robert Aish, 'MasterArchitect: An Object-Based Architectural Design and Production System'. *Proceedings of the CIB W74 + W78 Seminar*, Lund, Sweden, 1988.

12 Robert Aish, 'Extensible Computational Design Tools for Exploratory Architecture', in Branko Kolarevic (ed), *Architecture in the Digital Age: Design and Manufacturing*, Spon Press (London), 2003.

13 Robert Aish and Robert Woodbury, 'Multi-Level Interaction in Parametric Design', in Andreas Butz, Brian D Fisher, Antonio Krüger and Patrick Olivier (eds), *Smart Graphics, 5th International Symposium*, Springer Verlag (Berlin), 2005.

14 Martha Tsigkari, Adam Davis and Francis Aish, 'A Sense of Purpose: Mathematics and Performance in Environmental Design', in *Mathematics of Space – AD* (*Architectural Design*), Vol 81, No 4, 2011, pp 54–7.

15 Fabian Scheurer and Hanno Stehling, 'Lost in Parameter Space?', in *Mathematics of Space – AD* (*Architectural Design*), Vol 81, No 4, 2011, pp 70–79.

16 Robert Aish, 'DesignScript: Origins, Explanation, Illustration', *Design Modelling Symposium*, Springer Verlag (Berlin), 2011.

17 Robert Aish and Aparajit Pratap, 'Spatial Information Modelling of Buildings using Non-Manifold Topology with ASM and DesignScript', *Advances in Architectural Geometry*, Paris, 2012.

18 Robert Aish, Al Fisher, Sam Joyce and Andrew Marsh, 'Progress Towards Multi-Criteria Design Optimisation using DesignScript with SMART Form, Robot Structural Analysis and Ecotect Building Performance Analysis', *ACADIA*, 2012.

**TEXT**

**IMAGES**

Figures 1, 2 © MIT; Figures 3, 4 From drawings by Christopher Alexander; Figure 5 © Robert Aish; Figure 6 © Robert Aish, redrawn by the author, with permission, from Alan Borning, 'The Programming Language Aspects of ThingLab, a Constraint-Oriented Simulation Laboratory', *ACM Transactions on Programming Languages and Systems*, Vol 3, Issue 4, October 1981, pp 353–87; Figures 7, 10, 11 © Autodesk; Figure 8 © Foster + Partners; Figure 9 © Hopkins Architects Partnership LLP; Figure 12 © Michael Steele/Getty Images

# PARAMETRIC EVOLUTION

**BRANKO KOLAREVIC**

Branko Kolarevic is editor of *Architecture in the Digital Age: Design and Manufacturing*, a key text in the field of digital design and highly relevant to the Smartgeometry (SG) community. Kolarevic was an invited keynote speaker at the 2012 SG conference. In his chapter he offers a contextualisation and explanation of some of the key parametric projects that have influenced and inspired this generation of architectural designers.

*'After all, nothing is more fundamental in design than formation and discovery of relationships among parts of a composition.'* William Mitchell and Malcolm McCullough[1]

It was in the late 1980s and early 1990s that a profound shift took place in architectural design. For the first time in history, architects were designing not the specific shape of the building but a set of principles encoded digitally as a sequence of parametric equations by which specific instances of the design can be generated by simply varying the values of parameters.

Instead of working on a composition (*parti*), the designers would construct a parametric, computational system of formal production, create on-screen controls that affect its outcomes, and then select forms that emerge from the operation of the system. In this *digital morphosis*, a system of generative rules, relations and/or constraints is defined first (*in-formation*), and its interactive controls specified; the resulting structure of interdependences is often given some generic form (*formation*), which is then subjected to the processes of *de-formation* or *trans-formation*, driven by those very same relations and rules embedded within the system itself.

In a radical departure from centuries-old traditions and norms of architectural design, digitally generated forms are not designed or drawn as the conventional understanding of these terms would have it, but they are calculated by the chosen generative computational method using different parameter values. Instead of just modelling an external form, designers first and foremost articulate an internal generative logic, which then produces, often in an automatic fashion, a range of possibilities from which the designer could choose an appropriate formal proposition for further development. Models of design capable of consistent, continual and dynamic transformation replaced the static norms of conventional processes.

In parametric design it is the parameters of a particular design that are declared and not its shape. By assigning different values to the parameters, different objects or configurations can be created. Equations can be used to describe the relationships between objects, thus defining an *associative* geometry in which geometric elements (points, lines, shapes etc) are mutually linked. That way, interdependences between objects can be established, and objects' behaviour under transformations defined.[2]

Parametrics provide for a powerful conception of shape and form in architecture by describing a range of possibilities, replacing in the process stable with variable, singularity with multiplicity. Using parametrics, designers could create an infinite number of similar objects, geometric manifestations of a previously articulated schema of variable dimensional, relational or operative dependencies. When those variables are assigned specific values, particular instances are created from a potentially infinite range

1 Gehry Architects, Vila Olímpica Complex, Barcelona, Spain, 1992.
The 'Fish' structure sits at the entrance to the Vila Olímpica complex on Barcelona's waterfront.

2 Gehry Architects, three-dimensional model of the Vila Olímpica Complex, Barcelona, Spain, 1992.
The model was produced in CATIA.

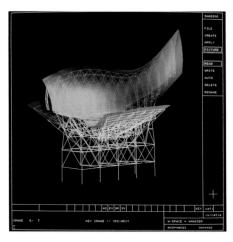

2

3 Grimshaw, International Terminal, Waterloo
Station, London, UK, 1993.
The design has 36 dimensionally different but
identically configured three-pin bowstring
arches.

4 Grimshaw, International Terminal, Waterloo
Station, London, UK, 1993.

of possibilities. Fixed solutions are rejected for an exploration of infinitely variable potentialities.

Parametric design is now well established in both the profession and academia. It is commonly understood as an enabling digital technology for infinite variation of shapes and forms, either through the embedded, inherent ways in which geometry is represented within the chosen drawing and modelling software or via visual programming aids or scripting.

### PARAMETRICS: THE EARLY PROJECTS

Two projects completed in the early 1990s heralded the new possibilities and opportunities that the digital technologies of parametric design (and fabrication) made attainable: the Olympic 'Fish' in Barcelona (1992) by Frank Gehry and the International Terminal at Waterloo Station in London (1993) by Nicholas Grimshaw.

The Barcelona 'Fish' project was the first 'paperless' project executed in Gehry's office in the early 1990s using computer-aided three-dimensional interactive application (CATIA).[3] It was relatively simple, involving cladding on the structural steel, the geometry of which was parametrically defined within CATIA. The design, fabrication and construction of the project were all coordinated through the computer model. Reportedly, there were only about six drawings by hand and a computer model for the entire process, which was used for tracking parts, design and the layout of the system.

Grimshaw International Terminal at Waterloo Station clearly demonstrated the conceptual and developmental benefits afforded by the parametric approach to design. The building is essentially a 400-metre-long glass-clad train shed, with a 'tapering' span that gradually shrinks from 50 metres to 35 metres. Its narrow, sinuous plan is determined by the track layout and the difficult geometry of the site, which is the main source of the project's complexity and which gives such potency and significance to Grimshaw's design, especially its spectacular roof. The roof structure consists of a series of 36 dimensionally different but identically configured three-pin bowstring arches. Because of the asymmetrical geometry of the platforms, the arches rise steeply on one side with a shallower incline over the platforms on the other side. Each arch is different as the width of the roof changes along the tracks.

Instead of modelling each arch separately, a generic parametric model was created based on the underlying design rules in which the size of the span and the curvature of individual arches were related. By assigning different values to the span parameter, the 36 arches were computed and inserted in the overall geometric model. The parametric model was extended from the structural description of arches to the elements that connect them and to the corresponding cladding elements – that is, to the entire building form. Thus, a highly complex hierarchy of interdependences was parametrically modelled, allowing iterative refinement – that

4

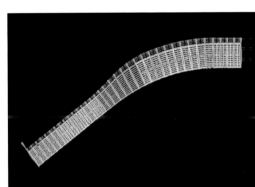

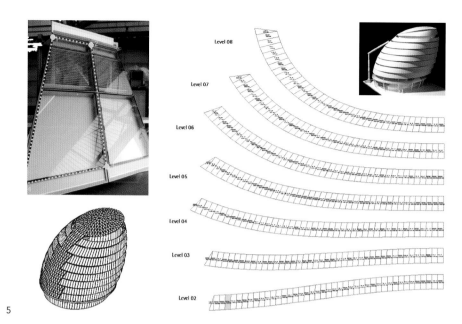

5

6

7

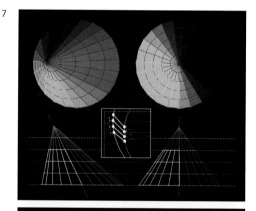

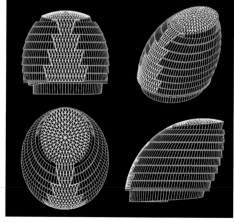

5 Foster + Partners, City Hall, London, UK, 2002.
The flat-patterned drawing of the glazing solution for City Hall.

6 Foster + Partners, City Hall, London, UK, 2002.

is, the dimensional fine-tuning of the project in all stages of its development, from conceptual design to construction.

A few years later, in 1998, Norman Foster's practice established a Specialist Modelling Group, led by Hugh Whitehead, whose brief from the outset was to develop parametric models of geometry for various projects the office had at the time, such as London's City Hall. For that project, the group started by developing a 'parametric pebble', which was essentially a sphere, whose 'minimal control polygon' was connected to a parametric control 'rig' in Microstation, so that the form could be adjusted by using proportional relationships. The creation of such 'variational templates' for direct use by the design teams then became standard in the practice. Hugh Whitehead reported at the time that it would take several hours for his group to produce a custom-built parametric model which would then often be used for several months by the team to produce alternatives for testing during design development.[4] Different parametric models were generated for the City Hall project, including the glazing system, which was based on a stack of sheared cones. The team developed a software macro that enabled automatic generation of the glazing solution, with the glazing frames fanning backwards with the rake of the building, producing a dynamic visual effect. To estimate the costs, the original macro was extended to lay out the glazing panels in a flat pattern, automatically scheduling all areas of the facade, and listing panel node coordinates. That particular technique of generating flat-patterned drawings quickly became rather important in the work of the group, because fabricators or contractors could use them in pricing, manufacturing and on-site assembly, regardless of the complexity of the form. Such flat-patterned drawings also enabled the mass-customisation of components – in this case, glazing frames – all of which were topologically identical and dimensionally different.

These projects were the harbingers of the parametric revolution that followed. Parametric design is now commonly understood and broadly used in practice to vary and dynamically explore the geometry and spatial articulation of building designs. While the notion of parametric variation is easy to convey and understand, the actual organisation or structuring of dependencies and relationships in designs is in a state of free-for-all where no particularly established methodologies exist beyond the already familiar grids and modules. This is in large part due to a relative absence of a proper discourse that addresses the role of *topology* versus *geometry* in architectural design.

### TOPOLOGY VERSUS GEOMETRY

The wide adoption of parametric design led to something much more profound than the re-emergence of complex, curvilinear forms (or the proclamations of new style driven by parametrics) – a shift of emphasis from geometry to *topology*.

According to its mathematical definition, topology is a study of intrinsic, qualitative properties of geometric forms that are not

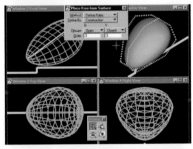

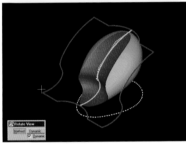

8

7 Foster + Partners, City Hall, London, UK, 2002.
The glazing solution for City Hall is based on a stack of sheared cones.

8 Foster + Partners, model of City Hall, London, UK, 2002.
The 'parametric pebble' model of City Hall.

normally affected by changes in size or shape – that is, which remain invariant through continuous one-to-one transformations or elastic deformations, such as stretching or twisting. A circle and an ellipse, for example, or a square and a rectangle, can be considered to be topologically equivalent, as both a circle and a square could be deformed by stretching them into an ellipse or rectangle, respectively. A square and a rectangle have the same number of edges and the same number of vertices, and are, therefore, topologically identical, or *homeomorphic*. This quality of homeomorphism is particularly interesting, as focus is on the relational structure of an object and not on its geometry – the same topological structure could be geometrically manifested in an infinite number of forms.

The notion of topology has particular potentiality in architecture, as the focus shifts to relations that exist between and within elements of the geometry. These interdependences then become the structuring, organising principle for the generation and transformation of form.

What makes topology particularly appealing in architecture is the primacy over form of the structures of relations, interconnections or inherent qualities which exist internally and externally within the context of an architectural project. But what defines a topology of an architectural project? Is there some kind of universal set of relationships and interdependences that define forms and spaces? How should those relationships and interdependences be structured – as hierarchies or networks? How should they be visually manifested and manipulated?

Then there is the issue of *topological* operations, which affect first the internal relational structure and then, as a consequence, the resulting form(s). As a rather simple example, a rectangle could be transformed into a triangle with a single topological operation of deleting one of its vertices. Syntactically and semantically, this is one of the simplest operations that could be carried out. Obviously, the repertoire of topological operations will in large part be determined by the topology of the project, ie that which associates elements of the geometry to each other.

Historically, in architectural design, shapes that delineate spaces were frequently constructed within some graphic context which was set at a basic compositional level by abstract organisational devices, such as grids, axes and construction lines. For example, Jean-Nicholas-Louis Durand (1760–1834) and Louis Sullivan (1856–1924) relied heavily on grids (patterns of construction lines) and axes (construction lines of specific importance). The work of Le Corbusier (1887–1965) from the Purist period around 1920, both in architecture and painting, was guided by the application of '*les tracés régulateurs*' – regulating or construction lines that provided at a basic compositional level an organising framework for establishing positions and relations of line segments within and between shapes. Such 'construction' lines, however, could become much more useful and interesting when used not just

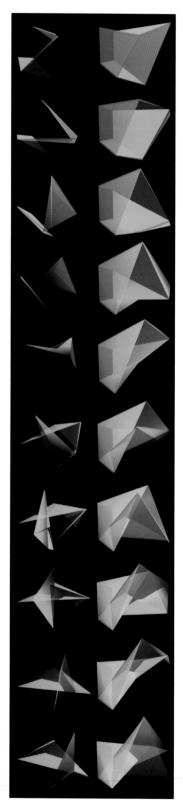

as a rigid skeleton for the delineation of shapes, but to regulate the behaviour of a drawing (or a model) and to maintain its essential structure as its parts are manipulated.[5] In other words, by allowing some elements of the geometry – in this case the 'construction' lines – to control positions and orientations of other elements through their geometric relations and dependencies, we can structure the behaviour of the object being designed under transformations. As a consequence, models can become semantically charged and can be manipulated in a semantically sophisticated fashion. A computer-based design tool can record and maintain already established relationships, even recognise the emergent ones, and compute the consequences of design transformations while preserving the semantic integrity of the drawing or the model.

Using geometric relations, a designer can enforce desired spatial configurations of building components and spaces – the project's topology. The established relations constrain the design possibilities; they structure possible manipulations. The choice of relationships applied in a *parti* may result in dramatically different designs even though a small set of possible relations and a few transformations are available. How the composition is assembled, structured, or restructured, determines its developmental potential. As William Mitchell observes: '[T]he choice of modeling conventions and organizational devices that will structure the internal symbolic model [...] will determine how the model can be manipulated, and what can be done with it.'[6]

The structuring of dependencies – the topology of the parametric model – determines how it transforms as the parameters are varied. A designer must understand the underlying topological (ie organisational) structure of the model to operate successfully upon it. This understanding is required on a basic, pragmatic level: if an interconnected element is moved, what other elements will move too. However, if the topology of the model – that is, its composition or the underlying organisational structure – is too complex, applying a transformation to it might be difficult to control and envision. In other words, the consequences of propagating changes to the model after applying a certain transformation (or a parameter variation) could sometimes be very surprising. Resulting configurations can be genuinely new and, in some instances, might trigger an innovative approach to the project. A parametric model can thus become a vehicle on a path from known to unknown, from predictable to unpredictable.

### TOOLS OF PARAMETRIC DESIGN
In the computer-aided design research community of the 1980s there was a rather obvious recognition that using digital tools to discover and create new spatial organisations and forms is a different task than drawing or modelling a known, existing or already conceived form. It was commonly understood that what was needed were computer-based design systems which could treat the form or object being created as an entity subject to continuous manipulation and change.[7] For those systems to be effective, they

9 Homeomorphic (topologically equivalent) figures.

had to provide interactive and dynamic creation and manipulation
of forms or objects being designed with the level of transparency
and fluidity common to traditional techniques. Most importantly, for
these computer-based graphic systems to become actual design
systems, they had to be versatile and thought-provoking.

It used to be that much of the creative discovery in architectural
design took place in the two-dimensional realm of study
drawings. An apparent contradiction, however, emerged in
closer examination of that process. The act of drawing, as well
as other traditional ways of communicating spatial information
in architectural design, is inherently static, producing snapshots
of an evolving design concept. The act of designing, however, is
intrinsically dynamic. Shapes depicting an evolving design concept
are seldom static – they change constantly. The recognition of this
disparity between drawing as a static and design as a dynamic
activity provided an impetus for a number of researchers, both in
academia and in the industry, to search for dynamic design media.

A variety of systems was developed over the past two decades
to facilitate sophisticated structuring of geometric models and
their parametric variation. The early experiments in relations- or
constraints-based modelling led to robust commercially available
systems that provide for powerful conceptions of form and spatial
organisation. In addition to myriad tool palettes and option boxes
that provide for interactive creation and manipulation of geometry,
many offer ways to extend the system's capacity via some kind of
programming or scripting language. Some provide ways of visually
programming the underlying structure of the geometry, meaning
that in some programs the coding is no longer required.

Developing a parametric model is in fact programming: entities are
defined that form larger assemblies, relationships are established,
values are assigned to parameters. Some designers do this
through scripting (ie programming) and some use sophisticated
modelling software that features visual programming. Regardless
of the way in which it is done, effective parametric design requires
abstractions, definitions of relationships – more than the simple
knowledge of syntax of some programming or scripting language
or the features of some modelling software. Once the project's
topology is articulated, the geometry can be either procedurally
created (via programming scripts) or interactively modelled
using some visual context for establishing associations between
constituent elements of the geometry.

### PROGRAMMING BEHAVIOUR THROUGH TOPOLOGY
Parametric approaches to design conceptualisation benefit
designers by allowing them to efficiently and effectively
generate new information within the design task through graphic
processes – that is, by providing graphic means of generating
new but always contingent information within the design task
through dynamic manipulation of the parameter values and the
design object's relational structure. They expand the designer's
ability to speculate about possibilities. Parametric design places

value on explicit formulation – its use requires 'discipline' and an understanding of the relation-based approach to design as a method. Once the approach to the project's topology is understood, it can be used effectively to 'program' the 'behaviour' of a design object. It is on facilitating this process of topological modelling and structuring that much of the development of parametric design tools is currently focused.

## REFERENCES

1 William J Mitchell and Malcolm McCullough, *Digital Design Media*, Van Nostrand Reinhold (New York, NY), 1991.

2 Branko Kolarevic, 'Lines, Relations, Drawing and Design', in Anton Harfmann and Michael Fraser (eds), *Reconnecting: Proceedings of the Association for Computer Aided Design in Architecture (ACADIA) 1994 Conference*, Washington University (St Louis, MO), 1994.

3 James Glymph, 'Evolution of the Digital Design Process', in Branko Kolarevic (ed), *Architecture in the Digital Age: Design and Manufacturing*, Spon Press (London), 2003.

4 Hugh Whitehead, 'Laws of Form', in Branko Kolarevic (ed), *Architecture in the Digital Age: Design and Manufacturing*, Spon Press (London), 2003.

5 Branko Kolarevic, *Geometric Relations as a Framework for Design Conceptualization*, doctoral thesis, Harvard University Graduate School of Design, 1993.

6 William J Mitchell, 'Architecture and the Second Industrial Revolution', *Harvard Architecture Review*, Vol 7, 1989, pp 166–75.

7 Branko Kolarevic, *Geometric Relations as a Framework for Design Conceptualization*, doctoral thesis, Harvard University Graduate School of Design, 1993.

1 Installation for the exhibition 'Working Prototypes' following the SG 2010 workshops at IAAC, Barcelona, Spain.
The material systems for the network are composed of 3D printed components and three connector components featuring floppy, semi-rigid and rigid materials.

1

# MATRIX ARCHITECTURE

JENNY E SABIN

Architect Jenny E Sabin investigates the intersections of architecture and science, and applies insights and theories from biology, textile structures, computational design and mathematics to the design of material structures. A member of the Smartgeometry community for six years, first in 2006 experimenting with ideas of the mathematics of weaving, and most recently in 2010 when she investigated non-linear systems biology and design, her work signals a new collaborative and multidisciplinary direction for architectural practice.

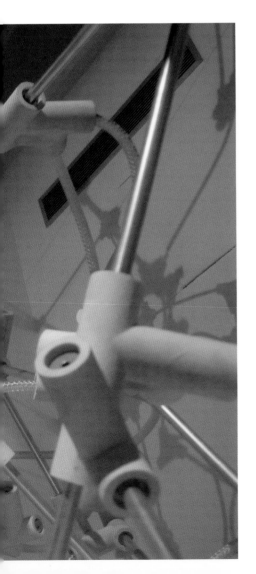

Collaborations between architects and scientists offer up potentials for productive exchange in design while revealing powerful models for visualising the intangible. As an experimental designer in practice, also engaged in research and education, my work-investigates the intersections of architecture and science. It applies insights and theories from biology and mathematics to the design of material structures. Through the visualisation and materialisation of dynamic and complex data sets, I have generated a body of speculative and applied design work that aligns crafts-based techniques with digital fabrication alongside questions related to the body and information mediation. It is an approach that may be referred to as *matrix architecture*, a hybrid term that bridges my collaborative work with matrix biologists with shared relationships between architecture and weaving. As exemplified in the work of Anni Albers at the Bauhaus (see below), this work renders the product of information tangible through context, material and form.

The material world that this type of research interrogates reveals examples of non-linear fabrication and self-assembly both at a surface and at a deeper structural level. In parallel, this work offers up novel possibilities that question and redefine architecture within the greater scope of generative design and fabrication. Project examples span my work as a researcher, educator and experimental architectural designer. Key examples link my early work on the mathematics of weaving – explored during the 2006 Smartgeometry workshop (SG 2006) – to intersections between architecture and science, exemplified in my SG 2010 workshop with Dr Peter Lloyd Jones entitled 'Nonlinear Systems Biology and Design'. Fundamental to all of this work is the integration of the human body as a primary point of departure into the conception, materialisation and making of complex form. Context matters, and the body provides numerous potent biodynamic models for addressing

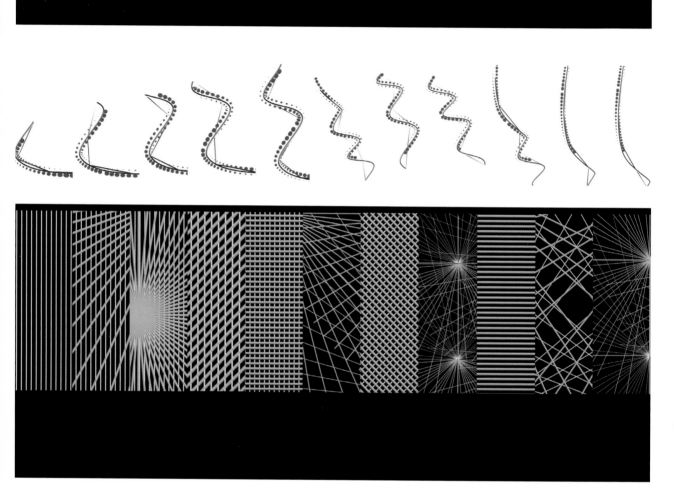

2 Jenny E Sabin, *Pattern Book*, 2006.
This project explored at SG 2006 captures a
potential spectrum of variegated forms via the
careful control of initial inputs.

practical concerns related to building performance while also expanding our perception of space and its combined components.

The pairing of architecture and textiles is not a new idea. Modern and historical examples that come to mind include the seminal and vast bodies of artistic and design work by Anni Albers (1899–1994), Gunta Stölzl (1897–1983) and Lilly Reich (1885–1947). In contrast to the current gender landscape of computational designers in contemporary architectural practice and research, it was women who generated the first examples of parametrically designed form in modern architecture. Importantly, the Bauhaus weavers marked a shift from expressionistic and individual handcraft compositions to mass-produced and rapidly manufactured prototypes for furniture, interior design and architectural elements. This shift led the way to a new approach to craft and making, one that was marked by the integration of pattern, material constraints, form and fabrication; perhaps offering up the first analogue examples of generative and parametric design work in the context of scaled prototyping and fabrication. Similar to many of the cutting-edge experiments happening in our schools and certainly at the annual SG workshops, the women in the Weaving Workshop at Dessau embraced the capabilities of the most current mechanised looms of the day and integrated this with a mathematical understanding of pattern and form generation. The 'pliable plane' was Anni Albers's term for this generative intersection between architecture and textiles.[1] This 'pliable plane' is a landscape of information made tangible through geometry and matter. The 'pliable plane' is matrix architecture. The women of the Bauhaus at Dessau indeed paved a new path for the development of a theoretical and architectonic practice rooted in textile.

My interest in weaving is in both tracing a long lineage of relationships between weaving and computation as outlined above, and in encompassing shared relationships between architecture and woven form.[2] It was during my first SG workshop in Cambridge, UK in 2006 that I merged these interests with a parametric environment through the use of GenerativeComponents. The technological and cultural history of weaving offers architecture a potent and useful relationship between design and digital fabrication. This *Pattern Book* of woven outputs, explored at SG 2006, captures a potential spectrum of variegated forms via the careful control of initial inputs and outputs. This is achieved through the manipulation of parametric software tools and custom-written scripts or algorithms.

After studying the parametric qualities of weaving at the SG 2006 workshop, I moved these models into an applied project at Artists Space in New York City. As part of the first instalment of the 'H_edge' installation by Arup Advanced Geometry Unit, Cecil Balmond and myself, *Fourier Carpet*, an 11-by-1.5-metre tapestry, productively contrasted the crisp edges of the three-dimensional quality of the woven tensegrity structure with a soft undulating and rhythmic pattern sequence in woven thread. Each section of the tapestry is generated by the same algorithm, but with subtle

4

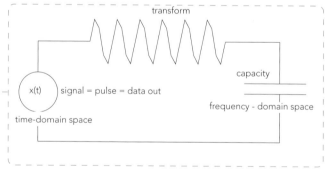

transform

x(t)    signal = pulse = data out

time-domain space

capacity

frequency - domain space

data

"30","-4.99314131707784e-013","0"
"29","-1.81635632001249","0"
"28","-7.69420884293869","0"
"27","-7.69420884293896","0"
"26","1.81635632001181","0"
"25","1.32473459285575e-012","0"
"24","-1.81635632001391","0"
"23","-7.69420884293814","0"
"22","7.69420884293793","0"
"21","1.81635632001453","0"
"20","-2.03817865362943e-012","0"
"19","-1.81635632001326","0"
"18","-7.69420884293379","0"
"17","7.69420884293767","0"
"16","1.81635632001306","0"
"15","-2.49657065853892e-013","0"
"14","-1.81635632001266","0"
"13","-7.69420884293782","0"
"12","7.69420884293823","0"
"11","1.81635632001368","0"
"10","-1.01908932681471e-012","0"
"9","-1.81635632001307","0"
"8","-7.69420884293806","0"
"7","7.69420884293799","0"
"6","1.81635632001327","0"
"5","-5.09544663407357e-013","0"
"4","-1.81635632001348","0"
"3","-7.69420884293811","0"
"2","7.69420884293814","0"
"1","1.81635632001338","0"
"0","0","0"
"30","-4.99314131707784e-013","0"
"29","1.12256994144903","0"
"28","-12.4494914244142","0"
"27","-12.4494914244137","0"

signal

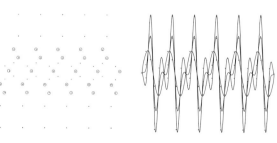

fourier spectrum as points                woven result

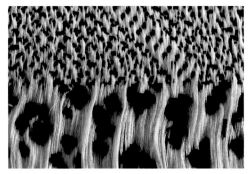

5

3 Jenny E Sabin, *Fourier Carpet*, 2006.
The *Fourier Carpet* was generated from
multiple Fourier series. Specifically, the Fourier
series is a transformation that changes data
from space/time to wave number/frequency
(ie time-domain data into frequency-domain
data). It is a mathematical filter with far-reaching
applications spanning many fields. One of the
well-known connections between mathematics
and music is the theory of the Fourier series.

4 Jenny E Sabin, *Fourier Transform*, 2005.
The Fourier series draws upon art and design
and combines architecture, weaving and
computational systems. The Fourier series is a
binary mathematical sequence for the analysis
of sound and colour, and is used in the *Fourier
Carpet* project to create carpets woven in wool
and synthetic yarns.

5 Jenny E Sabin, *BodyBlanket*, 2005.
In this project, the output is transformed into
a pattern block and woven. The intent is to
realise interfaces between patients, information
and the hospital setting by giving physical
and architectural form to patient data, thereby
making data directly perceptible. The woven
output is a skin that has both a front image and
a back image with a space between.

shifts in the designed parameters. These pattern studies informed
the final chunk of binary code that was used to weave the *Fourier
Carpet* on a digitised Jacquard loom.

*BodyBlanket* (2005) and *Fourier Carpet* (2006), based on the
Fourier series, a binary mathematical sequence for the analysis of
sound, are woven in wool using an early computational model for
computers, the Jacquard loom. As one traces the technological
and cultural history of weaving, a link is revealed between the
punch-card technologies used to automate these mechanical
weaving machines and the early binary systems used for
computation in the first computers. This link is rooted in the coded
binary patterning system of warp and weft. Because weaving
exists within the space of zero and one, it is possible to weave
computational designs that are rooted in a binary structure of data
points. This process seeks to understand and intuit spatial patterns
within data sets, patterns that through study and analysis lead to
architectural elements in the form of textile tectonics. The process
gives rise to questions about the visualisation of data, technology
and how we as people interface and interact with information.

The link between computation and weaving is still a very robust
one. One specific link defines a mathematical relationship between
the trigonometric terms sine and cosine. Basic trigonometry shows
us that the two terms are quadrature or orthogonal to each other
and are therefore fully independent of each other. A cosine wave is
just a sine wave whose phase is shifted by 90 degrees or precisely
a quarter turn of the full cycle. This orthogonal relationship allows
sine waves to weave with cosine waves. One such relationship calls
for the summing of simple sine and cosine waves to produce what
are called complex waves. This is called a Fourier series. A woven
Fourier series is mathematically complex.

Both *Fourier Carpet* and *BodyBlanket* were generated from
mathematical models that transfer sound, colour, harmonic
systems and dynamic data from the human body into woven
designs. The woven data is transformed into a computer-aided
design (CAD) file of binary block code, which is then fed into a
digitised Jacquard loom. With *BodyBlanket*, data provided by the
human body is woven. For example, when undergoing magnetic
resonance imaging (MRI), the human body emits a series of
frequencies that are then filtered through a transform called the
Fourier transform. Once filtered, the harmonic data emitted from
the body is converted into a static image. This type of material
transfer of data through geometry and form is shown in the
*BodyBlanket* project. *Fourier Carpet* and *BodyBlanket* are matrix
architecture, a momentary materialisation of dynamic harmonic
data. This dynamic space is also biological.

Similar to the mathematical dynamics of weaving, biology also
provides useful systems-based models for architects to study and
understand how context specifies form, function and structure.
While the end goals may differ in science and architecture, there
is a driving necessity in both disciplines to spatialise, model and

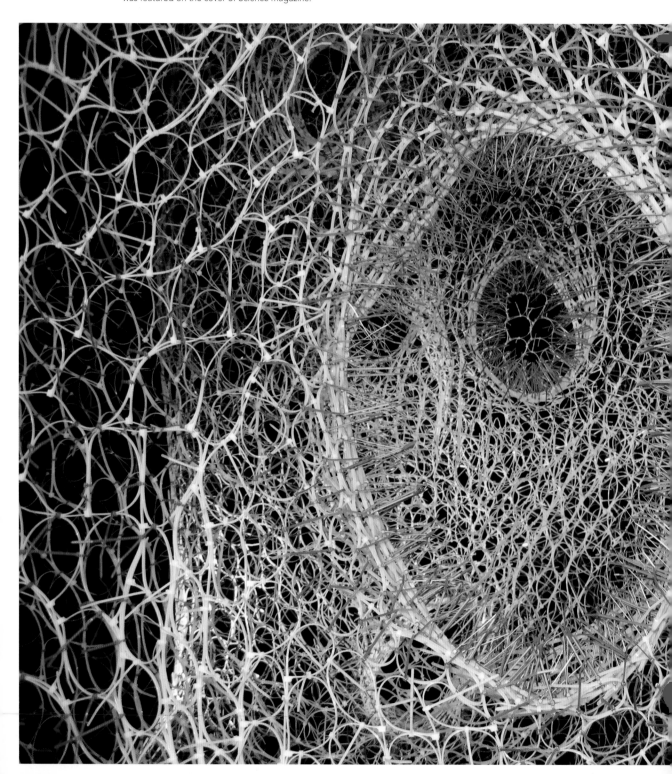

6 LabStudio (Jenny E Sabin, Andrew Lucia, Peter Lloyd Jones and Annette Fierro), *Branching Morphogenesis*, 2008. This image won the 2009 International Science and Engineering Visualization Challenge and was featured on the cover of *Science* magazine.

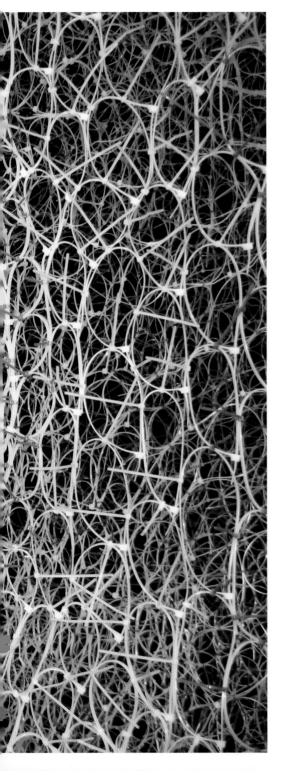

fabricate complex, emergent and self-organised systems. How do we intuit, see and inhabit complex wholes that are indiscernible from their parts? Models borrowed from biology show us that form is the product of complex interactions between contextual events and code over time and in space. This dynamic interplay between code and context enables the production of dynamic matrix architectures at multiple-length scales and oscillatory states.

As can be seen with weaving, the evolution of digital media has prompted new techniques of fabrication but also new understandings in the organisation of material through its properties and potential for assemblage. The scope of much of this experimental design work and research, probes the relationship between code and pattern, material and geometry, fabrication and assembly. The following work builds upon the material organisations and structural systems present within the weaving projects by integrating them with contextual constraints and robust feedback loops that are biological. These are frequently driven by diverse data sets arising from intersections found between science and architecture. The bringing together of code with context, through the study of natural systems, provides insight into relationships between form and behaviour. Frequently, the starting point depends upon the visualisation of complex data sets through the generation and design of computational tools. Here, material, geometry and environment are not separate from each other but rather share reciprocal and therefore ecological relationships through a comprehensive modelling of inputs and outputs.

Organic models such as those found in nature afford new modes for understanding issues of feedback, adaptation, growth and self-assembly as they negotiate truly dynamic environments. A rigorous understanding and analysis of these types of models will allow architects to retool and re-evaluate how we negotiate topics such as complexity, emergence and self-organisation in architecture. Rather than mimic or directly translate these scientific models to the human built scale and vice versa, this type of research requires a break from perceived pedagogical boundaries, thus giving rise to new modes of thinking and working in design and science. It is through this immersion that our design tools may become more flexible by engaging a thorough assessment of truly complex and emergent systems.

This immersion within transdisciplinary work found at the interface between architecture, computation and science has been substantially bolstered by my collaborative research with scientists, namely with Dr Peter Lloyd Jones, former Professor of Pathology and Laboratory Medicine based at the Institute for Medicine and Engineering at the University of Pennsylvania. Within the context of our collaboration, we co-founded a hybrid architectural-biological research and design network called LabStudio. We are primarily interested in architectural models and design tools that come forth through the study of cells and tissues within a tissue-specific dynamic extracellular matrix environment. More specifically, we are observing how micro environmental architectures, at the level

7

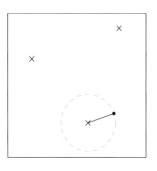

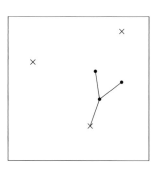

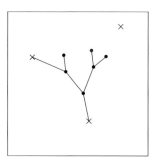

Step 1: Free-flowing Particles

Step 2: Anchoring Particles
to Matrix

Step 3: Branching

Step 4: Connecting

8

7 Generative rules from the 'Nonlinear Systems Biology and Design' workshop cluster at SG 2010, IAAC, Barcelona, Spain.
These diagrams show the generative rules created by participant Jacob Riiber.

8 'Nonlinear Systems Biology and Design' workshop cluster at SG 2010, IAAC, Barcelona, Spain.
With cluster champions Jenny E Sabin, Peter Lloyd Jones, Andrew Lucia and Erica Savig, the workshop focused on the simulation of nonlinear behaviour in cell biological systems and the translation of this behaviour into material systems and fabrication techniques, namely through 3D printing.

of the matrix, control cell behaviour, and how function follows form at the geometric, biochemical and biophysical levels. This matrix environment is a cell-derived woven and globular protein network that contacts most cells within the body – an architectural textile of sorts. Importantly, as I have come to learn from my collaboration with the Jones laboratory, this environment changes dynamically throughout development and disease, and we are specifically interested in models that show how these alterations feed back to control cell and tissue behaviour at the level of code and beyond, in multiple dimensions including time. This exchange of information between the inside of the cell and its exterior environment presents a potent architectural model for understanding how context or environment shares a reciprocal relationship with code, geometry and matter. Matrix architecture features formal and material attributes that are based upon interdependent relationships between environment and code.

In one project, we have developed advanced imaging and scripting procedures to generate new forms and structural organisations within architectural design. This project is titled *Branching Morphogenesis*, and was designed by myself and Andrew Lucia with Peter Lloyd Jones and Annette Fierro. It investigates part-to-whole relationships revealed during the generation of branched structures formed in real time by interacting lung endothelial cells. The study and quantification of this network allows for a greater understanding of how variable components might give rise to structured networks in both biology and architecture. The installation materialises five slices in time that capture the predicted force network exerted by interacting cells upon the neighbouring matrix. The time lapses manifest as five vertical, interconnected layers made from over 75,000 cable zip ties. Gallery visitors are invited to walk around and in between the layers and to immerse themselves within an organic and newly created 'Datascape'. Dynamic matrix change is fused with the body and human occupation, all through the constraints of a ready-made.

These ideas were further explored at SG 2010, which was held at the IAAC (Institute for Advanced Architecture of Catalonia) in Barcelona. As one of 10 workshops within the 'Working Prototypes' session, we focused our efforts upon simulation of nonlinear behaviour in cell biological systems and the translation of this behaviour into material systems and fabrication techniques, namely through 3D printing. Our cluster was titled 'Nonlinear Systems Biology and Design'. The workshop situated itself at the nexus between architecture and systems biology to gain insight into dynamic living systems for the development of novel computational design tools and material systems that are at once natural and artificial. This approach examines the nature of nonlinearities, emergent properties and loosely coupled modules that are cardinal features of 'complexity'. Through the analysis of biological design problems in specialised 3D designer microenvironments, students were exposed to new modes of thinking about design ecology through an understanding of how dynamic and environmental feedback specifies structure, function and form.

9

9 'Nonlinear Systems Biology and Design' workshop cluster at SG 2010, IAAC, Barcelona, Spain.
The team from left to right: Peter Lloyd Jones, Jenny E Sabin, Andrew Lucia and Erica Savig.

10 'Nonlinear Systems Biology and Design'
workshop cluster at SG 2010, IAAC, Barcelona,
Spain.
This workshop aimed to give insight into
dynamic living systems for the development of
novel computational design tools and material
systems that are at once natural and artificial.

For the first stage of the workshop, our efforts were focused upon abstracting and extracting the underlying rules and criteria for cellular networking behaviour. We are interested in abstracting behaviours as opposed to static form and cellular shapes. Additionally, we taught the students about the interdependence between environment, code and algorithmic processes. In biology, this is known as reciprocity. Before the start of the workshop, our testing ground included heavy use of our ZCorp 510 colour 3D printer. We were interested in prototyping components, not wholes. I was also interested in using the powder-based printer to rapidly prototype full-scale nonstandard parts instead of representational forms. We launched a 'node competition' with the accepted workshop participants before the start of the workshop.

ZCorp provided generous support in the printing and production of the components before and during the actual workshop. Similar to the working methodologies of Antoni Gaudí, we were interested in bridging behaviours abstracted from biology with material constraints, force transmission and actual fabrication and assembly as a continuous and unfolding loop. In the context of the workshop, there was a constant re-engagement of feedback, where constraints from the actual physical environment informed our virtual computational models. The final Working Prototype engaged a process of nonlinear fabrication informed by biological behaviour and novel fabrication techniques that incorporated 3D printing.

By immersing oneself in complex woven and biological design problems – such as those featured in this essay – and abstracting the inherent relationships of these models into code-driven parametric and associative models, it is possible to gain new insights into how mathematics and nature deal with design issues that feature part-to-whole relationships, complexity and emergent behaviour. As the women of the Weaving Workshop at the Bauhaus pioneered and certainly in the context of my work in LabStudio, collaborative pursuits expose us to new modes of thinking and making within a deeper understanding of form and function in context. This type of immersion is paramount as we continue to navigate, occupy and filter the vast terrain of computational design with increased urgency, criticality, specificity and sensitivity.

10

## REFERENCES

1 Anni Albers, *On Weaving*, Wesleyan University Press (Middletown, CT), 1993.
2 Ferda Kolatan and Jenny E Sabin, *Meander: Variegating Architecture*, Bentley Institute Press (Exton, PA), 2010.

## IMAGES

Figures 1, 2, 4, 5, 6, 7, 8, 9 © Jenny E Sabin; Figure 3 © Artists Space, photo by Whitney Cos; Figure 10 © Shane Burger

# METRICS OF HUMAN EXPERIENCE

## ROLY HUDSON AND MICHAEL WESTLAKE

Roly Hudson has been a participant and tutor at six Smartgeometry (SG) events, most recently at SG 2012 at the Rensselaer Polytechnic Institute, Troy, New York, USA. There he co-led the 'Transgranular Perspiration' workshop cluster, which used embedded sensors to design for and map heat flow in composite ceramic materials. He spent several years travelling and teaching the computational design software GenerativeComponents, which was a key part of early Smartgeometry workshops. Here with architect Michael Westlake of Populous, he explains his approach to developing parametric tools in integrated building practice, towards new ways of defining the geometry of sports experience.

1

Populous have been an early adopter of parametric software. Much of Populous's parametric work has originated in or has been previously presented at Smartgeometry events. The Aviva Stadium in Dublin was the result of the first parametric alliance, between Populous and Dr Roly Hudson, driven by the mandate for an enhanced spectator experience through novel form. Construction-based criteria had to be developed to support this formal approach. A second phase of work developed tools that captured formal guidelines and designer experience of generating stadium seating bowls based on spectator view quality. Following this, a Formula 1 track redevelopment project resulted in a process that captured vehicle crash physics to enable design of spectator facilities in crash zones. This initial use of physical simulation and graphical representation led to an architectural design tool that placed evolutionary structural optimisation on the architect's desktop. The SeatView project described in this chapter draws on this body of knowledge and enables a quantifiable metric of human experience to be used as a driver for design.

## PARAMETRIC DESIGN AT POPULOUS

Plotting the course of parametric activities at Populous over the last eight years indicates a trajectory that goes beyond geometry and emphasises developing tools and techniques that parameterise physical characteristics and now enrich measurement of human experience. This approach was initiated following a professional software workshop in London in late 2005. Populous commissioned a trial geometric definition of the Aviva Stadium with GenerativeComponents (GC), which eventually developed into a core part of the project workflow. The benefits of this approach had significant impact during design and construction. The partnership between academia and practice continued and further projects based on a parametric approach followed. The success of the strategic approach of these projects is in part indebted to the opportunity to informally discuss modelling challenges with leading architectural geometers at SG events. Further to this, the influence of the spirit and conceptual themes of the workshops and conferences must be acknowledged. In particular three aspects span the projects described in this chapter: cross-disciplinary collaborations; multi-application workflows; and embedding analytic data directly within three-dimensional representations.

1 Aviva Stadium, Dublin, Ireland: screen shot of model, 2007.
Generation of assembly construction data. A GenerativeComponents model was created to control design geometry, generate construction data, define structural geometry for analysis and track construction progress.

The Aviva project has been well documented as the first built project that used a commercial parametric design application to integrate design and construction across the project team.[1] Populous and structural engineers Buro Happold shared a parametric definition, custom made with Bentley's GC software.[2] The underlying geometric definition and control methodology benefited directly from informal architectural geometric discussions held at SG 2006 in Cambridge, UK. Implemented early in the design development phase, the shared model was used to refine conceptual geometry, generate data files for structural analysis, produce construction documentation, check proposed facade detailing, produce machine data for fabrication and check

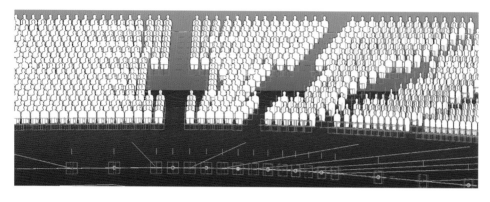

2

3

as-built geometry against the design.[3] The process sought to use advanced pragmatic, parametric modelling to deliver an architectural form that would enhance spectator experience.

## SEATING BOWL MODELLER

During the construction of the Aviva Stadium, work began on a second extensive parametric project, the stadium Seating Bowl Modeller (SBM) tool. SBM served as a vehicle to capture both formal design guidelines[4] and many years of combined experience of architects at Populous. The basis of this tool is the c-value method[5] which is used to define the seating bowl section. In addition to the c-value (which indicates spectator view quality), SBM also included egress as a driver for design. Geometric setting out of access and the resulting changes to stadium capacity was controlled by parameters defining evacuation times. SBM is therefore an application that embraces occupant experience at two levels: safety and quality of view. Inspired by current approaches showcased at SG, SBM provided a colour scale representation of view quality bound directly to the design geometry. A customised version of the SBM tool was used to undertake a series of design studies for the London 2012 Olympic Stadium.

## RACE TRACK MODELLER

The Race Track Modeller (RTM) tool[6] combined GC and a game engine to simulate driving around proposed Formula 1 track designs. Performance data from the simulation is combined with real data acquired from analysis of vehicle-mounted accident data recorders (ADRs). The output of the tool is a graphical representation of simulated stopping positions of vehicles that have lost control and left the track. This information directly informs the design of motor racing facilities. From the point of view of the spectator, the zoning of spectator facilities can be located closest to the most exciting parts of the race. From

2 Seating Bowl Modeller, 2008.
Screen shot showing placeholder spectators generated within the model. SBM captured both formal design guidelines and designer experience in a parametric tool driven by view quality and egress.

3 Aviva Stadium, Dublin, Ireland, 2010.
View of the north end of the stadium, which was the first built project that used a commercial parametric design application to integrate design and construction across the project team.

4 Seating Bowl Modeller, 2008.
Analytic output from software. Colour scale and numeric representation of c-value around the stadium is bound to the bowl geometry, enabling intuitive design decision making.

5

5 Silverstone circuit, Northamptonshire,
UK, 2011.
Track and spectator facilities around pit lane.
A customised multi-platform parametric
workflow enabled lead architects Populous to
develop a challenging new track and pit-lane
building.

6

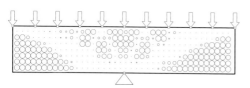 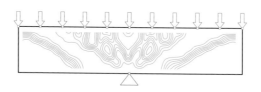

6 Interactive evolutionary structural desktop
design tool, 2010.
Graphical output from software. Holes in under-
stressed material and surface height field from
over-stressed zones are two possible techniques
for post-processing a structural data field.

**7 SeatView, 2012.**
Analysis method applied to lecture hall/cinema/
theatre configuration. Blue represents the
projected area of screen/proscenium and red
the projected area of view occlusion.

**8 SeatView, 2012.**
Analytic representation of data bound to 3D
model. Blue represents the a-value (projected
area of pitch) and red the projected area of
pitch occlusion.

7

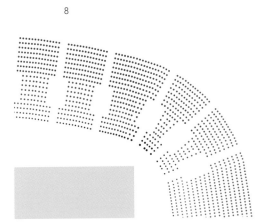

8

the point of view of the driver, various track configurations can
be tested to find the most challenging. To place spectators in
dangerous run-off zones (the area where vehicles are expected to
stop after losing control and leaving the track), RTM enables the
positioning and specification of crash barriers and appropriate
track surface material selection. RTM is a reflection of ideas that
were apparent in SG 2009 where data sets, hardware and various
software applications were combined in highly customised
workflows. The RTM was developed and successfully tested during
the redevelopment of Silverstone Race Track.

## INTERACTIVE EVOLUTIONARY STRUCTURES
The last project in this trajectory, popeso, integrated an
evolutionary structural optimisation (ESO) routine with custom
interactive tools for visualisation and control within a modelling
application. ESO is a design method based on the concept of
gradually adding or removing material from a structure depending
on stress patterns determined by analysis. The modified structure
is reanalysed and the process repeated for several 'generations'.
Using popeso, the designer can be interactively engaged in
specifying under-stressed (inefficient) or over-stressed material by
determining parameters that control the post-processing of a data
field. This data is the result of a novel structural analysis process
involving both finite element analysis and dynamic relaxation. The
tool implements core concepts that have recurred at SG events;
interactive structural exploration that provides conceptual geometry
and models for further structural analysis and physical prototyping.
In the context of parametric projects at Populous, popeso extended
the capacity to graphically interpret physical phenomena.

## THE SEATVIEW PROJECT
The objective of our current work is to critically revisit the SBM
project and to draw on the accumulated skill set, strategic
knowledge and technology in order to enhance the way spectator
experience can be used in design. The SeatView project's first aim
is to incorporate a richer measure of view quality into the design
of high-capacity tiered seating facilities. Secondly the goal is to
develop a further set of metrics of spectator experience for use as
design drivers. The current method specified by design guidelines
stems directly from a method for designing auditoria documented
by John Scott Russell in 1838. The section is defined using
sightlines that are perpendicular to the shoulders of the spectator
and constructed from the spectator's eyes to a static focal point
(the closest point on the sideline in field sports).

The existing method is two-dimensional; it does not acknowledge
the three-dimensional experience or the dynamic nature of sport.
The movement of spectators' eyes, heads and shoulders during
a game is not taken into account. The c-value method does not
account for height above the playing surface which provides a less
obtuse viewing angle of the pitch plane. Calculation of c-values
around the stadium provides information of how this metric varies
around the stadium but does not reflect ergonomics or three-
dimensional view quality. Our approach begins with the individual

spectator rather than an abstract section. We re-create a version of the spectator's view using their eye position as a camera location and the centre of the playing area as a view target location. Evaluating the area projected onto the spectator's viewing plane provides a new metric of view quality which is three-dimensional.[7]

Our goal is to develop an application that allows designers to generate alternative design proposals and assesses the occupant experience of these by graphical and statistical comparison. The statistical approach suggests a further objective that would enable the designer to select and weight specific criteria and run a goal-seeking routine to determine parameter values.

### SEATVIEW: TOOLS, WORKFLOW AND SOFTWARE

SeatView analysis runs as an application plug-in written in c#.net for Rhino 4.0. The plug-in requires a set of points defining spectator eye locations, a surface representing the playing area and surfaces representing heads and shoulders of other spectators. The generation of geometry and analysis take place independently. The geometry is either manually modelled, generated using Rhino's Grasshopper plug-in or created with our custom standalone application for defining seating geometry. This workflow leaves the design and evaluation process open to design teams operating with a range of computational and modelling capacity.

All the numeric data collected by the analysis routine can be output to a spreadsheet. The plug-in generates a folder structure for storing and comparing data from a series of proposed stadium designs in spreadsheet format. A summary spreadsheet is automatically created that cross-references the values from each set of variant design data files. The summary spreadsheet is set up to indicate and compare basic statistics derived from data measured in each design option. This provides the designer with access to hard data which may later be combined with proposed geometry or used for further statistical analysis.

### METRICS OF OCCUPANT EXPERIENCE

Parametric design enables exciting formal architectural possibilities through rationalised construction, speedy evaluation of multiple alternatives and refinement of physical building attributes. Adding the capacity to study experiential qualities shifts the design focus towards what is often missing in contemporary architecture: the occupier. The underlying algorithms implemented in SeatView and the possibilities for incorporating such a range of occupant-based metrics indicates great potential for parametric design of space to be driven from the perspective of the user. We urge other parametric designers not to limit modelling to evaluation of the physical performance of proposed designs but also to incorporate metrics that indicate the quality of occupant experience.

The success and developmental direction of SeatView draws directly on the trajectory of the projects that preceded it. The core issues that have informed our strategic approach to computation include the cross-disciplinary, multi-platform and bound analytic

9

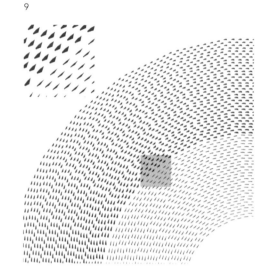

9 SeatView, 2012.
Composite graphic of 18,000 spectator views. The graphic shows differences in the visible green area (projected pitch) between upper and lower seating tiers, with detail of the transition between tiers.

techniques that have emerged in the first decade of SG. We now see great potential in applying these approaches to scenarios where building geometry results from metrics of human experience.

## REFERENCES

1 Roly Hudson, Paul Shepherd and David Hines, 'Aviva Stadium: A Case Study in Integrated Parametric Design', *International Journal of Architectural Computing*, Vol 9, No 2, 2011, pp 187–203; Paul Shepherd, Roly Hudson and David Hines, 'Aviva Stadium: A Parametric Success', *International Journal of Architectural Computing*, Vol 9, No 2, 2011, pp 167–85.

2 Paul Shepherd and Roly Hudson, 'Parametric Definition of Lansdowne Road Stadium', in *International Association of Shell and Spatial Structures*, Vol 1, CD ROM (Venice, Italy), 2007; Roly Hudson, 'Frameworks for Practical Parametric Design in Architecture', in Helmut Pottmann, Michael Hofer and Axel Kilian (eds), *Advances in Architectural Geometry 2008*, conference proceedings, Vienna University of Technology, pp 17–20.

3 Roly Hudson, 'Knowledge Acquisition and Parametric Model Development', *International Journal of Architectural Computing*, Vol 6, No 4, 2008, pp 435–51; Roly Hudson, 'Parametric Development of Problem Descriptions', *International Journal of Architectural Computing*, Vol 7, No 2, 2009, pp 199–216.

4 Geraint John and Kit Campbell, *Handbook of Sports and Recreational Building Design*, second edition, The Architectural Press (Oxford), 1995, p 68; Geraint John, Rod Sheard and Ben Vickery, *Stadia, Fourth Edition: A Design and Development Guide*, Taylor & Francis (Oxford), 2007.

5 HMSO, *Guide to Safety at Sports Grounds*, fifth edition, Stationery Office (Northwich), 2008, p 109.

6 Roly Hudson, Drew MacDonald and Mark Humphreys, 'Race Track Modeller: Developing an Iterative Design Workflow Combining a Game Engine and Parametric Design', *Parametricism (SPC) ACADIA Regional 2011 Conference Proceedings*, 2011, pp 175–83.

7 Alan Tansey and Michael Westlake, *A Better View*, research fellowship – internal investigation and report funded by Populous, 2010.

## IMAGES

Figures 1, 2, 4 © Roly Hudson, Populous; Figure 7 © Roly Hudson; Figures 8, 9 © Michael Westlake and Roly Hudson, Populous; Figure 3 © Populous, photo by Donal Murphy; Figure 5 © Darren Heath. www.darrenheath.com; Figure 6 © David Hines, Populous

# INTERACTING WITH THE MODEL

## NEIL KATZ, WITH BESS KRIETEMEYER AND TOBIAS SCHWINN

Architect Neil Katz first attended Smartgeometry (SG) in 2006 and has participated in and led workshops at many subsequent events including SG 2007 with Tobias Schwinn and SG 2012 with Bess Krietemeyer. Katz brings a highly valuable practice perspective to the workshops, as he has worked at Skidmore, Owings & Merrill (SOM) for many years using computational methods to tackle architectural problems, drawing on more than 25 years of experience with algorithmic and parametric modelling. Interested in everything from intricate tiling patterns to environmental simulation to the structural systems of skyscrapers, Katz's enthusiasm and expertise add much to the SG community.

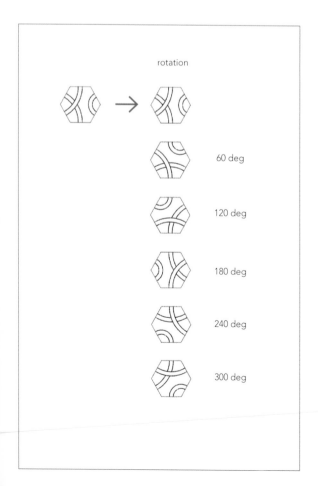

Parametric thinking has always been the defining factor in my work since studying architecture at Pratt Institute (where my primary mentor was Haresh Lalvani) and throughout my professional work at SOM. I define 'parametrics' as a logical method of generating forms with governing rules, variables and relationships, with a very prevalent influence of pure and simple geometry. My frequent advice to students, colleagues and myself is to *start simply and add complexity* or, *start simply and simplify even more*. An intriguing aspect of models created parametrically is their apparent complexity, yet if we examine how they are generated, we can be surprised at the simplicity of the process. Some excellent examples of this are the Mandelbrot set[2] and cellular automata, as described by Stephen Wolfram.[3] Similarly, my own tiling studies demonstrate how complexity can emerge from very simple rules of rotation and translation. As parametric frameworks grow in complexity, maintaining simplicity within the governing rules becomes essential.

My primary method of implementing parametric modelling in my work has been through scripting, which requires an abstraction of a design model. The design possibilities with scripting can range enormously, from creating a simple collection of application commands to a sophisticated set of rules. It can incorporate tests and decisions, iteration and recursion, and even communicate with other applications or data. Although some fear that scripting relinquishes control of a design, in my opinion it provides a different kind of control, one which has a very positive impact on the aesthetics, the design process, and especially the performance of a project. In many modelling tools, the designer will directly and intuitively interact with the model, as a sculptor might work with clay. In this process 'rules' are implicit to the designer but are not explicitly defined in the model. In contrast, scripting requires designers to make these rules very explicit. Many view this as an expansive design approach for creating, exploring and interacting with multiple information sets and scales.

While still studying in the early 1980s, I began working with SOM where I learned to use their proprietary software (DRAFT and AES (Architecture & Engineering Series)). At the time AES was being developed, computational power was much more limited than it is today, but the software was very flexible and (to me) intuitive. It also allowed what we now generally refer to as scripting. Scripting with AES particularly made repetitive tasks extremely time-efficient and it ensured a consistency in the model. As an interdisciplinary firm working in a highly collaborative environment, SOM embraced the AES software – it was designed to facilitate collaboration.

### PERSONAL INTERACTIONS: INSIDE THE MODEL
The 2006 Smartgeometry workshop (SG 2006) assembled a small world of designers interested in methods similar to

1 Neil Katz, tiling study, 2011.

On the left side, we see the tile edges, and can verify that each tile is identical; on the right side the edges have been removed, and the identical (simple!) pattern suggests one that is more complex.

1

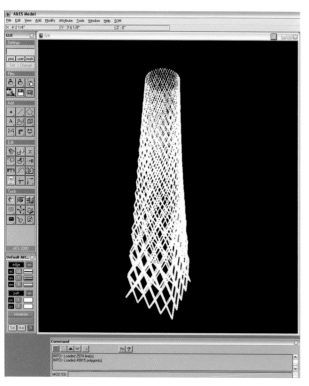

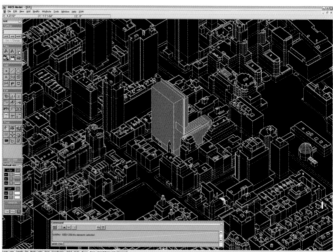

2 SOM, screenshots of AES interface, mid-
1980s.
Parametric tower study (left), which featured
a transforming tower with an external diagrid
structure, and generated with a script. Massing
study (right), showing our project in a context
model.

my own, and this was extremely exciting for me. Held in Cambridge, UK, the workshop was largely focused on the use of GenerativeComponents (GC), a parametric CAD software developed by Bentley Systems. GC was new for me, and, as required, I attended a training workshop at Stevens Institute in Hoboken, New Jersey in preparation. While I'd been collaborating with my colleagues at the office, for the first time I realised that I was also very isolated from other parametric thinkers. Many of those people have become coworkers and friends, including Kyle Steinfeld who was the instructor at that workshop.

Working with command files in AES, AutoCAD and Lisp scripts, I was comfortable interacting with two very different representations of a model: a 'graphic' representation in which the model could be designed visually; and the 'instructions' representation, the script itself. In addition, GC also offered a third representation mode: a 'relationships' diagram, or tree, which symbolically and graphically identified how parts of the model reference and depend on each other.

When I applied to attend the SG workshop and conference I was working on Lotte Tower, a competition for a super-tall tower in Seoul. During the competition stage the design and structures teams were collaborating closely, requiring abstractions of the design model to share information. The tower transformed in shape from a square plan at the base to a circle at the top, and had an architecturally expressed diagrid structural system. Since it was a problem I was very familiar with and for which I had developed various parametric modelling strategies and iterations, I thought it would be a challenging case study for GC.

In addressing the complexity of sharing abstract information, GC provided an excellent 'new' feature: it exposed the variables in the model, making them very easy to see and to modify. Previously, in order to change a variable with my scripts, I needed a text editor to modify lines of code with those variables (which I was comfortable with, but most of my colleagues and collaborators were not). The change was not immediately reflected in the model, so in order to see any new results, I needed to run it again and generate a new model. Although time-consuming, there is underlying value by interacting with the model in this way. The fundamental knowledge gained from this intimate design process reveals the power of building on simplicity.

So perhaps we can ask the question: 'What is the model?' Is it the graphic or virtual model of the geometry of a design or idea? Or can it be a more abstract representation: the script itself, a set of rules, a spreadsheet? Building Information Modelling (BIM) typically defines a building model as a database, where drawings are not static representations but live reports of the data in the 'model'. Perhaps even the three-dimensional 'model' can be a live report of a more abstract representation of the design. Working with scripting and GC illustrates two levels of interacting with the model: at a higher level we can describe the rules and

3 SOM, Lotte Tower, Seoul, South Korea, 2005.
The design for a super-tall tower in Korea features a transformation in form from a square to a circle, and a diagrid external structure.

4

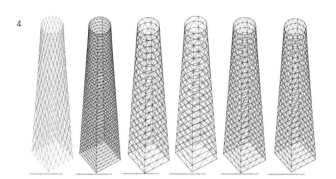

4 SOM, Lotte Tower, Seoul, South Korea, 2005.
At SG 2006 I explored design variations of
Lotte Tower that responded to structural and
architectural requirements. Shown here are
parametrically generated diagrid variations
for the building modelled with AutoCAD and
Autolisp.

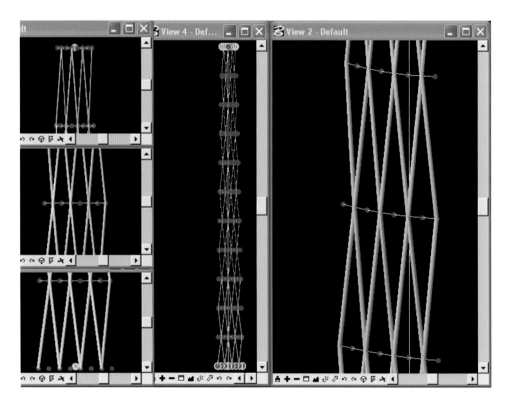

5a

relationships, and at a lower level we can describe how to use these rules to create, visualise and modify our model.

When I talk about my work, I often describe a process of solving a problem. I believe this process is independent of a particular software or programming language, or even whether we use a computer at all. Depending on the problem, the process might be faster with computational tools, and depending on the tools the process might vary slightly. But the process most importantly reflects a way of thinking about solving the problem. In presentations I often forget to mention the particular tools I used, and often get asked that question. The tools are less important than the process and intent.

### COLLABORATIVE INTERACTIONS: MULTI-SCALAR WORKFLOWS

Because SG 2007 took place in New York, more people from our SOM/NY office were able to attend, including Ajmal Aqtash, Kat Park and Tobias Schwinn. Our goal for this workshop was to use GC in a collaborative way, reflecting methods and tools that we use at our office and in our practice. DRAFT and AES were designed with collaboration in mind. When we began using AutoCAD at SOM in the early 1990s, however, the general paradigm was that one person worked on drawings one at a time, as if by hand. We created a 'shell' around the basic AutoCAD application to be able to work with our building information model in a more flexible and collaborative way.

Within our SOM group, we challenged ourselves to create a collaborative environment with GC. We divided ourselves into two teams: the *massing* team was exploring the form of the tower (a hypothetical project we created for the workshop) by using algorithmic and optimisation techniques to create a form that met certain criteria that we established; the *articulation* team also used algorithmic and optimisation techniques to develop a skin for that massing model, which could continuously adapt to iterative designs of the massing. This parametric linking of multi-scalar geometries required us to think about how the tools we were using supported our process and workflow. It also necessitated the setup of a virtual network for interacting with and exchanging data (something we take for granted at the office).

We established design criteria that required the skin to respond to the location and movement of the sun. We wanted both the form of the tower (massing and orientation) as well as the articulation (aperture size and orientation) to respond to this variable condition. While one design variable affected both aspects of the model, multiple design variables could also have been explored and specified as parameters, such as views, wind, aperture size and floor area constraints.

Working collaboratively has become increasingly important, and in some ways more difficult. With DRAFT/AES, collaborative interactions with the model occurred within the office using tools and formats designed to facilitate data exchange for modelling,

5b

5a and 5b Modelling Lotte Tower in GenerativeComponents (GC) at SG 2006, Cambridge, UK.
Views of the parametric model.

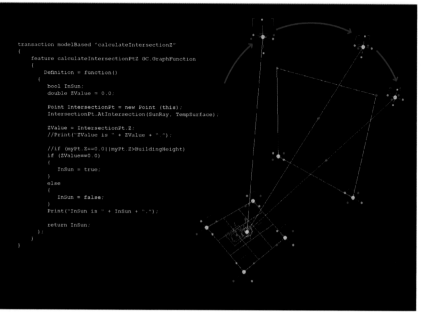

```
transaction modelBased "calculateIntersectionZ"
{
    feature calculateIntersectionPtZ GC.GraphFunction
    {
        Definition = function()
        {
            bool InSun;
            double ZValue = 0.0;

            Point IntersectionPt = new Point (this);
            IntersectionPt.AtIntersection(SunRay, TempSurface);

            ZValue = IntersectionPt.Z;
            //Print("ZValue is " + ZValue + ".");

            //if (myPt.Z==0.0||myPt.Z>BuildingHeight)
            if (ZValue==0.0)
            {
                InSun = true;
            }
            else
            {
                InSun = false;
            }
            Print("InSun is " + InSun + ".");

            return InSun;
        };
    }
}
```

6

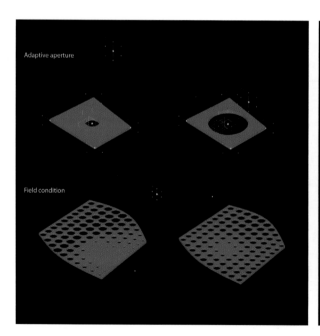

Adaptive aperture

Field condition

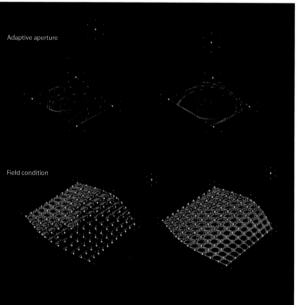

Adaptive aperture

Field condition

7

analysis and visualisation. When we worked with people outside the office, we generally collaborated in a traditional way (with physical drawings). Now we share data intensely with many people and among varied applications, which have their own formats and appropriate levels of detail.

When we consider these design collaborative interactions as paradigms, the question of defining the 'model' becomes a more and more difficult one to address. What are its boundaries and how is it characterised? Who 'owns' the model? The 'model' is no longer a single entity, but aspects of it can be manipulated by individuals with different concerns, criteria and tools. And with such flexibility and potential for complexity, how many scales of design criteria can be addressed, and how many disciplines can participate?

**IMMERSIVE INTERACTIONS: COLLABORATION BEYOND THE COMPUTER**
In previous years I was involved in SG workshops only as a participant, but in 2012 in Troy, New York, I participated as a workshop leader, or 'champion', where I was able to experience and help shape the event's evolution. The theme of our cluster was 'Bio-Responsive Building Envelopes', a proposal submitted by Anna Dyson and Bess Krietemeyer of the Center for Architecture, Science & Ecology (CASE). Other cluster 'champions' of our group included Sam Seifert, Satoshi Kiyono and collaborator Jim Krietemeyer.

The 'Bio-Responsive Building Envelopes' cluster stemmed from a research area at CASE that focuses on the transfer of emerging display technologies to a dynamic building envelope called the Electroactive Dynamic Daylighting System (EDDS). The EDDS embeds electropolymeric materials within the surfaces of an insulated glazing unit, creating programmable patterns that can respond to individual aesthetic preferences and exterior bioclimatic conditions. While environmental performance was an overarching criterion, our cluster experimented with a fully immersive design environment for exploring and testing information-rich patterning techniques. Simultaneously integrating both environmental data feedback loops and participant-generated interactions into the parametric design process was the primary focus.

Our cluster used a custom software – initially written by Bess for her PhD research – to simulate the bio-responsive building envelope (EDDS) and the immersive interior environment. The software was further developed by several collaborators throughout the workshop. One of the major focuses of the workshop was to interact with the dynamics of the simulated facade in a highly experiential way. This included designing and testing patterns that morphed over time based on environmental conditions or the preferences of individuals. Several pattern 'types' were developed based on algorithmic rules, each with their own set of parameters that could be modified by participants. For example, one pattern type was based on an 'image upload' function; another was designed as a 'solar tracking' layer, intended to dynamically adjust its pattern to block direct insolation in real time. To ensure that the pre-coded patterns would provide plenty of exploration

6 Custom-developed, project-independent GC component checking for shadows cast by adjacent buildings, explored by SOM at SG 2007, New York, USA.
From left to right: output console listing values of Boolean InSun variable; imperative representation of the model; interactive graphical model.

7 Study with hypothetical facade components responding to solar position and shading by adjacent buildings, explored by SOM at SG 2007, New York, USA.
A simple component with adaptive aperture to respond to varying levels of insolation and components incorporating recursive subdivision and aperture as a means for adaptation.

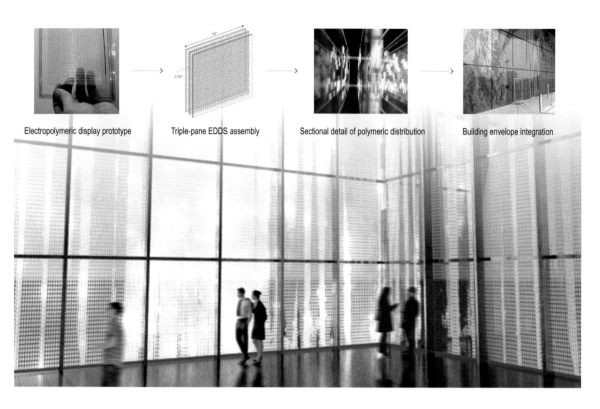

Electropolymeric display prototype · Triple-pane EDDS assembly · Sectional detail of polymeric distribution · Building envelope integration

9

8 Experiments using a proposed Electroactive
Dynamic Daylighting System (EDDS), prepared
for SG 2012, Rensselaer Polytechnic Institute,
Troy, New York, USA.
The EDDS is a dynamic bioresponsive building
envelope technology developed by researchers
at the Rensselaer Center for Architecture
Science and Ecology (CASE).

9 'Bio-Responsive Building Envelopes'
workshop cluster at SG 2012, Rensselaer
Polytechnic Institute, Troy, New York, USA.
Participants design and develop custom
patterns for the simulated bio-responsive
building envelope according to aesthetic
preferences and energy performance for
multiple times of day and year.

space, a wide range of parameters were available for modification. Despite the thousands of iterations readily available to explore, many participants were still eager and very adept at designing and coding their own. We incorporated physical interactivity using Kinect devices, which caused the simulated facade to shift perspective as participants moved around. We also varied the movement of responsive patterns using this technique, tracking people and creating viewing portals within the patterns.

What is our model in this paradigm? It is an immersive, dynamic and interactive environment, relaying information back to the designer on multiple levels. Three-dimensional lighting effects, performance feedback and interactive response combine for a definition of 'model space' that moves beyond the computer screen. Boundaries of the model are blurred as interaction with the design process is becoming much more experiential.

## THE EVOLUTION OF THE MODEL

In the 25+ years I've been working with algorithmic and parametric modelling, I've seen many aspects of this field evolve. Tools – software and hardware – are more powerful, sophisticated and intuitive. Complex digital designs created using software can now be physically realised through advanced fabrication technology, streamlining the design and evaluation process. More people are able to access these tools and participate in a process of design which was previously limited to early-adopters.

Evolving interaction methods continue to redefine our notion of the 'model' and our understanding of 3D modelling space. Collaborative workflows and immersive environments generate exciting opportunities to simultaneously design for multiple scales of performance criteria while emphasising the spatial and temporal experience of a particular design. Through these techniques we are interested in not only the physical aspect of our models, but also the behaviour and performance relationships among different aspects of the model. In this sense, 'visualising' the model does not just represent an image of the design's appearance, but it is an understanding of these non-visible characteristics. As evidenced by SOM's Lotte project, where Kat Park created a platform-independent master model to facilitate collaborative design,[4] our 'models' today reflect these changes through the enormous capabilities of our tools and in our attitudes about how we work. The 'evolution of the model' is not just in the model itself, but in how it is used and by whom. This evolution is exemplified in the projects and experiences described in this chapter.

SG workshops and conferences, among others, have reflected this evolution, and surely influenced it as well. Buildings designed in this paradigm can embody a visual complexity and performative dynamism not previously achievable. Perhaps more significantly, these buildings are able to respond to fluctuating environmental and human conditions in ways that were not possible before. New subfields have sprouted, focusing these

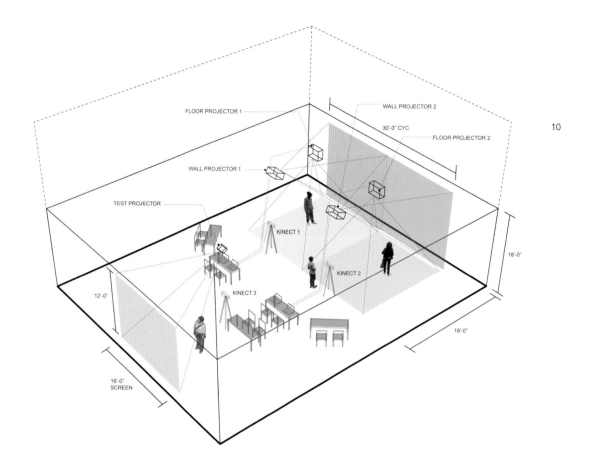

FLOOR PROJECTOR 1

WALL PROJECTOR 2

30'-0" CYC

FLOOR PROJECTOR 2

WALL PROJECTOR 1

TEST PROJECTOR

KINECT 1

18'-0"

KINECT 2

12'-0"

KINECT 3

18'-0"

16'-0"
SCREEN

10 'Bio-Responsive Building Envelopes' workshop cluster at SG 2012, Rensselaer Polytechnic Institute, Troy, New York, USA. The physical setup for the immersive design environment links multiple projectors, infrared motion sensors, and visualisation and analysis software.

11 'Bio-Responsive Building Envelopes' workshop cluster at SG 2012, Rensselaer Polytechnic Institute, Troy, New York, USA. Participant interactivity is incorporated using Kinect motion sensors and overlaps with individual pattern design to create emergent visual effects. Above, stills of a viewing 'portal' as it tracks a participant and opens locally for views; below, stills showing how the bioresponsive building envelope blends a solar responsive pattern and unique user interaction.

design processes in fascinating ways, including emergence, optimisation, biomimetics and robotics, among others.

Personally, I find it fascinating to work in this manner – to design in a slightly abstract way, or, in other words, to design the rules which generate the form. I find it extremely exciting when, as a result of a script, I am surprised at the result – I get a model which I didn't expect! This is also one of the most powerful aspects of this process – to be able to explore new possibilities in design, with tools and processes that facilitate this explorative experience.

## ACKNOWLEDGEMENTS

The SG 2012 workshop would not have been possible without the support of Rensselaer Polytechnic Institute, Skidmore, Owings & Merrill LLP, and the New York State Energy Research and Development Authority (NYSERDA) in collaboration with New Visual Media Group (NVMG). Many thanks to Robert Aish for his support and wisdom, and to other SG mentors and organisers who have made the workshops and conferences wonderful and inspiring experiences.

## REFERENCES

1 Benoit Mandelbrot, *The (Mis)Behavior of Markets*, Basic Books (New York, NY) 2004, p 125.
2 Benoit Mandelbrot, *The Fractal Geometry of Nature*, WH Freeman & Company (Oxford), 1982.
3 Stephen Wolfram, *A New Kind of Science*, Wolfram Media (Champaign, IL), 2002.
4 Kat Park and Nicholas Holt, 'Parametric Design Process of a Complex Building In Practice Using Programmed Code As Master Model', in *International Journal of Architectural Computing*, Vol 8, No 3, 2010, pp 359–76.

## TEXT

## IMAGES

# RESPONSIVE DESIGN:
## TOWARDS AN ECOLOGY OF OBJECTS AND PEOPLE

ANDRE CHASZAR,
ANTON SAVOV,
PETER LIEBSCH AND
SASCHA BOHNENBERGER

The 'MicroSynergetics' cluster at the Smartgeometry (SG) workshops in 2012 combined the usual variety of parametric modelling software, but also linked these to physical actuation to create a landscape of colourful machines. The parametric model became dynamic and the physical model similarly became a dynamic entity. These workflows not only suggest the ability of architects to create design tools to explore dynamic buildings, but also that through linking digital models and the building itself by utilizing sensors and actuators, the digital model has the potential to remain relevant and continue evolving beyond the design stage and into the life of the building. Here the leaders of this SG cluster explain some of their inspiration, theory, and some exemplary projects from this cluster's work.

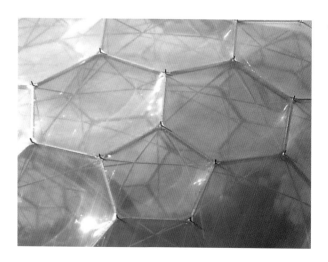

1

1 Grimshaw, Eden Project, Cornwall, UK, 2000.
The inflated ETFE cushion components adjust their insulating performance through changing air pressure to control the interior environment.

2 Att Poomtangon and Anton Savov, *Keep Something for a Rainy Day*, Venice Art Biennale, Italy, 2009.
The interactive installation achieves microclimatic adjustment of humidity through direct visitor engagement. Water is pneumatically pressurised via pedal pumps.

For us as designers, architects and engineers, perhaps the two most significant changes in the last 10 years are the merging of digital and physical and the omnipresence of information. The environments and materials we are designing are being embedded with ubiquitous computing capabilities. Furthermore the data generated and gathered is being stored, processed and communicated through increasingly open sharing platforms.

While early in the use of computers in architecture one needed to 'construct' a virtual model as a representation of a geometry or material property, nowadays we no longer need to remain in a digital realm to use the capabilities computers offer us. Computation or the 'cyber' has entered our world through various embedded devices, sensors, communication and collaboration platforms and social networks, all of which link the physical and digital worlds.

Through involvement in Smartgeometry (SG) we experienced the shift from a software training workshop towards full-scale prototyping, linking digital designs with their physical instantiations. In this article we reflect on some of those changes and look to emerging trends from our perspectives in practice and research.

### DESIGN PROCESS
Our work pursues interactive technological and collaborative social synergies. We create dynamic architecture using dynamic modelling environments and responsive physical artefacts. The ability of these modelling environments to feed back to the physical world through sensor-triggered interfaces allows us to implement prototypes with customisable material performances. Cloud-based sharing and processing of models and sensor data let us test real-time negotiation of environmental parameters. By combining these engagement levels we establish an inclusive ecology in the design workflow. The interactive technological synergies take us to the realm of *augmented composites*.

2

To explore this challenge, we brought our expertise together in a series of workshops. These culminated with one in February 2012 at Städelschule Architecture Class (SAC) in Frankfurt entitled 'Pasta in Bed', and another called 'MicroSynergetics' at the SG 2012 event held at the Rensselaer Polytechnic Institute, Troy, New York, USA. The results were a set of experiments and installations that aimed to squarely tackle this issue of interactive technological-material-social synergy via multiple perspectives and approaches.

### AFFORDABLE CUSTOMISATION OF MATERIAL PERFORMANCE
The invention of physical building components with desired characteristics often occurs by adapting materials and technologies 'alien' to the industry. As seen in the Eden Project (2000) in Cornwall, UK – an enclosed biosphere comprising interlinked domes – Grimshaw pushed the boundaries of ETFE (Ethylene Tetrafluoroethylene) foil, resulting in the icosahedral geodesic skin of hexagonal pillow-shaped components with up to 11-metre diameters.

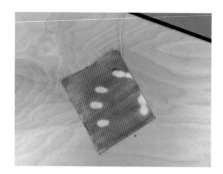

3

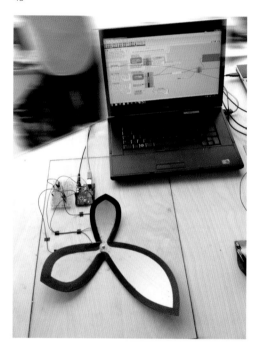

4a

4b

3 Thermochromic ink swatch on paper from the 'MicroSynergetics' workshop cluster at SG 2012, Rensselaer Polytechnic Institute, Troy, New York, USA.
Heat-sensitive pigments contribute to visual feedback on time and force of physical contact, as well as temperature.

4a and 4b 'Interactive flower' component, designed and made by Tore Banke for the 'MicroSynergetics' workshop cluster at SG 2012, Rensselaer Polytechnic Institute, Troy, New York, USA.
Conductive paint on veneer senses proximity and actuates shape-memory alloy (SMA) via Arduino and laptop.

The constant introduction of materials coming from other disciplines is readjusting the meaning of materiality in architecture and indicates a shift in the perception of the artefact. Materials are evolving from facilitating single functions to being multifunctional. Furthermore they also begin to enable in designers a new awareness of the built environment and the user. We propose a holistic approach whereby material is both physically and digitally surveyed. Design constraints are developed by the resulting knowledge aiming to create consciousness of the material among its designers as well as users. This allows discovering and combining intrinsic and extrinsic properties of different substances by means of simultaneous crafting and analysis. Thus the designer becomes familiar with parameters of the resulting 'augmented composite' to utilise its characteristics as design drivers.

### 'INTELLIGENT' COMPONENTS

Pursuing performance inherent to materials, we have been building on our own work, starting with a more mechanical approach as in Anton Savov's project *Keep Something for a Rainy Day* from the Venice Biennale 2009. This project achieved interactive microclimatic adjustment of humidity with water pneumatically pressurised through pedal pumps to create fog.

Such material performances can be combined into 'augmented composites' that offer functions such as sensing, actuating and interacting with external data. Those composites are by no means limited to the familiar plastic and fibre composites. For example, conductive paint can replace motion sensors, shape-memory alloys (SMAs) can be combined with regular building components, and phosphorescent/light-emitting or colour-changing materials can be used to communicate with the user in a passive as well as active manner.

In our work we take advantage of creating tailor-made components that can be assembled to fulfil specific tasks uniquely for a project. An example from our SG workshop used conductive ink to create a proximity sensor. Applicable to various materials in several layers, conductive paint creates its own magnetic field when current flows through it. This field interacts with the field surrounding the human body. When a certain programmed proximity is reached, the conductive paint closes the circuit,

5a

5b

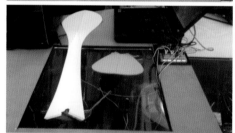

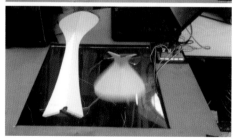

5a and 5b 'Perpetuum-mobile' component, designed and made by Stan Carroll for the 'MicroSynergetics' workshop cluster at SG 2012, Rensselaer Polytechnic Institute, Troy, New York, USA.

Folded paper 'arms' move to cover and uncover light sensors whose actuation via muscle wires depends on the measured light levels. The two components' movements result in aperiodic behaviour due to slight differences in sensor calibration and wire reactivity.

triggering the component. Another installation at SAC used metal mesh for the same purpose, actuating SMA wires to change the shape of a flexible enclosure.

The recognition that the built environment is a dynamic system rather than a static one poses the question: do we need to change the way we design architecture and the design methods we use? Materials that change their shape when heated, or solids that become liquid under external forces are examples of a material's regular mechanical properties, while a 'solid-state phase-changing' material can 'remember' its original shape and will therefore always return to its original form or appearance. To fully understand the behaviour of solid-state phase-changing materials, the physical experiments were extended with parametric and computational tooling.

## DYNAMIC SYSTEMS AND MODELLING

The potential for dynamism has existed since the outset of SG due to its foundations in parametric-associative modelling. While in the past, the explicit focus has been on exploring alternative designs, there has always been an implicit possibility that the alternatives produced could transform in time.

The concept of change over time had always been present but limited to the activity of the designers building and 'exercising' models. The normal, direct manipulation via parametric or scripted models to influence the resulting form takes place in time with a continuous, successive loop of observation and modification by the designer. This is partially overcome by a 'batch' strategy to produce a series of alternatives in a short time, achieved either by varying one or more parameters over some range or by an automation strategy with pre-coded preferences. For example, 'fitness functions' allow the selection of preferred versions. But in all of these cases the majority of versions, or 'states', remain virtual. In the exploration of variations, only one option is finally selected. Collections of similar forms arrayed over some collection of spatial locations also hint at dynamism. While the time element is missing after the exploration process has ended, traces are left via differences both visible and invisible occurring at different locations – thus implying potential for temporal change.

6

7

There has been less attention in practice to dynamic potential. Very few projects offer opportunities to realise designs incorporating mechanisms more complex than simple hinging, sliding, rotation or telescoping. The trend towards 'solid-state' behaviours, such as electrochromic control of glass translucency or thermal- and humidity-driven shape changes, addresses reliability concerns by avoiding moving parts or at least shifting the locus of movement to granular, cellular and molecular levels. In our workshops we tested how to design and operate interactive, dynamic systems using responsive materials in a participatory way, simulating interactive material and system behaviour with sensors which could feed back to the models as well as using models to drive physical systems' behaviour.

## USER AND SENSOR INTERFACING

'Augmented composites' are able to respond and react to changes in the surrounding environment in a controlled way. Wide application of sensors in the building industry started with the engineering practice of building 'health' monitoring, achieved by placing sensors in spaces and components, gathering data on their performance over time, and thus informing maintenance and subsequent projects. In the early stages of user-driven interaction the dynamic change and communication of an object was achieved by mediating light. A prominent example is the D-Tower (2003) in Doetinchem, Netherlands, designed by Nox and realised in collaboration with Bollinger + Grohmann (B+G). The BIX installation at the Kunsthaus Graz, another project of B+G with Peter Cook and Colin Fournier, also demonstrates interactive and informational potentials for building facades.

Making use of the latest developments in the field of micro-sensors, testing setups are becoming financially affordable and allow the designer to collect real-time data. Sensor techniques and microprocessors can be utilised to track how materials and design elements respond to external influences. With these sensors the creation of real-time feedback systems reacting to changes in material properties is becoming feasible.

In our workshops, we tested the combination of physical and digital data manipulation in parametric models such as one representing a roof opening directly linked to a microcontroller, light sensor and SMAs where skylights were controlled by light intensity. In this setup we now have two functions: first, the light sensor controlling the digital model, and second, an override mechanism that supports the particular needs of the user. By introducing remote control via a programmable interface designed in TouchOSC, the control of the skylight is handed back to the user. Sensors can thus complement material systems' 'natural' responses to environmental factors such as temperature, humidity and physical forces. The role of sensors and information as part of the system can contribute to both its inherent dynamic behaviour and also interactive modifications of that behaviour.

6 Nox Architects, D-Tower, Doetinchem, Netherlands, 2003.
Changing colours indicate emotions of the inhabitants of Doetinchem.

7 Light sensor and digital interface designed and made by Peter Liebsch.
Physical composite model in which the opening of the skylight is controlled by the intensity of light measured by a light sensor. A remote control via a programmable interface designed in TouchOSC lets the user override and therefore control the otherwise automated system.

8 'The Bar' installation at SG 2012, Rensselaer
Polytechnic Institute, Troy, New York, USA.

## TOWARDS AN ECOLOGY OF OBJECTS AND PEOPLE

We argue that with the advent of interactive technology and novel materials, synergic effects for architecture can occur. Custom tools and materials combined with sensors and design interfaces have the potential to support dynamic systems in architecture. 'Augmented composites' which sense changes in the environment anticipate an adaptive architecture that allows designers and users not only to interact with, but also learn from, environmental effects and can better address the needs of building inhabitants. Adaptive architectural designs could adjust their structure, properties or arrangement according to user demand or environmental changes. A dynamic system cannot be adequately explored via static drawings and key-frame simulation or analysis tools. The control and design of a physical data-driven material system is another interpretation of the notion of the craftsman. By working with a haptic-intuitive material exploration, the whole dynamic potential of the material can be discovered.

The experiences of organising an SG workshop cluster and attending other SG events have provided us with a great opportunity to contribute to the development of digital and physical collaborative workflows. Many questions remain concerning the respective roles in design of exploration and optimisation, as well as of decision-making and negotiation, but SG continues to provide a vital and relevant platform for exploring such issues.

## ACKNOWLEDGEMENTS

We wish to thank the 2011–12 first-year Masters students at SAC and the participants in the SG 2012 'MicroSynergetics' cluster for their contributions to the workshops. For their support and encouragement we also thank Bollinger + Grohmann, Grimshaw, SAC, RMIT-SIAL and the organisers of SG.

## IMAGES

Figure 1 © Grimshaw; Figures 2, 8 © Anton Savov; Figures 3, 5a, 5b © Sascha Bohnenberger; Figures 4a, 4b © Tore Banke; Figure 6 © Lars Spuybroek/NOX; Figure 7 © Peter Liebsch

# DESIGN FLOW AND TOOL FLUX

## ROBERT WOODBURY

Robert Woodbury was invited as part of the initial team of tutors at the first Smartgeometry (SG) workshop in 2003 and is a very influential member of the SG community. He participates in all SG events and provides his expertise and leadership for students and tutors alike. At SG he assists tutors to explore their own research questions, but he also researches SG itself. He is a pioneer in the field of computational design, able to theorise and contextualise the work of SG in professional and academic contexts. Here Woodbury discusses how the emergence of SG relates to developments in design exploration and methodology.

The psychologist Mihaly Csikszentmihalyi describes flow as a mental state we can achieve when we are fully and productively engaged in high-skill, high-challenge activity.[1] The flow-inducing activity becomes the centre of awareness and can block feelings of hunger and fatigue – people simply forget to attend to such 'mere' bodily functions. Designers know flow well. Through focus and skill, a design emerges on paper from the tip of the pencil and is seen over and over again through many sketches. It seems to refine itself. Only a few years ago, it would have been ridiculous to claim that computational design aided flow in any meaningful way. Today we see a different picture, one in which a bewildering variety of tools each enable flow in particular ways.

This is perhaps the greatest change in computational design: its tools have shifted from describing known ideas to creating new ones. SG has been more than a witness to this transformation: its events and members have been central players in conceiving and making new kinds of tools and in using tools in radically new and insightful ways. SG is not alone. Other creative fields find themselves in similar flux, as their computational tools become more attuned to the core work being done. Indeed, the term 'flux', which literally means 'flow', aptly describes how tools have changed.

We are in a time of many ideas affecting each other, quite unlike earlier times in which a few key ideas – such as interactive interfaces and constraints,[2] solids modelling,[3] shape grammars[4] and building information modelling[5] – emerged in sequence. Tools exist to improve work. They embody mostly simple and often singular ideas: a wrench is a lever arm with the centre of a bolt as its fulcrum; a knife is a sharp edge with a safe handle; an arc-welder channels electrical current through a point of contact. People refine tools, typically by holding the central idea constant and making it work better in a specific context. Thus wrenches become socket sets; we have knives just for sushi; and TIG welders enable extremely fine work in refractory metals. The number of seed ideas is much smaller than the number of tools available. Computer tools are no different – they embody a few good ideas. Here I argue for six central ideas that form the flux towards better design media: dataflow programming; ubiquitous scripting; the web of abstraction; symbol amplifiers; the web of mathematics; and human-in-the-loop data import and export. I omit a crucially important tool flux: the loop of bits to atoms and atoms to bits, confident that this idea is pervasive throughout this book. I conclude with an argument for the explicit representation of alternatives, an idea that is becoming important but has not yet matured.

## DATAFLOW PROGRAMMING

Computers work by executing algorithms. So do cooks, at least those who follow cookbooks. Indeed, algorithms are recipes; when used in computers, very precise recipes indeed. An algorithm works by processing instructions. But who does the processing? The usual answer given by most programming languages is that there is effectively a single entity (often called a thread of control) that executes instructions one by one. The entity gives the computer commands, thus the common label of 'imperative language' for Basic, Fortran, C, Java, C#, C++, Processing, Python and a host of others. All such languages privilege a view of computation as recipe; thus they make it difficult to see other points of view that people using computers to do work might better apprehend.

Chief among these other views is that of relationships, which are the core construct underlying the now familiar dataflow programming tools that have become so popular with designers. With these, people build programs by connecting objects: they literally 'wire' models together. Although Sketchpad, the very first computer-aided design (CAD) system, was relationship based, the systems that came to dominate the commercial CAD market supported recipe-based languages for algorithms, when they provided algorithm support at all. The technical picture today is very different. Almost without exception, the major CAD systems, at least those parts of them most heavily used, support algorithms through relationships more than instructions. Of course, many systems provide both.

The professional picture has shifted too. People now use computers to do design work at all stages of design and for a continually surprising variety of tasks. I argue that relationship-based, specifically dataflow, programming enabled much of the professional shift. I further argue that the reason for the shift lies in something called the 'attention investment model' combined with the 'gentle-slope system' hypothesis. Alan Blackwell's 'attention investment model' presumes that our attention is a highly valuable resource which we invest in a task by balancing our perceptions of the task value, its attentional cost and the risk of failure.[6] We bias the present: a bird now is worth two later. We avoid costly failure, even when its probability is low. We look at learning a complex new tool as a risky enterprise – if we fail to learn it fast or well enough, we have wasted the effort invested. We thus prefer tools and CAD systems that support incremental learning and require minimal setup.

Michael Dertouzos coined the term 'gentle-slope' to describe exactly such systems.[7] A gentle-slope system imposes low barriers to achieving new skills. The figure on the right compares fictional but representative systems offering similar capabilities.[8] The intent of the figure is to give a sense of the relative difficulty of using tools to achieve results. Though the three systems in the figure are abstract, their basic structure can be found in several CAD systems that were on the market in 2012. One such system, GenerativeComponents (GC) had an extended beta-test period through the early SG events. Although its designer Robert Aish did not know of the gentle-slope system hypothesis by name, he was very clear in describing his intentions for GC in eerily similar terms. GC is a complex system, with many small steps to mastery. Each step enables new capability and some need not be taken in order. The recent addition of visual programming in GC's graph view dramatically improves on Aish's initial vision.

## UBIQUITOUS SCRIPTING

Anyone who has worked with a dataflow system knows that it is not enough. At some point, we need more powerful tools and we turn to history for them. Imperative programming languages have received far more attention and have undergone far more development than any other language type. Notwithstanding arguments of their inherent worth, the fact of their maturity makes them the tool of choice for 'serious' computational work. Almost all major CAD tools provide access to a programming language. Predictably, if one believes in gentle-slope systems, the most successful such languages are relatively simple and are interpreted (providing immediate execution) rather than compiled (deferring execution). We have even coined the term 'scripting language', an otherwise meaningless new phrase, to describe programming languages that are directly connected to tools.

Technically there is little new here: AutoCAD had the language AutoLisp in the 1980s. What is new is the social expectation that comes with ubiquity and the social networks that support it. Put simply, serious contemporary designers are expected to script, are rewarded for it and gain stature by being good designers through it. Languages evolve from earlier languages so most share many features, reducing learning barriers. Many design tasks can be accomplished with modest scripts, indeed many SG workshops show that the core ideas and basic technique can be picked up in a few days. The polish of practice takes considerably longer, but receives an enormous boost from a simple social fact. We share code. And the Internet makes sharing code simple and fast. Indeed, the preferred working style for most designers who script is to find, copy and modify code made by others. A dramatic example of code sharing occurred during the third SG workshop (held in

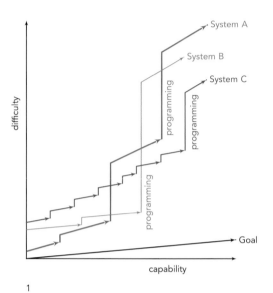

1

1 Comparison of systems offering similar capabilities.
The intent is to give a sense of the relative difficulty of using tools to achieve results. A good strategy for a system is to aim at a relatively large number of small steps in the capability/difficulty function.

Cambridge, UK) when Axel Kilian introduced the technique that became the 'Reactor Pattern' in my book *Elements of Parametric Design*.[9] Within hours, the code had found its way around the workshop via jump drive. Many began to play with Reactor-based ideas. Code sharing is not enough. Designers share larger ideas.

## THE WEB OF ABSTRACTION: PATTERNS, PACKAGES AND CLASSES

System developers supply general (and mostly complex) operations that they hope many will use. Designers write specific (and usually short) programs to achieve immediate tasks. The two do not always meet. Designers can imagine more computation than developers can make. Convex hulls and Voronoi diagrams; subdivision surfaces and conjugate meshes; genetic algorithms and swarm optimisation: each of these provides new tools for new design ideas. Independent developers have built a web of abstraction that explains and provides new functions at the fringe of commercial systems. Unlike the cottage industry of special functions for sale that briefly flowered in the 1980s, most of these are available for free on the web. The economy has shifted from money to fame (though a cynic might say that fame is simply a choice to defer monetary reward). The programming community has developed a range of concepts and tools that aid explaining and use.

Two of these are patterns and packages. A pattern is a generic solution to a well-described recurrent situation. It explains both context and solution. Most useful patterns come with example code, which people are free to copy and modify. The *Elements of Parametric Design* book and its companion website present a recent and salient example of patterns specifically for computational design.[10] Packages comprise a coordinated set of programs and instructions on how to correctly connect them to CAD data. To use a package is to figure out how to get data into it and how to understand its results. Good packages entice, either through ease or joy of use. Daniel Piker, the author of the popular Kangaroo package for Grasshopper, writes:

> I suspect a part of the wide success of Grasshopper is due to its toy-like nature. The playfulness of the interface makes it enjoyable to use, which aids learning and encourages experimentation and the development of new ideas. Though it may mislead some into underestimating it, this playfulness actually reinforces its usefulness. A lot of the same qualities that make good toys also make good design tools such as great flexibility and intuitive interaction.[11]

## THE WEB OF MATHEMATICS

Every university library has more mathematics books than a single person could read, much less master, in a lifetime. Understanding much of contemporary mathematics requires many years of study. The same being true for design, it is rare to find appreciable mathematical and design expertise in a single soul. Nonetheless, designers have done and used mathematics for centuries. The results tend to show in the forms created. Contemporary design

2

2 Example of sharing code on the Internet. Through his blog (http://buildz.blogspot.com) Zach Kron provides a large and growing catalogue of programming solutions and working code. Through often playful examples, he conveys useful and serious ideas for the scripter's craft.

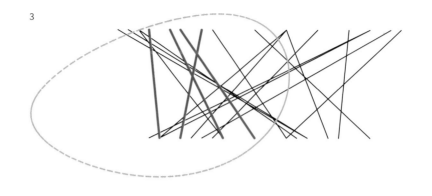

3

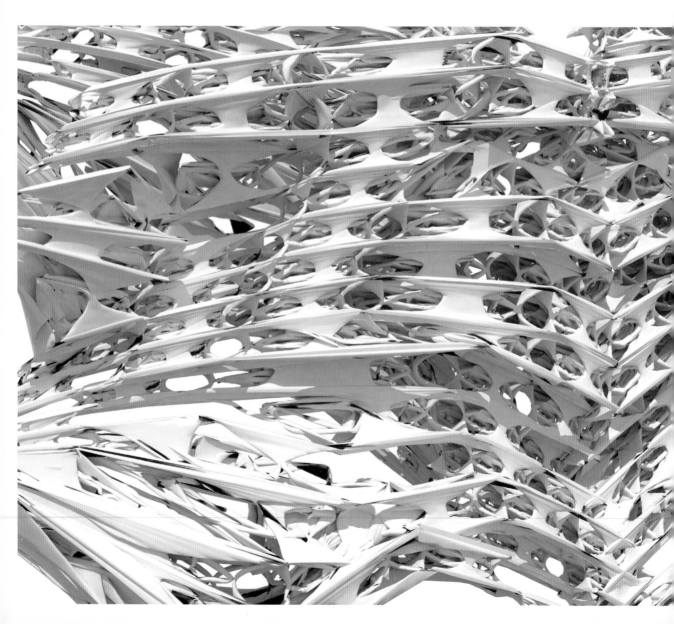

is no exception – mathematical structure can literally be seen in the surface of much curvilinear architectural form, and deeper examples abound as well.

What differs today is availability and access. Only a generation ago, finding and using mathematics involved library visits, book borrowing and largely solitary reading. Today a web search makes mathematics accessible to all. Entire sites such as Wolfram's MathWorld are devoted to widely disseminating mathematical concepts. Understanding enough is a different matter. Books such as *Architectural Geometry*,[12] *Essential Mathematics for Computational Design*,[13] *Geometric Tools for Computer Graphics*[14] and *Elements of Parametric Design*[15] aim to distil and convey key mathematical tools for design. The mathematics for, and of, design changes with time. As designers reach for new expressive forms they shift from smooth to subdivision surfaces; they find form with Delaunay triangulations and rediscover projection as a form-making tool. Indeed, even to use a parametric modeller well requires qualitative understanding of basic concepts of parameterisation, projection and vector arithmetic. To observe a designer today is to see such mathematics at play.

## SYMBOL AMPLIFIERS
In the 1970s George Stiny adapted computational grammar to create 'shape grammars': collections of simple rules that can collectively generate families of designs.[16] Shape grammars experienced a dramatic flowering in the 1980s and 1990s and then declined, at least outside academia. Their simplified cousins, which Stiny called 'set grammars', have recently made a dramatic resurgence. In a case of convergent evolution, techniques such as procedural modelling from computer graphics and distributed artificial intelligence have come to play similar roles in design. Each of these techniques expands terse design descriptions into complex form. Tools such as CityEngine are capable of nearly instantaneously creating plausible neighbourhood models, based on minimal input data. Whereas much of the mathematics of design has been concerned with things continuous and deterministic (smooth surfaces, complete tilings, force models), these symbol amplifiers inherently model discrete choice (Which building type sits on this corner? What facade elements? What room layout?). Ironically, spatial grammars were one of the early big ideas in computational design. As such, they demonstrate well that media can take unexpected trajectories, that concepts can take many computational forms and that important ideas can take a long time to find real application.

## THE WEB OF DATA
Below programming and patterns lies the 'stuff' on which programs operate. Contemporary CAD systems have provided a layer of such that simplifies many programming tasks. This layer comprises input and output. It is trivially easy to export data from most CAD programs in a wide variety of formats. Some, like comma-separated value format, are incredibly general, allowing almost any data to be exported as long as it follows simple formatting rules. Others, like Industry Foundation Classes,

4

3 Mathematical concept implemented as architectural design tool.
The Jordan curve theorem states that a point is inside a closed curve if a ray from the point crosses the curve an odd number of times. Applied twice, the theorem gives a simple and correct test for lines inside convex closed curves.

4 Complex form generated using swarm algorithm.
Robert Cervellione develops and shares (through www.cerver.org) distributed artificial-intelligence symbol amplifiers that can be applied at many levels of design. Shown here is a swarm system that deforms and changes an underlying parametric system based on swarm density, alignment and other rules embedded into the swarm system. The idea is to use the logic of a swarm system without the limitation of directly converting the system to geometry.

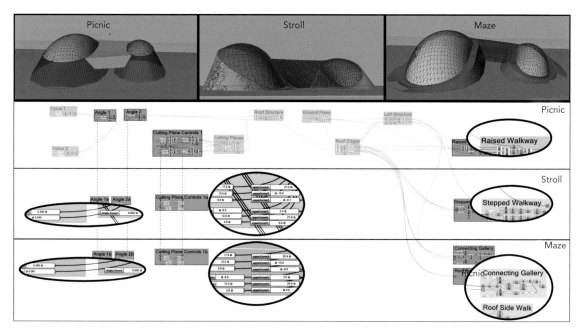

5

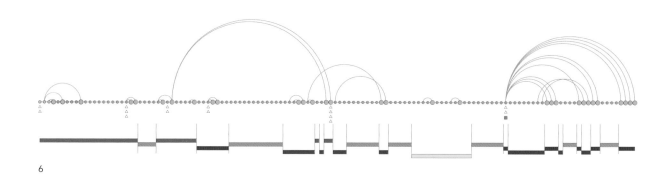

6

specify precise and rigid formats for particular kinds of objects. The specifics of these formats are much less important than what they enable: general data exchange among a variety of tools, commercial, open source and private. Such exchange begets new terms: 'data marshalling' and 'mash-ups'. To marshal data is to use simple tools to organise and reorganise data so that it can be used elsewhere. Probably the single most-used marshalling tool is Excel, in which a small set of functions (mostly vlookup, hlookup, indirect and the text functions) enables rapid and dramatic data transformations so that data produced in one format can be used in another. To make a mash-up is to combine and organise existing tools to create new applications. At any SG event much of what happens is making mash-ups through marshalling. In fact, the Copenhagen event of 2011 highlighted data as its theme and marshalling as its main technique.

### ALTERNATIVES, AN IDEA WHOSE TIME IS COMING

Researchers have long known (and some have forgotten) that people do complex work by searching in a problem space for likely solutions. They consider more than one idea: pursuing some, forgoing others and often merging solutions together into a new synthesis. Strangely, until very recently, computer interfaces in all fields have provided direct interaction with only one model at a time. As they always do when provided with poor tools, people have responded with workarounds. Multiple layers, versions of files, scripts with elaborate if-then-else constructs, manually programmed tables of alternatives: all of these attest to an unmet need for better support for alternatives. Perhaps the best demonstration of need is any good designer's sketchbook. Typically these can be read as a story of exploration, of a path through a space of possibilities.

Fortunately CAD is beginning to change. Tools like the Autodesk Showcase and SolidWorks ConfigurationManager take the first baby steps towards a future in which designers will routinely work with more than one idea at a time. Actually, the babies are taking strides while CAD toddles behind. Video games have long had elaborate interfaces for equipping characters with options such as armour, weapons, magic elixirs and faerie companions. To watch a 12-year-old move through a vast array of options is to see the future of design tools at play. Researchers in diverse fields are designing, developing and evaluating new interfaces for alternatives. At the 'Human–Computer Interaction' (HCI) conference in 2000, Ben Shneiderman proposed eight activities (including exploration) required for supporting innovation with human–computer interfaces.[17] In a seminal graphics paper Joe Marks et al describe 'Design Gallery' interfaces which aimed to 'present the user with the broadest selection, automatically generated and organised, of perceptually different graphics or animations that can be produced by varying a given input-parameter vector'.[18] The computational design group I run with Halil Erhan at Simon Fraser University has several active projects on interacting with parametric alternatives. So has the practice world, where presentations and professional papers now often

5 Naghmi Shireen, parallel interface study.[19]
A subjunctive dependency graph contains representations for alternatives directly in the dataflow. Naghmi Shireen's parallel interface shows that, in a model abstracting Foster + Partners' Elephant House at Copenhagen Zoo (2008), changing values for tori radii will result in parallel changes to the derived radii in the branch alternatives; whereas changes made to tori angles and cutting planes in the derived graphs change local states.

6 Rodolfo Sánchez, transaction interface study.[20]
The transaction interface supports alternative process flows, generating multiple design alternatives.

contain tables of alternatives as an integral part of design stories. Surely CAD must follow.

Returning to the theme of design flow and tool flux, every SG event richly demonstrates how designers are seeking new ways of being in design flow through engaging themselves in the ongoing flux of tool conception, design, development and deployment. Design does indeed live in an interesting time, in which all parts of the field: practice, CAD vendors and research; contribute new and vital ideas. For me it is sure that communities like SG are and will be an essential and integral part of computational design. My sole prediction is that, a decade from now, we will be surprised by the changes we have undertaken and experienced.

## REFERENCES

1 Mihaly Csikszentmihalyi, *Creativity: Flow and the Psychology of Discovery and Invention*, Harper Perennial (New York, NY), 1997.

2 See: Ivan Edward Sutherland. *Sketchpad: A Man–Machine Graphical Communication System*, Technical Report 296, MIT Lincoln Laboratory (Lexington, MA), 1963.

3 See: Bruce G Baumgart, *Winged Edge Polyhedron Representation*, Stanford Artificial Intelligence Report CS-320, Stanford University (Palo Alto, CA), October 1972; and Aristides AG Requicha, 'Representation for Rigid Solids: Theory, Methods, and Systems', *Computing Surveys*, Vol 12, No 4, December 1980, pp 437–64.

4 See: George Stiny and James Gips, 'Shape Grammars and the Generative Specification of Painting and Sculpture', in *Information Processing*, No 71, 1972, pp 1460–65.

5 See: Charles Eastman and Max Henrion, 'Glide: A Language for Design Information Systems', *Computer Graphics* (Proceedings of the SIGGRAPH Conference 1977), July 1977, pp 24–33.

6 Alan Blackwell and Margaret Burnett, 'Applying Attention Investment to End-User Programming', in *Proceedings of the IEEE Symposia on Human-Centric Computing Languages and Environments*, 2002, pp 28–30.

7 Michael Dertouzos, *What Will Be*, HarperCollins (New York, NY), 1997.

8 The figure is adopted from Brad Myers, Scott E Hudson and Randy Pausch, 'Past, Present, and Future of User-Interface Software Tools', *ACM Transactions on Computer–Human Interaction*, Vol 7, No 1, March 2000, pp 3–28.

9 Robert Woodbury, with contributions from Brady Peters, Onur Yuce Gun and Mehdi Sheikholeslami, *Elements of Parametric Design*, Taylor & Francis (Oxford), 2010.

10 Ibid; website: http://elementsofparametricdesign.com [accessed 5 January 2012].

11 Daniel Piker, *Project Kangaroo – Live 3D Physics for Rhino/Grasshopper*, 2010, http://spacesymmetrystructure.wordpress.com/2010/01/21/kangaroo/ [accessed 9 August 2012].

12 Helmut Pottmann, Andreas Asperl, Michael Hofer and Axel Kilian, *Architectural Geometry*, Bentley Institute Press (Exton, PA), 2007.

13 Rajaa Issa, *Essential Mathematics for Computational Design*, Robert McNeel Associates, 2010, http://blog.rhino3d.com/2010/03/essential-mathematics-for-computational.html [accessed 17 August 2012].

14 Philip J Schneider and David H Eberly, *Geometric Tools for Computer Graphics*, Morgan Kaufmann (San Francisco, CA), 2003.

15 Robert Woodbury, with contributions from Brady Peters, Onur Yuce Gun and Mehdi Sheikholeslami, *Elements of Parametric Design*, Taylor & Francis (Oxford), 2010.

16 George Stiny and James Gips, 'Shape Grammars and the Generative Specification of Painting and Sculpture', in CV Freiman (ed), *Information Processing 71*, North-Holland (Amsterdam), 1972, pp 1460–65.

17 Ben Shneiderman, 'Creating Creativity: User Interfaces for Supporting Innovation', *ACM Transactions on Computer–Human Interaction*, Vol 7, No 1, March 2000, pp 114–38.

18 Joe Marks, Brad Andalman, Paul Beardsley, William Freeman, Sarah Gibson, Jessica Hodgins, Thomas Kang, Brian Mirtich, Hanspeter Pfister, Wheeler Ruml et al, 'Design Galleries: A General Approach to Setting Parameters for Computer Graphics and Animation', in *Proceedings of the 24th Annual Conference on Computer Graphics and Interactive Techniques*, ACM Press/Addison-Wesley Publishing Co (New York, NY), 1997, pp 389–400.

19 From: Naghmi Shireen, Halil Erhan, David Botta and Robert Woodbury, 'Parallel Development of Parametric Design Models using Subjunctive Dependency Graphs', in *ACADIA 2012*, October 2012.

20 From: Rodolfo Sánchez, Halil Erhan, Robert Woodbury, Volker Mueller and Makai Smith, 'Visual Narratives of Parametric Design History: Aha! Now I See How You Did It!', in *Proceedings of the 30th eCAADe Conference*, Czech Technical University in Prague, Vol 1, September 2012, p 259.

# THE SOUND OF SMARTGEOMETRY

### BRADY PETERS

Brady Peters is an architect and co-editor of *Inside Smartgeometry*. A key member of the Smartgeometry (SG) community since attending the 2003 conference in Cambridge, UK, he has been a tutor from 2006 to 2012 and conference co-organiser of SG 2011 in Copenhagen. Formerly an Associate Partner with the Specialist Modelling Group at Foster + Partners in London, at SG 2010, 2011 and 2012 he has explored ideas relating to computational design, sound and simulation engaging with his PhD research on the potentials of complex geometry to create sound-defining surfaces.

1

2

1 SG 2010 workshop, IAAC, Barcelona, Spain. At SG 2010 there was a new terminology, and a new organisation. Participants were organised into 'clusters' headed by 'champions'. In four days, the challenge was not only to design, construct and evaluate a prototype, but also to allow participants to work at their own pace, bring their own knowledge to the project, and follow their own trajectories within the focused research brief.

2 'Manufacturing Parametric Acoustic Surfaces' prototype at SG 2010, IAAC, Barcelona, Spain. In collaboration with Martin Tamke, this SG workshop cluster examined how acoustic variables could be encoded into the architectural parametric design system, and how distinct acoustic spaces could be created through the use of sound-modulating panels.

Queuing up to get into the warehouse, it seemed like you were going into some all-night dance party. Hundreds of young people milling around, talking and smoking, waiting to get into a sold-out event held in an otherwise empty industrial part of Barcelona. Security checked everyone's ID and loud noises emanated from inside the space. Once inside the vast warehouse, groups of people were intently discussing things as they made their way to smaller rooms located around, and overlooking, the main space. Except these people weren't dancers, they were architects, and the glow didn't come from sticks, but from the hundreds of laptops running advanced and custom design software. There was no massive sound system; the noises instead came from the variety of digital fabrication machines that were running in every corner: computer numerical control (CNC) machines, giant laser cutters, fabric-cutting machines, industrial robots and 3D printers. Designers were collaborating and discussing and components were being built and tested. This was in strong contrast to quieter SG events held in carpeted meeting rooms at placeless luxury hotels and focused entirely on software. After six years of events, the SG 2010 workshop at the IAAC (Institute for Advanced Architecture of Catalonia) in Barcelona presented something entirely different. It felt like an architecture rave. This was the new sound of smart geometry.

## SOUND PROTOTYPES

Architects design the experience of space. While this experience inevitably includes sound, we have little understanding of and few tools to design for sound. There is surprisingly little research on sound in architecture, yet a wealth of knowledge from allied fields such as acoustics and engineering. Sound is not included in any digital design software. To address this problem, the focus of my PhD research has been to embed notions of acoustic performance in architectural design software, as a design driver, considering sound as a part of a project's design intent. SG has played an important role in this research through the construction of two experimental sound prototypes.

## PARAMETRIC ACOUSTIC SURFACES

Our experiment for SG 2010 was designed to allow all participants to engage with the computational model, so we needed to start with a simple model that had the ability to become increasingly complex as more parameters were added. While the design of the parametric and sound strategy was done prior to the workshop, all of the design and fabrication of the parametric acoustic panels was done at the workshop by the participants. The sound design strategy dictated what the performance of specific components would be in terms of whether they absorbed, reflected or scattered the sound; however, how this performance was achieved and the specific design of the panel components was left to the individual participants. This way of working, with different designers able to simultaneously design components to be added to a whole, is often used in offices to allow collaboration. The central parametric model allowed participants to engage with a larger research project as well as contributing their own designs for acoustic sub-components.

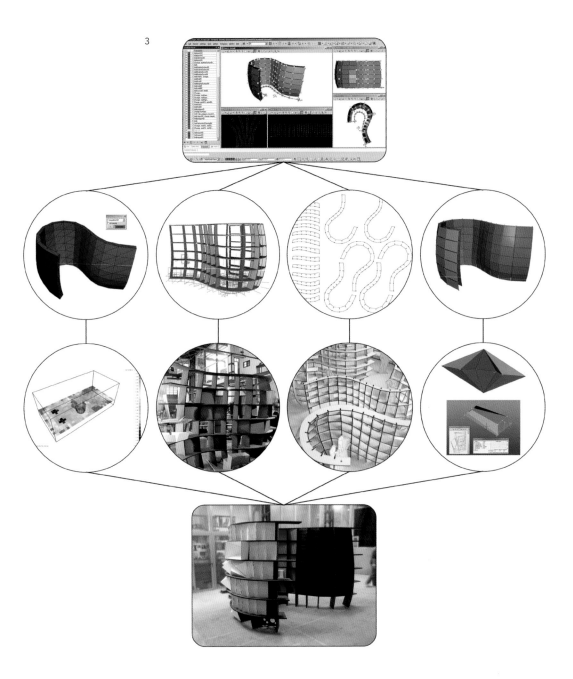

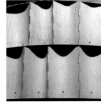

3 'Manufacturing Parametric Acoustic Surfaces' prototype at SG 2010, IAAC, Barcelona, Spain. Data representations within the parametric model were the acoustic simulation geometry, the structural model, the fabrication data and the placeholder surfaces. These representations linked to software (Odeon, GenerativeComponents, Rhinoceros), machines (laser cutter, 3D printer, CNC cutter) and collaborators.

4 'Manufacturing Parametric Acoustic Surfaces' prototype at SG 2010, IAAC, Barcelona, Spain: parametric acoustic modules.

There was a mix of pre-planning by cluster leaders (the wood superstructure was laser-cut at IAAC over three days before the workshop began) and the creation of an open framework that allowed participants to create their own designs which could produce unexpected results. Participants designed various acoustic components: sound-scattering panels, sound-reflecting and -focusing panels, sound absorbers, perforated screen absorbers and sound windows.

 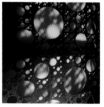

4

## REPRESENTATION AND SIMULATION

Sound is not currently part of the digital design environment. A strategy to understand the sound of our geometry is to look outside of this environment to hear our designs and understand their acoustic performance. Simulation software does not create geometry so it is necessary to draw this in another software and import it; this requires that the geometry be in the correct format. While this is perhaps a seemingly trivial point, it indicates a larger representational issue of what, how and why, we draw. At SG 2010 we worked with several representations of the project: the complete architectural model for visualisation, the placeholder shapes and related acoustic subcomponents, fabrication data, and the geometry for acoustic simulation. Drawings and models are necessary abstractions – they do not contain all of the information in the real world. To consider acoustic performance, it is necessary to understand how sound is abstracted, simulated, and how this impacts geometric representation.[1]

The current accepted mode of predicting acoustic performance is through geometrical acoustic simulation. This abstraction assumes that sound travels in rays, which contain sound energy and which lose energy (are absorbed) or change direction (are reflected or scattered) as they interact with the surfaces of the room. This abstraction excludes the wave nature of sound, and as a result there are limitations on what can be calculated. Geometric details smaller than the wavelength of sound are unnecessary and indeed have been shown to decrease accuracy, so only large surfaces should be included. As these programs compute ray intersections with surfaces, it is necessary to describe (and draw) the design in simple triangular meshes with little detail.

As architects, we need feedback from our drawings to understand how our buildings will perform. The acoustic performance for this installation was predicted using a simplified model of the actual installation, but what about the parametric components themselves? How can the acoustic performance of the complex geometry of the architectural surface be predicted? And then can this acoustic performance inform the surface geometry?

## MEASURING PERFORMANCE

The hyperboloid is a geometric surface used extensively in the Sagrada Família Basilica in Barcelona and is said to create a unique and diffuse soundscape in the church.[2] In the experiment at SG 2011, the construction of two sound-focusing walls – one flat, and one covered with hyperboloids – allowed the sound quality of the hyperboloid geometry to be experienced. Much of the workshop focused on the mathematical definition, computational description and fabrication technique of the hyperboloid geometry. In addition to these other concerns, we tested two techniques to predict the acoustic performance of these architectural surfaces: the measurement of sound-scattering physical models, and the numerical simulation of sound waves. This performance was then used to inform the modification of the surface through the participant's custom design tools.

5 Acoustic prototype at SG 2011, Copenhagen, Denmark: sound-scattering wall of hyperboloid geometries.
In collaboration with Mark Burry, Jane Burry, Daniel Davis, Alexander Pena de Leon, John Klein and Phil Ayres, the workshop this SG workshop cluster investigated the geometric definition, construction logic and sound-scattering properties of hyperboloid surfaces.

6 Working environment showing the two full-scale test walls, computers for generating geometry, 3D printed scale models for measuring performance and prototype hyperboloid wall components.

6

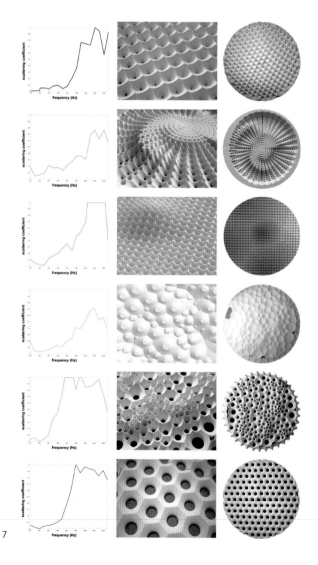

7 Acoustic prototype at SG 2011, Copenhagen, Denmark: six hyperboloid complex surfaces. Diagram showing the amount of sound scattering in relation to frequency with a detail of the 3D print, and plan views of the circular surface samples.

8 Acoustic prototype at SG 2011, Copenhagen, Denmark: workflow to integrate sound scattering into design.
Participants created custom computational design tools to generate the hyperboloid geometries. The complex surfaces were then 3D printed, and tested to determine their scattering properties. This data was then used to inform the design of the full-scale installation.

7

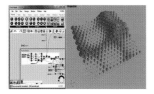

**design tool** hyperboloid geometric logic

v

**performance measurement** use experimental methods establish relationship between geometry and performance

v

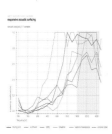

**performance-driven design tool** choose design option to construct

v

**construct 1:1 prototype** measure performance of sound scattering wall

Scale prototypes were tested using an established method.[3] This technique is used in practice and has been adapted for an architectural design process. The results in this experiment supported previous research and showed that the relational depth of surface components, and the amount and size of the surface detail, impact the sound-scattering properties in terms of the frequency, and the amount of scattering, respectively.[4] Critically, the data from these measurements can be used in acoustic simulations; therefore, while the geometry itself is not literally represented in the acoustic simulation model, the performance of the geometry is present through the measured scattering coefficient. The acoustic characteristics of the hyperboloid components could then be understood at the level of the surface, and also when arrayed in different configurations in a larger spatial situation. However, while the process of generating the data is fast, the fabrication of the model takes time (hours), as does the testing (more hours). And this is just for a single iteration; to extrapolate the performance of a variable geometry from a range of options takes days.

### INTEGRATING ANALYSIS

Sound is a wave. It occurs in a medium like air or water or steel – there is no sound in the vacuum of space. Sound occurs when a vibrating body transmits its energy to neighbouring particles, propagating in spherical waves. It is obvious that it is much too large a computational task to model every particle of air in a room and map the progression of the sound wave as it interacts with the materials and geometry of the surfaces. Unlike geometric acoustic simulation, numerical techniques attempt to model at least some of these particles. These simulations are quite computationally intensive, but they can be used to visualise the interaction of sound waves and surfaces, and evaluate their acoustic performance. A computer code was written that implemented the 'finite-difference time-domain technique'.[5] At SG 2011 we demonstrated a 2D version of this technique. It is faster than prototyping, and can be run within the architectural design environment, therefore giving feedback on the acoustic performance of complex surfaces as they are designed.

### TOWARDS ARCHITECTURAL SOUND DESIGN

The consideration of sound in the design process is often a matter of compliance with regulations, or it is related to the construction of concert halls. But the acoustic character of a space has the capacity to enrich our architectural experience beyond meeting building regulations and making music sound better. Reflecting on my work in this area, which has involved more than a dozen prototypes and design experiments, I can say that sound can be integrated into our digital design environment. The knowledge is there, it is just a matter of assembling the right tools and techniques.[6] But once sound is integrated, how will designers use this knowledge?

The two experiments at SG have contributed a great deal to my research. They have allowed me to pursue a focused design brief within a semi-structured environment while simultaneously getting feedback from designers. Many of these experiments have

9

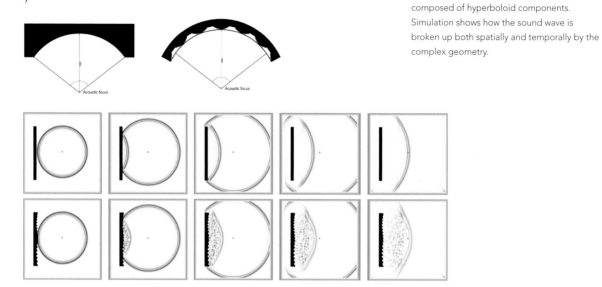

9 Acoustic prototype at SG 2011, Copenhagen, Denmark: finite-difference time-domain analysis of scattering surfaces. Comparison of flat surface versus surface composed of hyperboloid components. Simulation shows how the sound wave is broken up both spatially and temporally by the complex geometry.

10

10 *Distortion 2.0, GGG Gallery,* Copenhagen, 2012.

*Distortion 2.0* is an experimental research project designed to create visual and acoustic effects within an open-plan space. The project builds on the knowledge gained from the SG 2010 prototype and uses the sound as a key driver in the design process. Through its geometry and material, a complex wall surface creates spaces with different acoustic characterst. The project was designed specifically to probe two acoustic extremes: a sound-amplified zone, and a sound-dampened zone.

been focusing on the creation of design tools, techniques and methods. Sound design is more than just a design tool, a strategy for integrating sound into architecture. What we are searching for is a way to include sound as a part of the architectural design process, a part of its creative design intent. Sound design is about good sound, not about compliance. It is about developing a way of talking about the experience of sound and space. In order to achieve this we must draw, simulate and measure the sound of our smart geometry.

## REFERENCES

1 Brady Peters, 'Acoustic Performance as a Design Driver: Sound Simulation and Modelling at Smartgeometry', in *International Journal of Architectural Computing*, Vol 8, No 3, 2010, pp 337–58.

2 Jane Burry et al, 'Modelling Hyperboloid Sound Scattering: The Challenge of Simulating, Fabricating and Measuring', in *Proceedings of the Design Modelling Symposium Berlin 2011*, Springer (Berlin; Heidelberg), 2012, pp 89–96.

3 International Standard, ISO 17497-1, 'Acoustics – Sound Scattering Properties of Surfaces – Part 1: Measurement of the Random-Incidence Scattering Coefficient in a Reverberation Room', 2004.

4 Brady Peters and Tobias Olesen, 'Integrating Sound Scattering Measurements in the Design of Complex Architectural Surfaces', in *Future Cities: Proceedings of the 28th eCAADe Conference*, ETH Zurich, 2010, pp 481–91.

5 J Redondo et al, 'Prediction of the Random-Incidence Scattering Coefficient Using a FDTD Scheme', in *Acta Acustica United with Acustica*, Vol 95, 2009, pp 1040–47.

6 Brady Peters et al, 'Responsive Acoustic Surfaces: Computing Sonic Effects', in *Proceedings of the 29th eCAADe Conference*, University of Ljubljana, 2011, pp 819–28.

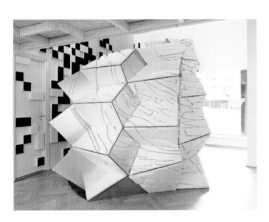

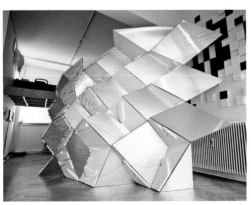

# DESIGN EXPLORATION AND STEERING OF DESIGN

### AXEL KILIAN

Axel Kilian is an architect and Assistant Professor at the Princeton University School of Architecture. He has a PhD in Computation from MIT. He is a key member of the Smartgeometry community, having been a tutor at workshops from 2003 to 2010 and a co-organiser of the conferences in 2008 and 2009. Kilian identifies and calls for increased multi-platform and open-source design tools with collaborative workflows that allow for the sharing of design algorithms. He argues that advances in computation should not be seen as replacing or limiting the role of the designer but rather as a means to enhance design exploration.

1

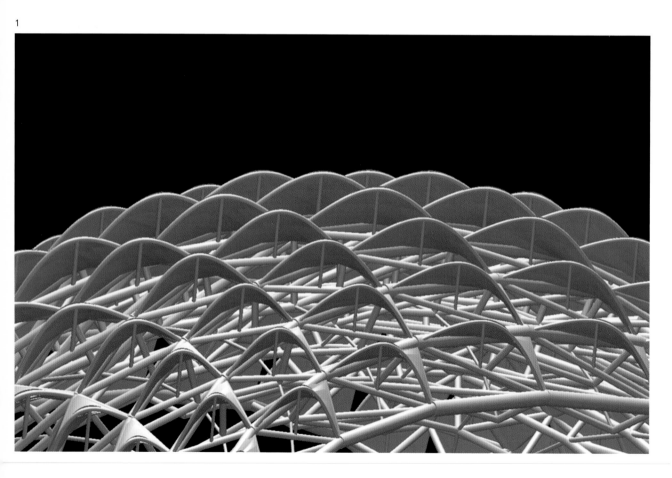

Coming from an academic background, the annual Smartgeometry (SG) events have always been a motivation to clarify my understanding of concepts I was interested in at the time – and a challenge to distill those concepts down to the essence in teaching examples. Some of these concepts became examples to illustrate possible uses of GenerativeComponents (GC) in its early iterations. The motivation for the examples was to encourage design discovery out of the simple connection of different design parameters through geometric dependencies. During the SG workshops the emphasis for me has always been on tutoring and less on developing my individual work. Seeing the value in the design proposal of a participant and attempting to develop it further with them was for many years the main motivation for me in tutoring the workshop. At the same time much effort went into reviewing and contributing to GC during its early years of development. As the community evolved rapidly, my knowledge became insignificant in comparison to the collective knowledge in the room and the new challenge became contributing to the direction of the overall event through the suggestion of speakers and themes. It became clear after a few years that a single software platform would never be sufficient to reflect the rapidly evolving idea-scape that was so central to the workshop events, just as the events were not dominated by any one single background or discipline. It has been fascinating to see the computational constructs and paradigms evolve over the past years at SG both in the workshops and at the conference. The initial reliance on a single platform and the dual paradigm of geometric dependency modelling and scripted design has widened to include electronics, robotics, actuation and sensing and a much wider range of 1:1 fabrication informed by computational design.

## DESIGN EXPLORATION

For many years digital modelling was lauded for the ability to generate designs that were impossible to build and therefore by definition avant-garde. Then a time followed where computation was in the spotlight mainly for making such novel designs buildable. What I would like to emphasise here is the use of computation to explore a wide range of possibilities with many of the co-dependencies between different factors of the design included in the evaluation. Computational design exploration can therefore go beyond form finding where the designer actively steers the process towards novel results in calibrating key design aspects. Recognising novel results is difficult, however, due to the lack of precedent to compare them to. Computational constructs can serve as an externalised design record in an exercisable form and as such aid in the rerunning and re-evaluation of the results. Creating such models of design is an important step to integrating different tangible and intangible design aspects and linking them algorithmically. But the definition of the design model also can limit its use, as is the case in the hierarchical dependency of a parametric model, where the dependency chain also determines which elements can define which other elements. Some of these limitations can be overcome, for instance for simplistic kinematic chains; but, if the driver and driven relationship is not known

2

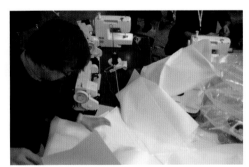

1 Adaptable roof shade study for SG 2003, MIT, Cambridge, Massachusetts, USA.
An early parametric adaptive shaded roof sketch developed in preparation for SG 2003 to test a series of components tied to an external constraint in response to a local changing geometry condition of the roof surface.

2 Hands-on fabrication at SG 2010, IAAC, Barcelona, Spain.
Inflatable fabric envelope studies were designed, fabricated and assembled.

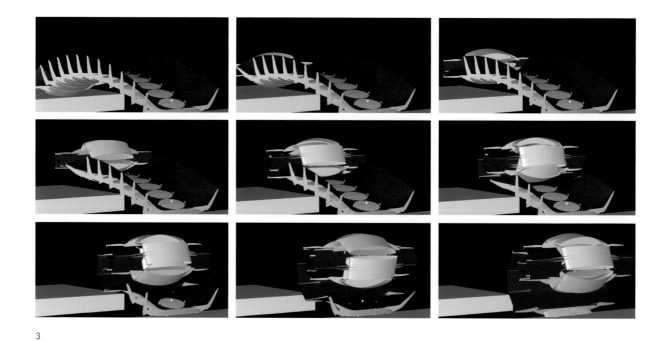

3

3 Curling bridge study, TU Delft, Delft, Netherlands, 2008.
Example of using parametric models to study kinetic constructs by simulating mechanics through geometric constraints.

4 Solver-based form-finding roof study, MIT, Cambridge, Massachusetts, USA, 2006.
Solver-based particle spring system used for form finding a free-form roof with structural members proportionally scaled based on local forces.

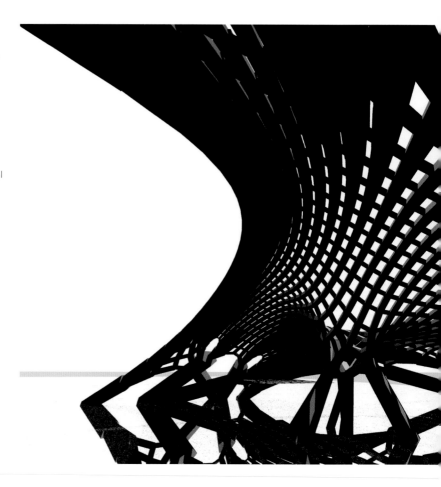

beforehand or can change during the design exploration, a computational solver model is needed.

My research interest in the use of solvers for design exploration started in using particle spring solvers for structural form finding. Observing the limitations of hierarchical associative parametric modelling platforms in education, and in workshops like SG, strengthened my interest in alternative computational models for design. Solvers make it possible to create non-hierarchical associations between design elements and create bi-directionally driven dependency networks unlike the one-directional parent–child relations in parametric associative design models. This makes them powerful as general constraint solvers in structural form finding but also generally in any type of constraint-based design model.

My PhD work addressed a few exemplary approaches to design exploration based on solvers.[1] To exercise such dependencies fluidly and in a bidirectional manner, much translation between different forms of abstraction is necessary. An example of a flexible approach is the use of solvers that allow for the bidirectional linking of design elements. But beyond the implementation limitations, substantially different types of design explorations exist that benefit from different computational approaches. In my PhD I discuss three design exploration case studies: firstly, fine tuning of established design problems; secondly, exploration as the definition of new design problems from scratch; and thirdly, exploration as exercising a computational instrument for design discoveries.

### MODELS OF DESIGN IN COMPUTATION

An implicit challenge of SG is the further development of models of design in computation. By bringing together people from different disciplines that represent the cutting edge of research and practice in their respective fields, the event acts as a catalyst for daring to go further beyond the comfort zone of day-to-day practice and research and test out new combinations of approaches in a pressure-cooker-type, high-intensity, four-day environment. Implemented computational models rely on underlying algorithms, and complex algorithms are hard to develop from scratch in a span of four days. But in response the computational design community has migrated to environments that favour open-source development, the sharing and reuse of design constructs in forms of algorithms and design definition, which allows the creation of at least prototypical new models of design by recombining components in novel ways. But to develop such sketches robustly usually requires long-term investment of time and expertise. The early SG events served in a way as an in-person social networking precursor for many of the computational forums, such as the Grasshopper online community. Much of learning and discovery in computational design today happens in such social networks, but the multi-day in-person collaboration during the SG workshops still is unique, especially in comparison with other conference and workshop combos. The respective in-depth expertise still resides in practice and research, but in the collaboration new interdisciplinary knowledge is created. SG continues to push the boundaries by

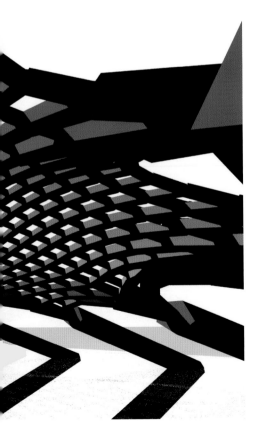

4

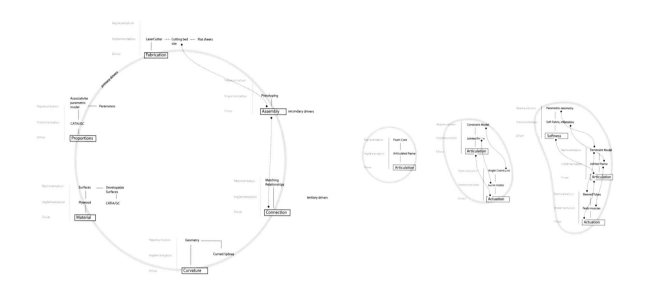

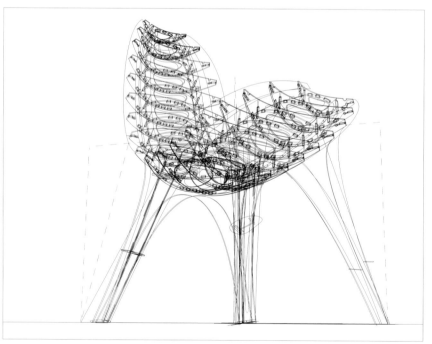

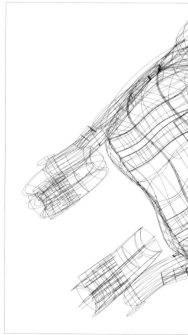

5

5 Three examples of design exploration
types, from PhD thesis, MIT, Cambridge,
Massachusetts, USA, 2006.
The three case studies of different design
exploration types explored in my PhD thesis,
*Design Exploration through Bidirectional
Modelling of Constraints*: a fine-tuning
exploration in the chair example, a design-
defining exploration in the concept car study,
and an exploration through a computational
instrument in the solver-based form finding.

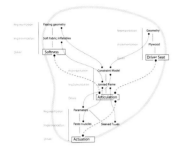

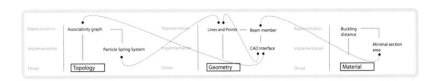

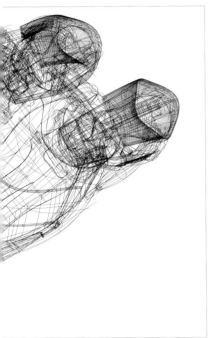

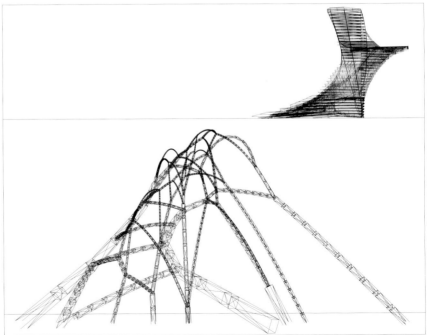

expanding beyond the physical four-day workshop event by using social media interaction between the participants in preparing for and post-processing the events.

The push to develop design-specific models is an ongoing one as the design challenges also continue to change. One change is the integration of more design aspects into the generative design process and also the creation of associations that do not just document these aspects but also allow them to have an active role in shaping the design. The SG workshops have always served as a test bed for emerging trends with potential clashes between design intent and computational implementations. Through persistence and connecting across disciplines and organisations, progress has been made to expose participants to new ideas and push existing perceptions of models of design forward. In more recent years, this has expanded even further to tangible prototyped implementations centred on a number of design challenges in so-called workshop clusters, with projects developed in a mixture of open source, design environments assembled on the fly, and the recombination of coexisting commercial platforms that hold much promise for the dynamics of design creation in the field.

### FROM COMPUTATIONAL TOOLS TO THE EXPLORATION OF IDEAS

In the early years of SG, the focus was on the mechanics of developing and testing the emerging software platform GC and on finding abstractions of design principles in computational and geometric ways. Working through geometric dependencies was an initial way to overcome the need to script design strategies. Instead, a series of design steps were recorded as an associativity graph that could be exercised for design refinement and exploration. At the same time a group around Chris Williams focused on algorithmically elegant design expressions in script form.

Different software packages existed that implemented parametric associative geometries such as computer-aided three-dimensional interactive application (CATIA), but they were not mainstream platforms at that point. The trend has been away from single platforms towards on-the-fly assemblies of computational constructs incorporating different software and hardware elements. Prototyping in physical form also became increasingly important from initial laser-cut and 3D-printed mock-ups to full-scale and fully functional physical constructs. This also exemplifies the transition from exploring computational tools to the exploration of ideas.

### THE AGE OF THE MODEL

What are the challenges for computational design in architecture and engineering today? A central one is how to represent designs that cannot be handled by our cognition alone. This class of design problem is becoming increasingly important with the complex interdependencies of performative requirements of architecture in connection with complex geometries. New computational models of abstraction are urgently needed.

The perception of computation in the discipline as a whole has changed during the past decade. The initial focus on digital drawing programs gave way to the fascination for all things visual. The research obsession with the production of images was followed by a focus on digital fabrication. The latest stage is the integration of the running computational processes of the design into the finished product, allowing the physical artefact to do more and different things. This is not a new trend, with feedback and control system having existed in robotics and aviation for a long time, but their turn into the low-cost mainstream is having a big effect on events like the SG workshops. But computational conceptual design intelligence has been neglected in these product-driven trends. A focus on computational intelligence does not mean the substitution of the human designer. On the contrary: it means strengthening the cognitive process with computational constructs to think with. Many precedents exist around the idea of digital tooling or design-specific applications. For instance many designers have used the processing environment to develop such sketch applications. Those are also externalised constructs to capture a thought process or a set of experiences into an exercisable form. But I think the next step is needed: to address the conceptual fluidity so crucial to the early design stages. For this to happen, computation has to become more integral to the design process and become faster, not in terms of processor speed, but in ease of formulating thought. This unique challenge is best addressed in a strong design environment with adjacent cross-disciplinary support.

This is the age of the model – here meaning the model of thought, not physical mock-up. In computational expression, some form of model is required. Such models are more established in science and are for now strongest where metrics are quantifiable and managing data is at the centre. But quantifiable data does not make for design, and neither does geometry alone. It is the integration of design intent into the computational models as an exercisable entity that is the biggest challenge in the domain of computational design today.

**REFERENCES**

1 Axel Kilian, *Design Exploration through Bidirectional Modeling of Constraints*, PhD thesis, MIT (Cambridge, MA), 2006.

**IMAGES**

Figures 1, 2, 3, 4 © Axel Kilian; Figure 5 © Collection FRAC Centre, Orléans, France

# GEOMETRY:
## HOW SMART DO YOU HAVE TO BE?

### CHRIS WILLIAMS

Chris Williams is a structural engineer known for his innovative work on the British Museum Great Court and the Savill Building at Windsor Great Park. A pioneer of design computation, he worked on the digital analysis and physical model testing of gridshell structures with Frei Otto and Ted Happold. His work integrating computation as a design tool influenced the creation of Smartgeometry (SG). He was a tutor for many of the early SG events and his work remains an important source of inspiration and knowledge in the community. Known for tackling design and computation problems from first principles, here Williams offers a mathematical discussion of parametric descriptions of geometry for design. He addresses not only how 'smart' geometry needs to be, but how much geometry we need to know and use as designers.

Throughout human history, new technology has made old skills and knowledge redundant. Bows and arrows made spears obsolete and the people who made or threw spears either had to adapt or find that they had no job. Expert spear makers and throwers would bemoan the loss of skills and the fact that young people no longer respected their special abilities.

However, it is not always the case that new technology replaces the old. The French painter Paul Delaroche (1797–1856) was premature when he said 'From today painting is dead!' upon seeing an early photograph in 1839. Bicycles exist alongside cars and a person might own and use both under different circumstances. In an inner city the older technology – bicycles – is more practical. Powered boats and ships have replaced sail for practical purposes, but people love to sail. The physical pleasure of cycling and sailing means that they will never die out.

All technologies require people with different skills; the person who makes the best spears is almost certainly not the best thrower. The making of buildings, bridges, cars and aeroplanes requires many skills, creative, intellectual, physical and organisational, and it is unlikely that they will be combined in one person. Even if they were, the client would not be prepared to wait for this one person to do all the work on their own.

Separation of 'creative' and 'intellectual' abilities is arbitrary, but it is intended to differentiate between the flash of inspiration and the long and painstaking task of preparing drawings and making sure that everything will work. Stereotomy is the application of three-dimensional geometry to architecture, originally the cutting of stone and timber. Thus in the creation of a cathedral we can imagine the architect, the 'stereotomer' and the stonemason working closely together, each respecting, but at times being irritated by the others.

Computers are no longer a new technology, but their implications for the ways in which people will work are still unclear. Up until about 20 years ago it was necessary for structural engineers to be able to construct an intellectual model of their proposed designs in order to make sure they worked. This model was in their minds and sketches, and they decided how they wanted their structures to function. Now computers are invariably used for structural analysis, and however illogical the structural layout, analysis is not a problem, at least if the mode of structural action fits within the limited palette of commercial software packages. Thus it could be said that structural engineering as an intellectual discipline is dead. However the increasing complexity of codes, standards and legislation means that civil engineers won't be out of a job: the regulations will provide the work, as they do for lawyers and accountants.

Architects are lucky in that one would imagine that the creative aspects of design are the least likely parts to be taken over by computers.

### THREE-DIMENSIONAL GEOMETRY

It is possible to do three-dimensional geometry by projection onto a two-dimensional drawing board, but it is difficult. It is also difficult to achieve the required level of accuracy – perhaps a few millimetres over a distance of 100 metres, so fractions of a millimetre at drawing scale. This means that one has to use analytic geometry to calculate lengths, angles and so on. Points in space are specified by Cartesian coordinates, lengths are calculated by Pythogoras's theorem and angles are calculated using the scalar product or vector product as appropriate. Naturally these calculations are done by a computer program and invariably the user is not the person who wrote the program. Thus the user does not have to know Pythagoras's theorem, because a tame mathematician has programmed it into the software for them.

### DIFFERENTIAL GEOMETRY

Differential geometry is the study of curved things, lines, surfaces and the space-time of general relativity theory.[1] A curve cannot be described by a single equation and it is usual to specify the Cartesian coordinates in terms of a parameter. A typical point on a helix would be described by

$$x = r\cos\theta$$

$$y = r\sin\theta$$

$$z = \frac{p}{2\pi}\theta$$

in which $r$ is the radius seen in plan and $p$ is the pitch or increase in height per revolution. $\theta$ is the parameter and as $\theta$ varies the point moves along the curve. However in the language of 'parametric design' $p$ and $r$ would be described as parameters controlling the shape and size of the curve.

The unit tangent to any curve can be found by differentiation

$$t = \frac{\frac{dx}{d\theta}\mathbf{i} + \frac{dy}{d\theta}\mathbf{j} + \frac{dz}{d\theta}\mathbf{k}}{\sqrt{\left(\frac{dx}{d\theta}\right)^2 + \left(\frac{dx}{d\theta}\right)^2 + \left(\frac{dz}{d\theta}\right)^2}}$$

Curvature is defined as the rate of change of $t$ per unit length, which can be found by differentiating again. Surfaces can be defined by a single equation. Thus,

$$\frac{x^2}{a^2} + \frac{y^2}{b^2} + \frac{z^2}{c^2} = 1$$

specifies an ellipsoid, or a sphere if the constants $a$, $b$ and $c$ are all equal. We can obtain $z$ from $x$ and $y$ :

$$z = \pm c\sqrt{1 - \frac{x^2}{a^2} + \frac{y^2}{b^2}}$$

but we have the problem that there are negative and positive values of $z$ for given values of $x$ and $y$ . Instead we can use the parametric form

$$x = a\cos\theta\cos\phi$$
$$y = b\sin\theta\cos\phi$$
$$z = c\sin\phi$$

in which the parameters $\phi$ and $\theta$ would correspond to the latitude and longitude on the Earth. $\phi$ and $\theta$ are also referred to as surface coordinates. We can choose whatever symbols we like for the surface coordinates; $u$ and $v$ , are commonly used:

$$x = a\cos u\cos v$$
$$y = b\sin u\cos v$$
$$z = c\sin v$$

Lines of constant $u$ and lines of constant $v$ form a net on the surface. We can get a different net on the same surface by instead writing

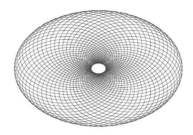

$$x = \frac{a\cos(u-v)}{\cosh(u+v)}$$

$$y = \frac{b\sin(u-v)}{\cosh(u+v)}$$

$$z = c\tanh(u+v)$$

to produce the spiralling surface coordinate net shown in figure 1. Note that to cover the ellipsoid fully $(u+v)$ has to tend to plus and minus infinity.

Before going any further let us change the symbols for the parameters or surface coordinates from $u$ and $v$ to $\theta^1$ and $\theta^2$. Note that $\theta^1$ and $\theta^2$ are two separate variables, not $\theta$ to the power 1 and $\theta$ squared. This seems very confusing and annoying to begin with and it is only gradually that the reason for doing so becomes clear. Thus we now have

$$x = \frac{a\cos(\theta^1 - \theta^2)}{\cosh(\theta^1 + \theta^2)}$$

$$y = \frac{b\sin(\theta^1 - \theta^2)}{\cosh(\theta^1 + \theta^2)}$$

$$z = c\tanh(\theta^1 + \theta^2)$$

Dirk J Struik's *Lectures on Classical Differential Geometry* is probably the most easily read book on differential geometry, and he uses $u$ and $v$ surface coordinates.[2] In their book *Theoretical Elasticity*, Albert E Green and Wolfgang Zerna use $\theta^1$ and $\theta^2$ for their surface coordinates and as well as doing geometry they cover the theory of shells.[3] It is here that the curvilinear tensor notation using subscripts and superscripts comes into its own. Note that the Cartesian tensor notation uses only subscripts, but it is best avoided since it cannot deal with curved objects and it gets you into bad habits in not using both superscripts and subscripts.

We can find the covariant base vectors on the surface by differentiating:

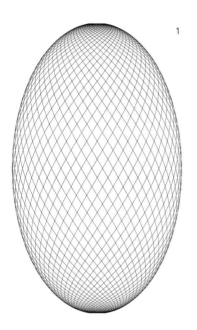

1

1 Plan and elevation of ellipsoid with 'spiral' surface coordinates.

$$\mathbf{g}_1 = \frac{\partial x}{\partial \theta^1}\mathbf{i} + \frac{\partial y}{\partial \theta^1}\mathbf{j} + \frac{\partial z}{\partial \theta^1}\mathbf{k}$$

$$= \frac{a\begin{pmatrix} -\sin(\theta^1 - \theta^2)\cosh(\theta^1 + \theta^2) \\ -\cos(\theta^1 - \theta^2)\sinh(\theta^1 + \theta^2) \end{pmatrix}\mathbf{i} + b\begin{pmatrix} \cos(\theta^1 - \theta^2)\cosh(\theta^1 + \theta^2) \\ -\sin(\theta^1 - \theta^2)\sinh(\theta^1 + \theta^2) \end{pmatrix}\mathbf{j} + c\mathbf{k}}{\cosh^2(\theta^1 + \theta^2)}$$

$$\mathbf{g}_2 = \frac{\partial x}{\partial \theta^2}\mathbf{i} + \frac{\partial y}{\partial \theta^2}\mathbf{j} + \frac{\partial z}{\partial \theta^2}\mathbf{k}$$

$$= \frac{a\begin{pmatrix} \sin(\theta^1 - \theta^2)\cosh(\theta^1 + \theta^2) \\ -\cos(\theta^1 - \theta^2)\sinh(\theta^1 + \theta^2) \end{pmatrix}\mathbf{i} + b\begin{pmatrix} -\cos(\theta^1 - \theta^2)\cosh(\theta^1 + \theta^2) \\ -\sin(\theta^1 - \theta^2)\sinh(\theta^1 + \theta^2) \end{pmatrix}\mathbf{j} + c\mathbf{k}}{\cosh^2(\theta^1 + \theta^2)}$$

$\mathbf{g}_1$ and $\mathbf{g}_2$ are tangent to the lines of the coordinate net and are therefore also tangent to the surface itself. Note that for a general surface and coordinate system $\mathbf{g}_1$ and $\mathbf{g}_2$ are not unit vectors, indeed their magnitude will vary from point to point. Also they will not cross at right angles.

The scalar products

$$g_{11} = \mathbf{g}_1 \bullet \mathbf{g}_1$$
$$g_{12} = g_{21} = \mathbf{g}_1 \bullet \mathbf{g}_2$$
$$g_{22} = \mathbf{g}_2 \bullet \mathbf{g}_2$$

are the components of the metric tensor, also known as the coefficients of the first fundamental form. The distance between two adjacent points on a surface is

$$ds = \sqrt{g_{11}(d\theta^1)^2 + 2g_{12}d\theta^1 d\theta^2 + g_{22}(d\theta^2)^2}$$

which explains the term 'metric tensor'. This equation can be written more succinctly as

$$ds^2 = \sum_{\alpha=1}^{2}\sum_{\beta=1}^{2} g_{\alpha\beta}d\theta^\alpha d\theta^\beta = g_{\alpha\beta}d\theta^\alpha d\theta^\beta$$

in which the summations $\sum_{\alpha=1}^{2}\sum_{\beta=1}^{2}$ are implied by the Einstein summation convention.

We can find the unit normal to a surface using the vector product:

$$\mathbf{n} = \frac{\mathbf{g}_1 \times \mathbf{g}_2}{|\mathbf{g}_1 \times \mathbf{g}_2|}$$

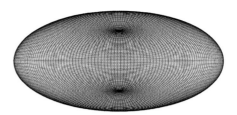

The normal can be differentiated and the scalar products

$$b_{11} = -\mathbf{g}_1 \bullet \frac{\partial \mathbf{n}}{\partial \theta^1}$$

$$b_{12} = b_{21} = -\mathbf{g}_1 \bullet \frac{\partial \mathbf{n}}{\partial \theta^2} = -\mathbf{g}_2 \bullet \frac{\partial \mathbf{n}}{\partial \theta^1}$$

$$b_{22} = -\mathbf{g}_2 \bullet \frac{\partial \mathbf{n}}{\partial \theta^2}$$

$$b_{\alpha\beta} = b_{\beta\alpha} = -\mathbf{g}_\alpha \bullet \frac{\partial \mathbf{n}}{\partial \theta^\beta}$$

are known as the coefficients of the second fundamental form. These coefficients tell us how the direction of the unit normal changes as we move on the surface, in other words the curvature of the surface.

Curvature is a symmetric second-order tensor. Stress is also a symmetric second-order tensor and therefore stress and curvature have the same mathematical properties, in particular we have two orthogonal principal curvature directions on a surface. The mean curvature $H$ is the average of the two principal curvatures and the Gaussian curvature $K$ is the product of the two principal curvatures. On a soap film or minimal surface (surface of minimum surface area for a given boundary), the mean curvature is zero.

By the fundamental theorem of surface theory the six quantities $g_{\alpha\beta}$ and $b_{\alpha\beta}$ fully define a surface, except for its position and a rigid body rotation. However $g_{\alpha\beta}$ and $b_{\alpha\beta}$ are not independent since they are all derived from differentiating just three equations for the Cartesian coordinates as a function of the surface coordinates. By differentiating yet again and using the fact that order of partial differentiation does not matter, we obtain three compatibility equations, known as Gauss's Theorema Egregium (Excellent Theorem) and the two Peterson–Mainardi–Codazzi equations.

Gauss's theorem shows that the Gaussian curvature can be calculated from just the three quantities $g_{\alpha\beta}$ and their first and second derivatives. Thus just measuring lengths on a surface tells

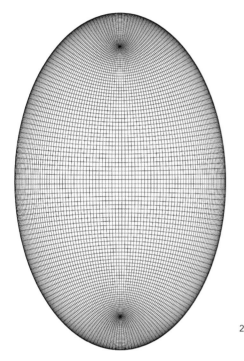

2

2 Plan and elevation of ellipsoid with principal curvature surface coordinates.

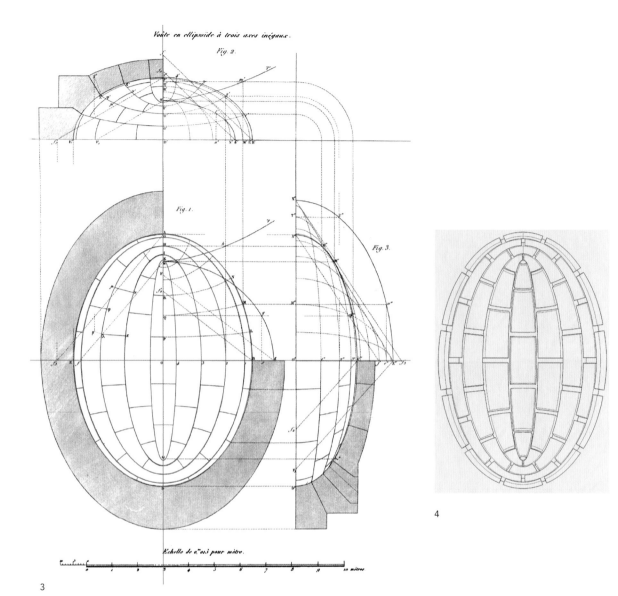

3 Ellipsoidal vault. Plate 44 from Charles-
François-Antoine Leroy, *Traité de stéréotomie*,
1870.

4 Computer-generated ellipsoidal vault: line
drawing.

us the product of its principal curvatures. This is truly remarkable and has all sorts of practical implications for architectural geometry and cutting patterns for tents and clothes.

Finally let us now change the surface coordinates on our ellipsoid yet again so that the coordinate curves follow the principal curvature directions:

$$x = a\cos\theta^1 \sqrt{1 - \frac{b^2}{a^2}\sin^2\theta^2} \sqrt{1 + \frac{b^2}{a^2}\sinh^2\theta^3}$$
$$y = b\sin\theta^1 \cos\theta^2 \cosh\theta^3$$
$$z = b\sqrt{\sin^2\theta^1 + \frac{b^2}{a^2}\cos^2\theta^1}\,\sin\theta^2\sinh\theta^3$$

Here $a$ and $b$ are again constants, although their numerical value would have to be changed to get the same surface. The third constant is $\theta^3$ and we shall see presently why the superscript 3 is used. This principal curvature coordinate net is shown in figure 2. It can be shown that this is indeed a principal curvature net by $g_{12} = 0$ and $b_{12} = 0$ .

The source code for the C++ computer program which produced this image is given in an appendix. The program produces .dxf files for drawing lines and faces and an .stl file for 3D printing. They are all text files and can be opened by all sorts of software. C++ is controlled by the International Organization for Standardization and one can be certain that a program written now will continue to work on any computer in the foreseeable future.

### ELLIPSOIDAL VAULT
Figure 3 is plate 44 from Charles-François-Antoine Leroy's *Traité de stéréotomie* of 1870.[4] It shows an ellipsoidal vault with the joints between the stone blocks following the principal curvature directions. I have superimposed numerically calculated curves in red, demonstrating the accuracy of Leroy's drawing.

Figures 4 and 5 are computer generated using a program very similar in principle to that in the appendix. However the program is somewhat longer due to the fact that each block is defined by six curved surfaces defining its faces. In the equations

$$x = a\cos\theta^1 \sqrt{1 - \frac{b^2}{a^2}\sin^2\theta^2} \sqrt{1 + \frac{b^2}{a^2}\sinh^2\theta^3}$$
$$y = b\sin\theta^1 \cos\theta^2 \cosh\theta^3$$
$$z = b\sqrt{\sin^2\theta^1 + \frac{b^2}{a^2}\cos^2\theta^1}\,\sin\theta^2\sinh\theta^3$$

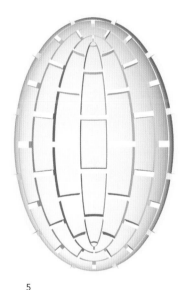

5

5 Computer-generated ellipsoidal vault: rendering.

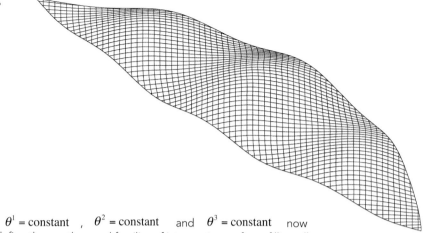

$\theta^1 = \text{constant}$ , $\theta^2 = \text{constant}$ and $\theta^3 = \text{constant}$ now define three orthogonal families of intersecting surfaces filling all space. The surfaces are hyperboloids of one sheet, hyperboloids of two sheets and ellipsoids.

### GENERAL THEORY OF RELATIVITY

PAM Dirac's *General Theory of Relativity* (1975) describes the mathematics of Einstein's theory in just 68 pages.[5] He uses $x^\alpha$ instead of $\theta^\alpha$ and now $\alpha$ takes the four values 0, 1, 2 and 3 for four-dimensional space-time. The equation

$$ds^2 = g_{\alpha\beta} d\theta^\alpha d\theta^\beta$$

still applies, except now $ds$ is the time interval experienced by an observer who is present at two adjacent events in space-time.

Most people are aware that mass curves space-time to produce gravity. In fact it is not just mass, but the stress–energy–momentum tensor which curves space-time, producing a complete unification of mechanics and geometry.

Geodesics on a surface are lines that have zero curvature when viewed normal to a surface. The shortest distance between two points on a surface is a geodesic. The differential equation for a geodesic on a surface is exactly the same as it is in space-time, except for the change of the number of coordinates. The planets move along geodesics in space-time.

### HOW MUCH GEOMETRY DO YOU NEED TO KNOW?
The question here is: How much geometry do you need to know to do it yourself rather than rely on someone else's software?

This is a bit like asking 'How good do you have to be at cycling to go by bike rather than by bus with someone else driving?' The answer is: 'It all depends.'

Geometry is such a large and varied subject that even professional mathematicians specialising in geometry only know bits of the whole picture. Thus to specify a minimum knowledge threshold is ridiculous.

6 Geometry of the Savill Building, Windsor Great Park, UK, 2006 (Glenn Howells Architects, Buro Happold, Green Oak Carpentry).

You don't have to be Bradley Wiggins (the British cyclist who has recently won the Tour de France and an Olympic gold medal) to ride to the shops. On the other hand, you have to be sufficiently competent for the risks of an accident not to be too great.

Thus with geometry, provided you get your building to fit together, it does not matter how much you do or don't know. If you find a nice curve or surface somewhere with interesting properties you can incorporate it into your design. This was very much the approach I adopted for projects like the British Museum Great Court (Foster + Partners, Buro Happold, Waagner-Biro; 2000) and the Savill Building at Windsor Great Park (Glenn Howells Architects, Buro Happold, Green Oak Carpentry; 2006). The section of the Savill Building is based on the damped sine wave:

$$z = e^{-\frac{x^2}{a^2}} \cos\left(\frac{2\pi x}{\lambda}\right)$$

in which the wavelength, $\lambda$, is a function of $x$.

Geometry does not just mean curves; there is also proportion applied to rectilinear objects. One might obtain inspiration from the golden ratio or plastic number. The plastic number corresponds to the limit of the Padovan sequence[6] in the same way that the golden ratio is the limit of the Fibonacci sequence.

REFERENCES

1 See: PAM Dirac, *General Theory of Relativity*, John Wiley & Sons (New York, NY), 1975.

2 Dirk J Struik, *Lectures on Classical Differential Geometry*, Dover Publications (New York, NY), second edition, 1988.

3 Albert E Green and Wolfgang Zerna, *Theoretical Elasticity*, Oxford University Press (Oxford), second revised edition, 1968.

4 Charles-François-Antoine Leroy, *Traité de stéréotomie: comprenant les applications de la géométrie descriptive à la théorie des ombres, la perspective linéaire, la gnomonique, la coupe des pierres et la charpente*, Gauthier-Villars (Paris) 1870: text and plates (*planches*) in separate volumes.

5 See: PAM Dirac, *General Theory of Relativity*, John Wiley & Sons (New York, NY), 1975.

6 Richard Padovan, *Dom Hans van der Laan: Modern Primitive*, Architectura & Natura Press (Amsterdam), 1994.

IMAGES

Figures 1, 2, 4, 5, 6 © Dr CJK Williams; Figure 3 Courtesy of Dr CJK Williams

## APPENDIX: ELLIPSOID COMPUTER PROGRAM

```cpp
#include <iostream>
#include <fstream>
#include <cmath>
#include <cstdlib>
using namespace std;
#define halfStep 2
#define step    (2 * halfStep)
#define m       (50 * 2 * step)
#define n       (2 * m)
double x[m + 1][n+ 1],y[m + 1][n+ 1],z[m + 1][n+ 1];
void makeSTLTriangle(int,int,int,int,int,int);
ofstream Julia("Ellipsoid.dxf");
ofstream Constance("EllipsoidLines.dxf");
ofstream Madeleine("Ellipsoid.stl");
int main(void)
{
    double a = 1000.0;
    double b =  600.0;
    double ratioSq = (b * b) / (a * a);
    double delta = 4.0 * atan(1.0) / (double) m;
    double w = 0.5;
    for(int i = 0;i <= m;i++)
    {
        double u = (double) i * delta;
        for(int j = 0;j <= n;j++)
        {
            double v = (double) j * delta;
            x[i][j] = a * cos(u)
            * sqrt((1.0 - ratioSq * sin(v) * sin(v)) * (1.0 + ratioSq * sinh(w) * sinh(w)));
            y[i][j] = b * sin(u) * cos(v) * cosh(w);
            z[i][j] = b * sqrt(sin(u) * sin(u) + ratioSq * cos(u) * cos(u)) * sin(v) * sinh(w);
        }
    }
    Julia<<"0\nSECTION\n2\nENTITIES\n";
    Constance<<"0\nSECTION\n2\nENTITIES\n";
    Madeleine<<"solid Ellipsoid\n";
    for(int i = 0;i <= m - 1;i++)
    {
        for(int j = 0;j <= n - 1;j++)
        {
            Julia<<"0\n3DFACE\n8\nEllipsoid\n";
            Julia<<"10\n"<<x[i   ][j   ]<<"\n";
            Julia<<"20\n"<<y[i   ][j   ]<<"\n";
            Julia<<"30\n"<<z[i   ][j   ]<<"\n";
            Julia<<"11\n"<<x[i + 1][j   ]<<"\n";
            Julia<<"21\n"<<y[i + 1][j   ]<<"\n";
            Julia<<"31\n"<<z[i + 1][j   ]<<"\n";
            Julia<<"12\n"<<x[i + 1][j + 1]<<"\n";
            Julia<<"22\n"<<y[i + 1][j + 1]<<"\n";
            Julia<<"32\n"<<z[i + 1][j + 1]<<"\n";
            Julia<<"13\n"<<x[i   ][j + 1]<<"\n";
            Julia<<"23\n"<<y[i   ][j + 1]<<"\n";
            Julia<<"33\n"<<z[i   ][j + 1]<<"\n";
            makeSTLTriangle(i,j,i + 1,j,i + 1,j + 1   );
            makeSTLTriangle(i,j,     i + 1,j + 1,i,j + 1);
        }
    }
    for(int i = 0;i <= m - 1;i++)
    {
        for(int j = halfStep;j <= n - halfStep;j += step)
        {
            Constance<<"0\nLINE\n8\nEllipsoid\n";
            Constance<<"10\n"<<x[i   ][j]<<"\n";
```

```cpp
          Constance<<"20\n"<<y[i    ][j]<<"\n";
          Constance<<"30\n"<<z[i    ][j]<<"\n";
          Constance<<"11\n"<<x[i + 1][j]<<"\n";
          Constance<<"21\n"<<y[i + 1][j]<<"\n";
          Constance<<"31\n"<<z[i + 1][j]<<"\n";
      }
  }
  for(int i = halfStep;i <= m - halfStep;i += step)
  {
      for(int j = 0;j <= n - 1;j++)
      {
          Constance<<"0\nLINE\n8\nEllipsoid\n";
          Constance<<"10\n"<<x[i][j    ]<<"\n";
          Constance<<"20\n"<<y[i][j    ]<<"\n";
          Constance<<"30\n"<<z[i][j    ]<<"\n";
          Constance<<"11\n"<<x[i][j + 1]<<"\n";
          Constance<<"21\n"<<y[i][j + 1]<<"\n";
          Constance<<"31\n"<<z[i][j + 1]<<"\n";
      }
  }
  Julia<<"0\nENDSEC\n0\nEOF\n";
  Julia.close();
  Constance<<"0\nENDSEC\n0\nEOF\n";
  Constance.close();
  Madeleine<<"endsolid Ellipsoid\n";
  Madeleine.close();
  cout<<"DXF and stl files written, end of program\n";
  return 0;
}
void makeSTLTriangle(int iA,int jA,int iB,int jB,int iC,int jC)
{
  double vector1[3],vector2[3],normal[3];
  vector1[0] = x[iB][jB] - x[iA][jA];
  vector1[1] = y[iB][jB] - y[iA][jA];
  vector1[2] = z[iB][jB] - z[iA][jA];
  vector2[0] = x[iC][jC] - x[iA][jA];
  vector2[1] = y[iC][jC] - y[iA][jA];
  vector2[2] = z[iC][jC] - z[iA][jA];
  double sumSq = 0.0;
  for(int xyz = 0;xyz <=2;xyz ++)
  {
      int xyzp1 = xyz + 1;
      int xyzp2 = xyz + 2;
      if(xyzp1 > 2)xyzp1 -= 3;
      if(xyzp2 > 2)xyzp2 -= 3;
      normal[xyz]
      = vector1[xyzp1] * vector2[xyzp2]
      - vector1[xyzp2] * vector2[xyzp1];
      sumSq += normal[xyz] * normal[xyz];
  }
  if(sumSq > 1.0e-6)//To remove zero area triangles
  {
      double length = sqrt(sumSq);
      for(int xyz = 0;xyz <=2;xyz ++)normal[xyz] /= length;
      Madeleine<<"facet normal";
      for(int xyz = 0;xyz <=2;xyz ++)Madeleine<<" "<<normal[xyz];
      Madeleine<<"\nouter loop\n";
      Madeleine<<"vertex "<<x[iA][jA]<<" "<<y[iA][jA]<<" "<<z[iA][jA]<<"\n";
      Madeleine<<"vertex "<<x[iB][jB]<<" "<<y[iB][jB]<<" "<<z[iB][jB]<<"\n";
      Madeleine<<"vertex "<<x[iC][jC]<<" "<<y[iC][jC]<<" "<<z[iC][jC]<<"\n";
      Madeleine<<"endloop\nendfacet\n";
  }
  else cout<<"Zero area triangle\n";
}
```

# GENERATIVE COMPONENTS AND SMARTGEOMETRY:
## SITUATED SOFTWARE DEVELOPMENT

VOLKER MUELLER
AND MAKAI SMITH

Software developers Bentley Systems have been a key part of the
Smartgeometry (SG) community since the first workshop in 2003, providing
financial and organisational support, expertise and software. Yearly
SG events provide a unique setting of dedicated high-level users for
sharing cutting-edge intellectual and technical ideas in architecture and
engineering. GenerativeComponents (GC) is among the programs used
by leading academics and practitioners who explore their designs through
developing creative parametric tools. Here, Volker Mueller (Research
Director for Computational Design) and Makai Smith (Product Manager
of GenerativeComponents) explain how Bentley Systems engages with
advanced users at SG, pushing continued developments in GC software.

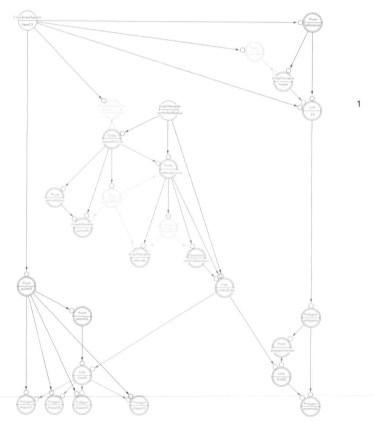

1

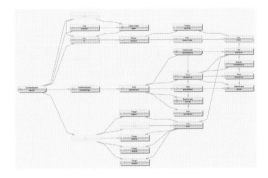

2

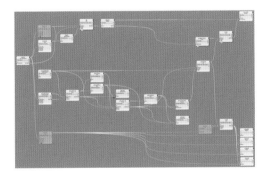

3

Over the past decade, there has been a strong link between the development of Bentley's GenerativeComponents (GC) software and the SG community. The two have developed together, allowing users to influence the software development and the software to impact design practice. The authors have an insider's and an outsider's view: for the first few years of GC's development, both used GC in practice in architecture and digital fabrication. Since 2008 and 2007, respectively, they have been directly involved in the development of GC at Bentley Systems.

## SOFTWARE DEVELOPMENT AND USER GROUP INPUT

The development of a groundbreaking design tool for the architectural domain with its long-standing traditions harbours challenges that cannot be discovered and solved in isolation: a close connection to users is fundamentally important. GC users work in innovative design practices, architecture and engineering alike, that are agile, adopt new processes, and adjust them competently to their specific needs. Adaptability is a core concept in GC. It has a means to create new object types and behaviours on the fly (hence, GC was initially called CustomObjects). Functionality like 'generated feature types' does not spring from a vacuum. It arises from intensive communication with and validation by users.

Starting with the Cambridge, UK workshop in 2003, SG provided close contact with forward-thinking user firms. At the core of the SG community are its founders and intellectual sustainers, the SG directors, tutors and other contributors. Around this core group there have been annual gatherings, at the SG events, of curious, adventurous and forward-thinking researcher-practitioners of design from architecture, engineering, industrial design, mathematics, natural sciences and the arts, and other cross-disciplinarians from beyond; and students, practitioners, educators, or any combination thereof. This unique group has been providing insights into the evolving practice of computational design to the GC design and development team. Bentley discovered early on that supporting SG provides the benefit of access to a unique community of individuals, institutions and firms. Therefore, Bentley has been the main sponsor of SG events, has provided extensive organisational support, and facilitated access to software and supplementary training.

Because SG attracts attendees from many disciplines, it spreads feedback about software usability beyond discipline-specific boundaries. It also drives home the point that there are different approaches to computational design, three of which have been incorporated in GC and are continually enhanced: a coding-oriented approach through scripting and programmatic extensibility; a diagrammatic or graphical programming-oriented approach through the Graph (previously called Symbolic View or Diagram); and a geometric computer-aided design (CAD) modelling approach through the model view. These three different modes of creating or interacting with the conceptual 'model' respond to the idea of multiplicity as a requirement for design software.[1]

1 Symbolic View in early versions of GC captured from GC 08.09.04.51, released in 2008.

2 Symbolic Diagram in v8 versions of GC captured from GC 08.11.08.260, released in 2011.

3 Graph in v8i beta version of GC captured from GC 08.11.09.110, as used at SG 2012. This graph allows placement of nodes without all inputs present, making it useful as a conceptual diagrammatic sketching canvas.

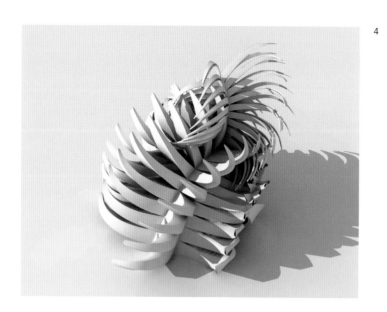

4

4 Martin Krcha at SG 2008 in Munich pursued artful serendipity.

5 At SG 2008 in Munich, Dirk Krolikowski from Rogers Stirk Harbour + Partners in London implemented typical megaframe connections on The Leadenhall Building, a development by British Land and Oxford Properties.

6 Screen capture of GC captured from GC 08.11.09.110, as used at SG 2012, Rensselaer Polytechnic Institute, Troy, New York, USA. This shows Transactions, Script Editor for scripting, the Graph for graphical programming, and the Model View for interaction with the geometric model.

5

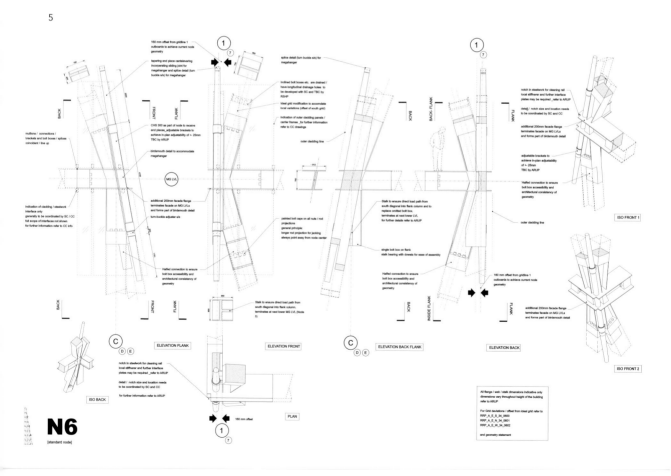

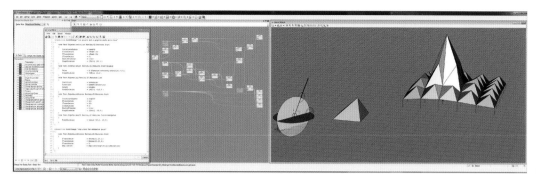

## 6

By its one-to-many nature, the relationship of software makers to their users makes it difficult to distinctly hear users' voices. The antidote to this is frequent contact between tool-maker and users in situ. The partnership of SG and Bentley has helped to individualise the many users' objectives for GC – it is a forum in which software use and architectural culture crystallise into requirements for software development. It also provides an intense and efficient environment for the collection of user feedback. SG 2008 recorded more than a hundred people using GC simultaneously for four intense days: this amounts to nearly two person-years of work. To experience so much effort compressed in space and time affords our software team an unparalleled opportunity to spot trends and form a cohesive picture about what is important to the users' projects.

## MUTUAL LEARNING PROCESS

Until 2009, the workshops were organised to serve a dual purpose: familiarising participants with software in development, as well as exploring and inventing an emerging approach to modelling using a parametrically controlled, dependency-driven change propagation system, concisely termed parametric modelling. Parametric modelling is very different from direct modelling, allowing an approach that tends towards thinking and designing with an eye to abstract, conceptual underpinnings rather than the representational level. SG is at the epicentre of a transition in architectural discourse from a focus on one-off drawings to accurate, computable models that support design investigations.

Feedback on usability and suggestions for new functionality allow the development team to learn about evolving design processes based on the parametric paradigm. The conference days following the workshops at each SG event provide further insight into practice and theory of parametric design, with presenters such as Patrik Schumacher, Helmut Pottmann and Brett Steele at SG 2008 in Munich, or keynotes from practitioners such as Hanif Kara, Ben van Berkel and Enric Ruiz-Geli.

Another important aspect of SG events is the opportunity to explore requirements for parametric design education. Collaboration with researchers and educators such as Dr Earl Mark and Dr Robert Woodbury has increased our understanding of the cognitive challenges a switch to parametric design poses.[2]

cleaning rail
150 mm x 150 mm

mega hanger

Mega LVL beam

birdsmouth detail to
accommodate megahanger
subject to further investigation
during stage E

additional 200mm facade flange
terminates facade on MG LVLs
and form part of birdsmouth detail

halfed connection to minimise
node overall size / craneage
weight while ensuring bolt
box accessibility

mega hanger bracket

floor beam

bracket for cleaning rail

node 7

## BETA-TESTING VERSUS USABILITY LABS

SG workshops are similar to free-form beta testing, but with consistently advanced users and a topic of inquiry provided by the organisers. These workshops also enjoy deep support from Bentley colleagues. In terms of development feedback, the concentration within a few days of intense pursuits is the outstanding benefit that such an event provides compared to the slow trickle of feedback that happens in free-form beta testing. This concerted feedback delivers a concentrated profile of the state of the software in the context of practical demands, enhanced by the voluntary deadline pressure of workshop participants desiring to produce presentable results within the workshop time frame.

Beginning in 2010 we started to supplement the feedback collected at SG with GC usability labs, pairing a lab at 'Be Together' (the Bentley user conference) with a follow-on event in London, UK. In contrast to SG workshops, usability labs are focused on testing one or two ideas thoroughly within a much shorter time period, typically 90 minutes. Following detailed scripts, users are observed to validate the software developers' assumptions implemented in the software. There are no instructions beyond the ones in the script; if supplemental information appears necessary, it is noted why and when it is inserted into the lab process; the colleagues conducting usability labs are there to closely observe the participants and take note of challenges users encounter and how they overcome them, and of any other noteworthy events. Chronological tracking is crucial to the evaluation of the lab log. After tasks, and especially after the lab concludes, the experiences are discussed. The usability labs that have been conducted investigated discoverability, GC's new Graph, and Node Groups. Lab results are summarised for the development team so that insights gained are incorporated into the development plans.

## CO-EVOLUTION

GC as an application of technology developed for the design of smooth and complex forms has grown up. It passed through the phase in which its fundamental mathematical and computer-graphic underpinnings stabilised. Now, a second wave of technology transfer is emanating from its users as GC and the SG community push into new territories of design investigation, charting pursuits into interactivity, materiality and invisible realms. Evidence is found in experiments with links between GC software and physical computing (actuators and sensors), and a melding of descriptors of form with predictors of behaviour (the model and its performance). At the same time, the nature of the workshops has evolved from being largely a geometric and algorithmic pursuit to one about performance and feedback explored through physical prototyping. SG has moved from the computationally abstract to the tangibly real while, ironically, shifting from problems derived from real projects to more abstract pursuits of pure research.

Looking at nearly a decade of SG conferences reveals a consistent vision for the future of computational design – a

7

vision that anticipates users moving away from employing computational design as a means to produce conventional architectural representations and towards something more. It is a search for ways to expand the scope of what may be represented computationally. Material, energetic and informational aspects accumulate and are brought into a transactional, dependent relationship with established design elements of geometry, program and notation. This approach takes advantage of the blossoming of computational power, but to do so it must confront the physical reality of architectural practice, which is not always so sanguine.

## DESIGN PURSUITS SHAPING SOFTWARE DEVELOPMENT

Conventional wisdom holds that design processes are iterative and nonlinear. These processes, however, are very often limited to just a few alternatives that are developed in parallel, and only for several iterations. Moreover, they are hampered by the inclination of designers to keep largely invalid design variants because they incorporate compelling solutions to parts of the challenge, without lending themselves to separating strengths and weaknesses because they intermingle responses to conflicting goals. Another factor is the thought and labour already invested in them. Parametric modelling helps avoid these pitfalls of direct modelling and lifts them to the conceptual level.

Design aspires to move from initial ideas to more refined versions that meet the design goals in increasingly improved ways. Parametric design allows design teams to include in the model design goals and the expectations for these goals expressed as performance measures. This requires a mapping of design goals to building behaviours, defining metrics that allow the measurement of these behaviours, and determination of their performance goals. Building behaviours can be simulated and analysed, or performance can be directly computed from the model.

## TOWARDS MULTI-OBJECTIVE DESIGN REFINEMENT

Given a set of parameters that drives a building model, even with limited parameter ranges and low granularity, the set of possible designs, or 'design space', described by that parameter set grows exponentially with the number of parameters used. Therefore, it becomes unfeasible for a user to traverse and explore a complete design space in order to identify all feasible solutions, the 'solution space', and within it the one design that meets all design goals in the best possible manner – that is, the optimal design. Consequently, an automated search approach is often more successful in identifying best-performing designs than a design team.

One also cannot expect a single optimal solution in design situations with multiple goals. At least some of those goals will be in direct conflict, and no single optimal solution exists. These are multi-objective situations. A proven approach to their resolution is multi-objective optimisation. Especially in engineering design, the term 'multidisciplinary optimisation' (MDO) is used synonymously,

7 The Leadenhall Building, a development by British Land and Oxford Properties, Rogers Stirk Harbour + Partners, London (Rendering).

8a and 8b Populous's Olympique Lyonnais
Stadium at SG 2008, Munich.
David Hines & Eduardo McIntosh of Populous
(formerly HOK Sports) investigated the
Olympique Lyonnais Stadium at SG 2008.

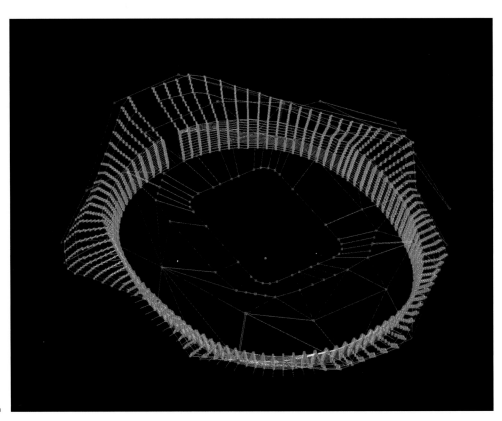

8a

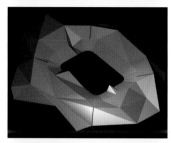

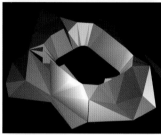

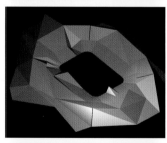

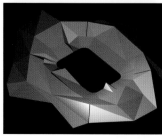

8b

implying that complex design challenges involve a variety of design and engineering disciplines, that different disciplines have different goals, and that these goals are often conflicting.

There are two major approaches to resolving conflicting goals. One approach prioritises goals and computes a single optimum.[3] The other looks for the relative best performers for each goal compared to the others. For performance measures of two goals plotted in a graph, a conflicting situation may appear as a curve – a so-called Pareto front – which lets the design team explore how the two goals compare, what the trade-offs are, and what the respective solutions look like.[4] In some cases the simulations or analyses necessary for performance evaluation take time as well, which makes a brute-force search through the entire design space unfeasible even with current computing resources. Therefore, the searches through the design space themselves need to be 'optimised'. One proven approach is the use of genetic algorithms.

Genetic algorithms are modelled after a simplified concept of evolutionary processes as a population's most successful individuals mating to create successive generations. They pass on properties encoded in genes, with mutations to the genetic code introducing arbitrary change or evolutionary opportunities. Continuous selection of successful individuals based on better performance drives improvements across successive generations. In parametric systems, genetic code is expressed by the system parameters; selection is based on calculations using various simulations and analyses or other metrics in combination with subsequent filtering for the best-performing individuals; mutation is modelled by applying some randomised spread to the parameters; and generational succession is modelled by splitting, mixing and mating the parameter sets extracted from the most successful individuals of a preceding generation to spawn new individuals for the next generation, creating evolutionary opportunities to prevent stagnation.

Successive improvement through many generations has strong parallels to iterative design refinement. The knowledge gained from examining the information generated by optimisation processes can then be used to refine the model iteratively by revising the design goals, revising the architectural design scheme, eliminating ineffective parameters, adding new parameters, modifying parameter ranges or parameter granularity, changing analysis or simulation parameters, and any other strategy imaginable.

Interest in optimisation using GC had become apparent at various SG events where attendees pursued optimisation schemes, either as geometric optimisation, including minimal surfaces and relaxation of particle spring systems, or as more complex iterations between a GC model and higher-end analyses such as structural analysis. For example, Populous (formerly HOK Sports) iterated the design for the Olympique Lyonnais Stadium

9

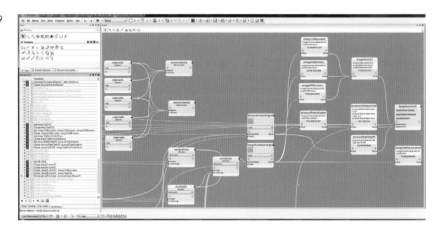

10

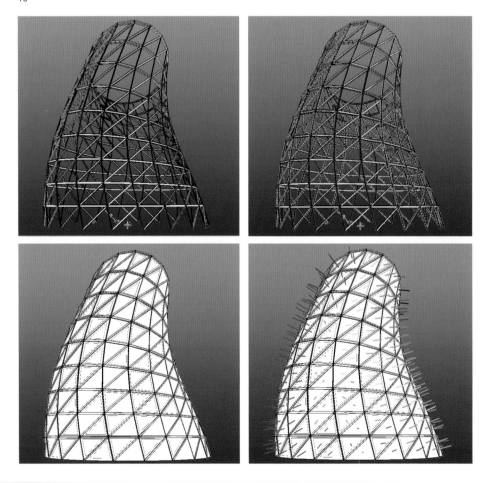

at SG 2008 to gain insight into parametric exploration of the stadium roof.[5]

## DESIGN DECISION SUPPORT

MDO addresses the challenges of generating design variations that illuminate sufficiently the potential range of the solution space by permitting the generation of many potential solutions, automating the substantive labour of selecting the most viable solutions, and eliminating those that do not perform well enough. With this filtering, MDO reduces the amount of time needed to narrow the choices down to viable solutions. In addition, with appropriate representations of the resultant evaluation of performance characteristics, MDO starts to support the design team's decision making.

With the introduction of thematic pursuits at SG 2010 held at IAAC, Barcelona, Spain, the relevance of cross-disciplinary explorations was made explicit, culminating in 2012 with the investigation of effective, optimal use of materials. This made the need for inclusion of optimisation as a component of GC even more apparent. For SG 2012, specialised node types were added to GC's vocabulary, including feature types needed for structural and energy analyses, such as structural members, building surfaces, nodes carrying project information, and structural and energy analysis nodes. Another node connected the model and its performance analysis results to the Darwin framework, which uses the Design Evolution genetic algorithm for multi-objective optimisation.[6] This enabled participants in the 'Material Conflicts' cluster to include material variations in their investigation of parametric designs with multi-objective optimisation for effective exploration of the solution space.

## ONGOING EXCHANGE

The partnership of SG and Bentley has helped to individualise the many users' objectives for GC into requirements for software development. SG events provide an intense and efficient environment for software testing and the collection of user feedback. Thus, for over a decade, GC has evolved as a result of a continuous dialogue between its developers and the advanced user community around SG.

This ongoing exchange between offered software capabilities, their usage in design processes, and desired capabilities to enhance support of innovative design approaches has advanced both the software and the practice of parametric design that requires this software. Clearly, future enhancements of design decision support, for example by close connectivity to analyses, simulations and optimisation algorithms, have risen above the horizon. Moreover, they offer the promise of a deepened understanding of the designed artefact before it is physically manifested with all its impact on the environment in general, and its surroundings and human users in particular.

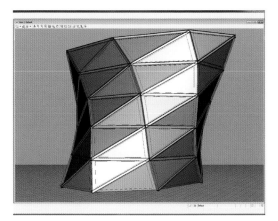

9 'Material Conflicts' cluster at SG 2012, Rensselaer Polytechnic Institute, Troy, New York, USA.
The cluster used structural and energy analyses with a genetic algorithm to explore MDO.

10 The analysis nodes feed the analysis results back into GC for further parametric consumption.

South elevation optimisation

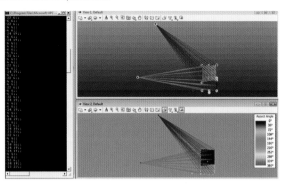

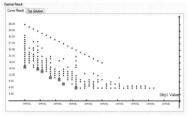

North elevation optimisation

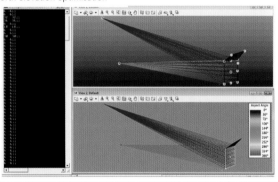

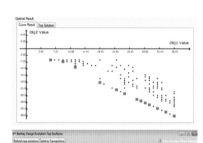

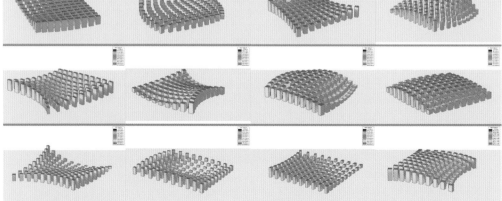

11 With help from Samuel Wilkinson, Greig Paterson investigated an urban design for maximum shading and minimum view obstruction (images recreated by the authors).

**REFERENCES**

1 Volker Mueller and Ivanka Iordanova, 'Rethinking Concept Design Tools: High-Level Requirements for Concept Design Tools', in *Circuit Bending, Breaking and Mending: Proceedings of the 16th International Conference on Computer-Aided Architectural Design Research in Asia (CAADRIA)*, Newcastle, New South Wales, Australia, 27–29 April 2011, pp 409–18.

2 Robert Woodbury, *Elements of Parametric Design*, Routledge (London; New York, NY), 2010 and Cheryl Qian, 'Design Patterns: Augmenting Design Practice in Parametric CAD Systems', dissertation submitted in partial fulfilment of the requirements for the degree of Doctor of Philosophy in the School of Interactive Arts and Technology, Simon Fraser University, Surry, BC, Canada, Summer 2009.

3 John Chachere and John Haymaker, *Framework for Measuring Rationale Clarity of AEC Design Decisions*, CIFE Technical Report TR177, Stanford University (Stanford, CA), November 2008; John Haymaker and John Chachere: *Coordinating Goals, Preferences, Options, and Analyses for the Stanford Living Laboratory Feasibility Study*, CIFE Technical Report TR181, Stanford University (Stanford, CA), March 2009.

4 Megan Neill, Roel van de Straat, Jeroen Coenders, 'Decision Support Tools for Parametric Design', in *Proceedings of the International Association for Shell and Spatial Structures (IASS) Symposium 2009*, Valencia, Spain, 28 September to 2 October 2009, pp 1145–53.

5 Roly Hudson, 'Frameworks for Practical Parametric Design in Architecture', in *Advances in Architectural Geometry (AAG): First Symposium on Architectural Geometry*, Vienna, Austria, 13–16 September 2008, pp 17–20.

6 Zheng Y Wu and Pradeep Katta, *Applying Genetic Algorithm to Geometry Design Optimisation: Improving Design by Emulating Natural Evolution*, Technical Report, Bentley Systems Incorporated (Watertown, CT), 2009.

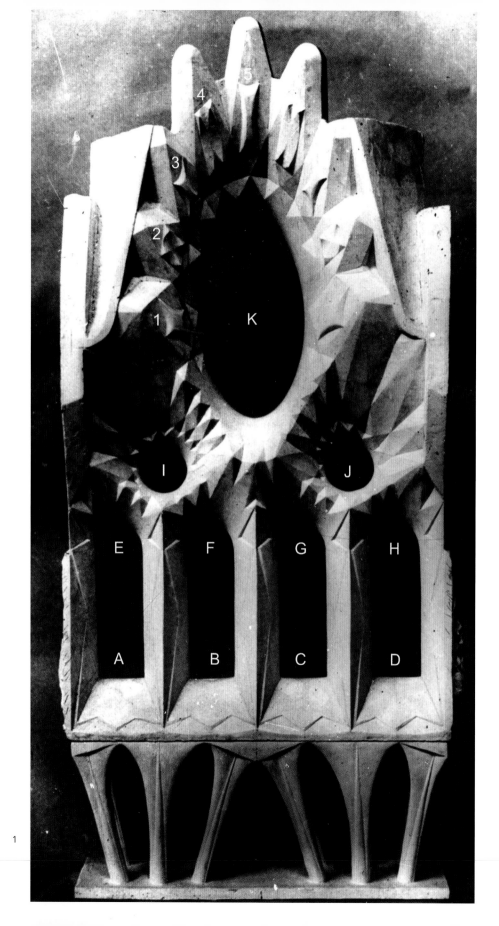

1

# FROM DESCRIPTIVE GEOMETRY TO SMARTGEOMETRY:
MARK BURRY

## FIRST STEPS TOWARDS DIGITAL ARCHITECTURE

Architect Mark Burry offers a personal account of his adventures in the world of applied architectural geometry – a journey that has gone from a solo experience to a shared experience. Since the first events, he has been an extremely influential and inspirational part of the Smartgeometry (SG) community, especially relating to his work completing Gaudí's unfinished masterpiece, the Sagrada Família Basilica, using bespoke digital tools. Here he reflects on over two decades of engagement with what he regards as an elusive concept: emerging digital architecture. He discusses how his work has gone from descriptive geometry, through computing and analysing geometry, to a collective notion of 'smart' geometry.

1 Sagrada Família Basilica, Barcelona, Spain, 1883–: Antoni Gaudí's 1:10-scale model of his final design for the clerestory window.
The letters refer to individual hyperboloids of revolution of one sheet.

I was fortunate to encounter Antoni Gaudí (1852–1926) at the operationally pointy end of that ultimate architectural adventure, that is, at a project level rather than just curiously observing his rather surprising oeuvre hands-off. In doing so in 1979 I was introduced to descriptive geometry in ways that I had had no such opportunity to engage with at high school nor subsequently during my architectural education. My further good fortune was to be doing this at least 10 years before architects typically could even think about acquiring a personal computer with appropriate software. 'Appropriate' refers to software styled around the software engineers' perspective of how they think designers think and operate. When I came to transfer my hard-won analogue descriptive geometry techniques to computer-aided design and drafting in 1989, no architectural software was remotely capable of the task that I had in hand, yet the software packages that had been developed for ship and aircraft designers could tackle such challenges with relative élan. I have Robert Aish to thank for his early recognition of the dimensions of my task and its opportunities, and a way forwards.

Twenty-three years on from my introduction to computers and architectural practice, the deficiencies of mainstream architectural software for certain types of experimental design research are still with us. The more exacting portions of the work we undertake to assist in the completion of Gaudí's major work, the Sagrada Família Basilica in Barcelona, continues to be aided primarily through the use of very high-end aircraft design software. What this means is that

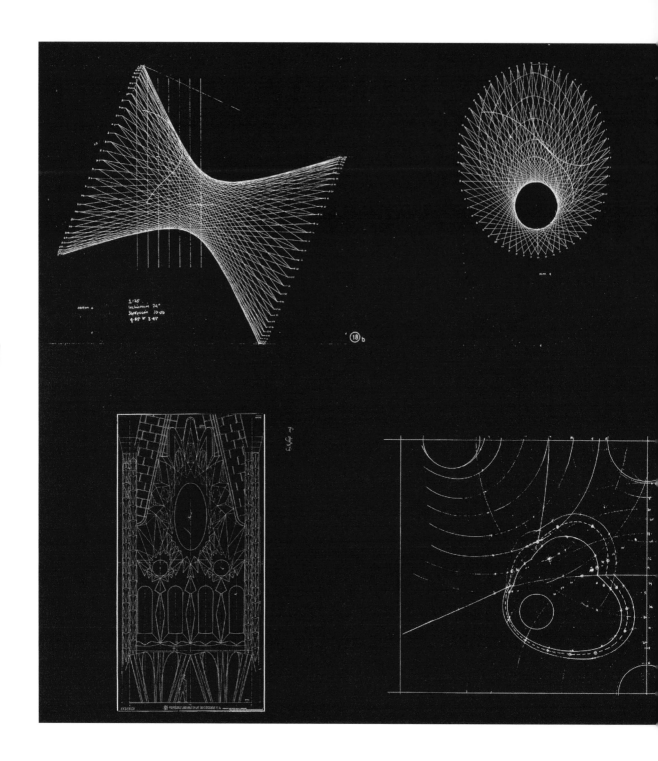

2 Sagrada Família Basilica, Barcelona,
Spain: hand-drawn projections seeking the
intersections between adjacent surfaces (drawn
by the author in 1979–80).

the task Gaudí set his latter-day successors between his engagement on the project in 1883 and his death in 1926 still sits outside the dominant paradigm of architectural practice, as evidenced by the deficiency of architectural software – its lack of any flexible efficacy for a design approach that is more sculptural than pragmatic. Eight decades later, even the best software is not equal to his formal and computational challenges. This is where the world of Gaudí converges with the world of the 21st-century Smartgeometer, because these deficiencies are the stuff that has forced us all to think and act outside the box, and ultimately form a community.

## DESCRIPTIVE GEOMETRY

My first incursion into descriptive geometry using the computer was conducted through a literal translation of my hand-drawn techniques. The problems I was tackling when I entered the Sagrada Família technical office were simple to describe: take a range of second-order (doubly ruled) surfaces and intersect them in space. Having done so, take the fourth-order curves of intersection between adjacent surfaces and identify points of their mutual intersection, which occur when three such lines intersect – the 'triple points'. Finally, select various rulings and, guided by the architectonic opportunities provided by the triple points and their component intersection curves, 'play' with the respective hyperbolic surfaces by introducing different doubly ruled surfaces. Thus if the primary intersections were between hyperboloids of revolution of one sheet, the interplay I describe between the surfaces would be selected from the remaining two members of a set containing only three possibilities: the plane and the hyperbolic paraboloid.[1]

Of course it is a touch disingenuous to talk of this being 'simple to describe' because the execution of the task was anything but an easy one. I had originally soldiered on, successfully constructing intersections between adjacent surfaces graphically by hand using strange (to me) drawing and measurement instruments in the manner of the 18th-century French stereotomers. I produced my traits through projecting various views simultaneously on paper.[2] It quickly became obvious that this almost tactile approach in straightforwardly adapting my manual drafting technique to the mouse and keyboard was an abuse of opportunity, and I was plunged into the world of design computation.

## COMPUTING GEOMETRY

As so often happens, this came about through a chance conversation. When we met in 1993 Peter Wood, an engineer in Wellington, New Zealand, seemed incredulous about my laborious (to him) approach to intersecting surfaces using a highly sophisticated parametric 3D solids modeller as if it were merely a digital version of my pen, ruler and compasses. Whereas I was carefully varying the parameters of prospective surfaces and computationally performing Boolean intersections using my chosen engineering software (CADDS5) to test the results against the painstakingly measured data extracted from Gaudí's original 1:10-scaled model fragments, he suggested that we collaborate around an optimisation technique through computation.

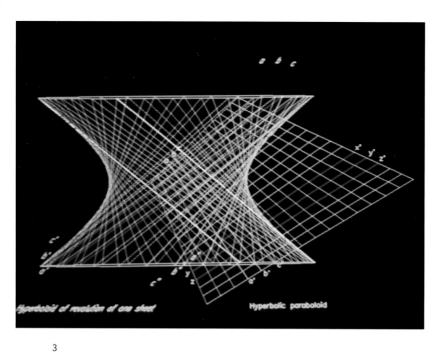

3

3 Sagrada Família Basilica, Barcelona, Spain: futile attempt to intersect a hyperboloid with hyperbolic paraboloid using mainstream architectural software (1989).

4

4 Sagrada Família Basilica, Barcelona, Spain: sequence of Xhyper app windows by which data files are read, parsed and processed by the software (1994).
With up to nine unknown parameter values, the app calculates the optimum hyperboloid in terms of most closely matching the selection of points measured from the surviving fragments of Gaudí's 1:10-scale plaster model. The panel on the right is a script generator translating the data from Xhyper directly into a digital model-maker.

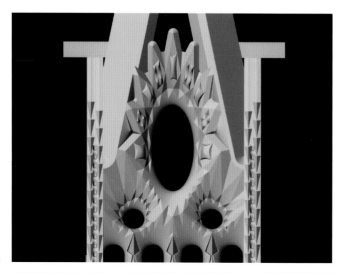

5

5 Sagrada Família Basilica, Barcelona, Spain: digital 'remastering' of Gaudí's 1:10-scale model for the clerestory, produced directly using the script generated by Xhyper in the previous image (1994).

6 Sagrada Família Basilica, Barcelona, Spain: sequence in the creation of planar decorative engravings in the hyperboloid surfaces capitalising on the constituent straight-line geometry (generatrices).

At that time (1992–5) I was working on the clerestory window (*finestral de la nau central*). With a model-making colleague based on site in Barcelona, we had spent six weeks first devising a measuring instrument then using it to find the positions in all three coordinate dimensions of 550 representative points in space on the model. The triple points and points around the collar of the hyperboloids were obviously primary measurements. Of secondary importance were points along the 3D curves of intersection between adjacent surfaces, and third in priority were points measured on the faces of the surfaces. The data for each surface was made into an input file and ranked hierarchically. Peter prepared a series of applets to run in UNIX (called 'Xhyper') which first read the data, then parsed it around the declared priorities and, using either of two genetic algorithms, homed in on a set of parameters for each surface as a 'best fit' solution. The reason for using two possible approaches ('Simplex' and 'hill-climbing') was to accommodate two potential extremes: relatively copious data and a high number of unknown parameters, and the opposite.

The points' relative importance allowed us to home in on optimal values prioritised to situations of allowable variability. Triple points, for instance, could not be flexible in position since they each implicated three intersecting surfaces. The collars, too, were non-negotiable as they were positioned according to Gaudí's highly resolved proportional system. The points on the surfaces were least important, and could afford to dance around a bit in space as the principal parametric variants were the angles of rotation relative to each other, and the proportions of their elliptical collars: almost all the surfaces are rotated away from their normal. Gaudí did not make it easy for himself or his collaborators.

The 3D parametric modelling software had a very powerful scripting overlay (for its day), allowing Xhyper to be tuned to produce an executable script that could build each geometrical solution automatically within the 3D modelling software environment, labelling and dimensioning the model as it proceeded. Despite the computational restrictions of the day (my US$50,000 workstation boasted 4MB of RAM, to the envy of my peers), the whole operation for each surface took less than an hour. It was not just a matter of reducing the task to manageable proportions or working to late 20th-century time frames; I believe that such techniques offered a design refinement simply not possible to this degree without the assistance of the computer in the way described. The reason that I make this claim is that despite the speed with which best-fit hyperboloids could be calculated, the subtlety of Gaudí's approach meant that the last steps had to be undertaken by hand-tweaking the parameters. The designer still had the last word.

### ANALYSING GEOMETRY
Moving on by almost two decades, I was startled to find history repeating itself. We have been working on unpacking Gaudí's design for the Glory Facade. There are surviving fragments of a 1:25-scale working model made from plaster of Paris which, combined with two surviving photographs, provide a detailed view

7 Sagrada Família Basilica, Barcelona, Spain, 1883–: the spires of the Nativity Facade completed just after Gaudí's death in 1926. Until 2012, the geometry of the tapering bell towers had not been identified.

8 Sagrada Família Basilica, Barcelona, Spain: matching measured drawings with point cloud data extracted from the actual building (Nativity Facade) (2010).

of his intentions for this, the Sagrada Família's principal facade. Unfortunately he had not completed the design model by the time of his death. Fascinating as this unfolding story is, it is beyond the scope of this paper to detail in full. Instead I will outline some of the techniques we have adopted in essentially a new trail of 'best-fit' geometrical outcomes and contrast them with our earlier efforts in order to provide a sense of the pace of change.

A key issue for interpreting Gaudí's intentions for the four campanile towers that form the facade's primary architectural elements is understanding the geometry of their profile, which clearly must refer back to those of the Nativity Facade, the only vertical elements completed in Gaudí's lifetime. In all our minds, these have been the idiosyncratic defining elements for the project as a whole for almost a century. As late as 2011 the profile of these highly original towers (described unflatteringly by George Orwell as 'hock bottles') had still not been derived.[3] Our approach was to scan the towers digitally to an overall accuracy of 5 millimetres, a technique that contrasts markedly with the six weeks full time it took two of us to measure the model of the clerestory window described above.

There are several competing theories as to the nature of the towers' vertical sectional profile curve. What is not in dispute is the presence of a 3D surface derived from a curve rotated about a vertical axis sitting seamlessly atop a cylinder such that both rotated and cylindrical surfaces are cotangent with each other. One theory is that the curve might be a vertical parabola with its apex cotangent to the vertical section of the cylinder rotated about the tower centre. Another is that it could be a hyperbola in the same orientation. A third is that it could be an ellipse.

We have used three methods to derive a credible understanding, all of which involved working with a 3D point cloud of the whole tower. The point cloud was 'cleaned up' as much as possible by scripting where appropriate, but regrettably a significant amount still had to be done manually.

The first approach we took was to work with that staple in our armoury of design computational tools: Microsoft Excel. This method was straightforward and is within the range of skills of most architects with regular mathematical ability. The measured curve profiles extracted from a typical section through the measured data were entered into the spreadsheet as 2D contour values, and the resulting interpolated curve compared with the three mathematical curves listed above, each calculated to have their uppermost and lowest points coinciding with the measured curve. Conditional formatting and automatic graphing allowed us to see the closest result at a glance.

The second method was to compare a point cloud in its entirety with a best-fit surface with a given geometry. Here the algorithm would build the surface from a given equation to match all the points as closely as possible. A statistical method compared each point's actual position with its proximity to the computationally derived best

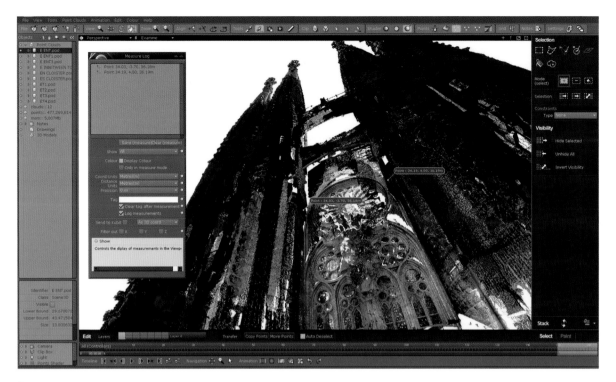

9

10

fit, and coloured according to its proximity. Ideally all the measured points would exactly match the calculated, and in the event we achieved a very satisfactory (ie close) result. As a means for double-checking, all the points were collapsed into 2D and a best-fit curve interpolated through the sampling. This allowed us to plot equation-derived curves with each end matched to the interpolated curve.

In fact our analysis yielded an ellipse in section (2D analysis) and an ellipsoid in 3D. The difference between a parabola and an ellipse for this set of values is really rather small. Given that the vertical axis for the parabola is infinitely repositionable with respect to the 'x' axis, whereas the ellipse axis is constrained to an axis centred on the tower, the closer match to an ellipse was quite satisfying for its geometrical precision; it also implies tighter thinking on Gaudí's part. Furthermore the ellipsoid makes more sense not so much for the Nativity Facade with its towers based on a circular plan but for the Passion Facade, its mirror opposite, proposed by Gaudí to have elliptical plans. Although constructed after Gaudí's death (completed in 1978), an ellipsoid that is derived from ellipses in all three planes is the only logical surface for a tower of this form that requires the cotangential intersection with the elliptical cylinders supporting them.

## SMARTGEOMETRY

In the time encompassing the two accounts above that are serving as bookends, much has changed but a lot has not. Starting initially with the proposed title '*Plus ça change … ?*', I had intended to catalogue a kind of digital impasse whereby the facility of our new tools were enfranchising a host of new participants who previously would not have been so venturous were they constrained to traditional media or early CAD software. I would have opined that the rapidly increasing power of the computers today, their drastically reduced costs, and the broader range of software were doing little more than further facilitate what we already do. That we could scan a whole Gaudí facade with such precision and speed, however, was a technical feat for us the designers, not an intellectual gain. I remember Professor Alan Bridges from Strathclyde University giving a 1999 conference keynote shortly before the birth of Smartgeometry. He showed hard drives the size of commercial washing machines bolted to the floor, capable of storing a massive half megabyte of information, if I recall correctly. In comparing this image from his pioneering days with the actual, his point was brutal: for all the increased power at our disposal, what was the new generation producing that was novel? But in the writing of this piece my title matured to one that looks at the moves we have made away from individual hero designers to collectives of creative individuals with widely differing personal skills, for whom computation offers a lingua franca. Plenty has changed in this regard.

As a codicil, I hasten to reassure the reader that my account here is not directed at explicating how to go about such analytical tasks on the path to synthesis but rather, what such spirited incursions into realms deep beyond the architect's training represent. For me it was the pivotal moment when my work moved away from ploughing a lonely furrow to understanding, for the first time, the

9 Sagrada Família Basilica, Barcelona, Spain: taking precise measurements from the Nativity Facade point data captured using a field 3D scanner.

10 Sagrada Família Basilica, Barcelona, Spain: in order to calculate directly from the measured data (point cloud), all extraneous noise has to be eliminated by hand.

11 Sagrada Família Basilica, Barcelona, Spain: best-fit curve optimised to match as closely as possible the 3D data converted to 2D.
The point scattering is shown in red, the best-fit ellipse in red, and the parabola is shown in cyan.

100M

90M

80M

70M

60M

50M

40M

privilege of working in teams whose members bring together remarkably different skills.

When I am asked what has been the most profound personal outcome from working on Gaudí's Sagrada Família Basilica, I reply that it has been the lessons that can be drawn from working in the shadow of a late architect who genuinely saw the entire design task as one that is holistic in nature. In terms of what I can apply from these lessons beyond this particular project, my response often causes surprise because I claim that it is not about helping others to create buildings that look like Gaudí's. Rather, I believe Gaudí's contribution helps develop an awareness that we have moved rapidly to a degree of complexity that requires a systematic approach to thinking and practising architecture, one that is not object (icon) oriented. In Gaudí's case the complexity he strove to resolve was more sculptural and cultural in ambition: architecture as plastic art.

In considering the 'smart' part of smart geometry, I define it not as the geometry itself working in a clever way to aid the architect otherwise bereft of any original ideas of their own (although geometry does often help in synthesis). Nor do I mean smart as in the sense of adroit individual human performance. I have taken the definition of smart in this conjunction with the word geometry to be the condition of transdisciplinary expertise seeking a common intellectual goal and achievement. Not forgetting the gifted people who brought us the computer and software in the first place, the smartness comes from the way we meld the skills of the spatial thinker and designer, mathematician, geometer and engineer. Thankfully the instinct for creative human endeavour still exceeds the imputed vital agency of our digital assistants in scale and value, despite the constraints of the slide rule and log tables having been set aside for ever. Smartgeometry represents the coming together of kindred spirits who have seen similar opportunities beckon in their individual domains but crave the human experience of the creative sharing that such movements offer. This represents, I believe, a quantum shift in the way we go about our business.

12 Sagrada Família Basilica, Barcelona, Spain: ellipses (vertical sections of ellipsoids) scaled and overlaid on a measured drawing of the Nativity Facade.

## REFERENCES
1 Mark Burry, 'Geometry Beyond Working Effect', in *Mathematics of Space – AD (Architectural Design)*, Vol 81, No 4, 2011, p 80.
2 Robin Evans, *The Projective Cast: Architecture and its Three Geometries*, MIT Press (Cambridge, MA), 1995, p 220.
3 George Orwell, *Homage to Catalonia* (1938), Mariner Books (Boston, MA), 1980.

## IMAGES
Figures 1, 7, 12 © Arxiu de la Basilica Sagrada Família, Barcelona; Figures 2, 3, 4, 5, 6 © Mark Burry; Figure 8 © Mark Burry, Brad Marmion and Michael Wilson; Figure 9 © Mark Burry and Brad Marmion; Figure 10 © Mark Burry and Michael Wilson; Figure 11 © Mark Burry and Peter Wood

# EXPLORING HUMAN–COMPUTER INTERACTION IN DESIGN PROCESS

## FLORA SALIM AND PRZEMEK JAWORSKI

Flora Salim and Przemek Jaworski's clusters at Smartgeometry (SG) 2010 and 2011 (co-organised with Hugo Mulder and Martin Kaftan) introduced the concepts of interaction and physical/digital connections to the SG community. Prior to this, workshop explorations centred largely around the mechanisms of geometry and their analysis. Most members of the SG community did not even consider interaction to be possible or see the potentials within their own work. Salim's and Jaworski's work has had a great impact on subsequent SG events and now many workshops integrate aspects of interaction. Here they explain their research approach and possible implications for the creation of new design tools and design workflows.

1a

Imagine a transdisciplinary design team in the early stage of design, brainstorming ideas, comparing design concepts and options, and trying to find the best solution space that will set the course of the project. This is not an old-school design team equipped just with their drawing pens and papers on a round table. This team employs a tangible interactive table to externalise their design thoughts, uses their phones and smart devices to gather and analyse data, performs rapid prototyping of models as they speak, presents their arguments using both digital and physical models that have just been fabricated on site. The models themselves are capable of producing live feedback, since they are equipped and connected with sensors, actuators and live data source from the project site. The whole collaborative design exercise is engaging, informative and hands-on – enabling better design decisions. This scenario describes our vision for the 'Parametrics and Physical Interactions' and 'Interacting with the City' clusters that we championed at Smartgeometry (SG) 2010 and SG 2011 respectively.

### REAL-TIME DATA

The ubiquity of computing has changed the way we interact with our world. This has not only influenced our lifestyle, but also shifted design thinking, methods and practice in a number of ways.

Firstly, since the wealth of data on the Net offers resources that can now be readily exploited to inform our design decisions, information flow is becoming an important concern for architects, not just for understanding people movement and vehicles, but also for conceiving conceptual space.[1] In the early architectural and urban design stages, where 80 per cent of major design decisions are made, it is essential to integrate online historical and real-time information related to the urban or site context we are designing for. Unfortunately, this is rarely the case. There is an opportunity to harvest and synthesise real-time weather and wind data, activities, movements at different places, roads, buildings and street blocks from online public feeds, social networks and mobile applications to inform our design processes. Historical and real-time data from the urban and social networks provide the potential for monitoring climatic and operating conditions of the city[2] and are particularly useful to inform new developments or retrofit projects of buildings, public spaces or transit hubs. By synthesising historical and real-time data with early-stage design models, 'what-if' urban scenarios can be established. The impact of a new development, at a specific urban site, on traffic, pedestrian flow or transportation demand, for example, can be analysed early in the project.

### HUMAN–COMPUTER INTERACTION

Secondly, the pervasive computing era has brought an evolution of human–computer interaction (HCI) that has also influenced our design process. Computers, which once looked like boxes with monochrome screens and required standardised tools of interaction such as the mouse or keyboard, are now embedded and embodied in everyday 'things'. Nowadays, the ways we interact with these 'things' are no longer limited to just keyboard

1a and 1b 'Interacting with the City' workshop cluster led by Flora Salim and Przemek Jaworski at SG 2011, Copenhagen, Denmark.

1b

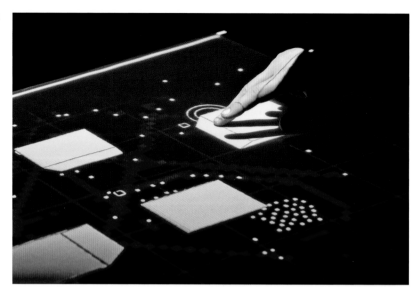

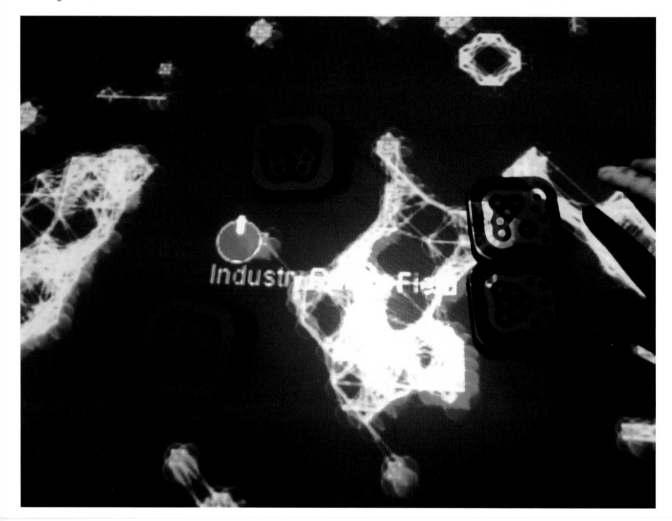

and mouse. Due to this new-found freedom of interacting with 'things', designers are also free to design their tools and methods of designing, for interacting with data, information, models and the real world. This is in order to generate better-performing products, models or buildings, or simply to engage the audience (clients, users, peers or other designers) with the design process.

## COLLABORATIVE WORKSPACES

Finally, these changes have paved the way for better support for collaborative design. In a classic perception of the design process, the designer's role is like someone putting coloured blocks (ideas) together, and making them work and perform best. It is like playing a Tetris game, making sure the blocks fit in space as closely as possible, minimising inefficiency, and maximising performance. In this state of things, the designer is 'connecting the dots', interpreting their meaning, and finding common interfaces ('plugs and sockets') between specific ideas, so they can work together. This could be called 'exploration and manipulation of a solution space', with many creative combinations and trial-error cycles. Sometimes this process is chaotic, sometimes more linear and organised – but it quite often resembles a guessing game.

Since a designer is often not acting alone, but part of a design team, it is important for every team member to be able to explore the solution space by externalising their design ideas to find the best design option that can be agreed upon by the whole team. They need to find a common platform for ideas to be externalised, expressed, exchanged and edited as a team. The digital manifestation of design intent can then be sculpted simultaneously by many people. Unfortunately, these people usually have different interpretations of key ideas driving the design, as they work away from each other, communicating poorly and sharing fragmented information. Various analyses, surveys, estimations and simulations of performance aspects of the project are being communicated – but it seems that all of them need to be translated, re-digested and made easy to use. Therefore new *collaborative workspaces* in a design process are required. The information-rich global networks fill society with this necessary knowledge, empowered by the open-source movement. In fact we have nearly all the solutions to resolve these problems and create efficient collaborative work environments. All this requires is a mental shift and openness to a new means of creation. The richness of available data and technologies is so vast, that capturing it and making sense of it for everyone requires new approaches.

## A NEW PARADIGM

There is a need to find a template for a design environment that integrates all data, all 'given' and 'unknowns', all questions and answers, and acts as a collaborative working space, allowing all participants to visualise data. They also need to be able to influence virtual design models in a natural, intuitive way. When we were organising our SG workshops we were looking for a clever means of visualising the design itself, not only its physical form, but also as a 'cloud' of all useful information, data streams,

2 Przemek Jaworski, Interactive Urban Table project, Lodz, Poland, 2011.
This is an example of augmented reality interfaces used in the design context – pedestrian simulation with flexible urban configurations modified by hand gestures.

3 Takehiko Iseki, Ur-Moeba Tangible Table project at SG 2010, IAAC, Barcelona, Spain.
Special markers induce generative behaviour in simulated urban fabric. When moved, the growth pattern of the city changes and new 'tissue' is added. The program uses cellular automata algorithms, and visual markers are recognised by a camera positioned above the projected image.

4a

4a and 4b Rafael Urquiza, Konstanze
Grammatikos and Filippo Ferraris, Bioclimatic
Responsive Skin project at SG 2010, Barcelona,
Spain.
The model reacts to changes in light conditions
and reconfigures the panels using servo motors.

simulations, so they can be updated whenever they are available, and seen in real time. But how to create and embed interactive tools into the new, emerging template of design process? Over two years at SG we conducted experiments in areas ranging from physical computing to interactive multimedia environments, including augmented reality and gesture/object detection, and investigated various programming tools related to live data streaming and visualisation.

The focus of our experiments was on enabling *tangible interactions* with design models or prototypes and obtaining *live feedback* from real-time data sources and from the interactive experience. Our research question was: How to create a design-oriented collaborative work environment?

This question was motivated by our previous experiences as design team members, where the flow of ideas and facts had many bottlenecks and was often broken or fragmented. Design team meetings around printed plans, or physical models, often needed additional means to visualise complexities and make them understandable to others. Work can flow more naturally when it happens in a new visual, interactive environment, created from scratch to accommodate key elements. The key elements are as follows: a common and accessible *virtual model* empowered by appropriate visualisation techniques; an intuitive *interface* for collective manipulation of design data and models; live *input* data streams from the Internet and/or sensors to enable the models to be responsive and/or adaptive to situational changes and site contexts; and *real-time output*, such as *live visual feedback*, kinetic or actuated outputs on physical models or haptic devices, to raise awareness of the consequences of design actions. This facilitates a rapid design decision-making process.

To make it possible, we had to tap into open-source libraries of augmented reality, gesture detection, data protocols and 3D rendering techniques. The do-it-yourself (DIY) electronic-arts community benefited from the rising popularity of the Arduino microelectronic platform. This has leveraged practical applications of interactive design prototypes. By combining the power of generative and parametric design, scripts, real-time data analysis, hands-on electronic prototyping and digital fabrication, at SG workshops we could manage to produce multiple prototypes and collaborative tools in just four days.

4b

### UR-MOEBA TANGIBLE TABLE. 'PARAMETRICS AND PHYSICAL INTERACTIONS' CLUSTER. SG 2010

The tabletop design interface for generative urban simulations enhanced the versatility of conventional computer-aided design (CAD) software as a design tool by connecting it with a more interactive, dynamic and visual environment. Users were able to touch and move markers on the table to drive generative growth processes, where city cells behave differently depending on the position of attractors. There were different types of attractors, each with its own growth pattern. These patterns could be adjusted

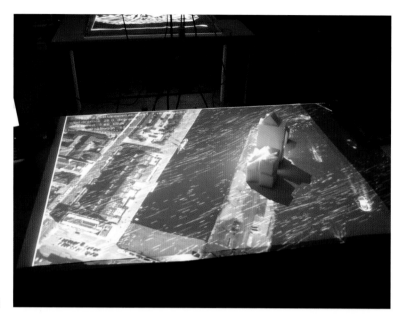

5 Raul Kalvo, Davide Madeddu and Jakob Bak, Ofelia Beach project at SG 2011, Copenhagen, Denmark.
Tangible manipulations of physical objects represent new urban design proposals for the site with wind simulations that get updated in real-time. The image is projected from above, and the installation uses a 3D scanner (Kinect) sensing positions of physical blocks in real-time.

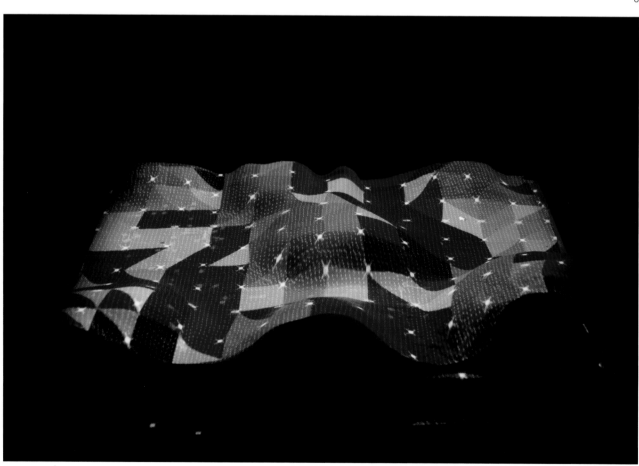

7

by rotating side markers to change properties, like speed and sensitivity towards neighbours.

## BIOCLIMATIC RESPONSIVE SKIN, 'PARAMETRICS AND PHYSICAL INTERACTIONS' CLUSTER, SG 2010

This project focused on physical, kinetic constructions and the interactive aspects of architectural elements. Most importantly, it demonstrated how the elements of a building could modify their own behaviour based on rule sets related to the human comfort zone. Each panel of the facade was equipped with light and temperature sensors and actuators that triggered movement – thus controlling interior temperature. User interactions also triggered movements on the panel. The idea, inspired by an origami game, was translated into a parametric CAD model with a scripted logic. The digital models were connected with the physical models post-fabrication. Changes in the parametric model (using attractor points) would trigger movement in the physical model and vice versa. The project achieved its main goal – to demonstrate that rapid prototyping in design could involve kinetic capabilities that performed sets of rules defining 'organic behaviour' as scripted in the parallel digital model.

## OFELIA BEACH PROJECT, 'INTERACTING WITH THE CITY' CLUSTER, SG 2011

Ofelia Beach is a real site on Kvæsthusmolen, in central Copenhagen. Environmental conditions such as strong wind caused this location to be problematic. The goal was to address complex analysis and simulation processes in a single tool that enabled access to, and manipulation of, flexible augmented models. This tangible interaction concept used real-time input from local weather stations and physical building blocks resembling new building massing. To visualise the scale and the local urban context, the satellite image from Google Maps was projected on top. Modular blocks could be moved around to construct a flexible physical model that could be digitised and reconstructed in 3D, in real time. As the blocks were moved, the dynamic nature of the wind, the flow direction, pressure, speed and turbulence, were visualised and projected back on the table around the building blocks. The project has shown that complex environmental and wind analysis can be tightly integrated into an interactive design workflow. This can become a powerful collaborative design aid.

### IUBI. 'INTERACTING WITH THE CITY' CLUSTER. SG 2011

iUrban Bioclimatic Informer (iUBI) is a 3D tangible interface which was used for designing the program of use and topography of an urban landscape, according to microclimatic parameters. Users could interact with soft elastic material (clay) to model the topography of the chosen site and receive real-time feedback about the environmental impact on the site that was then projected on top of the physical landscape model. The project emphasises the fact that collaborative teamwork can happen without keyboard and mouse. Thanks to instant visual feedback, designers can use their hands to sculpt and manipulate thin clay sheet and learn the consequences of their decisions in seconds. Augmentation of visual data into physical scenes created an opportunity to test how the use of new tools can change design workflows and improve team communication.

### FROM PHYSICAL TO VIRTUAL

Architects and urban designers have, for the first time, an affordable opportunity to create and participate in a tangible interaction platform for collaborative urban design. The projects described here attempt to push the potential of available technology to create tangible design interfaces in the context of urban design. In the early stages of design, tangible interfaces can be used to mediate expert and non-expert users in a collaborative environment and as an input device to 3D CAD software for digital modelling and further analysis.

These projects are examples of a new paradigm of design interface, which explores creative dialogue with natural input devices, streams of live data and simulations. These are enveloped in layers of visual and kinetic feedback, which are demonstrated to be a significant enabler for collaborative workspaces. As shown by the Ofelia Beach project, full weather information can be utilised during the simulation, thus depicting the model of the city almost 'as is' in reality in any given moment. Tapping into actual data streams becomes a relevant factor for understanding the city's mechanisms, which should be considered when investigating properties of the city as a system. Simulating behavioural properties on the physical models is also essential to visualise the impact of a design decision made by changing the physical models or surfaces.

Is this dialogue between physical and virtual going to enrich a designer's experience? Is it going to make collaboration easier? Yes, certainly. Of course there are still some issues, such as the conversion of scattered data sets and the need to integrate these into coherent working models. However, with focused effort and new technology, the creative process should start to resemble a multi-player computer game. Currently we are not that far off this simile: architectural workflows are now integrating building information modelling techniques, and geometry and data are becoming one.

## ACKNOWLEDGEMENTS
We would like to thank Hugo Mulder, co-leader of the 'Parametrics and Physical Interactions' cluster at SG 2010, and Martin Kaftan, co-leader of the 'Interacting with the City' cluster at SG 2011.

## REFERENCES
1 Malcolm McCullough, *Digital Ground: Architecture, Pervasive Computing, and Environmental Knowing*, MIT Press (Cambridge, MA), 2004.
2 FD Salim, J Burry, D Taniar, VC Lee, A Burrow, 'The Digital Emerging and Converging Bits of Urbanism', in *Future Cities: Proceedings of the 28th eCAADe Conference*, ETH Zurich, 2010, pp 883–92.

# DESIGNING INTELLIGENCE:
NICK PUCKETT
## DIY ROBOTICS FOR RESPONSIVE ENVIRONMENTS

Nick Puckett is the founder of AltN Research + Design
which develops custom software/hardware design tools and
interactive spaces. Others in the SG community have called
for democratisation of design computation tools; here,
Puckett extends these ideas and suggests a democratisation
of hardware, specifically robotics. In the spirit of newer
SG events linking physical and digital realms, Puckett has
provided ideas and technology linking computation to
physical assembly. He is currently an Assistant Professor in
the Digital Futures Initiative at OCAD University.

The 1964 exhibition 'Architecture without Architects', at the
Museum of Modern Art in New York, elevated vernacular structures,
or structures designed by people without architecture credentials,
to a level where the works could be situated within the greater
context of architectural history.[1] The show highlighted innovations in
material systems and construction techniques, and it illustrated the
potential of building technologies when they are given a different
set of needs and environments. Almost 50 years later, architects
are the protagonists in a world of *robots without roboticists*. Open-
source hardware and a community of electronic do-it-yourself
(DIY) enthusiasts have created the tools and knowledge base that
allows a 'non-expert' in robotics to design and create interactive
intelligent systems. This shift allows designers to enter the debate
of how physical and digital worlds relate and creates a new medium
for designers to consider: intelligence. It is no longer enough to
simply shape an object; its behaviour and personality also drive the
experience in the environment. Intelligent devices alter the way
we inhabit and navigate the physical world, so it is necessary for
architects to bring forms of intelligence into spaces.

In the late 1990s, work with gaming and special-effects software
provided new form-making potentials and created the tool
set for developing highly specific digital design tools. These
frameworks lowered the technical hurdles of traditional software
development, allowing designers to develop the digital tools
they needed rather than waiting for the software to be released.[2]
This approach provided new methods to directly engage other
disciplines such as engineering in the digital design process, thus

turning consultants into collaborators and increasing the scope and potential of our designs.

These ideas and methodology drive my own research and projects including those explored at Smartgeometry (SG). AltN Research + Design is a collaborative practice that engages technology as a design challenge rather than a technical issue. AltN undertakes projects that arise from research development that seek a design output or by working with other designers to prototype design ideas that would otherwise stay theoretical. In either case, the development process is focused around the creation of experimental prototypes that test and engage technologies within a design agenda. The work investigated at SG used robotics as a gateway to more disciplines, including biology and chemical engineering, which were previously perceived as 'off limits'. The projects rely on open-source tools and methods, but they do not preclude the need for experts. Instead, they provide flexibility, allowing the technology to evolve during the design process. The SG clusters provided an opportunity to open the research for interaction, expansion, and the creation of new strands of work upon which to build.

## LOGICAL AND CHEMICAL INTELLIGENCE

Over the past 10 years, my research has focused on how new tools and technologies can radically alter the process and product of design. Working in collaboration with architects, designers, engineers and scientists, we have developed prototypes that address how issues of interaction, behaviour and intelligence affect all stages of the design and production process. At the heart of this work lies an ongoing interest in finding ways to balance the relationship of control and surprise within an intelligent system. The Xiamen Energy Masterplan and the RoboFold manufacturing system were developed prior to the work at SG and laid the groundwork for the research questions that would ultimately be explored during the cluster workshops.

The Xiamen Energy Masterplan Model, developed in collaboration with CHORA, is a 4-metre by 4-metre interactive planning tool used to illustrate the potential of new energy initiatives in the city of Xiamen, China. The model consists of a 1:10,000 representation of the city created from 122 selective laser sintering (SLS) printed tiles. The tiles are underlaid with a network of 650 LEDs that visually depict the proposed energy projects in relation to the city and each other. The Model operates as a physical, responsive diagram of the Energy Masterplan and acts as a planning/design tool for the city, developers and the general public. The LEDs are divided into four colours representing each typology of information displayed – energy networks, energy efficiency, renewable energy and pilot projects – and the specific projects within each type can be distinguished through their unique 'light animations'. The animations were developed in parallel to the design of the physical structure in relationship to the material properties of 3D printed tiles, and an interface was created to allow any member of the team to design and craft the sequences.

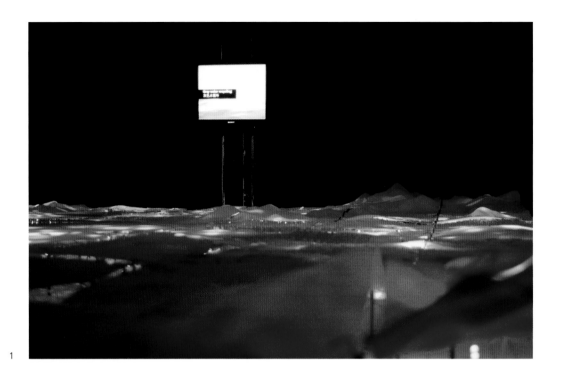

1

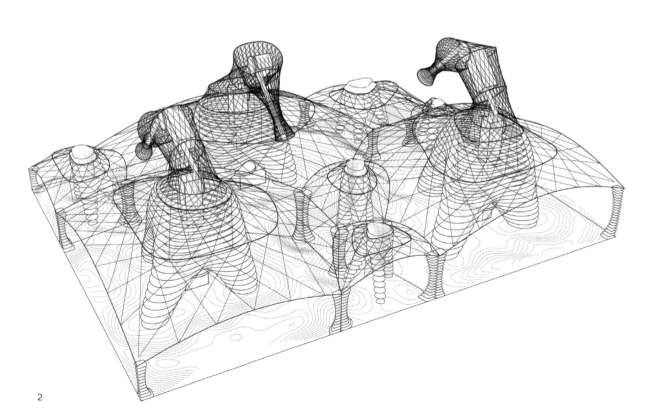

2

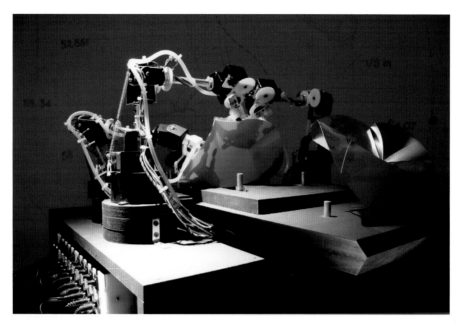

3

Though the exhibit is interactive, its primary function is to clearly display the energy projects through the design of the various light animations. The animations are very precise, giving the overall behaviour of the model a great deal of variety based on the combination and timing of the user's interactions.

The methods of physical animations that arose from the Xiamen Energy Masterplan were further developed in collaboration with RoboFold. This project developed the first working prototype of RoboFold's manufacturing system at a 1:5 scale. The prototype served as both a proof of concept and a platform on which to test the limits and potentials of the proposed manufacturing method. The principle behind the production technique uses curved score paths to bias the material and cooperative robots to fold the material into a desired shape. This production technique uses approximately one tenth of the energy of traditional forming methods and eliminates the high cost of producing a master mould for each shape. Since the production process itself was new, we focused on how generic educational robots could be retrained to fold by creating a custom hardware and software controller. Rather than writing new software, the approach created the manufacturing process as a physical animation using digital animation tools to control the movement of the robots. To achieve a fold, 29 individual actuators must be coordinated precisely over time, but within this system they are simply the outputs of a single animation sequence.

1 Xiamen Energy Masterplan Model.
The Xiamen Energy Masterplan Model is a 1:10,000-scale model of the Chinese city of Xiamen that uses a network of LEDs to create animations that visualise the planned energy programs in the city.

2 cyber-Garden v4.0 at SG 2011, Copenhagen, Denmark.
The project was designed as a multilayered network of flexible mesh, robotic arms, sensors and bacteria colonies. The arms function to tend the growth of the bacteria while embedded sensors guide their movement.

3 Second prototype for the RoboFold production system.
This 1:5-scale system was used to test the potentials of the folding system as a means of production.

These two strands of research, animated manufacturing and physical display systems, that arose from the work with CHORA and RoboFold were brought together for the development of cyber-Garden v4.0. The cyber-Gardens are a series of experiments conceived by Claudia Pasquero and Marco Poletto and developed by ecoLogicStudio. Over the course of the SG 2011 workshop,

4

5

6

7

4 cyber-Garden v4.0 at SG 2011, Copenhagen, Denmark.
The bacteria colonies were cultivated to a usable size before being transferred to the model.

5 BlackBox version 1.0 by AltN Research + Design, 2011.
This custom-built machine uses high-intensity UV light to cure sheets of shape-memory polymer. The production system allows the response temperature of the polymers to be designed in the lab and produced at a size viable for prototypes.

6 Shape-memory polymer experiment produced using BlackBox version 1.0 by AltN Research + Design, 2011.
This test laser cut a series of panels into the sheet that open or close based on the current temperature.

7 Shape-memory polymer sample created by AltN Research + Design, 2011.
The ratio of the polymer solution determines its response temperature. The solution is poured into a mould and then cured to solid.

three robotic gardening arms were designed, fabricated and trained to control the growth patterns of the embedded bacteria colonies. The prototype explored the relationship of electronic and biological intelligence as a closed loop of information and response.

Project BlackBox is a production system developed for the design and manufacture of responsive polymer surfaces by AltN Research + Design with the Bioactive Devices Lab in the Department of Chemical Engineering at the University of Kentucky. To achieve this we designed and built a machine that uses high-intensity UV light to cure sheets of polymer. The overall form and mechanism of the machine is designed to fit within a standard chemical engineering laboratory but provides a new capacity to create large-scale material for 1:1 architectural components. Responsive polymers can be programmed at the chemical level to respond to a specific temperature range by deforming in shape or volume. To produce responsive polymers, liquid monomer and cross-linker are combined at a given ratio that determines the response temperature of the polymer. The solution is then cured to a solid using either heat or UV light, as in the case of BlackBox. Typically, chemical engineering labs focus on creating small material samples which are tested and catalogued. The goal for Project BlackBox was to alter this relationship by creating large sheets of the material in the lab to be used as a prototype. Given the high cost of laboratory equipment, the machine was built using basic actuators and an Arduino microcontroller. Equipment in the lab measured the intensity of the UV light produced from the machine to ensure it was sufficient for curing the solution. The machine performs a simple function, but the potential outcomes are vast.

The machine was tested in the 'Beyond Mechanics' cluster at SG 2012. It was set up in a chemical engineering lab at Rensselaer Polytechnic Institute to allow the participants to design responsive clothing/cladding, starting with creating the material at the chemical level through to the finished prototype. Exposing the process to many other users opened up new potentials that were previously unseen. Over the course of the four days, a new curing process yielded what was initially seen as an error. At resting or room temperature, the cured sheets curled on themselves, but when heat was applied, the sheets relaxed into a flat shape.

Following the SG workshop, the causes and potentials of the curling behaviour were further tested and are serving as the basis for continued research. Converting a research idea of responsive materials into a machine that could be implemented, tested and altered by talented designers with a range of backgrounds allowed innovative solutions to emerge. By developing the technology in parallel, it also allowed these discoveries to be fed back into the design of BlackBox 2.0, which will ultimately be tested by a different set of users. The overall goal for Project BlackBox is to develop an open-source system and knowledge base that allows designers to program and prototype at a level that is similar to what we now have with electronics, allowing the responsive systems of the future to operate without electricity.

8

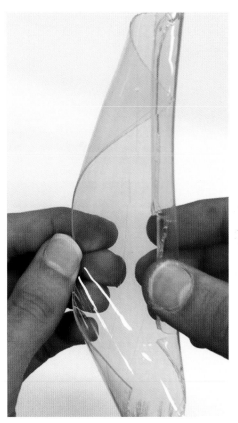

8 'Beyond Mechanics' workshop cluster at SG 2012, Rensselaer Polytechnic Institute, Troy, New York, USA.
During the SG workshop new properties of the polymer emerged whereby it would curl on itself. When heated, the material would relax the curling and could be held flat. Initially seen as an error in production, this material property is serving as the basis of ongoing research.

9 The cyber-Garden model created at SG 2011, Copenhagen, Denmark.
The model was designed at a scale of 1:200 to test the idea of bacteria as a responsive shading device. Small colonies were placed within the canopy components and as the colony grew, the component became more opaque. Sensors in the base of the model registered these changes and altered the path of the robotic gardening arms.

10 Results of the 'cyber-Garden' cluster at SG 2011, Copenhagen, Denmark.
The three robotic arms are embedded into a larger material system and manage the growth of the bacteria colonies.

9

In this world of robots without roboticists, it is the speed of feedback to implementation that makes these innovations possible. These quick, small steps allow iterations to move towards what would seem to be insurmountable technical hurdles.

# MARCO POLETTO AND CLAUDIA PASQUERO (ECOLOGICSTUDIO)

### CYBER-GARDEN V4.0

The cyber-Garden series tests design as a form of cultivation where the designer operates as a cyber-gardener by choreographing and breeding artificial ecologies composed by robotic, biological, social and urban systems. The cyber-Garden v4.0, developed at SG 2011, tested this with a 1:200-scale architectural model. During the workshop, participants engaged directly with the design of the form, the material organisation and the behaviour of this system to create a new type of space: a living expression of material, biological and electrical intelligence.

10

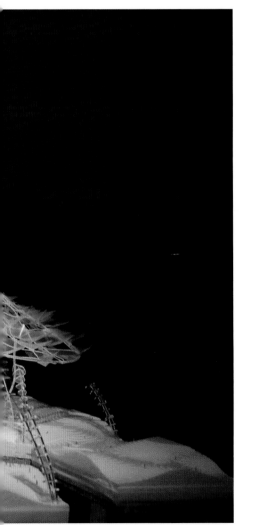

cyber-Garden v4.0 is a multilayered and sensitive architectural prototype, able to capture and filter light information in real time and programmed to become self-sustaining. Emergent digital patterns, which define the garden's 'photosynthetic plan', influence the positioning and behaviour of the robotic gardening structures. The robotic structures then cultivate the biological skin, with the goal of balancing its growth in relationship to microclimatic conditions. In this respect the cyber-Garden is an artificial ecology animated by the fundamental living mechanism of the 'feedback loop'; its augmented nature affords an extended interaction with human artificial systems, turning the prototype into a tool of systemic design. Within the cyber-Garden, digital and physical realms are interrelated, and the work of the architect operates across them both; digital design technologies are merging back with the world they re-describe; architecture can therefore be conceived in 'real time'.

The final prototype consists of a network of 24 radiation sensors, three custom-designed/programmed robotic structures, a parametric digital model, a set of woven fibres, and two bacteria colonies. The bacteria colonies are hosted by approximately 600 Petri dishes that function as tiles for the architectural skin. The more the bacteria grow, the more light is shaded on the ground; sensors record the process of shading and feedback the information to both the parametric model and the robotic structure. As a consequence, the cyber-canopy cultivates itself, providing light and nutrients to foster growth. This affects the digital plan and triggers the emergence of other gardening components. The flow of light and nutrients, human care and physical contact, or ecological stress analysis contribute to the growth and evolution of an augmented architectural model, a 1:200 representation of a 'real-time cyber-Garden city'.

# MARIANA IBAÑEZ AND SIMON KIM

## BEYOND MECHANICS, AND THE DESIRE FOR THE KINETIC

The purpose of this research workshop was to provide the opportunity for architectural designers to participate in the formulation, manufacturing and implementation of responsive architectural devices. The catalyst for the workshop agenda was the intersection of the clothing/cladding research that was previously developed by Ibañez Kim Studio and the Project BlackBox production system developed by AltN Research + Design. The workshop investigated methods for designing the form and behaviour of multi-scalar prototypes from a molecular level through to material assemblies. The entire process from chemical formulation of materials to the testing of prototypes was brought to SG 2012 and allowed the participants to engage directly with each stage of the process to develop innovative new approaches to responsive, kinetic systems.

Shape-setting materials provide a new set of potentials for designing dynamics in objects and systems. This type of kinetics goes beyond the traditional scope of actuation by mechanical movements. Unlike traditional kinetic systems that rely on separate and discrete parts working together under force, we are positioning a design discipline of smart material that can create movement through its singular chemistry and geometry.[3] Dynamic materials also promise a break in conceptualising movement through a model of engineering. With smart materials, the reliance on a mechanical frame and surface is dispensed with, so that a more direct line is established between production and application. For this workshop, the focus was on the design production of shape-memory polymers (SMPs). SMPs can be trained into a position, baked to that form, and then manipulated into another shape. A stimulus, such as heat, moves the material back to the original shape within its atomic structure – without external hinges or gears. The resultant movement is softer and resembles organic motion.

## PROTOTYPING BEHAVIOUR

For architects and designers, this chemical reaction opens up an entirely new methodology of design. Rather than rely on mechanical systems for which engineering expertise is required, architects may develop working prototypes with the use of predetermined mixes of a monomer, cross-linker and photo-initiator. Over the course of the workshop, participants developed a series of wearable temperature-responsive prototypes using SMPs. To achieve this, the cluster operated a fully functioning materials lab in addition to the design space of the workshop. This parallel approach allowed the participants to develop the behaviour of the system from the chemical level through to the finished prototype and examine how the polymer could be combined with other materials to influence the final result.

11 Project BlackBox curing a polymer sheet during SG 2012, Rensselaer Polytechnic Institute, Troy, New York, USA.
The cluster operated a lab within the department of chemical engineering at Rensselaer Polytechnic Institute to produce the polymer materials.

12 Results of the 'Beyond Mechanics' workshop at SG 2012, Rensselaer Polytechnic Institute, Troy, New York, USA: ruff collar by Daria Kovaleva; shirt by Daniel Davis and Marc Hopperman.

11

### REFERENCES

1 Bernard Rudofsky, *Architecture Without Architects: A Short Introduction to Non-Pedigreed Architecture*, UNM Press (New York, NY), 1964.
2 Greg Lynn, *Animate Form*, Princeton Architectural Press (New York, NY), 1999.
3 Sarah Braddock Clarke and Marie O'Mahony, *Techno Textiles 2*, Thames & Hudson (London), 2007.

12

# ENCODING DESIGN

## FABIAN SCHEURER

Fabian Scheurer is a computer scientist and founder of designtoproduction. He participated in Smartgeometry (SG) for the first time in 2006, when he was researching self-organising systems in building design at ETH Zurich, and has since been a participant and invited guest speaker at SG events. He lives in Zurich with his lovely wife and two kids, neither of whom he got to know over the Internet.

1

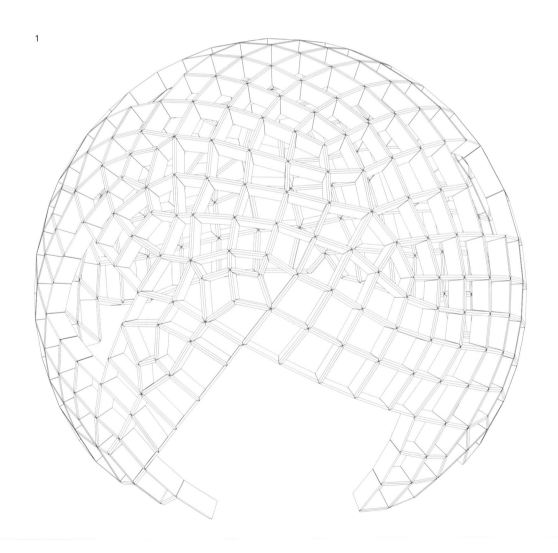

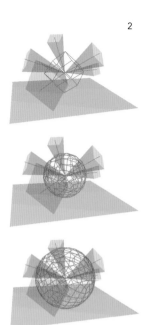

2

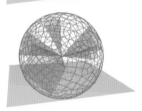

1 Final view of the detailed Swissbau Pavilion, Basel, Switzerland, 2005.
For every face of the generated mesh a four-sided wooden frame was built from CNC-cut plywood boards, leaving blank the faces inside the openings.

2 Meshing a sphere for Swissbau Pavilion, designed at the ETH Zurich's CAAD Chair with digital workflow from design to fabrication by designtoproduction, 2005.
The Swissbau mesher grows a quadrilateral mesh on a sphere, so that its edges align with openings (red) and the floor (orange).

Sometimes even netizens from the outset need an old-fashioned newspaper to discover evident connections between analogue life and the digital realm. Although I've been using e-mail for more than 20 years now, it would never have occurred to me that generative design and online dating struggle with the same basic problems – until, one morning on the train, I read an article on human leukocyte antigen (HLA) testing.[1]

The story is this: HLA molecules play a central role in controlling the immune system, which in turn is an essential factor for producing robust offspring. The bigger the variety in the parents' HLA genes, the more likely the children's immune systems will find the appropriate measures to whatever bug is trying to challenge them. In order to facilitate the pairing of Mr and Mrs Right, evolution has hooked up the immune system with the olfactory sense in a way that genetically different candidates like each other's smell better. As a result, when looking for DNA to recombine with your own for the sake of healthy descendants, close your eyes and follow your nose. Empiric studies show some evidence that this will lead you directly to a stable and productive long-term relationship. The mechanism is so subtle that it has been working well concealed for ages and was given romantic code names before science had a chance to become aware of it.[2] Unfortunately now, the chemical brothers taste and olfaction are the two out of five senses that completely resist digitalisation and thus pose a huge problem in online dating. Skype lacks a smell channel to pick out well-suited candidates.[3] But, thanks to advancements in gene sequencing, nowadays a workaround for this problem is available for just under US$250.[4] This is how much it takes to translate your HLA genes into a perfectly e-mail-compatible format and compare them to the DNA of prospective dates all over the world. So – without odour nuisance – you can separate the wheat from the chaff before you invest in precious airline tickets to meet personally. It also helps the climate.

### WHAT'S ALL THIS GOT TO DO WITH SMARTGEOMETRY?
My first encounter with Smartgeometry was in 2006, just after I had invested a couple of months into programming a 3D-physics simulator that grew a self-organising quadrilateral mesh on a sphere.[5] From scratch. In Java. About half of the effort was a fierce struggle against Java-3D and graphical user interface (GUI) issues until it finally worked the way I wanted it to. And just a few weeks after a pavilion had been designed with my generative system, built from timber cut using computer numerical control (CNC) and exhibited at the Swissbau 2005 fair in Basel. I had to realise that this part of the battle had been a complete waste of time – simply because I managed to recode the basic functionality on top of GenerativeComponents (GC) within a two-day SG workshop in Cambridge, UK. And by now, less than 10 years later, there are Grasshopper and plugins like Kangaroo, which would allow any interested undergraduate student to wire together such a system within a few hours. Generative design definitely has become as mainstream as e-mails and online dating.

3 Assembly of the Swissbau Pavilion, Basel, Switzerland, 2005.
The 320 prefabricated frames were stacked and fixed to each other with simple bolts to assemble the pavilion.

However, the other half of the many, many weeks of work had been eaten up in the conceptualising and careful redesigning of the algorithms, tweaking the parameter values and balancing the fitness criteria over and over again. This happened until a point when the generated outcome – in its full unpredictability – matched the initial idea of building a spherical pavilion out of 300 quadrilateral wooden frames. And that, I'm afraid, hasn't changed a bit. Even though the availability of more sophisticated tools makes it easier to test ideas, the development of these ideas and their verification and iterative refinement still does not come for free, any more than picking the right spouse and starting a family can be done via a simple mouse click on Facebook.

3

## GENERATIVE SYSTEMS ARE NOT SOLVING PROBLEMS

Phrasing an infallible lonely-hearts ad is probably far more difficult than programming a good generative system – at least for the average nerd. How do you describe what you are and what you're looking for in a concise yet entertaining way that evokes just the right reactions? Basically the same questions guide the development of a computer program.

Far too often, computers are still mistaken for being incredibly smart. Actually they are just incredibly quick and embarrassingly obedient and both are being utilised to cover up how slow they are on the uptake. Their biggest handicap is that they cannot handle ambiguities, so you have to explain everything to them in much more detail than to a three-year-old child. You have to untangle simple tasks like 'turn red when you bump into one of your neighbours!' into totally explicit step-by-step fool-proof instructions, written in a painstakingly dry computer language (a so-called 'formal language'), correct down to the last closing bracket. By definition there is no room for interpretation or creativity inside an algorithm. Once started, it is just deterministically running down a paved road, choosing directions at every crossroads based on predefined rules and continuing until it hits a stop sign or a blue screen. Even series of random numbers are in fact generated – one might say faked – by a deterministic rule, which leads to repeatable results when started with the same input. And there is no difference when you avoid typing the code and instead start wiring visual components like in GC or Grasshopper. In the end it's all deterministic software running on deterministic hardware.

Generative systems are algorithms and consequently they are completely ignorant to qualities they are not taught to measure and totally incompetent to find solutions outside their solution space. Let alone writing a really good sonnet or catchy advertising copy. Algorithms are not solving problems in just the same way that ads are not finding spouses. When they are well assembled, they describe the problem to resolve and a strategy that leads to a solution. Many of these strategies are based on the ability to quickly scan incredibly vast solution spaces and find good candidates that fulfil certain fitness criteria. To achieve this in reasonable time, probabilistic and/or dynamic approaches are

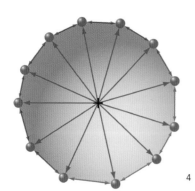

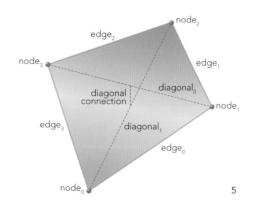

4

node₂

edge₂

node₃

edge₁

diagonal₀

diagonal
connection

node₁

edge₃

diagonal₁

edge₀

node₀

5

6a

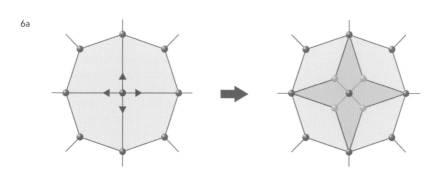

6b

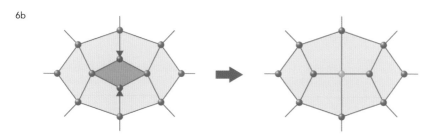

6c

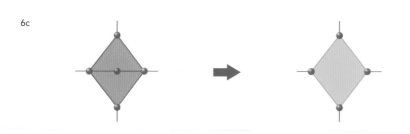

useful and often lead to results that surprise the audience. Mainly because they are a bit off the reductionist suggestions a typical engineer would come up with. But looking different does not necessarily mean that they are working better. And, in contrast to an algorithm, a good engineer often has the ability to actually solve problems by thinking outside the box. If you are able to explain the problem to them, that is.

## THE TOOLS ARE DEFINING THE PROBLEMS

From a reproduction perspective, chatting to the whole world online without a travel budget is just an entertaining waste of time. It probably results in an even lower reproduction rate than sitting in the local mall and trying to look cool. Tools don't deliver when they don't fit the problem or the available resources.

An algorithm is both a description of the problem and the solution. The Swissbau pavilion had to be spherical, because it is much cheaper to move points on a sphere than on a free-form surface, at least when you have to program everything on your own because no Grasshopper is anywhere in sight. Instead of defining a shape via knots and weights and writing a whole Java library of non-uniform rational B-spline (NURBS) functions, I just had to declare a centre point and a radius and do a bit of simple vector maths. The focus on quadrilateral faces on the other hand was a deliberate decision (everybody can do triangles!) and led to a rather special approach to meshing and to the introduction of openings that should disturb the otherwise all too regular patterns. The size of the sphere and the length of the face-edges were given by outside conditions like the available exhibition space and fabrication constraints. The tool was literally built around both the definition of the problem and the strategy for the solution.

Tools are always constraining the solution space. When using existing tools, this often becomes a question of balance. Where powerful digital tools meet weak human design decisions, fashion emerges. This is why we have been seeing too many Voronoi structures and UV-populated NURBS surfaces out there in the wilderness, which actually is a zoo, nicely fenced by downloadable tools. We have to be aware that existing tools are rarely producing new solutions but only the pursuit of new solutions is creating new tools. Fortunately, our tools develop at an enormous pace, partly because the number of users has exploded over the last decade but mainly because more and more of them start to create their own tools after a short phase of experimenting with the existing ones. That leads to new ideas. But then they all face the same challenges.

## IS THE PROBLEM REALLY THE PROBLEM?

Mating based on HLA gene matching might lead to healthy descendants but not necessarily to a partner with the same sense of humour. Even though the gene-sequencing industry is trying to suggest the opposite, there are serious doubts as to whether the olfactory system is able to trigger the release of enough endorphins for sharing a breakfast table until the kids fledge. Sometimes the fitness criterion chosen is just a right answer to a wrong question.

4 Encoding a sphere.
Keeping points on a sphere is pretty simple. Just tie them to the centre point with virtual threads.

5 Encoding a mesh face.
In order to keep all the quadrilateral faces close to a certain size and as quadratic and flat as possible, their four edges and two diagonals are working like springs, with a seventh string tying together the diagonals.

6a, 6b and 6c Encoding growth.
To maintain the four-sidedness of all faces during alterations of the mesh, three rules are defined and applied whenever a face meets certain conditions:
(a) too much tension on a node – add four new faces
(b) too narrow aspect ratio – delete a face
(c) too collinear nodes – join two faces.

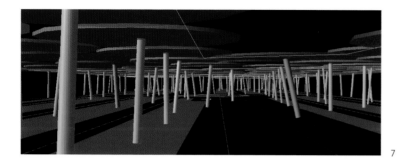

7 The Groningen Twister in action.
The Groningen Twister generated non-regular configuration of slightly leaning columns for a bicycle parking garage in front of the train station of Groningen, Netherlands. It was an interactive system, allowing the designer to guide the self-organising process with user interventions in real time.

7

8    habitat                                    agents

slab edges
(repelling)

openings
(repelling)

paths
(repelling)

bearing radius

top mass

distance
(repelling)

inclination
(erecting)

bottom mass

9

**8 The Groningen Twister: encoding distribution.**
While the tops of the columns in the Groningen Twister are repelled by dilatation joints and holes in the slab, their bottoms try to get away from the walking and cycling paths. The distance between two columns is dependent on their load-bearing capacity and every column tries to stay as upright as possible while it is being pushed around from all sides.

**9 KCAP Architects, Stadsbalkon Groningen, Netherlands, 2007.**
The Groningen Stadsbalkon by architects KCAP provides parking space for 4,000 bicycles underneath a pedestrian area which is supported by a 'forest of columns' designed with a generative system, the Groningen Twister.

**10 The Groningen Twister: user interface.**
The interface shows the myriad of value sliders necessary to avoid premature design decisions during programming time.

10

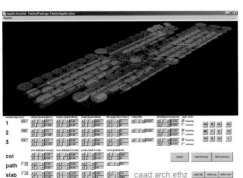

One of my first generative design systems, the Groningen Twister, had to arrange columns in an underground bicycle parking facility in an arbitrary pattern, while at the same time it had to ensure that they transferred the loads of a 3,000-square-metre concrete slab to the ground. Following the rules given by the designing architects, the columns were attracted towards the areas of the bike stands where they would be out of the way. Unfortunately that left a large portion of the ceiling unsupported because it had no bike stands underneath. By identifying the actual objective as 'keep clear of walking and cycling paths' and changing the implementation accordingly, this problem was instantly solved.

This rather simple example shows how difficult it is to define the right objectives for optimisation and how easy it is to get misled, especially when the algorithm designer already has an idea about how the solution could look. Finding an unbiased definition of the qualities needed is the first challenge. Defining a quantitative measure for how good or bad something is, poses the next one. And things get really complicated when a number of contradicting objectives have to be balanced. One look at the user interface of the Groningen Twister shows the full debacle: following the old programmer's rule to never hardcode any parameter value, there are about five dozen sliders to adjust input parameters, fitness measures etc. Less would definitely be more in this case. This also gives a hint to all the enthusiasts who think adding more and more optimisation criteria to the list will produce better outcomes. Experience shows that the result in most cases will be entropy: a dull compromise that fulfils all needs just equally little and none really. Design is all about decisions. Delegating them to an algorithm always means following a predefined path (see above), and you ought to be pretty sure that it leads somewhere you actually want to end up.

### IS IT MORE TROUBLE THAN IT'S WORTH?
So, you've invested a substantial amount of money and waited a few weeks after sending in a cotton bud with a sample of your oral mucosa, just to find out which of your many chat-partners out there presumably smells nice. Your nose, on the other hand, comes for free and is able to do the same in fractions of a second without even distracting you from other sensual impressions. Why not redirect the US$250 towards the local bar, where it could buy quite a few drinks to attract new acquaintances?

Who would use a complex digital system to solve a simple problem? In a studio at the AA I once was confronted with elaborate computational fluid dynamics (CFD) simulations of wind streaming through a back yard. In order to get input for their design, two out of five groups of students had independently assembled digital models of the surrounding area for their design and presented impressive images of red and blue vector fields in ANSYS. Interestingly, the main wind directions in both models were almost opposite. And when I looked over my shoulder I could see the nice 1:50 cardboard model of the whole situation and had to ask myself: why don't they just go down to Tottenham

Court Road to buy a blow dryer and some woollen yarn and use this for a BYO wind tunnel? The results would be equally significant, but the process would be fun for the whole group instead of just for the two geeks.

Physical simulation software has become ubiquitous. But apart from the fact that setting up good simulation of the real world needs quite a bit of know-how about the physics behind it – and reliable input data in the first place – it comes with another big drawback: cost of computation. One of the goals of the Groningen Twister was to ensure that the columns would bear the load of the pedestrian zone above it. Computer-aided engineering software is pretty good at simulating concrete structures, but nevertheless a halfway significant finite element method (FEM) simulation of a 3,000-square-metre slab supported by 150 columns with different sizes and inclinations still takes more than a few seconds. And that is far too much time if the intention is to build an interactive tool that needs at least 12 updates per second to show halfway smooth movements on the screen and react to user input without too much delay. Therefore the Groningen Twister did not use FEM but a few simple geometric rules of thumb, checked by the engineers, to ensure a more or less stable structural configuration. The system made sure that the designers stayed within the solution space of the engineers, who then only had to do one thorough analysis for checking after a good candidate had been produced.

Unfortunately – and this is the second big misunderstanding about computers – this problem is not going to fade away with ever more powerful processors. Although mostly unknown outside computer science – and completely ignored by software marketing departments – computation is not easily scalable. The field of computational complexity theory, founded in the 1930s and well established since the 1960s, has brought an astonishing insight to the world: many of the interesting problems cannot be computed in reasonable time, no matter how many transistors are squeezed onto a silicon chip. This is because even for seemingly simple tasks, like for example detecting collisions between moving objects, the computing time climbs non-proportional to the number of inputs. When done with a 'brute-force' approach the growth is quadratic,[6] which means if you can check 100 objects in 1 second, 200 objects will take 4 seconds. And collision detection is one of the cheapest problems. Finding the shortest route through a number of cities makes a trip to all your online dates a real brainteaser. This is known as the 'Traveling Salesman Problem' and its complexity is $O(n!)$, which means the computing time rises with the factorial of the number of cities. For only 15 cities there are 43,589,145,600 possible solutions to check in order to find the shortest route. Just one extra city adds 610,248,038,400 further solutions to this list.

### ENCODING DESIGN
Is that thing called love encoded in our HLA genes? Can the missing parent of our yet-to-be-born offspring actually be found more quickly and efficiently by an algorithm than by just wandering

growing

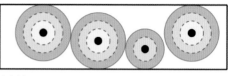

shrinking

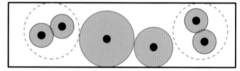

splitting

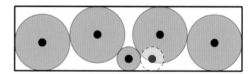

dying

11

11 Groningen Twister: encoding growth. The number of columns in the Groningen Twister changes according to the 'pressure' inside the slab area. When there are not enough columns to fill the area, they grow in two steps and during the third step split into two small columns. In reverse, when there are too many columns, they shrink and eventually remove themselves from the system.

the world open minded? Or is that no more than a good marketing stunt? I guess everybody has to find the answer based on their personal beliefs. The SG community of course is more concerned with a different question: Can good design be encoded in generative systems?

The human genome contains about 3.2 Gigabits of information and has been managing to self-replicate for over 50,000 years now, which I would regard as pretty successful design encoding. But to do something similar with digital computers will remain difficult, mainly because:

- computers as we know them are deterministic, not creative
- tools don't find solutions, solutions produce tools
- simulations are never as real as the real thing
- computers will never be fast enough.

Those four points I find pretty reassuring, because they leave the creative designer in the centre of the picture. When we move on from designing buildings to designing algorithms that design buildings, we are just changing the level of abstraction, but not the level of responsibility.

## REFERENCES

1 Laurina Waltersperger, '*Etwas Speichel für die grosse Liebe*', *Zürcher Tages-Anzeiger*, 6 August 2012, p 23.
2 Notably though, the German idiom for 'I hate so-and-so's guts' is '*Ich kann ihn nicht riechen*', which translates to 'I can't stand his smell'.
3 Admittedly it also lacks a touch channel. There have been promising experiments since the 1990s, but most of them clearly address the post-dating stage of a relationship …
4 See for example www.genepartner.com.
5 Fabian Scheurer, 'Getting Complexity Organised: Using Self-Organisation in Architectural Construction', *Automation in Construction*, Vol 16, No 1, 2006, pp 78–85.
6 When trying a brute-force approach, there are $\frac{1}{2} \times (n^2-n)$ possible collisions between n objects to check.

# WORKING PROTOTYPES, CREATING KNOWLEDGE

## SHANE BURGER AND XAVIER DE KESTELIER

Shane Burger and Xavier de Kestelier are practising architects and long-standing members of the Smartgeometry (SG) community. In 2010, they were appointed co-directors of SG, joining the original three founders to guide the community vision and plan the annual events. De Kestelier is a partner at Foster + Partners in London within the practice's Specialist Modelling Group. New York-based Burger is currently the Director of Design Technology at Woods Bagot, after years at Grimshaw. Here the duo reflect on the evolution in concept and organisation in SG through the years towards the current format which sees the workshops as places for both digital and physical experimentation and prototyping.

1 SG 2010 workshop space, IAAC, Barcelona, Spain.
Locating the workshop space within a former factory, adjacent to materials and fabrication equipment, enriched the design process through the infusion of physical prototyping.

In 2004, a Smartgeometry (SG) workshop was held at the University of Waterloo in Ontario, Canada, in partnership with ACADIA, the international conference for digital designers and researchers. It was the first SG event held at a school of architecture, but this initially did not have a significant influence on the character of the workshops. Many of us spent the four days in front of a laptop, in unremarkable classrooms producing digital designs. But looking back, this Waterloo event did end up influencing SG workshops to come, because a handful of participants began to take advantage of workshop facilities, including a laser cutter and an early-model 3D printer. For example, workshop participant Mark Cichy, a student at the University of Waterloo, explored a number of formalistic studies around the parametrics of interlocking shapes. The specific kind of interlocking he developed could only be fabricated through an additive fabrication process such as 3D printing. Oliver Osterwind, an engineer at Buro Happold, also explored digital fabrication. Working in collaboration with Chuck Hoberman, he intended to model the scissor-like components that Hoberman is known for in his adaptive architecture and extend the geometry from pure circular motion to a more complex elliptical geometry. Digital simulation was deemed insufficient. The software we were using at that stage was the first-ever working version of GenerativeComponents (GC) which, although more capable than other associative modelling tools of the day, lacked a physics engine. To test the feasibility of his design, he constructed

2

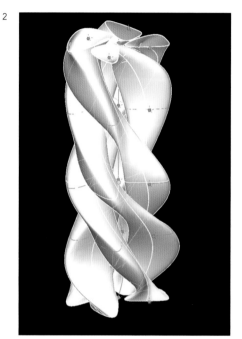

3

a physical model with the architecture school's laser cutter, the result serving as the physical verification of the prototype's movement. Following the Waterloo event, the use of small-scale digital fabrication became a constant in the SG workshops. Most were representational: a physical copy of the digital model's form. Furthermore, early workshops and conferences (New York, Munich, San Francisco) were often held in hotels and conference centres that were not conducive to the often messy processes of physical prototyping.

As directors planning SG workshops, we would often receive requests from academics inquiring about hosting SG at their university. In 2010, SG explored this option in earnest by asking various architecture schools to come up with proposals to host the workshops. From all those received, the IAAC (Instituted for Advanced Architecture of Catalonia) programme in Barcelona stood out. Affiliated with MIT's Fab Lab network, IAAC is based in an old factory, east of central Barcelona, and has a large, open manufacturing hall with adjacent high-end fabrication facilities. The availability of this space initiated a new style of workshops. To fully utilise the equipment at IAAC, we decided to focus the conference on digital prototyping and fabrication. However, utilising high-end equipment such as full-bed three-axis milling machines and high-voltage laser cutters brought with it some constraints. Typically, workshops included around 120 participants and 20 workshop tutors; sufficient 'machine-time' for 120 individual projects was not feasible. Our response was to make a significant shift from autonomous projects to those developed in a collaborative capacity by organising groups of 10 to 12 people into workshop 'clusters'.

Although driven by practical and organisational reasons, this shift towards fabrication and prototyping was a crucial change within the development of SG events. In past events, participants came with a certain design problem to solve through computational or parametric techniques, seeking the advice of a collection of experts who 'tutored' at the workshops. This individual work did not naturally lead to the cross-fertilisation of projects and knowledge. Capitalising on the wealth of techniques developed by individuals in previous events, a conscious decision was made for SG 2010 in Barcelona to restructure the event towards a collaborative workshop framework. While those engaged in the workshops brought with them individual ideas and experience, the new framework empowered group-based research around a collective concept. Ultimately, this environment is more reflective of design as a team effort while attempting to explore new models for computational collaboration.

Beginning with the 2010 event, each year SG has seen more than 40 teams that put together proposals to 'champion', or organise, a workshop cluster, with 10 selected for each year's event. Championing a cluster seems to be an attractive endeavour, but why? Serving as a Cluster Champion is a unique opportunity to bring together talented international participants, to explore a design brief the Cluster Champions have set out for the four

2 Mark Cichy, interlocking forms, SG 2004, University of Waterloo, Ontario, Canada.
Digital model constructed in GC and 3D-printed physical model from a series of formal studies of interlocking parametric surfaces.

3 Oliver Osterwind, experiments with linkages, SG 2004, University of Waterloo, Ontario, Canada.
Digital model constructed in GC and laser-cut linkage model. The linkage model expands and contracts. It was constructed to test the feasibility of the design and served as a verification of the prototype's movement.

4 Acoustic prototype from the 'Reactive Acoustic Surfaces' workshop cluster at SG 2012, Rensselaer Polytechnic Institute, Troy, New York, USA.
Subject-matter experts join with collaborators from a diverse array of disciplines to explore design around a central premise. The creation of prototypes reflects this diversity, widening the opportunities for development and feedback.

days of the workshop. Similar to workshop participants, Cluster Champions source from diverse backgrounds: universities, small and large architecture and engineering firms, software companies and technology start-ups. It is often these young start-ups that bring the best results – their time is extremely valuable in that they need to spend every moment they can on their new business. The SG workshops serve as their research and development hub. For example, Bruce Bell, a founder of Facit, a small design firm pioneering digital fabrication for residential housing, led a workshop cluster at SG 2010. His D-Process is a construction method whereby walls and floors are constructed from customised wooden box sections fabricated through a single, on-site, three-axis computer numerical control (CNC) machine and standard plywood. Bell came to SG to see if he could use the same setup of standard plywood and an inexpensive three-axis CNC machine to develop complex and adaptable formwork for in-situ concrete. In only four days, Bell and his team of workshop participants were able to develop a parametric system for modelling this formwork, building a physical prototype as a proof of concept.

Bell set out a brief or trajectory, but there was no guarantee of success within the four workshop days. Workshop participants do not come to SG to work in a teacher/student role. Cluster Champions and participants become a temporary collaboration for the duration of SG, and it is during the actual workshop that new knowledge is developed collaboratively and shared. In this manner, the generation of new knowledge capital in the workshops is quite different from the current models in practice and academia, in that it focuses intensely on a singular topic in multiple dimensions. Each participant brings their own skill set, expertise, experience and energy to contribute. Cluster Champions, serving as a topical catalyst for the workshop, collaborate with others interested in that topic to create something wholly new, far beyond the sum of its parts.

Community contribution and knowledge sharing is a key part of the ethos, a quality it shares with other open-source communities in software (Processing) and hardware (Arduino). Regular SG contributor Robert Woodbury notes that amateurs in computational design engage the 'copy and modify' process as a core methodology for learning programming and new design systems.[1] In acting on this shared belief, all the content developed in SG events is made available online for free in the hope that it will serve as the foundation for the next level of innovation.

### HARDWARE MASH-UPS
The visual and physical environment for design has long been ripe for revision. Neither the computer mouse nor the traditional computer-aided design (CAD) user interface provides us with an intuitive and playful design environment. Pragmatist philosopher Richard Sennett directs criticism towards the use of CAD technology in architecture as a technology that separates the mind and the hand.[2] The result, he argues, is a weakening of intuitive design due to a loss of intimacy with the physical nature of its

4

5 Custom sensors from the 'Urban Feeds' workshop cluster at SG 2011, Copenhagen, Denmark.
The 'Urban Feeds' workshop cluster developed a low-cost environmental sensor from open-source hardware. Participants walked around Copenhagen to record the local environment of urban spaces, noting temperature, carbon dioxide levels, humidity and solar data mapped via GPS, and wirelessly transmitting their findings back to the workshop.

6 Interfaces from the 'Interacting with the City' workshop cluster at SG 2011, Copenhagen, Denmark.
The use of tangible interfaces consisting of touch screens, 3D cameras and projectors have enabled architects and engineers to redefine the designer's UI (user interface) and realign it with physical intuition.

5

6

medium. In reaction to this, reconnecting the design environment to the physical world has recently emerged as a dominant thread in SG workshops. Reflective of the popular use of the word 'mash-up', computational designers have begun to reappropriate software and hardware platforms that were never made for design into a unique ecosystem. Gaming-based hardware like Microsoft's Kinect, combined with the community-developed graphics programming language Processing, enabled one workshop team at SG 2011 to display live wind analysis projected onto an adjustable physical model of multiple buildings. This same tool was later used within Foster + Partners' office as an active and agile system for early building design within an urban environment.

Wiring up diverse software platforms and tinkering with hardware is a pervasive and cultural extension of SG's origins. The early creation of custom functions and associations within one platform (GC) naturally evolved into external software applications and like-minded hardware-based communities. The last four years have seen a significant growth in the DIY culture of open-source hardware platforms like the Arduino microprocessor, as well as increased access to disparate commercial and web software applications through the public availability of APIs. These systems are often low-cost or free, well documented, and with strong user communities. Each of these factors lowers the barrier to access for the creative and curious. Our industry must engage with this as an opportunity to extend the design environment beyond the current operations, graphic representations and hardware interfaces provided by pre-built CAD tools and off-the-shelf computer workstations. The future of design environments is agile, extendable and most importantly, playful.

Each year new technologies and processes from disciplines outside of architecture find their way into SG workshops, enabling new innovations in the design environment. As noted above, rapid prototyping equipment, previously associated only with product design, made an early appearance at the workshops and led to new techniques in the evaluation of form. Low-cost web cameras and open-source electronics hardware platforms such as Arduino started off small in 2010, but quickly became part of the standard toolkit for design by enabling easier methods of data gathering and bridging the digital–physical divide. Theoretical biologist Stuart Kauffman termed this concept the 'adjacent possible' within the context of evolution.[3] SG actively enables exploration of the 'adjacent possible' through a constant search for new technologies and processes that sit just outside the discipline, especially those that serve as a stepping stone for new possibilities in the design exploration process.

### EVOLUTION

As the SG community has matured, its reach has become wider whilst simultaneously preserving a young edge. Some of the earliest collaborators have gone on to lead computation-based movements at the top architecture and engineering schools around the world, and many have forged successful careers in

7

7 3D printed nodes from the 'Nonlinear Systems Biology and Design' workshop cluster at SG 2010, IAAC, Barcelona, Spain.
Progressing from an earlier focus on form-based design iterations, workshops began to use the 3D printer to create rule-based parts for an overall prototype, in this case nodes for an emergent structure.

8 Working environment of the 'Authored
Sensing' workshop cluster at SG 2011,
Copenhagen, Denmark.
Beyond just the computer, the new designer's
environment contains physical prototypes
through digital fabrication, tangible interfaces
and electronics. Each extends the design space
for creative exploration.

practice, building significant structures. With earlier generations serving as mentors to the next, the 'new blood' participating in workshops each year brings greater levels of experience and a stronger infusion of core computational culture. Year after year, we have seen future design partnerships being formed at the event; these workshops often plant the seeds of future collaborations.

The research carried out at SG workshops is led by design, not technology. Each year we engage in questions about design and the built environment, enabled by and manifested in technology, building on the knowledge gained in previous years. As co-directors of SG, we do not *direct* the topic of exploration for a given year. We do not believe any singular technique is the answer, and do not prescribe a particular style. The yearly workshop 'challenge' is sourced from the community, a model we feel will continue to engage the most experimental topics of the day and provide years of influential dialogue. We seek new threads running through the design process and promote their exploration, debate, thoughtful reflection and application in new design futures.

8

**REFERENCES**
1 Robert Woodbury, *Elements of Parametric Design*, Routledge (London), 2010.
2 Richard Sennett, *The Craftsman*, Allen Lane (London), 2008.
3 Stuart A Kauffman, *At Home in the Universe: The Search for the Laws of Self-Organization and Complexity*, Oxford University Press (New York, NY), 1995.

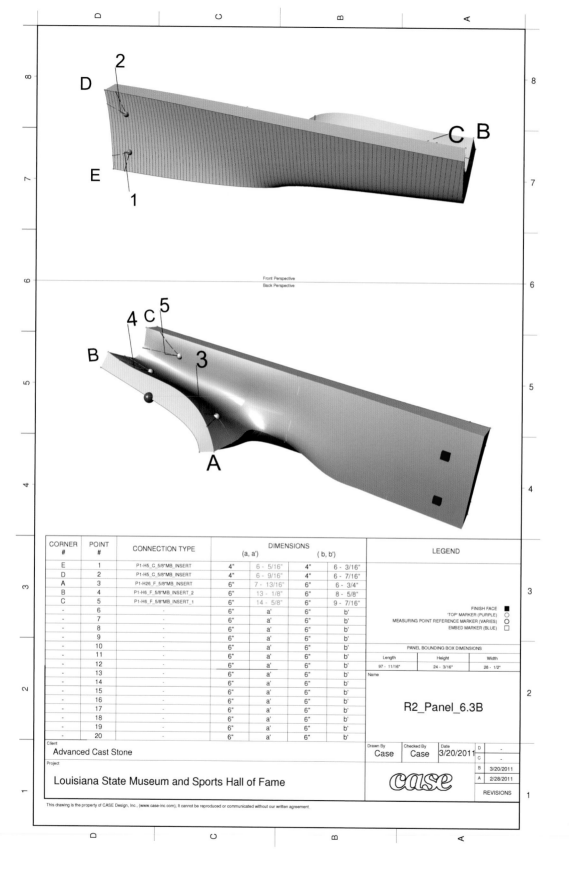

Front Perspective

Back Perspective

| CORNER # | POINT # | CONNECTION TYPE | DIMENSIONS | | | |
|---|---|---|---|---|---|---|
| | | | (a, a') | | ( b, b') | |
| E | 1 | P1-H5_C_5/8"MB_INSERT | 4" | 6 - 5/16" | 4" | 6 - 3/16" |
| D | 2 | P1-H5_C_5/8"MB_INSERT | 4" | 6 - 9/16" | 4" | 6 - 7/16" |
| A | 3 | P1-H26_F_5/8"MB_INSERT | 6" | 7 - 13/16" | 6" | 6 - 3/4" |
| B | 4 | P1-H6_F_5/8"MB_INSERT_2 | 6" | 13 - 1/8" | 6" | 8 - 5/8" |
| C | 5 | P1-H6_F_5/8"MB_INSERT_1 | 6" | 14 - 5/8" | 6" | 9 - 7/16" |
| - | 6 | - | 6" | a' | 6" | b' |
| - | 7 | - | 6" | a' | 6" | b' |
| - | 8 | - | 6" | a' | 6" | b' |
| - | 9 | - | 6" | a' | 6" | b' |
| - | 10 | - | 6" | a' | 6" | b' |
| - | 11 | - | 6" | a' | 6" | b' |
| - | 12 | - | 6" | a' | 6" | b' |
| - | 13 | - | 6" | a' | 6" | b' |
| - | 14 | - | 6" | a' | 6" | b' |
| - | 15 | - | 6" | a' | 6" | b' |
| - | 16 | - | 6" | a' | 6" | b' |
| - | 17 | - | 6" | a' | 6" | b' |
| - | 18 | - | 6" | a' | 6" | b' |
| - | 19 | - | 6" | a' | 6" | b' |
| - | 20 | - | 6" | a' | 6" | b' |

LEGEND

FINISH FACE ■
'TOP' MARKER (PURPLE) ○
MEASURING POINT REFERENCE MARKER (VARIES) ○
EMBED MARKER (BLUE) □

PANEL BOUNDING BOX DIMENSIONS

| Length | Height | Width |
|---|---|---|
| 97 - 11/16" | 24 - 3/16" | 28 - 1/2" |

Name

R2_Panel_6.3B

Client
Advanced Cast Stone

Project
Louisiana State Museum and Sports Hall of Fame

| Drawn By | Checked By | Date | | |
|---|---|---|---|---|
| Case | Case | 3/20/2011 | D | - |
| | | | C | - |
| | | | B | 3/20/2011 |
| | *case* | | A | 2/28/2011 |
| | | | REVISIONS | |

# MIND THE GAP: CASE
## STORIES OF EXCHANGE

The technologists at CASE are immersed in the realities of building on a daily basis. As long-standing members of the Smartgeometry (SG) community, members of CASE have participated in many of the early SG events. Their work uses computational methods to create, coordinate and communicate building information to make complex building projects happen. Here they share their experiences of two current projects in the office and provide a critical reflection on the current direction of SG that has shifted away from practice and building toward research and experimentation.

1 Trahan Architects, Louisiana State Museum and Sports Hall of Fame, Natchitoches, Louisiana, USA, 2012.
CASE automated the production of shop drawings of over 1,000 unique cast-stone panels showing structural connections for the panel fabricator, Advanced Cast Stone.

As New York-based designers and technologists working at SHoP Architects, our first exposure to Smartgeometry came from the early presentations of Shane Burger's work on Grimshaw's Fulton Street Transit Center (due for completion in 2014). The visualisations that Shane produced to describe the geometric approach to that project were inspirational to the small group of computational design enthusiasts in New York at the time. This work began at the second SG workshop held during the 2004 ACADIA Conference at the University of Waterloo, Ontario, Canada.

The next conference and workshop held at Cambridge University, UK in 2006 was where founding partner of CASE, Steve Sanderson, first experienced the focus and intensity of the event as a participant. Over the course of several long days and nights, Steve had the opportunity to work directly with some of the leading practitioners of computational design at the time, including the SG founders, Chris Williams (Bath University), Judit Kimpian (Aedas) and Marty Doscher (Dassault Systèmes, formerly of Morphosis). The event concluded with a conference held at the British Museum, where the Great Court by Fosters & Partners served as an elegant backdrop from the pre-GC era of computational design. Keynotes delivered by Hanif Kara of the structural engineering firm Adams Kara Taylor, inventor and engineer Chuck Hoberman, and Spencer de Grey, the partner-in-charge of the Great Court project at Foster & Partners, helped situate the focused explorations from the workshops within the broader context of architectural practice, reminding the participants and conference attendees of the amazing confluence of talent and resources needed to realize any significant work of architecture.

Steve continued his involvement with SG the following year, returning as a tutor for the workshop and conference held in New

York where Federico Negro, another founding partner at CASE, attended as a participant. The tutors were largely comprised of a mixture of returning tutors and participants from previous workshops, with a balance of practitioners from larger design and engineering firms and academics. The workshop participants however saw a noticeable shift towards students and professors. The conference presentations saw a similar reduction in external points of view, with only presentations from Matthew Herman of Buro Happold, Rob Whitlock of KPF and Bill Sharples of SHoP Architects to provide some broader context. Furthermore, these presentations simply reinforced, through projects, many of the same principles and ideologies put forward by the workshop tutors and participants. Increasingly SG was in danger of suffering from groupthink.

The next two events in Munich and San Francisco, where Steve continued his involvement as a tutor, exhibited many of the same patterns that were present in New York; with tutors, participants and presenters increasingly made up of academics. Subsequent events, beginning with Barcelona in 2010, saw significant changes to the overall structure and organisation of SG, with the introduction of new directors and an emphasis on a series of curated clusters organised around a central challenge that established the overall theme of the event. It is at these events where the shift towards academia is most pronounced; to the extent that by the 2012 event in Troy, New York nearly all of the cluster champions and participants were made up of educators and students.

These recent workshop challenges have placed emphasis on physical prototypes, resulting in a scale of investigation and execution suited for temporary installations, rather than the production of building-scale systems and components, which require far more time, labour, capital and expert knowledge to realise. The work produced is probably more rewarding for both tutors and participants, and the installations make for more interesting cocktail-party conversations, but these events lack the engagement with practice of earlier events. Unfortunately this arrangement perpetuates many of the flaws of architectural education, where the act of design is largely disconnected from the messy realities of practice and many of the rich conversations (and compromises) are suppressed in favour of design exploration.

As the industry begins to redefine itself in relationship to these new tools and processes, it is through the complex negotiation of these external forces that we believe that architects stand to gain or lose the most. As an organisation that was instrumental in establishing the role of computation within architecture, SG is uniquely positioned to provide leadership and direction within this shifting technology-enabled landscape. Ten years ago SG initiated a movement that changed the profession. It is our belief that it stands the best chance at doing it again. Our practice was built on many of the lessons we learned during those formative years of the event.

## THE CASE FOR CASE

Computation has had a profound and lasting impact on architectural design. Open any publication or visit any design website and you will encounter page after page of renderings that were unimaginable before the advent of computational design tools. Yet, the impact that these technologies have had on architecture's influence over the built environment has been less clear. The promises of direct fabrication, mass customisation and robotic construction have yet to alter the complex social fabric of building design and construction in any significant way.

Despite some advances in prefabrication and modular construction, primarily in commercial structures where architects have minimal involvement, and an increasing interest in design-build and integrated project delivery (IPD) contract structures in time-critical projects; the production of the built environment has changed very little. All of the major stakeholders in the process, owners/clients, architects/engineers and contractors/fabricators, continue to operate in more or less the same way as they did before the introduction of these technologies. Architecture has yet to capitalise on the process gains demonstrated in the manufacturing world, where many of the platforms currently used by the industry originated.

The reasons behind this resistance to change are interesting and complex enough to justify tomes dedicated to the topic, but the area that we would like to focus on in this essay is the role of computational design. The availability and accessibility of computational design tools have exploded over the last decade. What used to be the exclusive domain of a handful of entrenched software vendors has become an ecosystem of developers, hackers and designers, where the next big thing could come from a heavily funded research group or college dorm room. These changes have mirrored similar trends in the web development world, where application programming interfaces (APIs), low-to-no-cost development platforms and community-driven learning websites have drastically lowered the barrier to entry.

This has led to the emergence of specialist roles within architecture firms focused on the application and development of these tools towards architectural design. These roles have grown from niche, technical positions that few firms could afford to large groups in most major design firms. Entire academic programs (AA Emtech, AA DRL, Institute of Computational Design), organisations (SG, ACADIA) and countless conferences (Advances in Architectural Geometry, Shape to Fabrication, FORMATIONS) now focus exclusively on this topic. Within architecture, computational design is the new black.

However, this has not yet altered the role of the architect in the building design process. Architects are not fully leveraging the downstream value created using these processes to increase their value in the production of the built environment. Unless computational designers and the firms that employ them are

2 Allies & Morrison/OMA, Commonwealth
Institute (The Parabola), Kensington, London,
UK, due for completion in 2014.
CASE provided cross-disciplinary BIM
coordination for all members of the design
team, including the architects Allies & Morrison/
OMA, engineering consultants Arup and
landscape architects West 8, on behalf of the
project developer Chelsfield.

3 Allies & Morrison/OMA, Commonwealth
Institute (The Parabola), Kensington, London,
UK, due for completion in 2014.
CASE led the development of the project's
BIM Execution Plan, which described the level
of detail for all components of the design
coordination model.

2

3

4

AGGREGATED MODEL

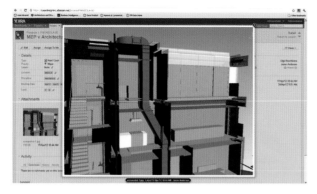

5

willing to step away from the keyboard and engage fully in the translation of information with the various stakeholders involved, their role and influence over this process will continue to diminish. In response to this, new technology consultancies have recently emerged that are beginning to apply these specialised skill sets more broadly across the entire building process.

Rather than being enamoured with the formal aspects of these technologies, these consultants emphasise the informational aspects. Instead of being fixated on process, these consultancies focus on results. We started CASE in late 2008, as the global financial crisis was in full swing, because we believed that technology offered a better way to design, construct and operate buildings. Our experience working as designers, project managers and educators focused on the application of emerging technologies to architectural design provided a unique vantage point into the potential of these new processes. Empowered by this knowledge, we decided to leave our jobs as designers in order to share this expertise with the rest of the industry.

### CASE STUDY 1: THE COMMONWEALTH INSTITUTE

The Commonwealth Institute is a mixed-use development adjacent to Holland Park in the Royal Borough of Kensington and Chelsea in London. The project seeks to reuse the existing Commonwealth Institute structure to house the new home of the Design Museum of London. In addition, three new residential buildings will be completed in the surrounding landscape. The project is a joint venture of Allies & Morrison (London) with OMA (Rotterdam) for Chelsfield, a London-based developer. Arup is the consulting engineer for all building systems, facade and structure. West 8 is the landscape architect. CASE was brought in by Allies & Morrison to provide technology process support and comprehensive model-based design coordination for all design disciplines on behalf of the owner. At the time of writing in August 2012, the project is nearing completion of design; construction is set to begin at the end of 2012, with completion anticipated in 2014.

The motivation to adopt a model-based approach on this project stems from broader industry movement in the UK towards more

4 Allies & Morrison/OMA, Commonwealth Institute (The Parabola), Kensington, London, UK, due for completion in 2014.
Using models authored by all design disciplines, CASE produced a complete virtual representation of the project that was used for design coordination and quality control.

5 Allies & Morrison/OMA, Commonwealth Institute (The Parabola), Kensington, London, UK, due for completion in 2014.
CASE adapted software used for tracking bugs during software development, to increase transparency and accountability for all disciplines on the design team.

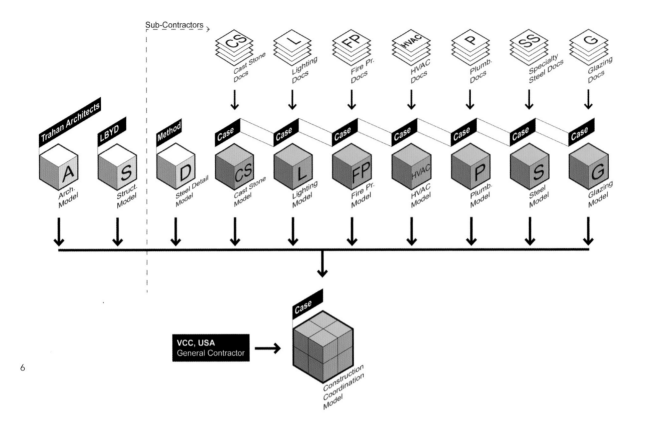

Sub-Contractors →

Trahan Architects
A — Arch. Model

LBYD
S — Struct. Model

Method
D — Steel Detail Model

Case
CS — Cast Stone Model

Cast Stone Docs

Case
L — Lighting Model

Lighting Docs

Case
FP — Fire Pr. Model

Fire Pr. Docs

Case
HVAC — HVAC Model

HVAC Docs

Case
P — Plumb. Model

Plumb. Docs

Case
SS / S — Steel Model

Specialty Steel Docs

Case
G — Glazing Model

Glazing Docs

VCC, USA
General Contractor →

Case
Construction Coordination Model

6

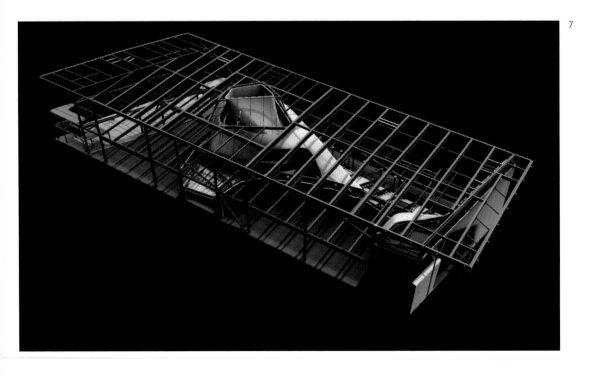

7

6 Trahan Architects, Louisiana State Museum and Sports Hall of Fame, Natchitoches, Louisiana, USA, 2012.
CASE provided two distinct services on the project: 3D modelling for the various subcontractors and construction coordination for the construction manager, VCC USA.

7 Trahan Architects, Louisiana State Museum and Sports Hall of Fame, Natchitoches, Louisiana, USA, 2012.
Due to the complexity of the design, the models produced by CASE were critical in coordinating all the mechanical systems of the building.

efficient methods of project delivery. Recently, the UK government initiated this movement by requiring 'fully collaborative 3D BIM [building information modelling] as a minimum by 2016'[1] on all public projects. While the Commonwealth Institute is a private enterprise, the owner had every intention to stay ahead of the general market and issued a project-specific requirement for 3D model-based delivery. The team, comprising architect, engineers and builders who had begun investing in BIM, saw the client-driven request as an opportunity to further their collaborative pursuits. With a clear objective to use BIM to eliminate friction in information exchange across parties and project phases, the owner directed the team to prepare a model-based approach that would eventually be used in the facility's operation. This directive formed the basis of the overall strategic and tactical goals of the BIM process defined by CASE, as well as establishing expectations for all those involved.

Ahead of any production, a framework for collaboration was defined by CASE through a BIM Execution Plan (BEP). The objective of the BEP was to provide a comprehensive guideline for participation in model-based collaboration. Through this process, high-level objectives were defined: an overall project strategy was developed; a plan was defined to implement this strategy; and finally, a set of protocols were outlined to ensure clear methods of exchange across all parties. Within this document, a Design Responsibility Matrix was developed that outlines elements to be included in the model; identifying who is responsible for their development and to what level of detail they are required to be developed. These documents, produced as a collaborative effort by every participant, set forth a clear scope of work for the delivery of a 3D Design Intent Model.

The exchange process was designed to be agile, providing the members of the design team with continuous feedback as their designs progressed. To facilitate this process, each participant was required to provide weekly updates of their models. This ensured that the design models were exchanged among the various disciplines and analysed by CASE on a regular basis. CASE provided analysis of the geometric aspects of the models: identifying potential conflicts, errors, omissions, clearances and general model quality. It also consisted of keeping a close eye on element categorisation, identification and other metadata used to track elements within the building.

This process allowed for increased transparency and accountability. The typical design process whereby teams work in relative isolation with infrequent, antagonistic exchanges was replaced by one with dozens of model-based interactions throughout all stages of design. It went a long way to minimise the risks inherent in traditional design methodologies by identifying issues, conflicts and unknown conditions before they became detrimental to either design intent or project delivery objectives.

Throughout our involvement on the project, CASE identified more than 200 distinct issues that were resolved before final design

8 Trahan Architects, Louisiana State Museum and Sports Hall of Fame, Natchitoches, Louisiana, USA, 2012.
Rendering of the interior atrium.

9 Trahan Architects, Louisiana State Museum and Sports Hall of Fame, Natchitoches, Louisiana, USA, 2012.
View of light fixtures being tested. The red dots are the protection covers on the sprinkler heads coming through the skin.

10 Trahan Architects, Louisiana State Museum and Sports Hall of Fame, Natchitoches, Louisiana, USA, 2012.
Installing a 'jamb' panel.

9

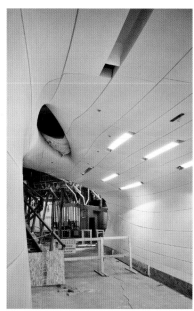

10

submission. The design team found tremendous value in having minimised unknowns to almost zero. Issues remained and requests for information (RFIs) are still expected, but there is general consensus that the team's understanding of their own design was more complete than it otherwise would have been.

**CASE STUDY 2: THE LOUISIANA STATE MUSEUM AND SPORTS HALL OF FAME**

The Louisiana State Museum and Sports Hall of Fame (LSMSHF) is a 2,400-square-metre (26,000-square-foot) copper-clad structure located in Natchitoches, Louisiana and the new home of the state's sports teams' memorabilia. The project was designed by Trahan Architects for the State of Louisiana. The construction manager was VCC, USA who hired CASE to provide comprehensive digital modelling and construction coordination services for all trades. The primary design feature of the building is the entrance, circulation and central atrium space defined by a free-form cast-stone system fabricated by Advanced Cast Stone, who hired CASE to provide all fabrication modelling services. The project is slated to be completed in winter 2012.

The motivation behind model-based coordination arose from the inability to properly represent the design's complex geometry using traditional methods. The building was designed using 3D animation software and, due to the number of atypical conditions that this created, the process of translating each condition into a 2D representation was not only inefficient, but also prone to error and misinterpretation. The architects realised that a model-based fabrication and construction coordination process was the only way to maintain their design intent. Their primary obstacle was the contract structure of state projects that required the acceptance of the 'lowest qualified bid', where contracts were not awarded based on demonstrated ability to realise similar projects, but on the ability to realise the project cheaply. To offset the potential of the design intent being compromised, the architect convinced the state to add a requirement for model-based fabrication and coordination across the entire construction phase as part of the bid process.

As a result the bid specifications were clear: all trades that interfaced with the cast stone were required to submit a 'fabrication level' (LOD 400)[2] 3D model of their entire scope, and were required to participate in the overall 3D coordination process. The cast-stone system, consisting of more than 1,000 unique panels ranging in size from 0.6 by 1.8 metres (2 by 6 foot) to 4.2 by 4.2 metres (14 by 14 foot), had to meet stringent surface integrity specifications. In this case, models were not just a requirement; they were a necessity. The fabrication models that CASE created from the architect's original design surfaces were used for coordination with other trades, as well as to finalise the support structure, resolve panel conflicts and robotically fabricate the final moulds for the cast-stone panels. The light fixtures, support structure, primary structural connections, glazing, stairs and handrails, air registers and terminals were all trades that used models produced by CASE in support of this process directly for fabrication. These systems would have been impossible to coordinate and fabricate using any other process.

Compared to the design coordination process for the Commonwealth Institute, the 3D construction coordination process for LSMSHF was far more piecemeal. Although all parties were contractually required to participate, the time in which they engaged the process was driven by their individual contracts and the overall project schedule, which had been defined before the 3D coordination process was implemented. In many cases, this would have minimised the influence of many trades that were brought in later in the process, but because the 3D model was so central to the overall construction coordination process, many trades that would not traditionally have had a voice were given an opportunity to contribute their expertise. This process was facilitated through weekly remote coordination meetings that were managed by CASE in order to identify and resolve conflicts ahead of fabrication and construction.

This model-based process provided a critical bridge between virtual representations and the field. The model was used to finalise design issues, release trades for construction, track progress, test out prototypes, plan installation and lock-out conditions, visualise sequencing, perform structural analysis and numerous other critical processes. Despite all of this, the project came across numerous problems due to limitations of the contract structure that have led to schedule overruns. Yet all of the trades involved in this process agree that without model-based delivery, the issues would have been more numerous and severe. In fact, it was frequently reiterated that this project could not have been realised without model-based delivery.

## TOWARDS A NEW COMPUTATIONAL DESIGN

The proliferation of computational tools within architecture has undoubtedly changed the landscape of the architectural profession by impacting both design processes and delivery methods. And yet, while the computational community has significantly expanded through the numerous venues mentioned above (including SG), the overall effect that these venues are having on the profession has diminished noticeably since their heyday in the early 2000s. The ubiquity and accessibility of these tools and processes has shifted the emphasis away from the exclusive domain of designers, towards a more scalable, inclusive discourse that is centred on problem solving through collaboration between numerous stakeholders.

This is where the narrow definition and interpretation of the SG challenges has most notably impacted the range of participation in recent years. An extremely limited portion of the industry has anything more than a passing interest in imagining '… the design space of architecture was no longer at the scale of rooms, walls and atria, but that of cells, grains and vapour droplets'[3], as most of us grapple enough with the difficulties of designing, building and occupying spaces at the macroscopic scale. Unsurprisingly, the clusters that were chosen in response to this challenge were equally pretentious. Can one imagine a building owner participating in one of these clusters? How about a builder? Nope. We couldn't either.

As an emerging core competency of design thinking, it has become critical to engage in a discourse that includes computation as an essential component of the building process: one that clearly demonstrates downstream value and emphasises participation and collaboration from all stakeholders. As a diverse group comprising individuals from many aspects of the architecture and engineering community, SG has an opportunity to lead an expanded research agenda that drives innovation through the collaborative potential of computational design, by focusing on a more inclusive, industry-focused approach to the identification of event challenges.

### REFERENCES
1 Cabinet Office, *Government Construction Strategy*, Cabinet Office (London), May 2011, p 14.
2 American Institute of Architects, Document E202-2008 Building Information Modelling Protocol Exhibit, American Institute of Architects (New York, NY), 2008.
3 Smartgeometry, *Smartgeometry Challenge 2012: Material Intensities: Simulation, Energy, Environment*, www.smartgeometry.org.

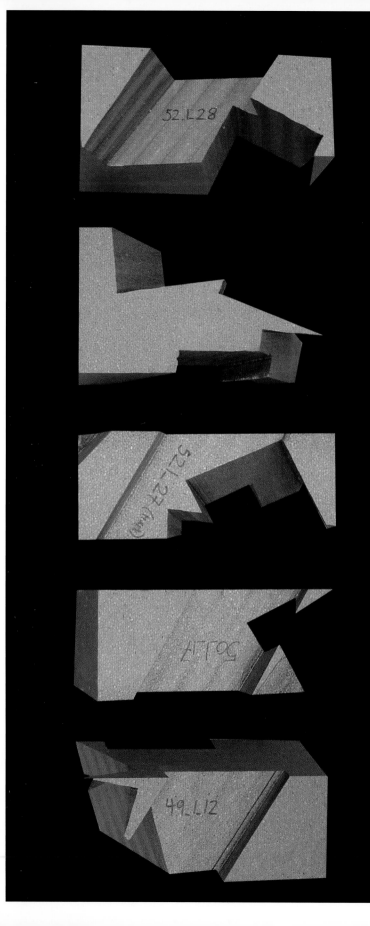

1 Individually cut block geometries from 'Explicit Bricks' workshop cluster at SG 2010, IAAC, Barcelona, Spain.
In order to follow the overall geometry, all Styrofoam blocks are uniquely shaped.

1

# DESIGNING ROBOTIC ASSEMBLIES

## TOBIAS BONWETSCH

Tobias Bonwetsch was a Senior Researcher at ETH Zurich's Laboratory for Architecture and Digital Fabrication chaired by Gramazio & Kohler. Together with Dr Ralph Bärtschi, he now heads R-O-B Technologies where he continues to develop robotic-based design and fabrication processes. At Smartgeometry (SG) 2010 he co-led with Bärtschi and Andrea Kondziela the 'Explicit Bricks' cluster where a combination of custom digital tools and an industrial robot were used to test different interlocking systems of complex geometrically shaped bricks. Here he outlines the potentials of using robotic techniques for architectural design.

Industrial robots have gained the interest of architects and designers in the last couple of years. On the one hand, this is due to their universal nature. Like other computer-numerically controlled (CNC) machines, industrial robots allow for a digital control of the fabrication process. By using them in combination with digital design tools, architects can transfer design information directly to fabrication machines. But what is more, unlike common CNC machines, the physical process itself – the actual material manipulation – can be customised. On the other hand, industrial robots lend themselves especially well to assembly tasks. This puts them close to the actual reality of building.

In the context of Smartgeometry (SG) it is this ability to control and manipulate the building process by both digital and physical means that is of interest to us. Provided that architecture manifests itself in physical reality, robots establish the link between computational design and the actual construction of architecture. Moreover, the definition and engineering of a specific robotic assembly process can inform the design and become part of the design process. In that way industrial robots emphasise construction as an integral part of architectural design.

The widespread use of digital design tools eases the creation of complex geometries and non-standard design solutions. Especially in the early years, these possibilities opened up by software lacked an equivalent on the side of physical execution. Realising such projects was mostly a top-down process, whereby the overall geometry had to be broken down into manageable parts that follow a constructive logic – a process that harbours the risk of compromising one's initial design idea.

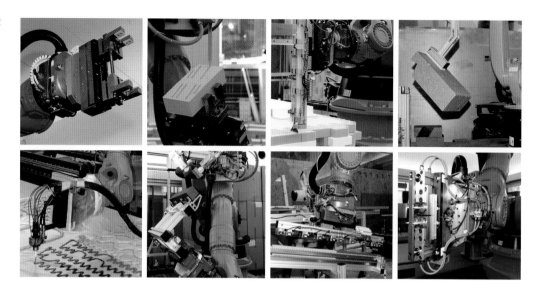

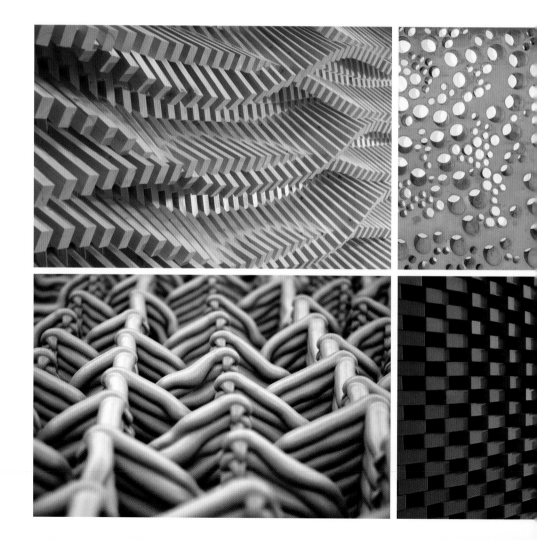

2 Examples of 'end-effectors' for industrial robotic arms.
Different custom-designed tools allow the robot to perform a multitude of different material manipulations.

3 Examples of robotically fabricated construction and material systems.

3

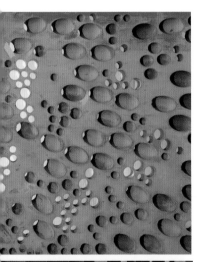

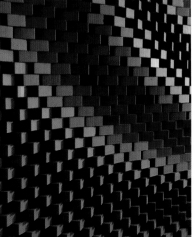

In our work the construction process stands at the beginning of a project and shares equal significance to the specific design intent. In defining the digital and physical control of an assembly process ourselves, we allow the creative and explorative part of making to facilitate the design process. When building specific tools for the robot to operate, we already frame possibilities and constraints of the fabrication process and thus the possible design space. In our approach industrial robots are not a mere tool for automation, but allow us to explore a multitude of different construction and assembly processes. In contrast to a traditional craft approach, where the knowledge of making is to a large extent embodied in the maker, when using the industrial robot, the knowledge of making has to be made explicit in the form of code. The manipulation of the explicit description of the fabrication process sets the basis for our design explorations. This is facilitated by computers and their ability to manage and process a large volume of data. We can design assemblies that consist of a large number of parts and are precisely defined down to their smallest constituent element, while the industrial robot provides the tool to transform this information into a physical process. Therefore, in our projects form is not primarily derived from computation or an overall geometry, but is developed out of the logic of construction and reflects the sequential steps of the specific robotic assembly process.

## ROBOTS AS UNIVERSAL FABRICATION MACHINES

Industrial robots can be understood as universal fabrication machines that can be adapted to perform nearly any desired material manipulation. In their generic nature industrial robots are comparable to computers, with the difference that actions are performed on physical entities. George Devol, considered to be the father of industrial robots, termed the object of his invention patented in 1954 as 'universal automation' and drew a direct analogy to computers. Where the latter is a 'universal machine' for office work – and nowadays almost all aspects of our lives – the former equals for fabrication: a general-purpose machine.[1]

Especially in the early years, although conceived as highly flexible machines, industrial robots were not applied as such, but mainly used for automating standardised processes. SG 2010 in Barcelona illustrated how today fabrication technology in general is much more accessible for the designer and thus allows for a change in the conceptual approach. Architectural practice is no longer imaginable without the aid of information technology, and CAD/CAM allows design information to be easily transferred to fabrication data. At the same time industrial robots have become a commodity that can easily be controlled using off-the-shelf personal computer technology. Given this combination, designers are able to unleash the flexibility inherent in the machine.

## PROGRAMMABILITY

Key to the flexibility of industrial robots is their programmability. Here lies the analogy of 'universal business machines' drawn by Devol. But, while the computer is made specific through the

4

5

particular software that runs on it, the programmability of the robot is twofold. Firstly, the control software plays a crucial role. The multi-axis robotic arm can move to any point in space within its kinematic range. The sequence of its movement is defined through coded commands controlling the robot's actions. As with other CNC machines, the robot's control software enables one to manufacture objects directly from their digital description. Secondly, and this sets industrial robots apart from common CNC machines, the user is able to define the actual physical material manipulation. An industrial robot can perform an arbitrary task because its task is dependent on the specific tool the robot is equipped with. Unlike CNC machines that are specialised in a single manufacturing operation like milling or laser cutting, the action and actual processing of material performed by an industrial robot is not predefined. These tools, or so-called 'end-effectors', can be highly specific and unique for a particular fabrication process. They can be designed to perform a physical material manipulation, but also to gather information for example by probing, scanning or measuring.

Many current examples use robots as universal fabrication machines, but in such a way that they only mimic existing CNC machines. But the application of industrial robots becomes truly powerful when its intrinsic potential is activated. That is, the design of user-specific, customised, physical processes. As the ability to program allows the architect to create his own design tools, freeing him partially from any concepts rooted in a specific CAD software, designing a robotic fabrication process opens up the freedom to follow physical processes outside the given frameworks of common CNC machines.

### ASSEMBLY DESIGN VERSUS COMPONENT DESIGN

Apart from engineering customised fabrication processes, another relevant aspect distinguishes industrial robots from common CNC machines. Where the manufacturing process of CNC machines is component based, the kinematics of industrial robots, which resemble the dexterity of a human arm, lend themselves particularly well to assembly tasks. CNC machines have their origin in the automation of machine tools and are therefore developed to machine components, mainly through cutting or deformation. A component-based design follows the logic of industrialisation. The intelligence and complexity of fitting is integrated in the component, such that the final assembly on site can be performed by an unskilled workforce. Digital control of these machines now allows realising non-standard designs, where every single component is different. Nevertheless, these components still need to be assembled – a task that can become quite challenging, especially for a large quantity of components, which are all potentially uniquely shaped.

This aspect of a component-based design is illustrated quite well through our 'Explicit Bricks' cluster at SG 2010, held at the IAAC (Institute for Advanced Architecture of Catalonia) in Barcelona. The goal of the four-day workshop was to design a constructive

4 Robotic Research Facility at ETH Zurich, Zurich, Switzerland, 2010.
Robotically controlled hot-wire cutting of Styrofoam blocks.

5 Screenshot of catenary arch prototype from 'Explicit Bricks' workshop cluster at SG 2010, IAAC, Barcelona, Spain.

6

7

system composed out of uniquely formed Styrofoam blocks. Different interlocking systems were tested in 1:1 prototypes. The individual blocks were robotically fabricated in a custom hot-wire cutting process, while the assembly was performed manually. One of the propositions developed in the workshop envisaged a constructive system in which the blocks spiral around a catenary arch and thereby support the stability of the overall structure. In such a system all blocks, although they follow the same interlocking principle, are uniquely shaped. While the digital process from generating the design to fabricating each individual block proved no difficulty, the assembly of a prototype arch was too complex and failed at the first attempt. Only in a second round, after a sophisticated assembly strategy was developed, could the structure be put up. While the potential of the robot to apply a project-specific fabrication process was exploited, the workshop also revealed the complexities that arise in assembling constructions that consist of a large amount of individual parts.

Applying industrial robots to assembly tasks embraces the construction process. Thus, robotically controlled assembly processes establish a close link to actual building practice, as construction can be described as the assembly of different parts and materials. The construction process can now be manipulated and digitally controlled. In the case of the numerous robotically assembled brickwork projects realised by ourselves and the group of Gramazio & Kohler at ETH Zurich over the last few years, non-standard designs can be realised using a standard component.[2] The basic brick units are identical. Diversity is introduced through the digital control of their assembly process.

### ASSEMBLY-BASED DESIGN
Industrial robots give the architect the digital and physical control over the assembly process, thereby facilitating a reconnection of design and making. This connection had dissolved as buildings became more complex, thus causing a separation and specialisation of disciplines within the building trades. The knowledge of making can lead to innovative and novel design solutions. There are numerous examples in architectural history where architect-builders developed their designs directly out of assembly processes, such as Filippo Brunelleschi (1377–1446) in the early Renaissance, Pier Luigi Nervi (1891–1979) and Félix Candela (1910–1997).[3] This does not imply that the act of making is the only thing of value, and that architecture should be reduced to a constructional craft. Questioning 'what' and 'why' to make is just as important.[4] But rather, the knowledge of making, and the choosing and manipulating of a fabrication process, are not only questions of problem solving or mere technical aspects in the process of realising architecture, but can act as a stimulus for design and instigate novel design solutions.[5]

### INTEGRATING ASSEMBLY PARAMETERS INTO THE DESIGN PROCESS
Parameters of the assembly process are specified by the robotic setup. This includes the reach of the arm and the specific geometry of the end-effector, which sets constraints on the

6 Assembly of prototype arch from 'Explicit Bricks' workshop cluster at SG 2010, IAAC, Barcelona, Spain.
The manual assembly of the individual blocks proved to be too complex.

7 Prototype from SG 2010, IAAC, Barcelona, Spain.
The 'Explicit Bricks' workshop participants used a hot-wire cutter attached to a robotic arm to cut individually shaped foam pieces. The 1:1 foam brick prototypes were assembled to construct an inhabitable pavilion.

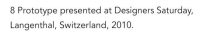

8 Prototype presented at Designers Saturday,
Langenthal, Switzerland, 2010.
Only after the workshop and having developed
an assembly strategy could a second prototype
structure be put up, which proved the concept
of the chosen interlocking strategy.

9 Kerim Seiler, *Gulliver* brick sculpture,
Pfungen, Switzerland, 2009.
The sculptural idea was developed with the aid
of a software tool, which embedded parameters
of the robotic assembly process.

10 Gramazio & Kohler in cooperation with
Bearth & Deplazes Architects, Gantenbein
Vineyard Facade, Fläsch, Switzerland, 2006:
robotic assembly process.

10

dimensions of the single piece processed and how it can be placed. Also to be considered are the specific characteristics of the material and semi-finished products processed and how these relate to the assembly process. It is important not only to account for a structurally sound final structure, but also to ensure that a stable equilibrium is achieved in each step during the build-up process. Once the fabrication parameters are identified and made explicit, they can be incorporated into software tools that open up a design space for exploration. In such a design space, bounded by fabrication constraints, the design exploration is deeply rooted in constructive principles and the physical reality of building. Given the ability to manage and process large volumes of data, the computer can inform a design, which the robot can then transfer into a physical process. The physical manifestation of a design can therefore be highly informed and precisely defined down to its smallest constituent element. This creates the opportunity for a new materiality that features richness of detail and in its logic expresses the possibilities of the computer.[6]

### FLEXIBLE FABRICATION MACHINES

Industrial robots are highly flexible fabrication machines. The parameters set by a specific fabrication process define the scope of the design space. At the SG workshop in Barcelona we were able to explore the architectural potential of a custom robotically controlled hot-wire cutting process. In this case, due to the tight time frame of the workshop, the participants were confronted with a predefined process; though we believe that truly novel design solutions emerge in combining the act of making and design. In creating custom robotically controlled processes, architects gain control over the building process. The definition of the assembly process and the specific material manipulation performed by the robotic system becomes part of the architectural design process.

11 Gramazio & Kohler, West Fest Pavilion, ETH
Zurich, Zurich, Switzerland, 2009: fabrication
process.
The robotic setup defines the maximum length
of the wooden slats that still can be processed.

12 Gramazio & Kohler, West Fest Pavilion, ETH Zurich, Zurich, Switzerland, 2009: photograph after completion.
The openings developing at the tops of the columns are a direct result of the dimensional constraints which were dictated by the robotic setup.

Robotic assembly processes in particular emphasise construction as an integral part of architectural design. In a digitally controlled process, each individual step of an assembly has to be made specific in order for the robot to transform that information into physical movements and actions. The manipulation of the explicit assembly description is the basis for a design exploration. This enables the introduction of diversity, even when the constituent elements are all the same. Although industrial robots are much more accessible, in the future, in order to facilitate this connection of design and making we need tools that on the one hand aid us to easily set up and control custom robotic processes, and on the other hand make the specific parameters of fabrication available in the design process. Thereby, form is not primarily derived from an overall geometry or computation, but from a physical process.

## REFERENCES

1 George Charles Devol, 'Programmed Article Transfer', United States Patent Office, 13, United States, 1954. In 1954 Devol applied for patent on Programmed Article Transfer that introduced the concept of *Universal Automation* or *Unimation*; US Patent 2,988,237 was issued in 1961. Available online at http://www.google.com/patents?vid=2988237 [accessed 30/11/12].
2 F Gramazio, M Kohler and J Willmann, 'Towards an Extended Performative Materiality: Interactive Complexity and the Control of Space', in N Oxman and R Oxman (eds), *Theories of the Digital in Architecture*, Routledge (London), due February 2013.
3 Steven Groak, *The Idea of Building: Thought and Action in the Design and Production of Buildings*, E & FN Spon (London; New York, NY), 1992.
4 Markus Breitschmid, *Can Architectural Art-Form Be Designed out of Construction? Carl Boetticher, Gottfried Semper, and Heinrich Woelfflin: A Sketch of Various Investigations on the Nature of 'Tectonic' in Nineteenth-Century Architectural Theory*, architecture edition (Blacksburg, VA), 2004.
5 Bob Sheil, 'Transgression from Drawing to Making', *arq: Architectural Research Quarterly*, Vol 9, No 1, 2005, pp 20–32.
6 Antoine Picon, 'Architecture and the Virtual: Towards a New Materiality?', *Praxis: Journal of Writing + Building*, No 6, 2004, pp 114–21.

# THE PRACTICE OF SMARTGEOMETRY

### HUGH WHITEHEAD

Architect Hugh Whitehead joined Foster + Partners to set up the Specialist Modelling Group (SMG) in 1998 with the aim of carrying out research and development in the intense project-driven environment of the office. Known for his computational investigations into designing design methods for architecture, he is also a co-founder of Smartgeometry. Here Whitehead explains his approach to using mathematical techniques as an aid to design, using examples from the SMG's early seminal projects.

1 Foster + Partners Specialist Modelling Group, 2009.

The Specialist Modelling Group (SMG) was established as an architectural research and development group within the office of Foster + Partners by Hugh Whitehead in 1998. Smartgeometry (SG) is an international collective of architects and researchers founded by Hugh Whitehead, Lars Hesselgren and J Parrish in 2001. The founders facilitate the workshops and conferences and, while not directly leading or participating in workshops, they have directed the organisation and guided its philosophy and framework since its inception. While the trajectories of SG and the SMG have an interdependence, they seem to weave like strands, which converge and diverge, periodically crossing over. SG is all about synergies, often between competing individuals and organisations, but for the period of the workshop it is gloves off, while we collaborate in collective exploration.

SMG has helped to deliver radical projects which were launched during a period of growth in which Foster + Partners doubled in size. In development terms the effect of the projects was cumulative, each one providing a springboard to the next. The idea of learning to build tools, as an integral part of the design process, involved new attitudes of mind through which we began to formulate a coherent strategy in response to new challenges focusing on the following concepts: geometry as a mechanism; rationale as a strategy; rules as proportional relationships; curvature as rate of change; the sketch as a metaphor; architecture as a team game; and computers as amplifiers of the intellect.

### GEOMETRY AS A MECHANISM

The approach of using 'geometry as a mechanism' is a direct reference to our first project which was the Swiss Re HQ, 30 St Mary Axe building (2004) – that most perfect of mechanisms, which is as precise as a Swiss watch. Although computers were used extensively to explore and fine-tune the concept and then to generate the implementation, the initial ideas were developed

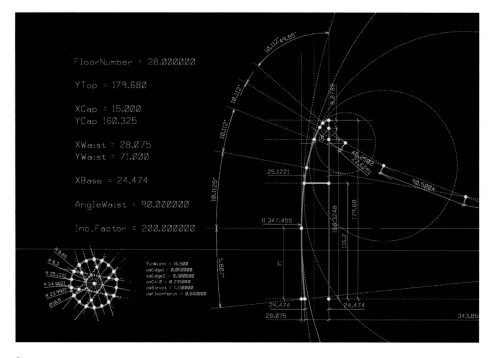

FloorNumber = 28.000000

YTop = 179.680

XCap = 15.000
YCap 160.325

XWaist = 28.075
YWaist = 71.000

XBase = 24.474

AngleWaist = 90.000000

Inc_Factor = 200.000000

fanWidth = 16.500
osEdge1 = 0.050000
osEdge2 = 0.300000
osCol0 = 0.235000
osStruct = 1.130000
osFloorPerim = 0.560000

2

3

2 Foster + Partners, Swiss Re HQ, 30 St Mary
Axe, London, UK, 2004.
Parametric setting-out model constructed using
MicroStation's Dimension Driven Design.

3 Foster + Partners, The Sage Gateshead,
Gateshead, UK, 2004.
Parametric setting-out model constructed using
MicroStation's Dimension Driven Design.

4 Foster + Partners, Swiss Re HQ, 30 St Mary
Axe, London, UK, 2004.

5 Foster + Partners, The Sage Gateshead,
Gateshead, UK, 2004.

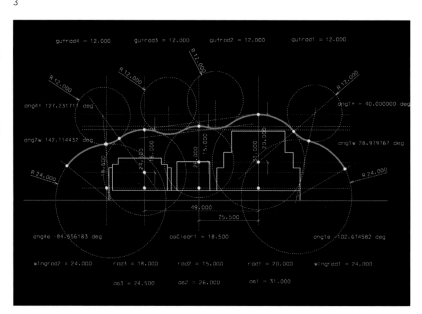

using cardboard models and raw intellect. The design was in effect completely pre-rationalised, but the result was a building that could never be drawn – only modelled in terms of rule-based relationships. We needed a form of shorthand that could automatically codify a massive amount of variation. At every floor the rules and offsets were the same, but the detail was always different. However, the variation could be specified and derived from a changing relationship between structural node and cladding node, which in turn were determined by the changing curvature of plan and section.

Parametric plans, sections and profiles were developed and linked using geometric projections and shared parameter sets. These formed inputs to Excel where the node coordinates were calculated, and then exported back to graphics where scripts generated a schematic 3D model which could then be populated with detail. The principles of this approach were developed and extended to carry us through the series of the first six projects. We also pioneered the use of a Geometry Method Statement. This is like the explicit DNA of a project and is issued to surveyors, contractors and fabricators, many of whom have their own parametric production systems. By explaining the rule-based derivation of setting out information, rigorous checking procedures could be implemented which ensured precise coordination in a way that transferred accountability.

### RATIONALE AS A STRATEGY
The next two projects could be described as exercises in post-rationalisation. Free-form double-curved surfaces needed to be panellised in a way that would make them both buildable and affordable, which required planarity and repetition. The Sage Gateshead (2004) was resolved by the subdivision of seven arcs swept around three arcs. The new London City Hall (2002) used facets of sheared cones between offset circular floor plates that reduced with height.

Chesa Futura (2004) was a new departure in free-form design, where the rationale became embedded in the tools that were used to create the form. There was no need for panellisation – what was required was a solid shell that could be sliced to create the curved ribs of a timber frame and then layered with accurate offset solids to represent internal skin, insulation, weatherproofing, battens and a cladding of timber shingles.

It was found that offsets from B-spline surfaces depend on a tolerance, so that with every operation the control polygon densified until the resulting solids become unworkable. By using variational profiles composed of tangential arcs, the solid modelling kernel in the software recognises the arc definitions and generates mathematical offset surfaces with no degradation. Accurate edge curves could be extracted and passed directly to advanced computer-numerically controlled (CNC) machines to create the components of the frame. An important aspect of design for fabrication is to develop modelling procedures that interface

4

5

6

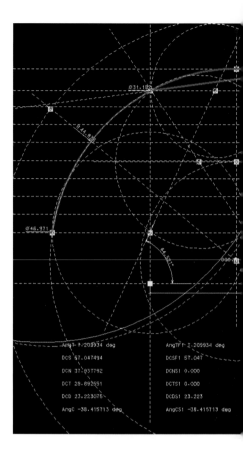

7

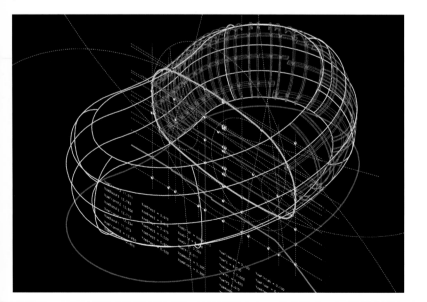

6 Foster + Partners, City Hall, London, UK, 2002.

7 Foster + Partners, Chesa Futura, St Moritz, Switzerland, 2004.
Parametric setting-out model constructed using MicroStation's Dimension Driven Design.

8 Foster + Partners, City Hall, London, UK, 2002.
Parametric setting-out model constructed using MicroStation's Dimension Driven Design.

9 Foster + Partners, Chesa Futura, St Moritz, Switzerland, 2004.

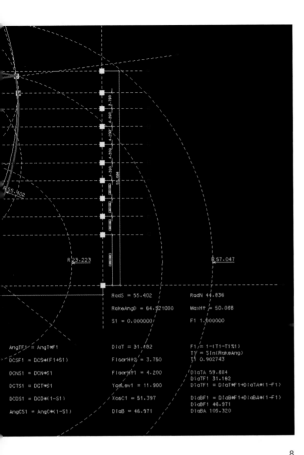

8

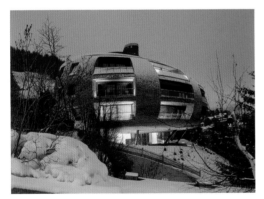

9

cleanly with downstream production processes. We learned to consider rationale as an integral part of the design strategy.

### RULES AS PROPORTIONAL RELATIONSHIPS
We also experimented with the idea of expressing rules as proportional relationships. In this way components could be designed which become adaptive to their context and exhibit nested system behaviour, which could then be varied by changing the driving ratios or even the expressions. Some of these related to structural properties or environmental considerations while others controlled spatial configurations.

### CURVATURE AS RATE OF CHANGE
These experiments then led to the idea of controlling curvature directly in terms of rate of change. But instead of using differential equations, which would have been opaque to most people, we proposed using law curves and law surfaces which could be sampled at any interval and provide a graphical interface to managing transitions or transformations. This approach produced control mechanisms that were intuitively understood by designers. Successful tool building is not just about generating results more quickly. It is also about externalising a thought process in a way that engages the team in the evolution of ideas.

Systematic procedures based on underlying logic and rationale are of great value once a design has reached a stable configuration. But successful results depend on a carefully planned premeditated approach, which must always derive from clear understanding and interpretation of the design intent. Commitment to a prescribed workflow cannot be allowed to constrain creativity by locking people into convenient processes, which may even have become irrelevant due to some lateral shift in thinking that exposes new potential.

During the early stages of design, most of what is produced becomes discarded or superseded very rapidly, so agility is of prime importance. During the later stages, as more detail is added and the team grows larger, the effort of maintaining the integrity of long chain dependencies can become counterproductive. We realised that parametrics and associativity tend to make their strongest contribution during the middle stages of a project. To try to understand what kind of tools might provide support for concept design, we proposed using 'the sketch as a metaphor'.

### THE SKETCH AS A METAPHOR
What is the purpose and nature of a sketch, both as an activity and as an artefact? We pick up an implement, which may be pen, brush or chisel and apply it to a medium, which could be paper, canvas or stone. What is significant is that the motor skills required have been in place since we were about four years old, so there is no distraction from the task in hand. The activity directly engages the hand, eye and brain loop in a way that taps deep into the subconscious. Without premeditation we just start, and allow what

10 Hugh Whitehead, Head of the Foster + Partners Specialist Modelling Group.

we see to trigger both the evolution and expression of ideas. So in answer to the first question we described a sketch as 'a way to externalise a thought process'.

There seemed to be no point in trying to mimic the sketching process with a digital equivalent, but perhaps we could learn something by examining it as a series of actions, where what is important is the order in which they occur. We observed that designers first make a mark, and then describe what it means. Next they modify the mark – and then change their mind about what it meant. By talking while drawing, the sketch ends up as something that communicates on many levels and is eloquent in its own right.

### ARCHITECTURE AS A TEAM GAME

Rapid iterations of the sequence trigger the evolution of ideas, but it is the order of operations that gives it fluidity and agility. Imagine if relationship modelling could support such a sequence. But what would be the CAD equivalent of a mark – some kind of unformed gesture to which any meaning can be ascribed after its creation? Certainly the selection from a list of geometric primitives or prescribed update methods does not qualify in this respect. It just forces us to describe form in terms of a historical status quo, instead of helping us to explore the behavioural characteristics. Sometimes a better approach to form-making can be to use physics-based simulations. Geometry is still employed, but as a means of description rather than the essence of form itself. Already we have crossed the boundaries between several disciplines, which is why increasingly we need to play 'architecture as a team game' and engage diverse skill sets in new combinations.

### COMPUTERS AS AMPLIFIERS OF THE INTELLECT

The final heading is a reference to an early mentor, Professor Tom Maver who founded ABACUS – Architecture and Building Aids Computer Unit, Strathclyde. When asked to justify investment in computer technology, he replied: 'We cannot afford not to. Computers are the amplifiers of the intellect.' Relating the story of this famous quote to Bill Mitchell, the Dean of MIT, he laughed and said: 'But if there is no signal there in the first place – it does not matter how much you amplify it!' The reply to this was: 'Yes – and if the only signal is noise – then all you get is more noise.' At the same seminar Bill Mitchell warned us: 'In my experience, software is a deeply conservative force.' We see this in practice and in schools of architecture where students strive to be different by seeking out new technology. The speed of uptake is now so rapid that good ideas spread like a virus and the work can end up appearing surprisingly similar.

### THE DESIGNER-SCRIPTER

Technology has the potential to transform not only the way we do things, but also what we do. While significant insights were gained from the early projects, they were laying the foundations for an era when scripting would become commonplace and generative design would go rapidly from niche to mainstream. There was a progression from parametrics to computation using algorithmic procedures.

10

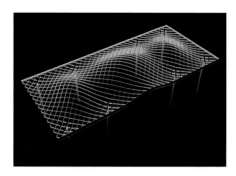

There are now multiple choices available and people tend to gravitate towards systems that are either very easy or very difficult to learn. The best scripters are usually self-taught and take pride in their ability to develop new skills and capabilities through their own efforts. While this generalisation has been beneficial, it has also become important to find ways to promote code sharing. Projects cannot afford to become vulnerable to isolated pockets of expertise, which may become bottlenecks in the design or production process. The experience of collaborating in SG workshops helps people to understand the significance of new ways of organising people and data flow.

It has been said that software developers are like walking code vaults. The only problem is when they decide to walk – which sometimes they do! In 2007, Robert Aish left SG and in 2011 Francis Aish left the SMG. Bentley succeeded in releasing GenerativeComponents (GC), but there were new players in the market and a three-year lead had disappeared. Both SMG and SG continue to flourish and intersect, while developing new agendas under new leadership. An era has passed but the voyage of discovery continues.

Today SMG combines a broad range of skill sets with people from different backgrounds. These include geometry, form finding, fabrication, building physics, fine arts, material science, environmental design, simulation, fluid dynamics and sustainability research. All are underpinned by a fluency in parametrics, scripting and computation. It is the combination of diverse skill sets which continues to push the boundaries, helping to deliver high-performance design based on radical new concepts.

We acknowledge the contribution of countless friends who have put their shoulders to the wheel and helped to turn geometry into a living mechanism.

**TEXT**
© 2013 John Wiley & Sons, Ltd

**IMAGES**
Figures 1, 2, 3, 4, 5, 7, 8, 9, 10 © Diagrams Foster + Partners, photos by Nigel Young/Foster + Partners; Figure 6 © Dennis Gilbert/View; Figure 11 © Timothy Hursley; Figure 12 © Brady Peters

12

11 Foster + Partners, Smithsonian Institution Courtyard, Washington DC, USA, 2007.

12 Foster + Partners, Smithsonian Institution Courtyard, Washington DC, USA, 2007.
The geometry for the courtyard enclosure was generated using a computer script written in VBA in MicroStation. This generating script used the centrelines of the columns, a set-out grid, and a B-spline surface as input. The code was over 5,000 lines long and had 57 parameters.

# DIGITAL CRAFTING:
## PERFORMATIVE THINKING FOR MATERIAL DESIGN

## METTE RAMSGARD THOMSEN AND MARTIN TAMKE

Mette Ramsgard Thomsen and Martin Tamke of the Centre for Information Technology and Architecture (CITA) in Denmark explore the notion of 'digital craft' through the construction of full-scale 'demonstrators' that investigate the relation between design, computation, performance and making. CITA, a research unit within the architecture school, hosted the 2011 SG conference in Copenhagen and its members regularly participate in SG workshops. Here they present a selection of research projects that have intersected with SG workshops which they relate to a new understanding of material and the new role of the designer as a 'steerer' of material properties, and therefore architectural performance.

The understanding of materials as active, whether compressed, under tension or flexed while handled, is at the root of all craft traditions. The ability to work a material, to saw and chisel wood, to weld and hammer steel or to weave and knit yarn relies on a profound understanding of its performance. It is through this material understanding that we come to shape the world of artefacts and structure that surrounds us.

The last thirty years have seen an increasing use of computationally steered fabrication technologies.[1] Computer-controlled fabrication now informs most of western manufacture across multiple different scales and materials. This increasing application of digital fabrication technologies has optimised today's industrialised building practice and created the new economic platform for our built environment.

1 Prototype from the 'Composite Territories' workshop cluster at SG 2012, Rensselaer Polytechnic Institute, Troy, New York, USA.

But digital fabrication is more than an optimisation tool. It also allows us as designers and architects to reconsider our conceptual and material practices. Digital fabrication has a direct consequence on the way that material is considered in design, shifting material thinking into the core of design intention. If architecture has predominantly been understood as a formalist tradition, where formal concerns preceded material thinking, designing for digital fabrication challenges this ideal. Instead material, craft and performance become inherent queries present already at the start of the design phase. What is at stake is not only the systematic control of variation or even a return to the

2 Prototype from the 'Manufacturing Parametric Acoustic Surfaces' workshop cluster at SG 2010, IAAC, Barcelona, Spain.

3 Distortion 1.0 Pavilion at Distortion Music Festival 2010, Copenhagen, Denmark.
The SG workshop cluster 'Manufacturing Parametric Acoustic Surfaces' is part of a larger research project in which further demonstrators were produced. Distortion 1.0 was a mobile acoustic space installed at five locations during the Distortion Music Festival in 2010.

2

richness of ornamentation, but equally a fundamental change to a *performative* understanding of materials.[2] Rather than thinking of materials as static or inanimate, materials are seen through their capacity to perform: to bend, flex and stretch. In this way *digital crafting*[3] allows architects to reconsider the traditions of fabrication and to investigate how new processes of folding, twisting or pleating materials can lead to new structural systems.[4]

During the last three years, members of the Centre for Information Technology and Architecture (CITA) at the Royal Danish Academy of Fine Arts School of Architecture in Denmark have been a part of the Smartgeometry (SG) community, and have participated in the workshops as a way of sharing and developing these research questions. In the three workshops presented here, we have explored the particular intersections between digital fabrication, material practice and design. The workshops are embedded parts of existing research projects. They therefore learn from the interdisciplinary collaborations and partnerships that have produced these inquiries and employ the methods, tools and techniques developed here. Open-ended and speculative, the workshop environment is a playful search into the further possibilities and questions that these research projects have posed.

3

### THE CHALLENGE FOR DIGITAL PRACTICE: FEEDING BACK INTO THE DESIGN CHAIN

The three SG workshops we have participated in relate to our ongoing research at CITA. They query the new expanded digital design chain that creates new interfaces between analysis and simulation, design and fabrication. This new way of working can lead to real differences in the way we conceptualise, design and build architecture. The ideal of working *for* and *with* a performative understanding of materials allows for designers to rethink our material practices. Rather than thinking of the digital only as a means of organising standardised practices, it becomes a possibility to rethink how materials are used, detailed and manufactured for our built environment. Our use of the term 'digital crafting' suggests a new engagement in the small scales of material specification, leading to a new practice in which architects and designers become the designers of the materials themselves as well as of buildings or artefacts. As our production industry enters a new era dominated by increasingly engineered materials, it becomes possible to ask how architecture could be constructed from site- or use-specific materials made directly in response to locally defined design criteria. What are the tools we need to devise these materials, how do we employ these new hyper-specified materials and what models can we use to understand these practices? As such, digital crafting and the interest in capturing the potential design innovation promised by design with material performance leads to new challenges to our design traditions, tools and techniques.

### MANUFACTURING PARAMETRIC ACOUSTIC SURFACES

The first challenge addressed in the workshops is the question of how to integrate analysis and simulation. The expanded

4 Visualisation of code for CNC knitting machine and the related knit of a prototype from SG 2011 in Copenhagen, Denmark.
The coding of production information allows for a direct link between the design space and the manufacturing.

5 Prototypes from the 'Performing Skins' workshop cluster at SG 2011, Copenhagen, Denmark.

4

5

6

7

digital chain promises a new level of feedback between design environment and the possibility of analysing and simulating environmental effect. The challenge is to integrate these simulations in the early design phase where they can be of real consequence for design. This means that as designers we need to devise new iterative design protocols by which insights from these simulations can be fed back into the design and interfaced with other spatial, programmatic or site-informed design criteria in meaningful ways. It is important to find ways in which the circularity of spatial and material design decisions can have an impact on their local environment. By linking simulation through design to material specification, detailing and fabrication, these complex feedback loops become apparent.

At SG 2010 at the IAAC (Institute for Advanced Architecture of Catalonia) in Barcelona, CITA led the 'Manufacturing Parametric Acoustic Surfaces' cluster in order to explore these ideas of materials and performance as linked to simulation. The two tutors were Martin Tamke, an architect and associate professor at CITA, with research expertise in the field of digital fabrication and design, and Brady Peters, an architect and PhD student researching the architectural implications of sound and complex surfaces. The workshop was part of the Distortion research project on the digital design, simulation and manufacturing of architectural surfaces in order to create specific acoustic spaces. Using off-the-shelf materials such as wood, plywood and Di-bond, the workshop employed parametric techniques and computer-numerically controlled (CNC) milling to produce individually shaped elements. Located at their calculated positions in a basic structure, the components were able to create local acoustic atmospheres through resonant absorption, reflection and scattering of sound. The workshop participants explored the transition between sonic effects through the grading of key parameters in the surface modules. Physical prototyping allowed for the testing of materials and enabled us to embed these into the elements underlying the parametric model. This was the basis for the precise production and assembly of the perforated and folded components. Key in the rapid development of the prototype was the immediacy of design, simulation and making. Finally the designed acoustic effects could both be experienced and measured in the full-scale prototype. The project furthered our understanding of the necessary digital tools for design and production and the required scale and detailing of a spatial structure in order to create perceptible acoustic atmospheres.

## PERFORMING SKINS
The second design challenge we addressed through the SG workshops was how these kinds of feedback loops challenge the scale of architectural design concern. By asking how local environmental information can inform the design of materials, their material composition, structure and performance, the question becomes what kind of design tools we need to create so as to enable this practice? How can we devise design methods for incorporating data from the local environment, what are the

6 Knitted prototype from the 'Performing Skins' workshop cluster at SG 2011, Copenhagen, Denmark.

7 Prototypes from the 'Performing Skins' workshop cluster at SG 2011, Copenhagen, Denmark.
Using the Arduino platform, the sensors integrated into the knitted surfaces could constantly feed back into the design environment.

8

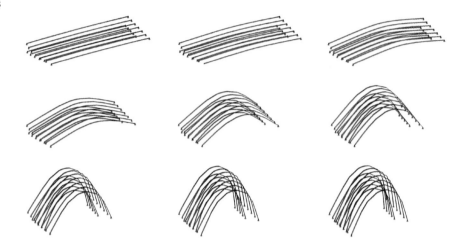

9b

8 Finite element (FE) simulation of the
bending process of the bespoke composite
material strips from the 'Composite Territories'
workshop cluster at SG 2012, Rensselaer
Polytechnic Institute, Troy, New York, USA.

9a and 9b Prototype from the 'Composite
Territories' workshop cluster at SG 2012,
Rensselaer Polytechnic Institute, Troy, New
York, USA.

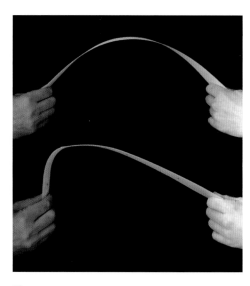

interfaces we need to create and what does it mean for the way we employ materials, our understanding of their life cycles and use? The practice of embedding sensors into material is well established in the larger context of the built environment as a way of monitoring material decay.[5] But could integrated sensors also allow us to gain a better understanding of how materials are performing, what their localised design criteria are and therefore how materials could be designed? Rather than simulating their performance, how could we 'read' their behaviour in real time and how could these readings become part of a design process? The creation of active materials – or *smart composites* – that bring together computational and material performances challenges our understanding of materials as standardised and homogeneous, leading the way to a new practice in which materials are highly differentiated and graded in respect of their context or use.[6] Considering materials not as standardised and uniform but as designed to change their performance, becoming denser, stiffer or thicker, broadens the possibilities of design.

The SG 2011 workshop cluster 'Performing Skins' was led by Mette Ramsgard Thomsen (CITA), Ayelet Karmon and Gabi Schaeffer (Shenkar College of Engineering and Design, Tel Aviv). It was based on their ongoing research into architectural textiles and the interface between the architect's design environment and digital production techniques. Linking the making of bespoke textiles through CNC knitting machines with the design space of architects, the workshop's aim was to find new ways of defining material specification and to define material compositions in direct response to accumulated local information harvested by integrated sensors. In the workshop, the design teams were asked to imagine the textile membranes as building skins detailed in response to environmental impact. We developed initial diagrams by which the material variegation in the knitted surfaces was defined. The diagrams allowed the specification of structural as well as material changes and the strategic inlay of sensor bands in the form of knitted-in conductive yarns. The use of digital tools to create computational models, and their concepts of precision, scale and performance were demonstrated through the creation of physical prototypes of membrane materials. Using the CNC knitting machine allowed for quick feedback in the design process. The stream of data from the embedded sensors was fed back into new active diagrams, changing them in real time with response to the contextual conditions of the surface. This produced differentiated geometrical definitions for the production of new material iterations. In this way we were able to expand our thinking of material specification to incorporate environmental data as design feedback.

### COMPOSITE TERRITORIES

The third design challenge that we investigated at SG questions how this engagement with the small scales of material design can inform the larger scales of structural design. To design with material performance means to understand the interactions between scales and their interrelated performances.[7] Learning

10 Material samples from the 'Composite Territories' workshop cluster at SG 2012, Rensselaer Polytechnic Institute, Troy, New York, USA.
Composites allow for the fabrication of materials with bespoke properties. In the workshop we examined the bending behaviour where a gradient in material strength shifts the material's behaviour fundamentally.

from parallel practices in material science such as multi-scale material modelling, in which the computational modelling of materials at small scale are used to parametrise models at larger scale, the question becomes how to best implement material performance in structural solutions. This brings back the importance of material simulation and its integration into the design chain. To work well with material performance necessitates good simulation tools so that these structural forces can be calculated and anticipated. Current design tools are conceived to calculate standardised materials in traditional load-bearing structures. As we come to work with more complex structural performances dependent on small-scale material performance such as self bracing, flexing and tensioning, we need new tools by which these calculations can be calibrated. At first, a problem arises in the mere increase in complexity. Material simulation and continual variation necessitate more complex algorithmic calculation and higher computer power. But a second, perhaps more fundamental problem, lies with the division of these design tools into carefully segregated professions, each with their own culture of problem definition and solution finding. If designers are to work intelligently with material performance, and thereby take full advantage of the shared digital platform and its linking of analysis, simulation, design and fabrication that grounds our material practices, we need to develop new tools by which the full partnership of designers, engineers and craftsmen can work together in the early design phases, creating material solutions for complex designs.

The SG 2012 workshop cluster 'Composite Territories' had at its base a workflow that linked the making of bespoke thermoplastic-based fibre-reinforced components with an architectural design- and engineering-based simulation process. The workshop combined the relationship between the stiffness of a structural element and its capacity to counteract or steer loads with the ability within the manufacturing process to give the polymer-based material a specific stiffness. This concept emerged in the ongoing research of CITA into fibre composites and was first materialised with the support of Knippers Helbig Engineering in the 'Composite Territories' installation in January 2012 at the ggggallery in Copenhagen. Shortly afterwards, the material research facilities at Rensselaer Polytechnic Institute (RPI) in Troy, New York enabled a further, more scientific exploration. The team of workshop leaders was hence interdisciplinary between CITA (Paul Nicholas, Martin Tamke, Mette Ramsgard Thomsen), Knippers Helbig Engineering (Hauke Jungjohann, Jan Knippers) and the hosts RPI (Ivan Markov).

While the basic concept emerged from the first installation, the tools and workflow of the cluster were developed among the group of tutors and participants before the actual workshop at RPI. It was, however, the exploration of material and making at the workshop that made further progress possible. Only this gave the necessary hands-on understanding of material parameters and the conditions for their behaviour. The material testing facilities at RPI allowed us to quantify the related material properties

11 'Composite Territories' installation at ggggallery, Copenhagen, Denmark, 2011. The SG 2012 workshop was a part of the CITA research project in the use of designed materials in architecture. A first prototype was set up in an exhibition in Copenhagen.

that helped us to calibrate its finite element (FE) simulation. The developed prototype focuses on the differentiated bending behaviour of strips of composite elements with bespoke stiffness. The combination of generative design tools, engineering analysis, material prototyping and testing established a flow of information in which an overall design informed the material properties of single elements and their fabrication. The complexity of the workflow limited distinctly the design space of the final prototype and affirmed the need to develop lightweight near-to-real-time simulation approaches in order to integrate material behaviour in the design process.

## PERSPECTIVE

To further digital design culture and to work effectively with the potentials of material performance, we need to find new models and methods by which we can support the feedback between scales. But how do we do this? In architecture, drafting at different scales has always meant engagement with different kinds of concerns, whether planning, spatial design, detailing or specification. But the logic of drawing – the system of projective geometry – remained the same. In working with material performance and in interfacing with material analysis, simulation, detailing and production, we need to find ways in which many different kinds of data, whether geometric, numeric or statistical, can be interfaced. As a practice, we therefore need to develop to modelling principles that allow for flexible, dynamic and interactive organisation of heterogeneous data streams. Most importantly, we need these models to be well integrated with the creative practices of architectural design. Architecture is characterised by its breadth of engagement. Not aligned with a single design goal, but instead always driven by a network of different and often opposing design concerns, architecture as a design practice must always find the best solution possible for a given context and at a given point in time. Our tools therefore cannot be understood as simple means of optimisation, but need to support the creative thinking of how a new material practice can fundamentally change the way we think of architecture, the way we live, work and interact as well as the quality of the spatial surroundings we create.

## REFERENCES

1 See: Christoph Schindler, *Ein architektonisches Periodisierungsmodell anhand fertigungstechnischer Kriterien, dargestellt am Beispiel des Holzbaus* [*An Architectural Model of Periods Based on Production-Related Criterias, Illustrated by the Example of Timber Construction*], doctoral thesis no 18605, ETH Zurich (Zurich), 2009.
2 See: Martin Tamke, Mark Burry, Phil Ayres, Jane Burry and Mette Ramsgard Thomsen, 'Design Environments for Material Performance', in *Computational Design Modelling: Proceedings of the Design Modelling Symposium Berlin 2011*, Springer (Vienna), pp 309–18; and David Leatherbarrow, 'Architecture's Unscripted

Performance', in B Kolarevic and A Malkawi (eds), *Performative Architecture: Beyond Instrumentality*, Spon Press (New York, NY), 2005, pp 5–19.

3 The term 'digital crafting' was developed by CITA and the Aarhus School of Architecture within the 2009–2011 research network of the same name. The network investigated how new digital design and production methods are instigating profound changes in the design and building of architecture. See: Mette Ramsgard Thomsen, Martin Tamke and Claus Peder Pedersen (eds), *Digital Crafting: A Network on Computation and Craft in Architecture, Engineering and Design*, The Royal Danish Academy of Fine Arts Schools of Architecture, Design and Conservation, School of Architecture (Copenhagen), 2012 (online at http://www.digitalcrafting.dk/wp-content/uploads/2012/08/DC-DigitalCrafting_Web_S.pdf [accessed 2 October 2012]).

4 Eric Van Every, 'Embedded Sensors for Life-Time Monitoring of Concrete', in *Proceedings of the 4th International Conference on Structural Health Monitoring on Intelligent Infrastructure* (SHMII-4), 22–24 July 2009, Zurich, Switzerland. See also: Limin Gao, Erik T Thostenson, Zuoguang Zhang and Tsu-Wei Chou, 'Sensing of Damage Mechanisms in Fiber-Reinforced Composites under Cyclic Loading using Carbon Nanotubes', *Advanced Functional Materials*, Vol 19, No 1, 9 January 2009, pp 123–130.

5 Marcelo Coelho, Sajid Sadi, Pattie Maes, Joanna Berzowska and Neri Oxman, 'Transitive Materials: Towards an Integrated Approach to Material Technology', in Anne Bajart, Henk Muller and Thomas Strang (eds) *Ubicomp 2007 Workshop Proceedings*, Innsbruck, Austria, 16–19 September 2007, pp 495–6.

6 Mette Ramsgard Thomsen and Ayelet Karmon, 'Informing Material Specification', in *Digital Aptitudes: ACSA 100th Annual Meeting*, ACSA Press (Washington DC; Boston), 2012, pp 677–84.

7 See: Eric Van Every, 'Embedded Sensors for Life-Time Monitoring of Concrete', in *Proceedings of the 4th International Conference on Structural Health Monitoring on Intelligent Infrastructure* (SHMII-4), 22–24 July 2009, Zurich, Switzerland. See also: Adriaan Beukers and Ed van Hinte, *Lightness: The Inevitable Renaissance of Minimum Energy Structures*, 010 Publishers (Rotterdam), 2005.

1

2

**1 Robotic prototyping.**
Simulating the linear extrusion process, a robotically controlled wire cutter shapes blocks of clay into individualised modules.

**2 Robotic wire cutting of clay.**
Prototypical assembly of blocks with ornamental surface texture geared towards maximizing the surface area to volume ratio to reap benefits for thermally active surfaces.

# DESIGN ROBOTICS:
## NEW STRATEGIES FOR MATERIAL SYSTEM RESEARCH

### MARTIN BECHTHOLD

Martin Bechthold is a Professor of Architecture at Harvard University and the director of the Graduate School of Design's Technology Platform. He first participated at Smartgeometry (SG) as a workshop leader of the 'Ceramics 2.0' cluster in 2012. The cluster explored and defined new possibilities at the intersection of computational design, digital fabrication and the world of ceramics. Here Bechthold traces the evolution of design robotics, looking at the beginnings of robotic technology in architecture as well as contemporary trends.

Ten years of workshops and conferences have established Smartgeometry (SG) as a respected platform for exploring novelty at the intersection of practice and the academy. As the integration of industrial robots into schools of architecture has advanced more broadly, SG has reflected this trend by persistently incorporating work in robotics. At the 2012 SG event at Rensselaer Polytechnic Institute (RPI), Troy, New York, the Design Robotics Group (DRG) at the Graduate School of Design (GSD) at Harvard University offered the 'Ceramics 2.0' workshop, a setting that allowed cluster participants to produce novel ceramic artefacts using a six-axis robot. Having previously untrained individuals use a standard industrial robot within the space of four days would have been technically unthinkable 10 years ago. Today the design to robotic manipulation process, once cumbersome and riddled with technical problems, has matured to a point that it permits exploratory design speculation, long the hallmark of SG, to occur within the compressed time frame of a workshop. Design robotics, with its focus on expanding design scope based on the rigorous study of a particular material system, has become the modus operandi that pervades DRG research and teaching alike.

### THE EVOLUTION OF DESIGN ROBOTICS

The initial pursuits to integrate robotic technologies into architecture are best described by the term 'construction automation'. This field, beginning in the 1980s, attempted to advance construction in ways that mirrored the integration of industrial robots in industries such as car manufacturing: treat design (by and large) as a given but attempt to improve the quality and productivity of construction. Worker safety and other concerns also played a role. The Japanese robotic construction systems, developed by large construction firms, robotically assembled high-rise buildings from prefabricated elements on site. Limited to

3

3 'Ceramics 2.0' workshop cluster at SG 2012, Rensselaer Polytechnic Institute, Troy, New York, USA.
The workshop cluster allowed participants to get hands-on exposure to both clay materials and robotic fabrication technology.

4

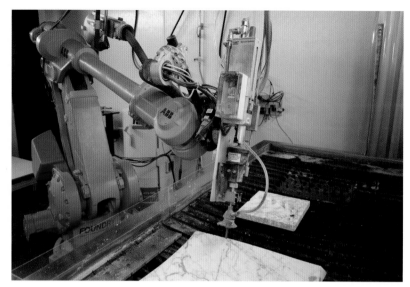

5

4 Robotically fabricated structural stone shell at the Graduate School of Design, Harvard University, Cambridge, Massachusetts, USA. 94 similar yet unique stone slabs were customised through perforations produced on a six-axis robotic waterjet.

5 Robotically fabricated structural stone shell at the Graduate School of Design, Harvard University, Cambridge, Massachusetts, USA. The finished shell allows location-specific views through the stone surface. Post-tensioned along the ruling lines, metal stiffeners between horizontal rows of stone stabilise the thin surface against buckling.

repetitive rectangular plans, they were maybe the largest and most comprehensive examples of construction automation. Automated material delivery and assembly systems were complemented by a plethora of smaller robotic applications for welding, fireproofing, finishing or painting, to name but a few. In this context Thomas Bock developed the notion of robot-oriented design (ROD) as 'a strategy in order to reengineer the construction process and redesign construction details and building components in such a way that it facilitates the implementation of construction robots'.[1] Robots in construction automation are meant to substitute human labour, and while this process may involve redesign of details and connections, it neither questions nor informs overall design expressions and architectural form.

At the opposite end of the spectrum of architectural robotics are recent trends towards largely academic installations that lean towards artistic endeavours. Not primarily geared towards improving production efficiencies but instead seeking to expand design scope, these projects pursue those geometric complexities, new kinds of tectonics, and ornamental material formations that are truly original to and only logical when using robotic technologies and their related digital design techniques. The GSD's robotically fabricated stone shell, a collaboration between Monica Ponce de Leon, Wes McGee and the author, gives testimony of this phase at Harvard. Erected in 2008, the shell features the first use of load-bearing thin marble. The overall surface is subdivided into 94 individual panels that have been post-tensioned into a rigid surface structure. Cone-shaped perforations generate ornamental light effects. Each panel is unique and derives its logic from the robotic fabrication process, a process largely indifferent to generating individualised or identical versions.

These efforts at Harvard and elsewhere have catalysed the field of digital design and its related, albeit now almost historic notion of parametrics. Projects may or may not include generalisable aspects, and as the field of architectural robotics enters into a third, more mature phase the value of such one-off installations will be increasingly measured by their associated contribution to knowledge that, once disseminated, can ultimately promote transformation and innovation in the building industry.

It is the focus on producing general knowledge that perhaps most clearly differentiates design robotics from the digital crafting of complex, speculative and inspiring installations, whereas the commitment to exploratory design distinguishes it most clearly from construction automation approaches. Work at the GSD since 2007 has touched upon both of the related approaches mentioned above, but is now firmly committed to their natural evolution into design robotics, a turning point clearly marked by the creation of the DRG in 2010; key members of DRG include Anthony Kane, Jonathan King, and Matan Mayer. Current work of the group is focused on the understanding and reconceptualisation of material systems, thus broadening established notions of material-based design. Research projects redesign a wide set of processes, relationships and techniques in order to address issues of performance through and with the methods of design. DRG work in material systems is best characterised as process-oriented, strategic and focused on performance.

It could be argued that the consideration of *process* is hardly new in architecture. Indeed, construction detailing has long considered construction process or assembly itself as a constraint that informs the relationships of parts to each other and to the whole. Examples for this time-honoured consideration of construction processes in design are the many detailing strategies for construction materials that lead to material-specific tectonics and expressions by largely determining the size, spacing and mutual connections of components. Concrete detailing is always aware of the need to remove formwork, and thus tends to avoid undercuts or tight spaces that obstruct access. Connectors in timber and steel construction are spaced to allow access for the human hand needed to tighten bolts. Part characteristics themselves, however, are not substantially questioned – standard bricks or lumber sizes become the basis of construction. Robotic research based on assembling standard parts exists at Harvard and beyond. Well documented are studies in various additive construction techniques, maybe best exemplified in the stacking of standard masonry blocks by industrial robots. Here the base unit – brick or block – remains the same industrially produced ubiquitous module. Beginning in 2005, Gramazio & Kohler at the ETH Zurich focused on the ability of industrial robots to stack non-standard patterns as quickly as traditional, regular patterns. Code generators on the software side created integrated digital workflows that supported the argument of 'digital materiality'.[2] The work departs from construction automation approaches as its focus is on adding value through design in the form of novel brick patterns.

## DESIGN ROBOTICS GROUP: REDEFINING MATERIAL SYSTEMS AND PROCESSES
Workflow tools of this sort have been developed and used extensively from the beginning of robotic research at the GSD. They are pieces of software that automate the creation of robotic instructions directly from the geometry data present in the parametric digital design models, thus expanding parametric abilities from the purely digital into the physical realm of material manipulation. Early GSD studies in robotic assembly of standard blocks were conducted in a course entitled 'Construction Automation' taught by the author. Taro Narahara at the GSD deployed bottom-up computational principles in allowing blocks to assemble semi-randomly as the most extreme case of non-standard patterns. He also integrated structural analysis directly into the digital process of forming the block pattern to ensure that any pattern remained stable based on the self-weight of the base unit. The software environment eventually produces all needed code to run a six-axis robotic manipulator and automatically assemble the blocks.

Departing from the robotic assembly of single-size modules as the next step in the evolution of design robotics is a sponsored

6

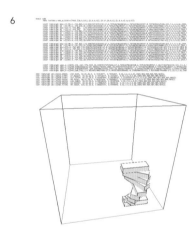

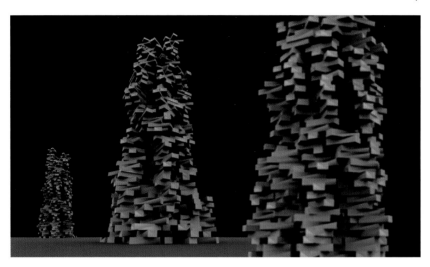

6 Study on semi-random block patterns by
Taro Narahara.
Structural stability is checked automatically
to ensure that physical blocks can be stacked
precisely as in the computational model.

7 Study on semi-random block patterns by
Taro Narahara.
Following a bottom-up computational
approach that mimics the way termites
build their structures, blocks are assembled
computationally for robotic stacking.

research project on robotic tile installation. Instead of using a
single tile size, DRG developed a robotic work cell that utilises
modular or randomly sized tiles for the robotic assembly of tile
mosaics. Preceding the system development, DRG conducted an
extensive analysis of economic, technical and market factors. The
supporting software, developed in collaboration with Professor
Panagiotis Michalatos (GSD), allows the import of images that are
analysed and translated into tile patterns. Variations in greyscale
in the image are replicated in the tile pattern by controlling the
relative amount of darker mortar and lighter-colour tiles. Darker
image tones are generated by placing smaller tiles that allow a
larger surface of darker mortar to be present. Other algorithms
allow various means of controlling semi-random tile patterns.
Projected implementation costs are compatible with industry
standards for manual placement. Tiles are to be installed on
backer boards that can then be rapidly mounted on site – a novel
approach that combines prefabrication with on-site techniques. As
a new business opportunity, the system would need to create its
own, new market for non-standard tile patterns.[3]

A recent student project illustrates – still within the context of
ceramics – DRG's ambition to engage robotics in the fabrication
processes for components. The flowing matter study by GSD
students Stefano Andreani, Jose Luis Garcia del Castillo and
Aurgho Jyoti rethinks the formation of the parts that make up
larger assemblies more substantially, and represents the expanded
mode of process-orientation characteristic of design robotics. The
project develops a geometric logic for blocks derived from the
linear movement of brick extrusion equipment common in the
industry. Blocks are shaped by cutting wires that are dynamically
angled as the clay is being extruded. Similar techniques are used
by potters who shape wet clay with wire tools – devices that
can be guided by hand or by a robotic manipulator. This simple
manipulation of the rectangular extrusions creates a surprisingly

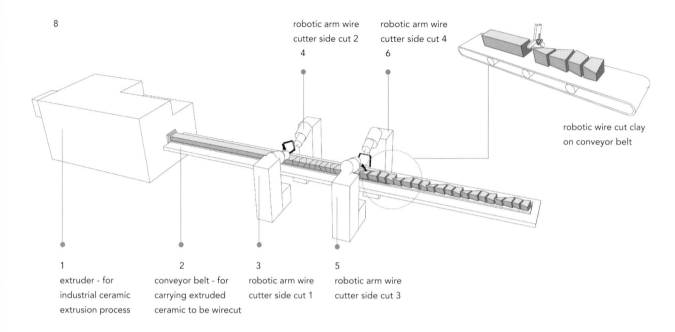

8

robotic arm wire cutter side cut 2
4

robotic arm wire cutter side cut 4
6

robotic wire cut clay on conveyor belt

1
extruder - for industrial ceramic extrusion process

2
conveyor belt - for carrying extruded ceramic to be wirecut

3
robotic arm wire cutter side cut 1

5
robotic arm wire cutter side cut 3

9

8 Flowing matter study.
Robotic wire cutting could be integrated into an industrial extrusion process.

9 Customised block units.
New forms of modular ceramic units are generated by integrating digital design with automated tooling for the robotic fabrication cell.

10 Flowing matter design study.
New structural and non-structural forms are enabled by combining individualised clay modules into larger assemblies.

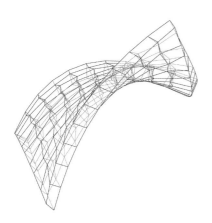

10

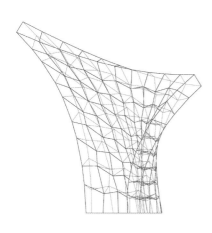

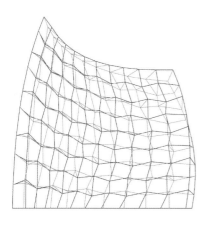

rich set of blocks of varying shapes. Normally planar mortar beds are now curved, ruling surfaces. Blocks are ideally assembled robotically because their similarity would make choosing the right block for the correct place difficult at best. Prototypical experiments confirmed the ability of robotically guided wire tools to shape clay blocks quickly and accurately. In lieu of extruded clay passing along a stationary wire, the linear movement of the clay was simulated by the equivalent movement of the six-axis robotic manipulator. While much remains to be explored, the study more than hints at the potential for block aggregations to be more substantially customised once the base unit itself has been individualised. Structural and non-structural patterns are equally feasible. The 'Ceramics 2.0' SG workshop cluster eventually used a similar tool and material support setup.

### THE STRATEGIC DEPLOYMENT OF ROBOTIC TECHNOLOGY

Considering construction processes and component fabrication as inseparable and interdependent elements of a single material system enables a second characteristic of design robotics – the strategic deployment of robotic technology. Initial analysis of the material system not only seeks to understand its characteristics in depth, it intends to identify the specific steps and elements in the fabrication and construction process that lend themselves to an integration of industrial robots and, most importantly, can maximise its value while minimising the need for custom robotic equipment. In the case of the flowing matter project discussed previously, the opportunity was identified through the analysis of industrial extrusion processes – a technique that currently deploys cutting wire, albeit only to cut elements to predetermine length.

Extrusion processes widespread in the production of thick ceramic tiles were investigated in a study by GSD students Mauricio Loyola and Jeremy Keagy. Observing the use of blade shearing techniques to cut extrusions to length or subdivide them into rectangular tiles, the team investigated prototypical methods to produce varied flat tile shapes. A simple angle tool blade was developed and tested using a six-axis robotic manipulator. The range of customisation options for flat tile shapes was substantial. It was further amplified once the extruded clay mass itself was not merely a slab of uniform thickness, but instead changed in thickness from one side of the extrusion belt to the opposite one. By using a fast robot to stencil out shapes from distinct portions within the linearly moving extrusion slab, a virtually infinite amount of tile shapes can be produced. Clearly this project could be combined with the robotic tile installation system, thus merging the strategic module variation with the robotic installation processes.

Much of the work in architectural ceramics has focused on increasing the ability of clay-based material systems to customise the end product systematically within the industrial context. The strategic deployment of robotic manipulation limits itself to affecting the fewest possible steps, leaving the major part of many well-established production techniques unchanged. A project that rethinks these techniques more substantially is a prototypical

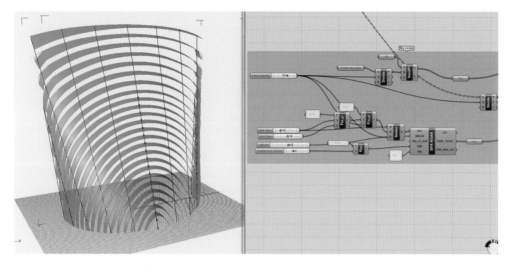

11

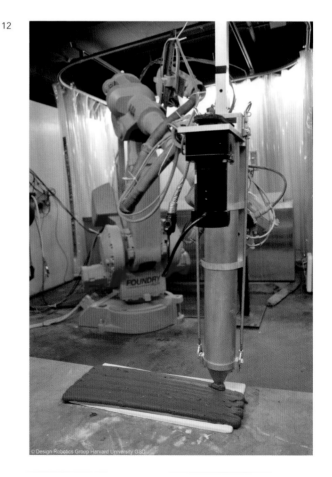

12

11 3D printing of ceramic shading lamellas.
The design interface allows environmental
design and design for robotic production to
occur without switching software. Parametric
variations can be easily visualised and, most
importantly, are accommodated within the
robotic fabrication system.

12 3D printing of ceramic tiles.
Using a custom extruder, tiles can be printed
onto a variety of mould surfaces including
plaster (shown), foam, or the newly developed
robotically adaptable mould.

software and related work cell that prints mass-customisable ceramic shading lamellas using standard robotic equipment. The lamella geometry is driven by performance needs: their form can easily be optimised for considerations of daylight and energy consumption while still allowing for desired views to the exterior. The design of the specific (curved, angled etc) orientations of the ceramic lamellas is facilitated by integrating shading and energy analysis in the design software. The environmental aspects of the workflow were developed by Prof. Christoph Reinhart. The digital workflow is streamlined by enabling the entire range of operations – from environmental design to robotic fabrication – to be prepared within a single software environment. Newly developed software components support the design for robotic fabrication steps which normally require cumbersome file transfer and numerous software platforms. Once a desirable shading geometry has been determined, the lamella surfaces can be thickened and subdivided to incorporate material- and project-specific constraints. Robotic code for the production environment is generated automatically. As a proof of concept, DRG designed and assembled a prototypical work cell centred on a robotic clay extruder that deposits clay onto a variable surface mould. The robotically adjustable mould geometry as well as the steps of clay deposition and surface post-processing are automated. The prototypical shading segment produced with the system is vested in design excellence while staying committed to enhancing building performance.

The project is strategic in that different portions of the overall digital workflow and the robotic production process can integrate as modules into existing industrial processes. Industrially extruded clay slabs, for example, could be shaped using the adjustable mould surface even without any of the other elements of the work cell. Robotic extrusion is also possible onto surfaces such as milled foam or plaster moulds. This project and certain other studies have been developed in collaboration with industry partners and remain under evaluation for further development.

### 'CERAMICS 2.0' WORKSHOP CLUSTER AT SG 2012
Much of the work in ceramics presented here prepared DRG for the 'Ceramics 2.0' workshop cluster at SG 2012. Here a small six-axis robotic manipulator was trucked to RPI and installed such that it provided a productive and safe work environment for all workshop participants. Run by Stefano Andreani, Jose Luis Garcia del Castillo, Aurgho Jyoti, Nathan King and the author, introductions to ceramic materials, products and, most importantly, to the industrial context of tile production were followed by software and machine tutorials. In order to allow immediate interaction with the material system, hands-on experiments with clay and hand-held wire cutters were encouraged. Despite the sophistication and relative ease of the robotic work cell the immediate, exploratory experience of handling clay was crucial. These analogue studies often challenged ideas that had been developed previously, and triggered new ideas based on the response of the material to a single tool, the wire. Adjusting wire

13

13 Prototypical facade segment.
As proof of concept, a facade segment was environmentally designed and individual lamellas were printed using the robotic work cell. The image shows a mock-up in the context of a conventionally produced extruded ceramic facade.

**14 Robotic wire cutting of clay.**
The precision and repeatability of robotically
wire-cut clay depends on the wire tension and
the consistency of the clay body. Shapes of
particular interest were those difficult to cut with
anything but robotic technology.

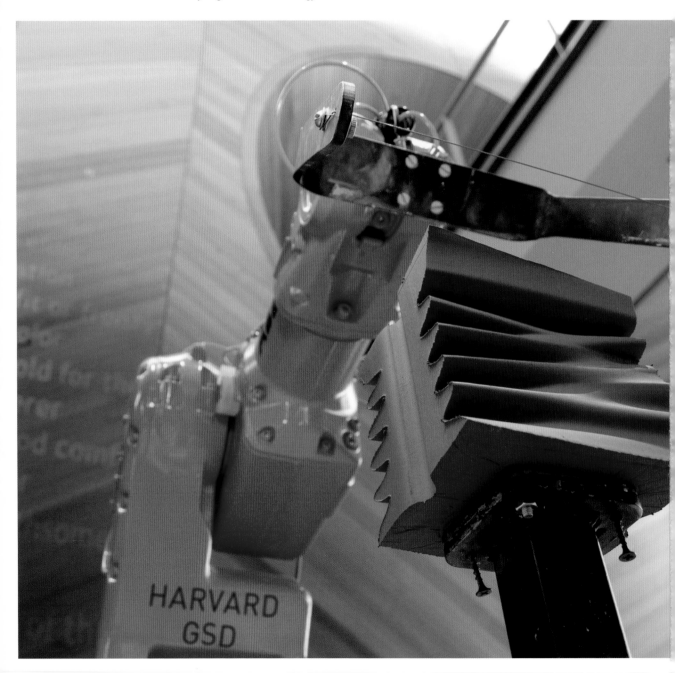

tension, for example, produced a range of interesting surface patterns that inspired their pursuit through robotic methods.

Going back and forth between manual and robotic clay manipulation, participants developed design intuitions that expanded beyond what would have been feasible when limited to either physical or computational methods. Given the precision of the robot juxtaposed with the variability of the wire tension and the elasticity of the clay, not all results were predictable. Exploring a material system in this open-ended manner generated a host of powerful ideas and much discussion. The workshop demonstrated that design robotics has matured to a point that brainstorming and sketching are now possible in newly hybridised modes that combine robotics with exploratory hands-on experiments. The SG venue, again, proved to be a fertile platform for developing and refining a forward-looking mode of design research.

## ACKNOWLEDGEMENT
Support for DRG's ceramic projects was provided by ASCER Tile of Spain.

## REFERENCES
1 Thomas Bock, 'Innovation in Construction by Automation and Robotics', *IAARC Newsletter*, No 5 (special issue), April 2006, p 1.
2 Fabio Gramazio and Matthias Kohler, *Digital Materiality in Architecture*, Lars Müller (Berlin), 2008.
3 King et al, 'Robotic Tile Placement: Tools, Techniques and Feasibility', *Proceedings of the International Conference on Construction Automation* (ISARC), Eindhoven, 2012, see www.gerontechnology.info/index.php/... gt.2012.11.02.498.756.

## IMAGES
Figures 1, 8, 9, 10 © Stefano Andreani/Design Robotic Group – Harvard Graduate School of Design: Prof Martin Bechthold, Nathan King, Jose Luis Garcia Del Castillo and Aurgho Jyoti; Figures 2, 4, 5, 13, 15 © Martin Bechthold; Figure 3 © Shima Miabadi; Figures 6, 7 © Taro Narahara; Figure 11 © Anthony Kane; Figure 12 © Nathan King; Figure 14 © Cat Callaghan

14

15 (Overleaf) Digital clay textures.
Varying wire tension differentiates the effect of identical tool paths through the clay body. Robotic control and material-related variation interact in generating rich surface patterns.